T0330242

GLOBALIZATION AND THE CULTURES OF BUSINESS IN AFRICA

GLOBALIZATION AND THE CULTURES OF BUSINESS IN AFRICA

From Patrimonialism To Profit

SCOTT D. TAYLOR

INDIANA UNIVERSITY PRESS
BLOOMINGTON AND INDIANAPOLIS

This book is a publication of

Indiana University Press
601 North Morton Street
Bloomington, Indiana 47404-3797 USA

iupress.indiana.edu

Telephone orders   800-842-6796
Fax orders   812-855-7931

Manufactured in the United States of America

Library of Congress Cataloging-in-Publication Data

Taylor, Scott D., [date]
    Globalization and the cultures of business in Africa : from pat-
rimonialism to profit / Scott D. Taylor.
        p. cm.
    Includes bibliographical references and index.
    ISBN 978-0-253-00266-2 (cloth : alk. paper) — ISBN 978-0-
253-00573-1 (pbk. : alk. paper) — ISBN 978-0-253-00581-6 (eb)
1. Business enterprises—Africa, Sub-Saharan. 2. Globalization—
Africa, Sub-Saharan. 3. Capitalism—Africa, Sub-Saharan. 4. Investments, Foreign—Africa, Sub-Saharan. 5. Big business—Africa,
Sub-Saharan. I. Title.
    HD2917.T39 2012
    338.70967—dc23
                                            2012017809

1 2 3 4 5 17 16 15 14 13 12

For my Father

CONTENTS

Preface   ix

Acknowledgments   xvii

PART 1. INTRODUCTION AND BACKGROUND   1

Introduction   3

1. African Business and Capitalism in Historical Perspective   22

PART 2. GLOBALIZATION AND POLITICAL
AND ECONOMIC TRANSFORMATION   43

2. Institutional Change in the 1990s
Economic and Political Reform   45

3. Business, the African State, and Globalization in the
New Millennium
Transnational Influences and Domestic Responses   64

PART 3. THE DIVERSITY OF AFRICAN BUSINESS:
PROBLEMS AND PROSPECTS   97

4. Foreign Investment beyond Compradorism and
Primary Commodities
The Role of the Global South   99

5. From Patrimonialism to Profit? The Transformation
of Crony Capitalists and Bureaucratic Bourgeoisies   130

6. Going Continental, Going Global
Africa's Corporate "Giants"   155

Conclusion
Prospects for Business in Africa and African Business   183

Appendix	189
Notes	193
Bibliography	221
Further Reading	235
Index	237

PREFACE

I should have known better. At the very least, I should have asked permission.

By the summer of 2010, having traveled to Africa as a student, researcher, and development consultant for more than twenty-five years, I considered myself sensitive to issues of privacy and voyeurism, objectification and power dynamics. But not on the day I found myself in search of the ideal image for the cover of this book—one of several that I hoped would suitably depict Africa's diverse business cultures.

Although small business and barely formal urban markets are not a central focus of this book, I decided to shoot a picture of downtown Lusaka's bustling Comesa Market (after the Common Market for Eastern and Southern Africa, behind whose headquarters the market sits). A few moments after I had snapped the photograph and left the market, I found myself pursued by one of the marketers. Furious, he assailed me and my party in Icibemba for what he assumed was my desire to objectivize what he called "our poverty": I was accused of wanting to return to the United States and use my photos to show others the poor and "undeveloped" conditions under which Africans live and work.

Although I was deliberately trying to obscure identities in the photo (I wanted *place* more than people), it is nevertheless true that his reaction was not only justified but was based on an astute understanding of how Westerners, and perhaps Americans in particular, have often conceptualized Africa and Africans as "backward," poverty stricken, and underdeveloped.

Perhaps in no location more so than in Africa's rough and tumble urban marketplaces is this conception more on display—or at least ripe for mischaracterization. This is, in many respects, the epitome of what Curtis Keim refers to as "primitive Africa"— an Africa that desperately needs to "catch up."[1] De rigueur in the past, arguably such views remain widespread today. It is precisely those assumptions and predispositions of a static and unchanging Africa that this book seeks to challenge, in particular by focusing on the opportunities for big business in contemporary Africa. Ironically, then, the merchant could not have been more wrong about my intentions. In fact, his interpretation was exactly the *opposite* of what this book aims to portray.[2]

I was aiming for a perfect collage of cover photographs that would display "African business" in all its fascinating contemporary variation, from the iconic stalls of the informal sector at Comesa Market to the soaring new office towers of Kigali, from the sellers of tourist objects to the whirring textile factories of Lesotho. The challenge is to transcend that vision of the informal market as the *sole* representation of business in sub-Saharan Africa. Although the photo collage ultimately did not work out logistically, this book seeks to illuminate the vibrancy, dynamism, resilience, and most importantly, the diversity of business cultures in sub-Saharan Africa, with a particular emphasis on medium and large-scale firms in the formal sector. Indeed, if I could locate him, I think my angry proprietor would be pleasantly surprised by this book.

Most studies of business activity in Africa tend to focus on the owners of micro- and small- and medium-scale enterprises (M/SMEs), and surely, those individuals can be downright impressive in their perseverance and intrepidity. Indeed, sub-Saharan Africa has become known for micro- and small-scale enterprises, and these perhaps form a central preoccupation of donors and international development practitioners. To casual observers, these occupations may be hallmarks of poverty and backwardness (as my market accuser feared), although to scholars they have been the scene of political ferment (John Heilbrunn); inventiveness and creativity (Janet McGaffey; Karen Tranberg Hansen); and vibrant entrepreneurship (Gareth Austin; Michael West; John Iliffe).[3]

Micro- and small-scale enterprises are hardly unimportant. Indeed, they play a critical function in subsistence—and more. They are critical sites of gender equity, even female senior authority, and many of these small businesses substantially exceed subsistence and generate measurable profits. Moreover, while this heritage is frequently overlooked, today's M/SMEs are the metaphorical heirs to a truly vast history of entrepreneurialism and capitalist practice in Africa that extends back into antiquity. With very few exceptions, however, I eschew small-scale or microenterprises in the informal sector in this book. First, these entities are already well covered in both scholarly and practical literatures on development, gender, and microfinance. Yet this preoccupation with M/SMEs in Africa, while not misplaced, is clearly one sided. Since M/SMEs are often geared toward subsistence and are predominantly based in the trades, they are, even under the most propitious conditions, inadequate vehicles for delivering technology transfer, capacity for reproduction and indeed, development itself. Of course, to label all small-scale business activity as "subsistence" flies in the face of considerable evidence.[4] Some of these players, such as the Mercedes-owning "Mama Benz" of Togo and elsewhere, have *accumulated* fabulous wealth. Yet while many individuals have thrived and exceptions clearly exist, by and large this grouping collectively has not been able to make the transition to larger business enterprises or diversify beyond trading. Their institutions have seldom been pillars of the "modern" economy nor have they been able to shape the state in the mode of a bourgeoisie. Thus, I see them as delinked from state structures or at least delinked from development imperatives as conceived in the contemporary era. In short, as important—indeed vital—as they are, Africa will not become renowned for its global business on the sturdy backs of market women alone.

In a way, therefore, the M/SME-centric image is an unfair depiction, or at least a misleading one, inasmuch as it belies the presence on the continent of a vast array of other business sectors, firms and operations, and opportunities that are obscured by the preoccupation with the informal (itself an unconscious depiction of a quaint, timeless and unchanged Africa, perhaps?). Hence, rather than focus on those small-scalers, the subject of this book is centered more squarely on medium and big business in Africa. These actors have not largely been the focus of analyses, in part because of our erroneous and outdated assumptions about the limits of the African private sector marketplace and its receptivity to larger formal business. Yet big business is not only present in Africa; it is also, I believe, more impactful.

This book argues that it is necessary to shift the paradigm through which large business in Africa is generally analyzed. Recent developments suggest a fundamental shift in the nature and practice of "African business." Evidence of this change is found in policy changes, the *Doing Business* reports published by the World Bank, and investment in new sectors, among other things. I draw on this data, news accounts, the still relatively scarce secondary literature on contemporary big business activity in Africa, as well as on insights from my own two decades of international field research in the area of business-state relations and private sector development.

The Cultures of Business is intended for students and scholars in a range of disciplines, including political science, economics, history, geography, business, and anthropology, for development practitioners, as well as for those individuals with a general interest in African affairs. The book eschews many of the conventions of a political science monograph, as it is less concerned with presenting data than it is with introducing arguments, which I hope are provocative. Moreover, this book deliberately avoids getting bogged down in disciplinary jargon that often consigns good books to the shelves of a handful of like-minded academics. Yet whereas I deliberately cross disciplines, drawing on the expansive literature by Africanist historians, cultural insights and observations from anthropologists, and of course business economics, I endeavor to stay true to my own disciplinary origins as a political scientist. Thus I regard the act of "doing business," perhaps especially in developing countries, as an endeavor that is inextricably linked to power and power dynamics, which shape, and in turn are shaped by, institutions. How state power is exercised is critical to understanding the fulfillment of Africa's entrepreneurial impulses and the expression of its diverse business cultures. Hence, the historical constraints on private sector growth in Africa can be understood partly as a function of the distribution of power: colonial states reserved that power to themselves and their citizens; postcolonial African governments saw unrestrained private sector growth as a potential threat to state power. Likewise, the lens of politics is also a useful one through which to view the general receptivity and welcoming attitude today of so many of Africa's elite political class to the *idea* of business and capitalism; where for generations the political economy was inimical to most large private firms, business now finds fertile ground.

DEFINITIONS, CONCEPTS AND APPROACH

Of course, "doing business" and "doing" capitalism is not quite the same thing, but the concepts of business and capitalism are nonetheless inextricably linked. Regarding capitalism, some scholars have found it useful to employ Max Weber's definition. "Modern capitalism, for Weber, is defined by the rational (deliberate and systematic) pursuit of profit through the rational (systematic and calculable) organization of formally free labor and through rational (impersonal, purely instrumental) exchange on the market, guided by rational (exact, purely quantitative) accounting procedures and guaranteed by rational (rule-governed, predictable) legal and political systems."[5] Its venerable provenance notwithstanding, I find this definition too limiting, however. Indeed, it serves as a convenient straw man to justify claims that Africa, which lacks many of these characteristics, has no capitalism. In fact, few contemporary economies would conform to such a rigid interpretation. Thus, I favor the more flexible definition employed by Ruth McVey in her study of Southeast Asia, which is both more supple and more applicable to "actually existing capitalisms" in the modern world.[6] McVey defines capitalism as "a system in which the means of production, in private hands, are employed to create a profit, some of which is reinvested to increase profit-generating capacity."[7] This definition incorporates agribusiness, banking, services, construction, trade, mining and other nonmanufacturing activities as well, "provided they are carried on in a capitalist manner *and involve domestic capital.*"[8] Certainly, this broader conception seems to have worked quite well for wide swaths of Asia, whose capitalist zeal few deny today. I will not hold Africa to a more exacting Weberian standard.

By "business" I refer primarily to formal, medium- and large-scale enterprises, both urban and rural. Although notions of what constitutes big business vary, I generally hew to the common definition, whereby medium-scale enterprises are those with fifty to three hundred employees. Small firms, by contrast, may have as few as ten employees. Yet even Africa's larger firms may be considered small by international standards, however.[9] I do differentiate between black and minority-owned business in Africa, where such distinctions are appropriate, although I include all of these domestic capitalists under the rubric of "African business." Conversely, the notion of *business in Africa* thus represents a broader category, which includes multinational firms doing business on the continent; each of these agents, domestic and international, informs the cultures of business in sub-Saharan Africa.

Importantly, this book is not intended as an analysis of a specific sector or industry.[10] Thus, the discussion includes firms involved in manufacturing, services (such as commercial trade), energy, telecommunications, finance, and transportation, for example, as well as large-scale commercial agriculture and mining, all of which enjoy substantial private representation in Africa today.

The country focus is similarly eclectic; although not completely pan-African in scope, it is self-consciously *multi*-African. Methodologically and stylistically, I refer frequently to country cases at the national and subnational levels for illustrative purposes throughout the book. However, these examples are integrated into the narrative rather than presented as discrete case studies or comparative country studies. Though somewhat at odds with the comparative method, my approach is stylistically consistent with those books I consider part of this genre, such as Steve Radelet's *Emerging Africa* or Vijaya Ramachandran, Alan Gelb, and Manju Kedia Shah's *Africa's Private Sector,* inasmuch as I try to avoid making claims about the entire continent. Like Radelet, I believe it is critical that we reject the idea of Africa as a monolith; indeed, the origin of much Afropessimist thinking lies in an inability or unwillingness to differentiate. In general, the companies I describe require polities that exhibit stability, a semblance of accountability (presumably democratic), and a market-oriented economy. At the same time, however, it is also necessary to explain change in some surprising locales as well. Since the book is as much company-based as it is country-based, a considerable portion of the discussion pertains to the capacities and adaptability of specific firms. Thus, while the national context is critically important, I also include examples of businesses that have thrived despite inauspicious domestic conditions.

The chronological focus of the book is on business and the business environment at the end of the twentieth century and first decade of the new millennium. During this time, I argue, we have seen a sea change, sparked by the political and economic transitions of the 1990s, that begs examination. But neither business activity of significant size and scope nor its study by scholars is a new phenomenon. Indeed, business, including trade and commercial enterprise, in precolonial times was vibrant and diverse and local, regional, and international in scope. Such activity prior to the colonial era has been painstakingly documented by historians such as Gareth Austin, Ralph Austen, Catherine Coquery-Vidrovitch, Toyin Falola and Alusine Jalloh, to name but a few. Indeed, there are rich studies on the Dyula and Hausa long-distance traders, for example, and on the myriad political and economic empires that fed the transatlantic and Indian Ocean slave trades. The growing presence of European firms, and eventually of those belonging to intermediary groups such as Lebanese in West Africa and Indians and others in East Africa, had cut sharply into the activities of black entrepreneurs by the first half of the twentieth century, although even then categories of so-called merchant princes and other entrepreneurs persisted. One need not subscribe to an Afrocentric view of history to appreciate the vital competitive role African business played in world commerce, especially in antiquity. Moreover, during the colonial era, minority-owned businesses established deep roots in Africa and thrived, albeit usually at the expense of their black counterparts. These are valuable insights for any serious student of African history.

Yet the prevailing reputation of contemporary Africa is that it lacks a strong business culture or competitive firms at the medium- and large-scale level. Hence, it is worth investigating both the explanation for and the accuracy of this reputation. What lessons can be derived from those firms and entrepreneurs that endure versus those that do not? What helps to explain their success or failure at reproduction and expansion, as *capitalists*? These are very much *twenty-first-century questions* that take on added importance in the wake of economic liberalization and a renewed focus on private sector development globally. In many ways, our theories have yet to catch up with important changes on the ground in a wide range of African countries.

I seek to reexamine theories of African capitalism by situating the analysis between neopatrimonialism and triumphalism or, if one prefers, between Afropessimism and Afro-optimism. These are essentially the two metanarratives that capture business in Africa and perhaps even the study of Africa as a whole. But there is often a missing middle. This book fills an important theoretical and practical lacuna between the triumphant views expressed recently by promoters of African business and capitalism, particularly in the development community, that Africa is unmistakably and rather uniformly "open for business" and those, among them many scholars, who would deny that the capacity for African business even *exists* on a measurable scale. Each of these extremes has garnered ample attention in the academic and practical literature, yet the middle ground is virtually ignored analytically—though perhaps not so by private equity firms and others. Indeed, there is a noticeable gulf between the triumphalism of some recent studies and the fatalism expressed perhaps most famously by Patrick Chabal and Jean-Pascal Daloz in *Africa Works: Disorder as Political Instrument*. Similar themes of course are also picked up in other works on African political economy and stress the hopelessness of business prospects in Africa: elites are too venal; states are too intrusive; markets are too immature.[11]

Steering a course between the poles of Afropessimism and Afro-optimism, this book aims to provide an unvarnished analysis of the prospects for bigger business and durable capitalism in sub-Saharan Africa. The book makes a case for reexamination of the evolving *cultures* of business on the continent and the impact of the history of African business and the theories long applied to it in light of contemporary forces impacting African business, including changes in the domestic and regional political economy and the emergence of new international business partners. These factors allow for a critical reappraisal of the potential of African business to contribute to development locally and internationally in an increasingly globalized world.

My argument rests on three principal foundations that are elucidated in each of the book's three parts. First, it rejects the determinism embedded in the (prevailing) cynical assumptions about African political economy and specifically about the African private sector. It challenges certain shibboleths about African capitalism and the continent's private sectors by interrogating the limits of these assumptions. While hardly a paragon of "mature" capitalism, the increased relevance of African private sectors in the 1990s is undeniable, such that we can now at least begin to talk about private sectors on their own merits rather than in terms of their parasitism vis-à-vis the public sector.

The second foundational premise holds that the more hospitable environment for business and entrepreneurship in contemporary Africa has been fostered by institutional change. In part, this results from the more beneficial processes of globalization. The phenomenon has varied and sometimes contradictory interpretations, but I refer to the transformative power of international norms and pressure—through the aid regime, lending policies, and the demise of Cold War ideological struggles—for the instauration of democratic practices and the enactment of pertinent economic reforms. My usage of the term globalization generally comports with Pádraig Carmody, who defines it "as the increased interconnectedness between places in terms of trade, investment, and information flows in particular," although to this rather economistic definition I would add both political and ideational components.[12] Globalization is not unidirectional, of course, but in the first instance, we consider its impact *on* Africa: the influences of structure and neoliberal economic ideology on African business, interactions between the forces of international and domestic capitalism and their impacts, and the various pressures for institutional change. (Globalization also refers to the expanded presence and visibility of a new array of international businesses in Africa today—for example, Chinese and Indian business interests.)

The transitions of the 1990s, which were further intensified by globalization, form a critical juncture in the prospects for an inherently African business sector. Even the most jaundiced observer of African political economy must accept, if grudgingly, that the private sector *climate* in Africa has shifted markedly in the past two decades and that political attitudes have changed in response to both domestic and international pressures. Indeed, private sector development activities and enthusiastic celebrations of African business, however premature, would be unheard of absent the key changes in the institutional environment that took place in the 1990s. A measurable degree of economic liberalization and democratization has played, in turn, a critical role in the visibility and viability of business actors.

The third underlying premise of this book is that African business has multiple sources and diverse origins. Hence, "African business" includes not just black-run firms but, as I've noted, settler and minority capital as well. Moreover, although this definition excludes multinational corporations (MNCs), they have an important role, both the ubiquitous Western multinationals and increasingly Chinese and other companies originating in the global south, including Africa's own large corporations. All represent potential partners for local firms as well as a basis for business operations in their own right. The sources of African business also include unconventional and unexpected ones, such as crony capitalists, whose inclusion here would shock the Afro-optimist contingent. Although these actors have traditionally been dependent solely on state largesse and patronage rather than production, they can in fact be channeled to more positive outcomes wherein they are motivated by profit and reinvestment rather than supported by a patrimonial system.

There are critical changes under way in contemporary Africa that tend to be over-looked by pessimists and overhyped by optimists. Recent analyses have noted the re-markable progress, yet we cannot be oblivious to the complex challenges that remain. Business, particularly larger firms, can play an important part of meeting those chal-lenges. The vibrancy, resiliency, and diversity of sub-Saharan Africa's business cultures enable a surprising number of firms, and perhaps many countries, to adapt to an in-creasingly globalized environment.

ACKNOWLEDGMENTS

Although this book bears my name, like most books it is ultimately a reflection of countless inputs and generous contributions from numerous individuals and institutions. At Georgetown, I had the privilege of working with a number of excellent research assistants over the course of this project. I would like to thank Mike Jobbins, Nicole Lewis, and Rahma Dualeh for their help in the early days of this book. Three research assistants deserve special thanks for their contributions at different stages of the project: the indefatigable Anita Ravishankar offered superb research assistance and helped give the book shape. Kristy Gray pointedly kept me on task and helped prepare and edit the first full draft of the manuscript. Ikepo Oyenuga was indispensible in the last stages of the project: without her help the road to final product would have been measurably more uphill.

I also benefited from participation in the BookLab at Georgetown University, under the capable leadership of Carole Sargent, director of the Office of Scholarly and Literary Publications. In the process, I received helpful feedback from Carol and my colleagues and fellow book group members Melissa Fisher, Kathleen McNamara, Andrew Natsios, Beverly Sauer, Tania Gentic, Leslie Hinkson, and Aparna Vaidik. All took time away from their own manuscripts to offer insights and much-needed encouragement.

I am thankful to Peter von Doepp and Deborah Brautigam for comments on conference presentations that informed several chapters. I am especially indebted to Toyin Falola and Callisto Madavo, who each generously read the entire manuscript and offered extensive comments and constructive critiques. Three anonymous reviewers for the press were also quite helpful. At Indiana University Press, Angela Burton and Sarah Jacobi ably steered the book to publication. My most heartfelt thanks go to Dee Mortensen, senior sponsoring editor, for her steadfast support of this project from the very beginning. I am grateful to her for bringing it to fruition.

Finally, I would like to thank my family for their constant support—and their deep reservoir of patience. During the time I wrote this book, my father, Timothy Merritt Taylor Sr., experienced a sharp decline in his health. Though I am saddened that he will never read this book, I will remember with great joy our conversations about so many others. This book is dedicated to him, with love.

GLOBALIZATION AND THE CULTURES
OF BUSINESS IN AFRICA

PART 1
Introduction and Background

INTRODUCTION

BUSINESS IN AFRICA

Barely a generation ago, most analyses of African development tended to regard the business community as inconsequential, treating business actors peripherally, if at all.[1] Indeed, in some quarters, the phrase "African business" might be regarded as something of an oxymoron still. Although most observers would now regard that assessment as unfair, even today the association of "business"—and certainly, *big* business—with "Africa" seldom conjures up images of modernity, indigenous industrial prowess, or even multinational corporate penetration, beyond the major extractive sectors such as petroleum and minerals mining enterprises.

More than a few indicators provide a foundation for the persistent belief that Africa is somehow incompatible with modern, formal business of sizable scale. In 2006, for example, not a single African-domiciled company from any sector was included in the *Fortune* Global 500 list of the world's largest corporations by revenue.[2] The World Bank's "Doing Business" initiative, which marked its seventh year of publication in 2009, reveals that just 7 of the 44 sub-Saharan countries in the study rank among the top half of the 180 countries evaluated on the basis of business climate. Moreover, it is widely known as well that African countries also rank among the world's highest in perceived corruption, fostering an environment in which even the most basic business functions may be a challenge to achieve.[3] Additional obstacles to business in Africa include underdeveloped capital markets, inadequate or decayed infrastructure, and structural constraints such as barriers to trade—the list goes on. These varied data would seem to indicate that Africa-based firms and economies would scarcely be considered in the pantheon of global business. Indeed, in a context of global capitalism, marked by the rapid ascension to international prominence of private firms from China, India, Brazil, and a host of other developing countries, African countries and their firms are often noticeably absent.[4] In other words, African businesses, regardless of whether they are associated with black Africans or resident minorities, are hardly recognized as being among global players; in fact, they are seldom even regarded as *continental* players in areas other than primary commodities.[5] What is more, with local economies often dominated by multinational firms and their affiliates, *African* businesses often are unappreciated as formidable players even in their respective *domestic* marketplaces. Simply put, Africa is not known for well-developed business sectors in which the preponderance of firms can demonstrate the ability to generate revenue and surplus and reinvest that surplus in productive enterprise (rather than merely engage in rent seeking), contribute to employment and perhaps the national treasury through payment of taxes, and provide other direct and indirect benefits to the local economy. On this array of shortcomings and set of underlying conditions a broad range of scholars and practitioners find common ground.

A more contested but nonetheless prevalent view holds that Africa does not have a strong business culture. This critique is aimed more squarely at Africa's black majorities, to be sure. Regardless, estimates of African business culture invariably come up short, especially when measured against those countries and regions that are regarded as archetypes, namely the United States and the West, Japan, and increasingly much of Asia. In those paradigmatic business cultures, profit and loss are taken seriously, the idea of productive gain is embedded in the belief system, and capital can be reproduced (or seeks to reproduce itself), whether in the family enterprise or on a national level. A vibrant business culture also promotes trust, thereby facilitating cooperation between entrepreneurs, which in turn allows interdependencies between firms, arm's-length contracts, loyalty, and the proliferation initially of small, highly productive firms.[6]

What explains Africa's enduring reputation for lacking a strong business culture and competitive medium- and large-scale firms beyond the traditional extractive sectors? Is African business as weak, unproductive, and corrupt as implied? More fundamentally, is a modern business culture that can precipitate the emergence of large-scale enterprises with at least the potential for global impact incompatible with African historical and cultural realities?

Responses to these questions fall essentially into two broad camps: Afropessimism and Afro-optimism. These are hardly unproblematic categories, and they mask a high degree of variation, but they nonetheless serve an illustrative purpose.[7] At its most extreme, Afropessimism is "the belief that Africa is irredeemably doomed to backwardness and chaos. Afropessimism embodies two tendencies—vilification of African experiences and valorization of Euroamerican engagements with Africa," grounded in the notion that "Africa is incapable by itself of historical progress and that any progress evident there is the result of Euroamerican interventions."[8] Within this broader Afropessimist discourse, however, I am particularly interested in the arguments that pertain to African economies and business more narrowly.

Toward that end, I interrogate the strand of Afropessimist thinking known as neopatrimonialism, a paradigm that gained considerable traction among a generation of political science scholars, and among a few anthropologists. To be fair, not all neopatrimonial theorists would classify themselves as "Afropessimists," but I argue that the devotion to the concept can lead to assessments of African economies, politics, and even culture that are ineluctably pessimistic.[9] Neopatrimonialism envisions a political economy beset by pervasive corruption and its attendant patronage and rent seeking rather than by rational economic structures (Chabal and Daloz; Thomas Callaghy). Taken to its logical conclusion, such a political-economic-cultural milieu necessarily undermines any prospect for modern capitalism and larger productive firms. Neopatrimonialism is a useful starting place for this analysis, since at its core are traditional cultural arguments that suggest a strong and negative linkage between "premodern" Africa and contemporary institutions and behaviors.

At the opposite end of the spectrum, Afro-optimists, by contrast, must guard against irrational exuberance about various positive trends on the continent. Indeed, some recent claims might lead us to believe that the questions about business viability themselves are irrelevant, and perhaps even invalid, because market conditions are in fact "marvelous" already.[10] What unites these disparate views is their tendency to misconstrue business in Africa, a subject on which analysts proceed from partial if not altogether false assumptions with alarming regularity. Even where these assumptions have a kernel of legitimacy to them, they are at the same time insufficiently nuanced to capture *generational change, diversity, and the possibility of further change in Africa's business environment*. Cronyism is a central tenet of Afropessimist discourse, for example, but I argue that cronies can actually fit within a more positive discourse and can be accommodated within our conceptions of African capital and what constitutes *legitimate business*. Afro-optimists insist that the present period establishes Africa as "open for business" and host to new economies likened to cheetahs, lions, and various other fleet-footed and hungry animals in the mold of the "Asian tigers" that preceded them. I am sympathetic to these interpretations, but the enthusiasm is often cast too wide and the seamier side of capitalist development is often wished away. Thus, this book aims to establish a middle ground by revisiting both Afropessimist and Afro-optimist assumptions, which mark the point of departure for this book.

THE AFROPESSIMIST-NEOPATRIMONIAL PERSPECTIVE: IMPLICATIONS FOR BUSINESS CULTURE

Those in the Afropessimist mold suggest that Africa's cronyist-neopatrimonial tendencies at all levels put a substantial brake on the kind of accumulation required for big business. Hence, because of patron-clientelism, weak institutions, and cultural norms that promote sharing and the payment of tribute to neopatrimonial "big men," black big business, arrived at through modern capitalism, is a virtual nonstarter.[11] Minority big business, while not comparably constrained culturally, nonetheless finds itself forever at the mercy of predatory neopatrimonial African elites.

Stressing the cultural or neopatrimonial dimension of African business (and states) promotes a determinism about African business whereby it is ineluctably corrupt: the very nature of patron-client ties in sub-Saharan Africa would appear to render the expansion of legitimate commerce extraordinarily difficult, if not impossible. The problem of African business therefore becomes an intractable one. And some in this intellectual tradition make an even more fundamental contention: that African capitalism—or, at least, capitalism as *practiced* in Africa—is simply incompatible with the expectations of firms and markets found elsewhere in the world. It is, in short, *culturally* distinct and culturally deficient.

Yet there are at least two reasons why such arguments against African business are unsatisfactory if not misleading. The first has to do with the notion of culture itself. A misconception about what "African culture" is leads to the erroneous conclusion that culture acts as a major constraint on the emergence of "legitimate" capitalism in Africa. In fact, the premise itself requires reexamination: there are many *cultures* in Africa; business cultures are similarly diverse. "African culture" cannot be reduced to monolithic caricature. "Africa" is comprised of fifty-five countries that are home to twenty-five hundred languages, representing half a dozen colonial experiences, three world religions, and hundreds of enduring traditional belief systems among its nearly one billion inhabitants. Yet there is an unmistakable tendency to speak of uniquely African phenotypes—almost always negative. Culture in Africa, or anywhere, is neither static nor monolithic but necessarily syncretic, that is, infused with the multiple and sometimes conflicting influences from a range of sources and traditions. It is hardly immutably bound up in some putatively "African" traditional practice. The same is true for business in Africa, whose multiple cultures are equally dynamic and diverse. Thus, this stylized notion of an African culture that appears in much of the literature needs to be fundamentally decoupled from the arguments about patrimonial capitalism.

When notions of culture (however overbroad) are deployed in African political economy writing and scholarship, the connotation is regularly pejorative, implying the existence of norms such as backwardness, slavish adherence to "tradition" and corruption, and a general lack of modernity. Yet the incessant "Africa as neopatrimonial basket case" trope is eerily reminiscent of the long-standing confusion about the role of "Confucian culture" in capitalist development in East Asia. The latter began, as Ruth McVey reminds us, by purporting to explain why Chinese were unlikely to make good capitalists. Ironically enough, one of the early purveyors of this thesis was no less than Max Weber, who "explored the relationship between Chinese ideology and social structure, and concluded that China's economic backwardness was fostered by the values inculcated by Confucianism," values at odds with the puritan ones enshrined in the Protestant work ethic.[12] Weber's characterization of the patrimonial form of authority forms the basis of the neopatrimonial argument in Arica.

With the economic successes of East and Southeast Asia (including ethnic Chinese within these economies), however, scholars recognized that the theory needed revision. Thus, eventually it was decided that Confucian "values of diligence, order, individual responsibility and so on *promoted* capitalist behavior."[13] As McVey rightly concludes, the misinformed arguments about "Confucianism," pro and con, were analytically weak and often suffused with racist assumptions about "Asian culture." Culture was both obstacle and enabler. In short, as with the misreading of Asian-Confucian cultures, the explanatory power of theories that purport to ascribe certain characteristics to an imagined "African culture" is equally lacking in analytical clarity.

The second reason why cultural arguments against African business fail to hold up to scrutiny is because they assume that *African* neopatrimonialism (and its offshoot, crony capitalism) is not only unique but an ineradicable feature of the African political-economic landscape. Neither of these appears to be correct. Neopatrimonialism and its analytical kin are based on Weber's forms of authority, but while Weber's original thesis remains robust after nearly a century, the "neo" variant has been stretched to its conceptual and intellectual limits.[14] Scholars employing the neopatrimonial framework have argued not only that it poses a fundamental barrier to transparency (non-corruption) and bureaucratic accountability but also that it is ultimately incompatible with modern capitalism.[15] Others, however, suggest that such (re)interpretations may in fact misread Weber, who perhaps "did not see the line between capitalism and the rent-seeking of power holders to be as absolute as many present analysts do."[16]

It is not necessary to discard the concepts of neopatrimonial and patrimonial capitalism altogether. Rather we must escape the Afropessimist cul-de-sac that results from uncritical adherence to such paradigms. Certainly, Africa has its share of crony capitalists, whose existence owes to clientelist linkages with the state rather than their intrinsic business acumen. Once again placing sub-Saharan Africa in a wider comparative perspective, however, it becomes equally plain that pervasive neopatrimonialism and its attendant cronyism in business practices are scarcely uniquely African pathologies. Furthermore, whereas corruption is undesirable, it is not incompatible with capitalist economic development. Thus, rather than assume these characteristics are sui generis in Africa, it is important to note that they are in fact quite common in developing and developed countries alike.[17]

Indeed, the role of such actors has been well documented in Asia, Eastern Europe, Latin America, and perhaps some OECD states as well. Importantly, polities in each of these regions witnessed both the emergence of cronies and their eventual transformation into if not always into "respectable" capitalists, then at least viable proprietors of functional businesses. Many examples can be found in recent studies covering everything from contemporary Korea to nineteenth-century New York City.[18] Like the robber barons of nineteenth-century America, Korean network capitalism, and perhaps even the organized crime syndicates that became pervasive in postcommunist Russia, Africa's patrimonial/crony capitalists can help to catalyze private sector development: business actors, even if their provenance is "illegitimate," may, over time, develop legitimate business interests and they will pressure (or create) states to protect those interests.[19]

This path of transformation will not be taken by all cronies. Thus it is vitally important to differentiate between those business actors that generally receive state favors and contracts but are nonetheless "going concerns" to begin with and those that are truly "briefcase businessmen" who lack even the rudiments of a company structure and are therefore utterly dependent on rents. Moreover, warlords who control politico-territorial entities through violence and the dispensing of patronage may be less willing to give up their lucrative and exclusive positions.[20] Likewise, although pure predation is usually unsustainable over the long term because patronage resources diminish, it is more easily maintained in areas of abundant natural resources, particularly in the established petro-states of Nigeria, Angola, Equatorial Guinea, Chad, and Sudan, where patronage resources are virtually inexhaustible. Conversely, in a context of finite resources, *coupled with a more democratic institutional environment,* illicit businesspeople cannot cannibalize their rivals ad infinitum.

In his 2005 book, *Syndromes of Corruption,* Michael Johnston reveals almost unintentionally that various forms, or syndromes, of corruption needn't derail formal, legitimate, modern capitalism in the form of large transnational business enterprises. To be fair, Johnson's primary focus is on the negative *political* impacts of various corruption syndromes and how they undermine accountability. He correctly points out that such syndromes are bad for democracy and erode the health of the polity.[21] But as his choice of developing-country case studies reveals, such syndromes do not necessarily have a detrimental impact on *business* emergence or on business's capacity to play a role in national development. Importantly, not even the most pernicious of his four syndromes precludes the emergence of a viable, even internationally renowned, business class in places like China or Mexico, for example.

At bottom, the determinism intrinsic to Afropessimism, whether derived by academics from neopatrimonialist interpretations of politics and culture or stemming from popular media, is deeply flawed. Its neopatrimonial variant is based on a misreading of Weber and of African culture. Neopatrimonial theorists see Africa as unique, which justifies their insistence that crony capitalism is an inescapable trap for sub-Saharan Africa, despite the fact that it has not been so limiting elsewhere. Finally, Afropessimism tends to overgeneralize "Africa," treating a diverse continent as an undifferentiated single entity. Consequently, Afropessimism cannot account for a number of recent trends in sub-Saharan Africa, nor for the new international *and* domestic interest in African business and the altered context for both business emergence and commercial transactions. As a columnist in the British newspaper the *Guardian* recently implored, "It's time the world listened to new stories out of Africa."[22] One story that has been surprisingly underplayed is the palpable new enthusiasm, both within Africa and to some extent globally, regarding the prospects for business development on the African continent.

THE GLOBALIZATIONIST-AFRO-OPTIMIST PERSPECTIVE

In contrast to those inclined toward Afropessimism, the Afro-optimists at least allow the possibility for confidence in and about African business. In fact, those adhering to an economic liberal or functionalist perspective, particularly representatives of the international financial institutions (IFIs) and the donor community, contend that the environment is not intrinsically hostile to business in sub-Saharan Africa. The members of this group, whom I refer to as "globalizationists," see the potential in globalization, at least in the interpretation of that phenomenon as increased interconnectedness.[23] Certainly in the twentieth century, however, the processes of globalization manifested themselves adversely in Africa. Indeed, even by this rather limited definition, from the period of slave trade and colonial extraction and exploitation to that of neoliberal structural adjustment programs (SAPs), globalization's impact was profoundly negative in Africa, arguably until quite recently.[24]

There remains widespread disagreement about the pros and cons of globalization. However, internal reforms and growth in sub-Saharan Africa and renewed interest in the continent on the part of investors and trade partners, the rise of China and donors (for example, through the promulgation of millennium development goals) in the current era hint at the possibility, at least, that this era can be more beneficial to Africa. Thus, even for those who regarded structural adjustment as a blunt and ineffective instrument for reforming African economies, today African countries are far better positioned to take advantage of current global interconnectedness. The global or external environment began to change fundamentally in the late 1990s, during which time neoliberalism underwent modifications and a greater emphasis was put on poverty reduction and debt forgiveness. Now that the domestic policy environment has improved, partly in response to these changes, the potential of African business can be unleashed. Although structure still matters, for globalizationists the principal obstacle is not external. African entrepreneurship has been constrained historically by hostile official state ideologies and their impact on the macroeconomy, a lack of investment, and a paucity of actionable ideas: rectify these problems, and Africa is "open for business."

Although the favorability of the current international environment for Africa is open to question and the benign nature of globalization remains contested, it appears that when it comes to issues of business in Africa, the globalizationists and the broader population of Afro-optimists have much more hang their hats on than their Afropessimist counterparts.[25] In fact, there are reasons for their enthusiasm. Indeed, the fairly recent barrage of promotional material and the emergence of institutions purporting to herald a new era in African business and—an important corollary—its attractiveness as an investment destination, particularly since 2000, is striking.

For example, numerous publications now analyze business practices and advise businesspeople and would-be investors, foreign and domestic. Among them, the scholarly *Journal of African Business* falls in the former category, whereas the UK-based magazine *African Business,* now in its fifth decade, falls into the latter, to cite just two noteworthy examples. Books, such as those by American businessman and author David Fick and business professor Vijay Mahajan, celebrate sub-Saharan Africa as a veritable haven for business. Although not about business directly, Steven Radelet's *Emerging Africa* heralds the renewed optimism and development opportunities in seventeen African polities, while the McKinsey Global Institute hails African economies as "Lions on the Move." Films, such as director Carol Pineau's 2005 documentary "Africa: Open for Business," praise Africa's new—or at least, newly recognized—private sector ethos; although it profiles just ten entrepreneurs from around the continent, they are regarded as genuinely representative of a larger phenomenon. Moreover, a broad range of Africa- and non-Africa-based entities have been set up to foster private sector growth. Two of the most prominent bodies were actually launched in the 1990s. One, the African Business Roundtable, was founded in 1990 by the Africa Development Bank with the aim of strengthening the private sector and promoting trade and investment. Another, the U.S.-based Corporate Council on Africa, established in 1993, aims to build commercial relationships between American firms and prospective African partners, presumably to their mutual benefit. Private sector business development has also been championed in recent years by the African Union, where it has been included among the self-identified "priority projects" of the Africa Union's New Partnership for Africa's Development(NEPAD). In addition, spurred on by the World Bank and the donor community, and certainly by a measure of domestic demand, virtually every sub-Saharan African country has adopted some form of private sector development (PSD) program.

Several other noteworthy features of the contemporary business environment in Africa lend support to the Afro-optimist/globalizationist view. Notably, various indicators suggest that a surprising number of competitive, apparently investment-friendly economies already exist in sub-Saharan Africa.[26] For example, the presence of several African countries among the top half of global economies according to the World Development Bank's Doing Business project clearly evinces both the existence of and a receptiveness to business that challenge many negative assumptions about the business climate. Of course, this ranking includes the usual suspects, Mauritius (17), South Africa (34), Botswana (45), and Namibia (66), which are often treated as "exceptional" in various analyses of Africa. But it also incorporates Rwanda and Zambia, with Ghana and Kenya (numbers 92 and 95, respectively) not far behind, whereas Liberia gains kudos for its aggressive reform.

But even the at times euphoric "new stories" out of Africa should be treated with some caution. Although the change in business cultures is readily apparent, the globalizationists tend to proffer overly optimistic programs rather than realistic assessments of the actual status of African business in various places around the continent. Though half a dozen African economies fall into Doing Business's top 100, six times that number do not. Indeed, some of the prescriptions that emerge from the relatively benign view of globalization suggest that merely introducing programs, such as the ubiquitous neoliberal SAPs of the 1980s and 1990s at the state level or those fostering entrepreneurialism in contemporary period at the private level, will unleash African business. Whereas the most uncompromising Afropessimists persevere with their theories despite countervailing facts, at least the optimists endeavor to explain new (positive) developments. But the latter's explanations are often sweeping and their prescriptions too wishful. Although the globalizationist perspective often features an admirable enthusiasm, the tenor of which I support, much of it remains untempered and formulaic.

Examining the actual track record in a range of countries across the continent, it is easy to conclude that the triumphalism accompanying PSD initiatives and similar programs is often unrequited in Africa, where many previous efforts, received with similar enthusiasm, failed to yield genuine results. In this vein, it is important to note that the level of political commitment within African governments to business and private sector promotion runs the gamut from demonstrable to merely rhetorical. To be sure, strong business cultures are present or emerging in parts of Africa, and states, donors, and formal private sector development programs will undoubtedly be important in channeling those cultures and ideas into actual enterprise. Yet while self-conscious, proactive, and programmatic efforts at private sector development are necessary for the emergence and expansion of African business, they are hardly sufficient.

In sum, most analyses of African business, whether inspired by Afropessimist-neopatrimonialist or by Afro-optimist-globalizationist worldviews, are plagued by incomplete diagnosis and correspondingly ill-considered prescriptions. In the end, I welcome the sentiments expressed by World Bank economist Daniel Kaufman in a 2007 address on debunking the Afropessimism myth. Arguing for more a centrist position, Kaufman insisted we must "challenge the notion of having irrational exuberance just because there [has] been recent good news in the [African] continent as well as other continents. If we focus too much on short terminism, that can lead also to a false sense of exuberant optimism, so we will take more on the middle view."[27] If one takes Kaufman's point to heart, it is easier to conclude that both the cynical determinism conveyed by the neopatrimonial-Afropessimist perspectives and the sunny optimism of the globalizationist perspective are overstated.

FOUNDATIONS OF A NEW ARGUMENT

This book seeks to weave a path between the two admittedly stylized extremes in order to present a balanced and realistic picture of business, principally larger business, in sub-Saharan Africa today. Although there are some authors who seek to navigate between Afropessimism and optimism, "big business" does not easily fit into our dominant Africa narratives. True, structural and historical conditions are inauspicious and infrastructure and human and financial capital are inadequate, but these should not blind us to the more complex realities of business in Africa. Yet the prevailing perceptions also lie partly in the way African business (and Africa as a whole) is portrayed to the world: perceptions and portrayal become mutually reinforcing.

Africa's portrayal includes a fixation on M/SMEs, especially at the level of donor agencies and international development organizations but also in the popular imagination of Westerners. It is perpetuated by what some marketing experts refer to as a misbranding problem, a misreading of African history (or an incomplete one), a lack of understanding of promising current trends and their causes, and, in the worst cases, a willful disregard for consideration of African cultural variables that explain anything other than "traditional" values that are antithetical to the expansion of modern capitalism. These negative stereotypes certainly feed skepticism about Africans' capacity for entrepreneurship and its ability to sustain business and especially medium- and large-scale business.

Notwithstanding the "good news" stories, which receive fuller attention in later chapters, Africa is replete with cronies, racially and ethnically segmented business sectors, self-interested political actors, beneficial as well as unscrupulous multinational investors. Yet these kinds of political economy endowments are not altogether different from those found elsewhere. Although, with rare exceptions, African businesses are not global players, and African states remain characterized by weak institutions, the ideological and even "cultural" space between business in Africa and elsewhere has narrowed considerably. Hence, business in Africa demonstrates important continuities and commonalities with other regions. African business, therefore, should not be studied as culturally distinct. The constraints attributed to history, structure, and culture have been either temporary obstacles or fundamentally misunderstood as insurmountable barriers to the continued development of "normal capitalism" in sub-Saharan Africa.

The book is organized in three sections, each of which corresponds to a central argument about contemporary business in Africa. The first argument is that the determinism embedded in the Afropessimist assumptions about African political economy and specifically about private sectors is unwarranted. It is necessary to challenge certain Afropessimist shibboleths about African capitalism and the continent's private sectors by interrogating the limits of these assumptions. At the same time, however, it questions the uncritical embrace of the globalizationist/Afro-optimist view. New and important currents are identifiable in sub-Saharan Africa, but in order to understand them we must derive different lessons from each of these worldviews. In brief, cultural barriers to the establishment of larger-scale, formal sector enterprises in Africa do not exist. If the existence of such firms today is not itself evidence of an intrinsic African capacity for capitalist practice, then the rich history of entrepreneurship in Africa should disabuse the cynics.

Yet patrimonial capitalism and the cronyism that characterizes it continues; the growing visibility of other forms of African business and capitalism does not mean that cronyism is necessarily on the wane, as the globalizationists imply. Indeed, a phalanx of "briefcase businessmen" whose existence depends on state largess is simply a reality across many countries. Therefore, scholars and others who focus on these characteristics have it at least partly right. But we need to look at the concept of crony capitalism more broadly, both to understand its relatively modern origins in Africa and its global nature. Moreover, across and sometimes within economies, it is possible to find cronies as well as successful cases of "legitimate" business practice in Africa.

The second claim this book is that institutional change has been a vital catalyst. In other words, the analysis holds that a more hospitable environment for business and entrepreneurship in contemporary Africa has been fostered by economic and political transformation. In part, this results from the more beneficial processes—and surely there are some —of globalization, including the transformative power of international norms and pressure via the aid and debt regimes, evolving international attitudes about the role of the state, and pressure for democratization as well as the enactment of pertinent economic reforms. Thus, the dual transitions of the 1990s formed a critical juncture that affected the prospects for an inherently African business sector. In important respects, the analysis affirms the view embodied in private sector development programs and comparable liberal initiatives that changes to the institutional setting are essential prerequisites. On the other hand, however, these institutional changes are scarcely sufficient for business to become formidable in a national, let alone regional, way. African businesses remain especially vulnerable to external shocks—for example, commodity price fluctuations, the vagaries of the international aid regime, and climatological pressures. Nevertheless, Africa's private sector climate has unambiguously improved in the past two decades, and political attitudes have changed in response to both domestic and international pressures. Africa's significant degree of economic liberalization and democratization establishes a critical foundation for business.

Economic policy changes make possible the expansion of business-generated wealth; political change increases the likelihood that entrepreneurs will keep it. Economic liberalization potentially provides access to credit, foreign exchange, and export markets; it fosters *opportunity* for entrepreneurialism and business success but not assurances thereof. Similarly, greater democracy allows participation by a wider range of private sector actors: business actors gain a *voice* that they lacked previously, enabling them to impact economic life, either through civil society organizations, such as business associations, or directly as key political constituents. In a "democratized marketplace," businesspeople will suffer less predation than under formerly closed, authoritarian— and in the recent African past, largely *anti*developmental—states. In turn, business actors, both collectively and severally, may pursue politics and policies that promote export potential, investment, favorable fiscal, monetary, and trade policies, and a political regime that welcomes their input. This does not make businesspeople *democrats.* Rather, a relatively higher level of democracy can be beneficial to actors who long suffered under the capricious policies of an authoritarian regime.

The third underlying premise of this book is that big business in Africa is diverse: it stems from multiple sources and varied origins and is embodied in a range of forms. These include the usual suspects, such as Western MNCs, as well as Chinese and Indian companies seeking investment abroad. All represent potential partners for emergent African firms and all could carry out business operations in their own right. Paradoxically, the sources of African business also include unconventional and unexpected ones, including Africa's own large corporations, whose existence is remarkably unappreciated outside of Africa, as well as so-called crony capitalists.

THE PLAN OF THE BOOK

Part 1 of the book, comprised of this chapter and the next, is concerned with identifying the roots of misperceptions about contemporary big business in Africa as well as with the recent historical constraints on business and the expression of business cultures (that is, the translation of intrinsic entrepreneurialism into operational firms). The chapters in this section define the terms that guide the analysis and examine the perceptions and misperceptions about business in Africa. Chapter 1 critically evaluates the various explanations for the relative paucity of large-scale manifestations of African capitalism. Much of the skepticism about African business that persists today derives from assumptions about a cultural incompatibility between African leaders and societies and modern business. However, this view conveniently ignores history, which chapter 1 attempts to rectify by briefly tracing the rich history of business and entrepreneurialism in Africa. Even in the precolonial period, a thriving business/merchant class of Africans existed in diverse locales across the continent. Colonialism tended to effect a major rupture in the further development and modernization of these activities even as it simultaneously elevated the European business interests of the metropole and of certain minority groups, such as South Asians and Lebanese.

Thus, the emergence of African private enterprise was retarded first by colonial restrictions on capital accumulation by blacks and subsequently by postcolonial regimes. Certainly, variation existed in regime types, in all countries—including those regarded as quintessential examples of African capitalism like Cote d'Ivoire, Kenya, and Nigeria—but the postcolonial state played an outsized economic role, whether as a result of ideology, corruption, or the continued incapacity of local entrepreneurs. The African state thereby crowded out local private investment, though nonblack African investors in many cases retained the substantial role they enjoyed prior to independence. Although minority-owned capital, sometimes referred to, not unproblematically, as nonindigenous or "settler" capital, often avoided direct state interference, their business operations were impeded nonetheless by poor macroeconomic policy.

The presence of economically dominant minorities (usually racial minorities) is widespread, affecting not only the obvious countries like South Africa, Kenya and Zimbabwe but also Tanzania, Mozambique, Sierra Leone, and beyond.[28] In short, although at times ill-fitting, settler capital is a vital component of business in Africa. Long the domain of white Europeans, Arabs, and the South Asian diaspora, these groups have lately been joined across the continent by hundreds of thousands of overseas Chinese. Many can claim international linkages and access to capital, breadth of experience and, paradoxically, a favorable relationship with African state actors who hail from the majority population. Yet the marginalization of majority (that is, black African) business interests can produce both economically suboptimal conditions and political instability. Furthermore, given their comparative disadvantage and limited market access, black businesspeople may regard cronyism—and an appeal to ethnoracial solidarities—as a rational alternative. These actors, at least initially, depend on their own position within the state or on state patrons ("big men") for their existence. Until the 1990s, in general, the economic and political institutional environment was inhospitable to the expansion of a genuine, more autonomous private sector development.

In part 2, chapters 2 and 3 explore the key transformative processes that have begun to unlock all forms of business in Africa, particularly those not tied to primary commodity sectors. These transformations are rooted, broadly, in factors that contribute to deepening a less injurious brand of globalization and economic and political transformation. Each chapter examines specific factors that have begun to contribute to business development and will continue to affect the direction of business success in Africa. The main concern is the transformation of the *context* in which business operates; most of these changes took place between 1990 and 2000, although several have occurred more recently.

The organization of the chapters in this section is essentially chronological. Chapter 2 focuses on the evolution of the African economic and political environment in the 1980s and 1990s and the impact of these changes on business. Although economic and political liberalization in this period produced mixed results and attracted considerable criticism, these programs proved foundational inasmuch as they helped usher in a fundamental shift in the ideological and institutional space for business in Africa.

Thus, although they were not designed as "probusiness" per se, the much-maligned SAPs of the 1980s and 1990s did contribute positively to a number of developments that, in turn, affect macroeconomic conditions across the continent. (Eventual refinements to the crude liberalization templates of early adjustment programs contributed to reductions in government expenditure and interest rates, significant opportunities for private investment, and, more recently, debt relief and PSD initiatives. These later dimensions are addressed in chapter 3.)

The political changes in sub-Saharan Africa during this period were even more profound. Prior to the democratization movements of the 1990s, the situation for private sectors in Africa was generally dismal; as Africa has become increasingly democratized, however, prospects for business appear to have improved as well. Business has emerged as both a supporter of democracy as well as a beneficiary. The impulse to support prodemocracy movements emerged from frustration with the constraint on accumulation imposed by the authoritarian state. Thus, many firms and business interest associations joined opposition movements in support of political liberalization. Business actors continue to support democracy around the continent, not out of deeply ingrained democratic tendencies, but simply because democracy has been *good* for business and business development in Africa. Importantly, democracy has not eliminated corruption, but it has introduced a measure of transparency, as well as the rule of law and respect for property rights, and has broadened opportunities for business actors historically outside the scope of the patronage machine. It has, in short, reduced political and economic barriers to entry. Although business support for democracy over the long term is hardly guaranteed and business sometimes thrives in the most undemocratic environments, in general, democracy and business development are mutually reinforcing.

In contemporary Africa, neoliberalism per se has become tainted because of its association with structural adjustment, which itself has been associated with increased poverty, a failure to boost economic growth in Africa, and widespread noncompliance. Yet a *new* mode of globalization now predominates, and this is the central focus of chapter 3. Economically, though Africa remains marginalized, this era of "post-Washington Consensus," debt relief, and poverty reduction strategies is in some respects more benign than its orthodox neoliberal forebears. Although poverty reduction through economic growth remains the ultimate goal, one of the key dimensions of the current era is an explicit focus on private sector development, which includes national and donor-supported programs aimed at expanding the supply of entrepreneurs, typically at the M/SME level. In all fairness, whereas PSD initiatives are likely to be an important component of a menu of measures intended to promote African business success going forward, its proponents, including many globalizationists, are often guilty conflating the *potential* performance of PSD with a demonstrated empirical record, as I have already noted. Nonetheless, the emergence of such policies and programs, especially at the national level (whether or not they are formally labeled "private sector development") indicates a fundamental shift in worldview at the level of African states and, importantly, in terms of the societal receptivity to the private sector.

Indeed, culturally, contemporary globalization has seen the inculcation in Africa of global norms of entrepreneurship and accumulation and (in many countries) an ideological embrace of the for-profit sector. Moreover, the Afrobarometer and other research reveal that democracy is now widely accepted as a political norm, despite the fact that many polities still fail to entirely live up to it. The combination of these economic, cultural, and political factors has helped to foster an environment in the twenty-first century that is substantially more auspicious for business in Africa than in any time since independence.

Part 3 of the book examines the diversity of African business and its prospects. An impressive array of diverse business actors—including multinational capital as well as the various forms of crony capitalism—is already part of the economic fabric of the continent. Evidence suggests a shift in both culture and opportunity that may alter the role and direction of crony capitalism, though we must generalize from the as yet few cases to a larger number of potential ones. Also overlooked in most studies of African political economy are those businesses in Africa that are *already* global players—the example of their own trajectories may prove useful for other firms and economies. These large corporations, mostly South African, have penetrated markets throughout the continent and, though to a far lesser extent, outside of it. Their dominance helps to explain the relatively strong performance of the South African economy, the largest and among the most diverse in Africa.

It is more than a little ironic that some of Africa's greatest business prospects in the near term may lie instead in yesterday's exploiters: larger-scale international investors in the form of MNCs, the continent's plentiful supply of crony capitalists, and Africa's own big business. The first of these, which pertains to various dimensions of foreign direct investment (FDI) and how it can be channeled to develop business beyond Africa's primary commodity sectors, is addressed in chapter 4. The chapter mainly takes up the theme of *the promise* of FDI first before examining the role of Western investment (historically and recently) and, finally, the more recent expansion of Chinese and Indian investment.

The bulk of FDI in Africa today continues to be aimed at the primary commodity sector, particularly extractives. Naturally, since the diversification of investment has not happened on an appreciable scale in fifty years of independence, all but the most committed globalizationists will be skeptical about the prospects for contemporary FDI to behave fundamentally differently from the way it has historically operated in Africa. A new pattern would result in measurable employment gains and in genuine technology and knowledge transfer, but the barriers clearly remain formidable. Yet important changes *have* occurred in the global political economy that introduce a new dynamism into these old platitudes. Relationships with the global south, principally China and India, but also Brazil, Malaysia, and others to a lesser extent, represent potentially vital contributors to the globalization of African business. China especially is proclaimed by its supporters as the vehicle through which African states and private sectors will acquire the information and technological advances necessary to achieve business success.

Outwardly, many Western observers claim that the Chinese have little regard for democracy, human rights, labor, or environmental regulation, and so on, and thus that the net effect of Chinese FDI in Africa will be detrimental.[29] Not surprisingly, African leaders regard such claims as disingenuous, at best. Indeed, leaders need only point to the rather dismal history of Western corporations in Africa—from their support for apartheid to their ignominious role in sustaining the brutal rule of Nigeria's Sani Abacha—to highlight the fact that Western FDI in Africa has seldom fulfilled a development function. By and large, African leaders continue to praise Chinese interest, at least publicly, and emphasize their own historical ideological connection and its own status as a "developing country." Supporters of an expanded Chinese and Indian economic presence in the region argue that it can result in technology transfer, employment gains, and other benefits for African business—as *partners*—and that it will promote the development of a flexible, multiuse infrastructure and linkages with Africa-based firms. Whether such interpretations of a benign or even salutary impact of China in Africa are accurate remains to be seen over time. Chapter 4 assesses the validity of the claims on either side of this emerging debate and considers the implications of this new investment, and to a lesser extent trade, for the broader business environment in the region.

Chapter 5 revisits in some detail the prevalence of neopatrimonialism and so-called crony capitalism, thus moving to the foreground a theme that forms part of the subtext in each of the preceding chapters. Neopatrimonialism suggests that "modern" state and market institutions in Africa are but a façade. Instead, elites systematically utilize public resources for private gain; power and position are based on personal loyalty to "big men" rather than adherence to the rule of law; and patron-client ties pervade every relationship from the level of the state president to the village elder. In short, those who consider African politics to be defined by neopatrimonialism assume that African business, at least business as conventionally understood in the West, is a highly dubious proposition because of the endemic corruption found in such environments; an autonomous private sector, they suggest, can scarcely develop within this context. This chapter confronts this assumption head on. I counter that it not only overstates the degree and permanence of neopatrimonialism and its related pathologies in Africa but also holds sub-Saharan Africa to a more exacting standard than other parts of the developing world by suggesting that the fundamental character of African political economy, and indeed "African culture" itself, is impervious to change.

I have emphasized that patron-clientelism, corruption, and crony capitalists are realities in contemporary Africa. Yet although pervasive corruption raises the cost of doing business, its existence is not an insuperable barrier to business success, as most economic liberals contend. What is necessary in order to create fertile ground for legitimate business is not the eradication of corruption or even of the neopatrimonialism that presumably gives rise to it but a transformation in the calculations of existing crony capitalists. In other words, erstwhile cronies, members of the so-called bureaucratic bourgeoisie and even, at the farthest extreme, warlords are capable of formulating medium- and longer-term interest horizons. Chapter 5 thus argues that changes in the economic and political institutional environments provide just such a catalyst for altering perspectives and reformulating objectives in response to new incentives. This is not true in all states, nor among all actors, but it is applicable in enough instances to warrant investigation.

In those places where the state's use of patronage resources are limited, as a result of a degree of democratization and transparency or as a result of economic hardship, for example, once favored groups cannot rely on state largesse ad infinitum: economic reforms contribute to a diminished *supply* of patronage, while political reforms render kickbacks, extortion, and other illicit means ever more costly. Moreover, reform has also engendered opportunities for business success that were foreclosed under the ancien regime. This is not to suggest that erstwhile crony capitalists, warlords, and the like themselves become personally virtuous; indeed, their personal attributes are largely irrelevant. Rather, their economic interests must eventually broaden and become more legitimate and outwardly focused and dependent on predictable access to capital, markets, and labor. Since at least 2000, African crony capitalists have found themselves confronting colossal changes in the institutional environment; accordingly, they will either adapt or die. Perhaps surprisingly then, many *do* adjust their economic behavior.

Finally, as we look longingly to a reformed crop of foreign investors or to the transformation of cronies, we often overlook Africa's existing corporate presence, large firms that are "indigenous" to the continent inasmuch as they were founded in Africa by Africans or residents—indeed, many of them are the heirs of the settler companies discussed in chapter 1. Chapter 6 examines companies that, within Africa, can be considered "giants," although that designation tends to apply largely in relation to other companies on the continent, given the scarcity of sub-Saharan African companies on various global business indices, for example. At the same time, some of Africa's largest and best known corporate entities seem to be outgrowing the continent: although its principal operations remain in Africa, mining conglomerate Anglo American has shifted its domicile to London; South African Breweries, now SAB-Miller after its unprecedented combination with the American brewery, has partners and investments in South America, the United States, Europe, and Asia; the mobile telecommunications firm Celtel, launched by a Sudanese entrepreneur and long identified with Africa (despite its provenance in the Netherlands), was acquired by the Kuwaiti firm Zain just as its reach was expanding continent-wide in Africa, and it is now owned by India's Bharti Airtel.

On one hand, these developments may foretell of a corporate flight from Africa that could rob the continent of its leading business interests at precisely the time that their focus and expertise are most needed to help shape new business expansion. On the other hand, however, they augur positively for a growing *global* presence of firms linked to Africa by ties more significant than the stereotype of MNC exploitation or extractive industries alone. Importantly, beyond the handful of firms perceived to be "de-Africanizing" their operations, it is possible to identify other companies that remain firmly rooted in Africa, attaining a continental presence if not always a worldwide one. In short, the emerging "global" presence of certain African companies, regardless of ownership, benefits all firms from the continent; the visibility of these giants is more than merely of symbolic value to emergent medium- to large-scale enterprises from sub-Saharan Africa. Indeed, it actually enhances the capacity of Africa *writ large* to market the very *idea* of African business by establishing precedents and partnerships and by portraying sub-Saharan Africa as a site of entrepreneurial activity. Such developments should decisively put to rest any residual notions of "African business" as oxymoron.

In the book's conclusion I reexamine the question of what it will take to develop locally, regionally, and internationally competitive businesses in Africa. Rejecting the naïve optimism expressed by numerous development community practitioners, I contend that the outlook is decidedly unfavorable for M/SMEs and the PSD initiatives that aim to promote them, at least in the near and intermediate term. Generating sustainable business enterprise through M/SMEs is both a difficult and long-term undertaking. M/SMEs, of course, can be an important route to business development on a case by case basis, but it is wishful thinking to expect that programs focused solely on M/SME development will promote a business culture or successful large business sectors: absent marked success early on, states, aspiring entrepreneurs, and the donors who purport to support them will abandon the effort. Such outcomes are even more likely in a context in which the domestic ownership of PSD programs remains in question, as it does in all but a few countries. For most countries, thus far, PSD programs have yet to secure a political constituency independent of donors. Yet we should be equally wary of overreach regarding the prospects for large-scale enterprises—the emergence of more than a few internationally competitive firms in the manufacturing, technology, and/or services sectors is unlikely anytime soon.

Nevertheless, "African business" *is* positioned for success in the long term. That Africa's answer, in the short term, lies more in big business (foreign and domestic) than in M/SMEs and as much in reformed cronies as conventional entrepreneurship is likely to prove controversial, not least because it hardly comports with development vogue. But given the constraints and opportunities presented by economic and political reforms, Africa's erstwhile cronies and international actors are best able to avail themselves of this dynamic environment. Previous studies have failed to grasp that this emergent business culture in Africa is both multifaceted and adaptable.

CONCLUSION

Over the long term, these multiple approaches—FDI and key multinational partnerships, reformed cronies and bureaucratic bourgeoisies, big business, as well as small enterprise development—represent a locally moored, if not necessarily *indigenous,* capitalism that is best positioned to experience success in sub-Saharan Africa. These approaches and the underlying actors charged with carrying them out are both "top down" and "bottom up." Importantly, this book demonstrates that, although rarely formidable in global terms, neither is African business moribund; a foundation of domestic and international enterprises exists on which to build. Nor is African business necessarily the captive of a hostile process of globalization with MNCs and domestic big business as its purveyors; these actors can be channeled to contribute to the generation of business opportunities and reproduction. Most notably, although the prevalence of corrupt—that is, falling broadly under the rubric of cronyism—business practices in Africa is well known, it is erroneous to extrapolate from this observation that African business is irretrievably corrupt or even necessarily antidevelopmental. To date, far too many observers have recited this mantra almost reflexively.

AFRICAN BUSINESS AND CAPITALISM IN HISTORICAL PERSPECTIVE

INTRODUCTION

Many contemporary observers tend to portray business in Africa as a fairly recent phenomenon or a colonial import. This ahistorical view has advantages for those subscribing to Afropessimist and neopatrimonialist positions, who use it to justify continued skepticism about the prospects for Africa, particularly for black business in Africa, as well as for the enthusiastic globalizationists, for whom it provides evidence of the novelty of business on the continent. This portrayal, of course, is inaccurate, as historians have documented the fact that business *in Africa* has thrived for centuries and has involved both indigenous African cultures and those from outside the continent. The trans-Saharan trade flourished from about the seventh through the sixteenth centuries and established the economic foundation for numerous African kingdoms and city-states. Later the Atlantic and Indian Ocean slave trades proved lucrative to Europeans, Arabs, and many African middlemen and kings alike. The period of "legitimate trade" that followed saw European coffers further engorged. And finally, during the late nineteenth and twentieth centuries, colonialism and imperialism yielded a tremendous increase in raw material flows to European factories and consumers, as well as the opportunity for European settlement and exploitation—which resulted in the establishment of many enduring commercial enterprises—in various parts of the African continent. Moreover, throughout each of these epochs, Africans continued to engage in commercial activity.

The focus of this chapter is on the forces and influences shaping big business in contemporary Africa; hence its chronological scope is mainly limited to the late colonial period and the colonial and postcolonial legacies. Yet the antecedents of African business cultures, particularly among indigenous Africans, are far deeper, span a variety of sectors, and a range of scales, ranging from what we would today label microenterprises to large-scale concerns. Drawing a *direct* line from this history to present-day business risks diminishing the critical role of recent events in shaping contemporary business cultures; without question, colonialism did considerable damage to black business interests, and independent African states themselves often harmed or impeded private sector activity writ large. Nevertheless, the historical legacy of entrepreneurship and business activity in Africa has not been lost completely.

Thus, a long view reveals that Africa has been a fount of commercial activity. Yet as the African encounter with the rest of the world deepened in modern times, this activity became more and more bifurcated, with black African business increasingly confined to small-scale and/or informal sectors, while larger, formal and more sustainable enterprises became the preserve of immigrant groups or foreign firms. Particularly since the colonial era, therefore, the competitive position of black would-be businesspeople on the African continent has been diminished relative to other profit-making actors, which is to say, outsiders. Because so many observers of contemporary Africa, arguably including more than a few scholars, are decidedly "presentist" in their thinking, there is a tendency to devalue or discount any intrinsic indigenous capacity for enterprise that predated colonialism.[1] Yet it is worth examining that history, both because it undermines any lingering Afropessimist assertions that Africans lack capacity for business and because we can identify certain qualities in Africa's history of indigenous entrepreneurship that resonate within contemporary business.

This chapter proceeds as follows. First, although the book's chronological focus is on developments in the colonial and postcolonial eras and its economic focus is on the constraints and opportunities faced by existing or aspiring big business, the chapter briefly revisits the vibrant history of business activity of varied degrees of formality and size in Africa, including that which predated the colonial experience. While a comprehensive investigation of this rich history is beyond the scope of this book, it is clear that the entrepreneurialism and business acumen of these actors unequivocally demonstrate Africa's historical and cultural capacity for business.

The chapter then turns to examination of the more recent limitations placed on African business by both external and internal forces, namely the colonial and postcolonial regimes. It is important to recognize that the marginalization of black African business—and any capitalist impulses—during the colonial period coincided with the ascendance of other outsider business interests, including colonial corporations, settlers, and intermediaries. The ascendance of these latter groups, to borrow an old phrase, actually helped to *underdevelop* African capitalism in many cases. But these external actors were not the sole constraint. Indeed, following independence, African states also contributed to the curtailment of nascent African capitalism, whether through deliberate policy, predation, or both. Thus, it is important to bear in mind that the relative frailty of contemporary African capitalism is very much a function of these quite recent historical structural constraints.

The third portion of the chapter considers the other groups, including MNCs and resident minorities, who were often allowed to fill the economic void created as business opportunities were denied to black Africans by the strictures of colonial practice and later by ideologically intolerant or otherwise hostile independent governments. Importantly, these groups did not represent political threats to newly independent regimes' fragile legitimacy. The activities of MNCs persisted in a surprising number of postcolonial states, even those espousing leftist ideologies, in part because they remained the principal economic link to the outside world.[2] At the same time, however, in most of sub-Saharan Africa, the environment, even for MNCs (and especially those operating outside of extractive industries), was less than propitious.

The role of MNC firms in contemporary economies is addressed more fully in chapter 4. This chapter instead focuses on the less mobile forms of minority-owned capital, including that owned by whites, Asians, Arabs, and others, whom I label privileged minorities. Although most prolific in former settler states, these communities are found throughout the African continent. Adopting a stance similar to that they took toward foreign corporations, relatively few postcolonial regimes sought to deliberately alienate these capitalists from the farms, factories, and other enterprises they had acquired under colonialism, official ideology notwithstanding.[3] In fact, many minorities were granted explicit capital-generating opportunities denied to their black counterparts. Today, these actors are far more than simply *geographically* African and rather are deeply intertwined in the fabric of business cultures on the continent. Hence the argument, first articulated in the introduction, that resident minority-owned business in Africa is, in fact, *African business.*

Fourth and finally, the chapter briefly addresses the rise of crony capitalism in Africa, explaining the ascendance of these actors, particularly in the form of a bureaucratic bourgeoisie, partly as a natural outgrowth of colonial and postcolonial restriction on more autonomous forms of accumulation. This book acknowledges that crony capitalism continues; however, it challenges those claims that see it as the only or even predominant form practiced by Africans. Indeed, a central theme of this book is that what we conventionally understand as capitalism has demonstrated viability in modern Africa. But this is not the sole route to credible business development and, by extension, national development. The discussion that follows should not be construed as an effort to validate or advocate crony or patrimonial capitalism. Instead, it is a call to recognize cronyism as a persistent global phenomenon rather than a uniquely African one and therefore as not necessarily antithetical to the emergence of modern capitalism as we know it.

When these various dimensions of historical inheritance, the rise of minority capital, and a more nuanced interpretation of cronyism are considered together, it is easier to understand the conditions under which contemporary larger-scale businesses emerged and continue to operate in Africa. The intrinsic viability and adaptability of business in Africa, along with a diversity of business cultures, was apparent from antiquity. Yet from the colonial era until recently, those business cultures often struggled to find expression within a context of inhospitable political and economic institutions. Black Africans faced the most severe constraints.

The Long History of Business in Africa

There is a vast literature on the emergence of commercial enterprise in Africa prior to the advent of colonialism and settlement. This literature stands in stark contrast to the caricature of the African continent as incompatible with business and capitalism. Indeed, it reveals business classes and actors that were honest, pervasive, durable, and most of all, prolific.[4] Although their business routes/empires were disrupted and in some cases destroyed by the imposition of colonial rule, their legacy persists in the entrepreneurial vigor found in both informal and formal sector black businesspeople in contemporary Africa. As Abner Cohen has noted, "Long before the Europeans arrived on the scene, the West Africans had operated truly international trade, with developed systems of credit, brokerage, insurance, exchange of information, transport and arbitration in business disputes. Law and order were generally maintained and strangers honoured their business obligations and deferred to the pressures of moral values and moral relationships of all sorts."[5]

Religion also played a major role, as the spread of Islam was instrumental in facilitating trans-Saharan trade and networks of trust that were essential to the expansion of business.[6] Historians such as Ralph Austen tell us that production and exchange systems emerged and proliferated throughout precolonial Africa—in agricultural commodities as well as around extractive industries such as iron, salt, and copper. These were hardly informal barter economies, as monetization also penetrated and became a key factor in formalizing market exchange.[7] Similarly, Ann Dougall notes an extensive credit system that was based on trust and facilitated these trade networks. Dougall concludes that although colonial rule led to a more forceful imposition of Western money and credit systems, these existed before the advent of colonialism.[8] Capturing the entrepreneurialism embedded in these cultures, as well as the potential for transformation to sustainable for-profit enterprise. Austen notes that "Africa subsistence producers were not unwilling to respond to incentives for material betterment provided that accompanying risks could be limited relative to the potential new gains."[9] Much of the growth in these incentives and greater specialization emerged as a result of Africa's encounters with non-African traders, however.

Numerous extensive precolonial trade networks in nineteenth-century West Africa, near the area of intersection between contemporary Mali, Mauritania, and Senegal, both among Africans and between Africans and outsiders, have been documented by Dougall.[10] One trade commodity was rock salt, which was purchased for cowries, loaded on camels in caravans, and exchanged throughout the network for grain, cloth, slaves, and kola nut further south. Other examples of trade networks include those found in the upper Guinea markets, where cotton goods, gold, salt, and slaves were exchanged, or in the east African littoral, where trade took place among indigenous Africans, Arabs, and later Portuguese and others.[11] As the slave trade expanded in the eighteenth and into the early nineteenth centuries, it marked an expansion of "big business" in parts of West Africa.

Although Joseph Inikori suggests that the Atlantic slave trade served to retard development of entrepreneurship in southeastern Nigeria, for example—and presumably in other areas—, others argue that colonialism was more damaging to black African business and entrepreneurship.[12] Neither encounter, however, eliminated black business, especially in West Africa. Indeed, Gareth Austin argues that the Atlantic slave trade actually brought business opportunities, even if these opportunities were primarily limited to rulers and large merchants. However, the period of "legitimate trade" that followed opened some opportunities for Africa's small-scale traders. On the coasts, for example, the transition from export of slaves to more legitimate commodities and the lower minimum capital requirements made it possible for small suppliers to enter the maritime export business in significant numbers for the first time.[13]

Although the trading empires of the precolonial period largely diminished with the expanded European presence, Austin challenges previous theories that nineteenth-century economic activity was limited to subsistence trading or that the markets that developed throughout West Africa were anything but formal business: "Trade and markets were no mere roof to a subsistence-walled house."[14] While businesses were generally organized at the household/family level rather than in "firms" per se, the reason why many did not develop "transgenerational continuity" as going concerns was less the result of institutional weaknesses than of a general instability arising from the risks of the operations themselves and from changes stemming from colonial occupation.[15]

In sum, the precolonial period was marked by the emergence of both legitimate trading empires and states and businesses sustained by the slave trade, as well as by a proliferation of small-scale traders. Most scholars agree, however, that the colonial partition of Africa after 1884 exacted a higher toll, immediately intensifying competition among traders and artisans and other black African businesses and ushering in nearly a century of European domination.[16]

THE IMPERIAL LEGACY

Colonial Exploitation

As Abner Cohen wrote nearly fifty years ago, "The first large scale European impact on West Africa was more disastrous than propitious," and this observation no doubt applies across the continent.[17] From Cecil John Rhodes and King Leopold II, to lesser-known explorers-cum-capitalists such as Carl Peters, Europeans availed themselves of Africa's abundant raw materials, cheap labor, sometimes slave labor, and high demand in the metropolitan countries to become fabulously wealthy through mining, commerce, and agriculture. Mining companies like the Belgian Union Minière du Haut-Katanga, the American Metal Company, and the Portuguese Diamang played major roles in colonial economies. The activities of the early mining magnates and entrepreneurs in the trades were complemented by those of financial services companies such as Barclays Bank and Standard Bank, large-scale commercial farming operations, and eventually manufacturing firms, which were subsidiaries or affiliates of MNCs, such as Cadbury and Firestone.[18] Later arrivals included companies such as Elf-Aquitaine, General Motors, and others. Thus, Western, mainly European and to a lesser extent, American, firms have long profitable roots in Africa. Moreover, from the earliest days of colonialism, European profit takers were joined by a merchant class of South Asians, Arabs, and other ethnic intermediaries who migrated from other imperial territories, such as British-ruled India and French-controlled Lebanon and Syria. These migrants became merchants and traders and occupied sectors either deemed undesirable or otherwise ignored by their European counterparts and were able to establish medium-scale business operations throughout Africa. Collectively, these foreign actors not only played a major role in the establishment of commercial enterprise in Africa but also contributed to linking Africa, however tenuously and dependently, to the global economy.

Yet all of these outsiders doing business in Africa operated in protected economic spheres. In other words, what the Europeans practiced in Africa in the late nineteenth and twentieth centuries was hardly the autonomous free market capitalism that some political scientists, early proponents of SAPs, and others prescribe for contemporary Africa—and have assailed Africa for not having.[19] Instead of an "invisible hand," colonial enterprises enjoyed the patronage of the state, whose benefits included access to land at reduced rates, access to labor, which was often effectively compulsory, loan guarantees, security, guaranteed export markets, the backing of the colonial state, and restrictions, if not outright prohibitions, on competition from noncolonial actors, whether black African or Asian.[20]

Thus, throughout the colonial era, the capacity of black African businesspeople to expand, diversify, or modernize was severely curtailed or proscribed entirely. In nonsettler-based economies, the profits, surplus, and labor pools of European-domiciled firms doing business locally were insulated from potential African competition, although Africans were permitted to enter relatively more sectors of the economy.

Restrictions were particularly severe in settler economies such as Algeria, Kenya, Angola, Mozambique, South Africa, South-West Africa, and Northern and Southern Rhodesia. As in West Africa and other nonsettler colonies, certain forms of black business persevered, mainly in smaller-scale informal trading and transport sectors. Even in apartheid South Africa, small-scale commercial traders and taxi drivers were able to establish and maintain an important economic niche.[21] Yet by both law and custom, Africans were prevented from entering key profit sectors—among them commercial farming, manufacturing, and other large-scale enterprises—where they might compete with local white businesspeople; in places like Kenya and Cote d'Ivoire, blacks were proscribed from sectors controlled by Indians and Lebanese as well. In Zimbabwe (Southern Rhodesia), white-owned firms were beneficiaries of subsidies and export incentive schemes, and associations of farmers, commercial entities, and manufacturers were well ensconced by the 1950s and had the ear of government. Conversely, legal prohibitions on black ownership of land and businesses, except in designated areas and sectors, were in place there until the late 1970s, thereby retarding incipient black capitalism. Zambia (Northern Rhodesia), despite its far smaller settler population, witnessed comparable discrimination against aspiring capitalist commercial farmers. Members of Zambia's Plateau Tonga community entered the commercial maize market in the 1930s, when they successfully produced and sold surplus. Their settler counterparts, however, resented the competition. So, with the support of the colonial government, settlers alienated Tonga farmers' land, forcing them onto inferior soils, which contributed to environmental degradation and ultimately destroyed Tonga commercial activity in this sector.[22] Similar restrictions on black business or farming activity existed in South Africa and Namibia until the late 1980s.[23]

It would be inaccurate, however, to infer that all countries experienced colonialism the same way. In territories of limited European settlement, such as in West Africa, the range of African opportunities was somewhat broader, although still largely limited to areas in which they did not compete with European trading operations or, to a lesser extent, with those run by Indian or Levantine interests. Asante men in British-ruled Gold Coast (Ghana) were able to operate in the profitable cocoa sector as farmers and brokers.[24] There were, however, periods during which colonial rulers expressed intense hostility toward African traders, in Ghana as in other territories. On the other hand, certain trading and formal and informal market activity flourished in Ghana during that period, where women played a prominent role. A similar vibrancy and penchant for collective action was found among Yoruba women traders in western Nigeria throughout its colonial encounter.[25] By and large, women have remained significant players in these markets.

Some interpretations of particular colonial-era policies differ among scholars. In the Kenyan case, for example, David Himbara insists that the idea that the colonial state hindered African business is "a myth," thereby challenging many of the seminal contributions to the so-called Kenya debate of the 1970s.[26] Himbara claims that colonial rulers in fact sought to provide infrastructure and engender "a business spirit" among Africans in the 1940s and 1950s through credit, provision of market stalls, establishment of African business chambers, and so on. With all due respect to the resiliency of African entrepreneurialism, Himbara is guilty of some romanticism here, as such initiatives were too little, too late. They came on the heels of on the eve of independence, after fifty years of marginalization, and did little to provide a foundation for the African consumers who lacked the capital and capacity to support these fragile businesses, which struggled as a result.

In the main, black entrepreneurship throughout the continent was not only discouraged under colonial rule but deliberately quashed, deprived of finance, access to free labor, a market in which to compete, and even of consumers, as blacks were disgorged from their land, heavily taxed, and subject to artificially low wages. Indeed, in most settler economies, the avenues open to Africans were restricted to the transport sector (mainly taxis and private buses) and small shopkeeping activities in urban townships variously referred to as "native areas" or "compounds." Where businesses did thrive they were largely confined to the small-scale and/or informal sectors, as noted. The line between these entities and contemporary big business, however, is a dotted rather than direct one: as subsequent chapters demonstrate, many of contemporary Africa's most prominent players in big business did not, in fact, grow from small to large. Nonetheless, despite the constraints imposed by colonialism, the perseverance and occasional growth of small firms during this era highlights the long-standing business cultures among black Africans that are not anathema to entrepreneurial spirit, profit, and sustainability.

According to some theorists, colonialism in Africa, while violent and destructive of African life and property alike, advanced the cause of capitalism in Africa (as Karl Marx's grudgingly acknowledged in his essay "On Imperialism in India" with respect to the demolition of traditional livelihoods in that colony). In this view, the intrusion of whites and colonialism may have had the advantage of undermining "many precapitalist institutions and practices," thereby creating the foundation for the emergence of a genuine African capitalism.[27] Yet this assertion is also a weak one. Europe introduced some aspects of capitalism to Africa, but it did not introduce modern capitalism *to Africans*. In fact, Africans were proscribed by their colonial masters from pursuing a more unfettered capitalism; choice and profit—albeit without competition—they reserved to themselves. European colonialism thus interrupted, deprived, and forestalled the entrenchment of African capitalism whose origins preceded it.

Those observers who insist on consigning contemporary Africa to some "gray zone" (to borrow from Thomas Carothers) of *adjectival capitalism*—crony-, patrimonial-, pre-, quasi-, and related variants—that has resulted from what they perceive as *cultural* constraints discount the lasting negative legacy of colonialism. This is not to suggest, however, that culture's impact is uniformly positive; such an assessment would be as erroneous as that of the neopatrimonial theorists. More importantly, the practitioners of colonialism were purveyors of mercantilism and socialism for whites, not market-based competitive capitalism; they allowed Africans to witness their version of global capitalism but fundamentally denied them an opportunity to partake of it.

At bottom, therefore, as independence approached, the paucity of black capitalists was clearly an artifact of colonial rule. Not surprisingly, this late start had the effect of retarding large-scale private sector development among black Africans. Yet however nefarious the institutions of colonialism and imperialism, it is also disingenuous to assign sole responsibility there. If the colonial state discouraged aspiring black capitalists, the postcolonial regimes often eviscerated any hope that a credible independent business class might emerge.

The Independent State and African Capitalism

The postcolonial business environment was particularly unpropitious, as African independence was accompanied by the proliferation of state-led development models, hostile and capricious political actors, a reflexive anti-entrepreneurialism, and conditions that continued to encourage welfare—or by the late 1980s, nothing at all—rather than wealth creation. In the more explicitly statist economies, African business interests were deemed antithetical to prevailing ideology. Thus, in those polities that followed dirigiste economic policies, the spread of capital was even further curtailed, as the state reserved for itself the profit motive, at least vis-à-vis black African private sector actors. Among the more famous examples, Ghana under Nkrumah, Tanzania under Julius Nyerere, and Zambia under Kenneth Kaunda erected a massive state machinery that arrogated business power to itself. The handful of Afro-Marxist states, most prominently, Ethiopia under the Dergue (1975–91) and Angola until 1991, were even more severe in their regard for private accumulation. It is worth noting, however, that none actually eliminated all private property—most famously Angola, which maintained extensive relationships with international oil companies, perhaps the quintessential bogeyman of neoimperialist plots, despite its ostensible commitment to communism.

Yet it is difficult to argue, as Paul Lubeck and colleagues did in the 1980s and scholars like Colin Leys did in the early nineties, that the scenario was fundamentally different in postcolonial Africa's nominally "capitalist" states at that time, principally Nigeria, Kenya, Botswana and Cote d'Ivoire. Certainly, there was a *business* class, of sorts, operating in these countries. But to characterize it as the quintessential capitalist class, an "African bourgeoisie," as the title of Lubeck's book pronounces, was more than a mild overstatement at the time. This "bourgeoisie" was, like other African business classes of the period, small, dependent on the state, and generally at the margins of the respective economies, as Ralph Austen demonstrates in his comprehensive book, *African Economic History*.[28] Furthermore, the business communities in each of Africa's putatively bourgeois societies, especially Cote d'Ivoire and Kenya, were dominated by minorities who had very few linkages to genuine black businesspeople at the time. Simply put, throughout the postcolonial era, even in states that pursued nominally free-market capitalist development paths, the accumulation of capital among indigenous, that is, black, African communities, frequently was stunted. It was crowded out by MNCs and minorities, frustrated by state predation and corruption and an adverse policy environment, and rendered uncompetitive by inadequate economic and financial infrastructure.

Throughout the continent, bureaucracies and state-owned enterprises expanded rapidly, and the African state became the bloated, overcentralized bureaucratic behemoth that was attacked by so many critics beginning in the 1970s and 1980s. This excessive statism affected all stakeholders. The number of people employed by Zimbabwe's state sector, for example, more than doubled from 40,000 to over 90,000 in the first decade of independence alone. Likewise, Tanzania's postcolonial bureaucracy ballooned to 191,000, nearly triple its previous size. Despite enjoying relative autonomy from societal influences, however, the bloated bureaucracies were stocked with cronies, undereducated, and underqualified staffs. Almost by definition, they lacked efficiency. They also lacked the necessary capacity to undertake and implement development strategies, regardless of the ideological blueprint provided them.

Certainly, much of this bureaucratic expansion was driven by patronage, but it was also a logical response at the time to development imperatives after nearly a century of colonization. The public sector was the only sphere of the economy that could be promptly Africanized by governments attempting to satisfy the political and economic demands of a newly enfranchised populace. Hence, Africanization laws demanded that companies, mainly foreign, divest a significant shareholding to local investors; because the state was typically the only African actor with capacity to acquire shares, it became enmeshed in business. This created something of a vicious circle: bureaucracies grew, new parastatals were formed, and the state expanded its remit over various aspects of commerce, including finance, import, export, and marketing. Yet while Africa's states were big (and bloated), they were hardly "strong," at least in the conventional political economy sense. Clearly, the African continent is not home to so-called developmental states often associated with East Asia. Nor does Africa contain exemplars of what Peter Evans has labeled "embedded autonomy," characterized by the meritocratic, prestigious, and efficient—"Weberian"—bureaucracies that have been attributed, often erroneously, to East Asia's economic success.[29] ("Asia" is as grossly overgeneralized and oversimplified, albeit positively, as is "Africa." Of course, to some extent, these characterizations become self-fulfilling.)

Postcolonial African countries were poorly positioned vis-à-vis the global economy at the time of independence. Subsequently, they were certainly guilty of corruption as well as bad policy choices. Yet, given their colonial inheritance, the weakness of (indigenous) private sector alternatives, and the urgency of development, it is a debatable point as to whether they really had any choice at all in pursuing strategies like state intervention, Africanization of bureaucracies, import substitution, and a host of policies associated with economic statism. Importantly, not all failure can be explained by the depravity of elites.[30] In fact, such statist strategies were likewise used in the East Asian countries, where they ultimately met with far more success, often despite entrenched elite corruption.[31] In Africa, the ultimate failure of these policies stemmed from various causes, including an unpropitious regional and geopolitical economic environment and a poor fit for the conditions, as well as corruption.

As the postcolonial African state inevitably became the engine of economic growth, little attention was paid to fledgling black private sectors; African business continued, but often at the margins. States largely maintained the status quo in their relationship with business, even where extant private sectors were dominated by a white settler minority, colonial-era intermediaries (such as an Asian or Levantine merchant class), or multinationals, and occasionally all three, although in some cases, new governments also intruded on minority ownership or sought to reserve certain sectors for blacks. Thus, indigenization or Africanization decrees ironically tended to cement this privileged role while also carving out an ownership position for the state. There are exceptions, of course, such as Idi Amin's Uganda, in which Asians were forcibly deprived of their enterprises and subsequently deported in 1972. Likewise, Mobutu Sese Seko's disastrous Zaireanization policies of the same period, which also involved expropriation, precipitated the flight of much of that country's European industrial and merchant class. The vast majority of Mozambique's 200,000-plus overseas Portuguese community fled the country voluntarily within two years of its independence in 1975. Although not victimized as in Uganda, Mozambique's minority businesspeople were driven out by the Frelimo government's Marxist rhetoric, as well as their own unwillingness to submit to black rule. Angola's white flight—and disinvestment—was of a comparable scale. Still, departures on such a scale in response to Africanization were generally rare.

In contemporary Africa, the presence of economically dominant minorities, as often as not, racial minorities, therefore is widespread, affecting not only the obvious countries like South Africa, Kenya, and Zimbabwe, but also Tanzania, Mozambique, Senegal, Sierra Leone, and beyond. In nearly all cases, these minority groups were vestiges of colonialism, and many arrived late in the colonial period. In fact, the largest numbers of white and ethnic intermediary group immigrants to Mozambique, Zimbabwe, and Algeria came between the mid-1920s and the mid-1950s, whereas South Africa saw renewed influx of white immigrants following the advent of black rule among its neighbors in the 1960s. Paradoxically, many members of these business communities have found themselves cosseted by postcolonial states, which have, at various stages, shown great hostility toward black or "indigenous" private sector development; the latter grouping was often regarded as a political threat.

PRIVILEGED MINORITIES: "SETTLER CAPITAL" AND THE CROWDING OUT OF BLACK ACCUMULATION

A Successful Niche

As suggested by the foregoing discussion, minorities have a long and complicated history in Africa. The forebears of the vast majority of these groups arrived early in the twentieth century, although in South Africa whites and other nonblack peoples began to settle on the continent some three hundred years earlier. One of the criticisms unfairly leveled at contemporary Africa as a whole is that it is inhospitable to business *generally;* the relative success of minority capital gives lie to these assumptions. Indeed, their presence is evidence that business is part of the economic fabric of many countries and of the vitality of certain economic sectors. Paradoxically, their presence and, typically predominance, in business creates challenges for their black business counterparts, but it also may foster opportunities for linkages, although admittedly these have been wanting historically.[32]

Certainly, Africa's minority entrepreneurs are often highly successful, evidenced by their longevity. Still, they have not survived independence, African nationalism, and Africanization programs, without engaging state and political actors; this includes, in many cases, participating vigorously in cronyism and corruption. By dint of their non-African heritage as well as their business acumen, however, minority businesses generally escape the harsh critiques leveled at their African counterparts; they manage to avoid characterization as practitioners of "crony" and "patrimonial" capitalism. Yet this stems not from their collective virtue but from our preoccupation with exoticizing Africa.

Nonetheless, the cumulation of these factors—the historical longevity, the positive and negative engagement, and the sociopolitical embeddedness—argues strongly for the inclusion of various minority business communities in our conceptions of African business, as I noted in the introduction. Indeed, because of their entrenched presence historically as firms and as members of the business community at large, their societal engagement, and their regular if frequently tacit engagement with political elites (including through corruption), these *minority businesses are African businesses*. Thus it is necessary to deal with them analytically as *part* of African business rather than treat them as *apart* from it.

The relative dominance of minority-owned capital, whether in Africa for generations or more recently arrived, has been a significant factor historically in the relative paucity of black African capital and the corresponding marginality of African businesses. Asian-, white-owned, and other businesses crowd out Africa businesspeople in several ways. In a political marketplace that is agnostic about advancing black private sector development (that is, one that eschews explicit state-led black empowerment schemes), minority-owned businesses are able to undercut would-be African competitors because they have a significant leg up.[33] In some countries this includes a hundred-year or more head start in business, although on average "indigenous" (i.e., black) and minority firms are the same age.[34] Minorities' firms are often significantly larger and better equipped to survive the vagaries of doing business in Africa, which include power cuts and water shortages. They also enjoy greater access to credit, especially trade credit via established supplier networks of coethnics based on trust, as well as access to their putative "homeland" networks in some cases.[35]

As a result of their long-standing presence, these minority communities often come to occupy certain established niches in the economy, whether financial services, food processing, commodity export, light manufacturing, or retail trades; success breeds success. Moreover, the combination of small market size and segmentation by ethnicity limits the entry of new competitors. These factors contribute to particular sectors becoming the preserve of particular ethnicities.

The Many Hues of Cronyism and Corruption

Members of Africa's white, Asian, and other minority populations participate in cronyism as a means to insulate themselves, to secure political protection of their established position in the economy. Businesspeople operating firms in sectors in which racial (or ethnic) minorities predominate have had to find creative ways of dealing with the state, in the interest of self-preservation. These range from the relatively unremarkable, such as country club relationships where public and private sector actors interact informally, to the more nefarious side payments to black politicians in return for political protection. Such schemes are hardly unique to Africa, of course; economic wherewithal buys access in virtually all polities. And on a continent in which wealth has rested historically with minorities, their conduit to the political class is little obstructed by the banalities of racial identity.

Among the more familiar names in this grouping include South Africa's Schabir Shaik, the corrupt businessman who was a close associate of President Jacob Zuma; Kamlesh Pattni of Kenya's Goldenberg International scam; John Bredenkamp and Billy Rautenbach of Zimbabwe, who seemed quite unfazed by the antiwhite rhetoric of their financial ally, President Mugabe; and financier Rajan Matani, who long enjoyed a largely beneficial, if occasionally temperamental, relationship with various sections of Zambia's ruling elite. Examples can be found throughout the African continent. Though the patterns may differ, in general, these individuals use their wealth as an entrée to cozy up to political elites; occasionally, the sweetheart deals they obtain become known publicly.[36] This is patronage politics, pure and simple, though it defies— and often escapes entirely—the sloppy characterization of patronage politics in Africa as a distinctly intrablack phenomenon. Among Africa's many racial minority communities, "traditional" patronage practices as conventionally understood (i.e., associated with shared kinship) are foreclosed because of ascriptive differences with the holders of political power. Although widely analyzed in the Asian context, very few scholars of Africa seem willing to acknowledge this issue of minority group corruption and its embeddedness in a patron-clientelism, let alone problematize it.[37]

For precisely the opposite reason, that is, because of their comparative disadvantage and limited market access, some black businesspeople may regard cronyism—and an appeal to ethnoracial solidarities—as a rational alternative to unbridled competition, at least initially. When Africans appoint their own to senior positions or reward "big men" from particular communities, analysts often call it "neopatrimonialism" and corruption and decry it as a dangerous African pathology. Indeed, these practices have attracted a slew of derisory labels—"patrimonial capitalism" (Weber), "pirate capitalism," "political capitalism," "state capitalism," and so forth (Thomas Callaghy, Paul Lubeck, Sayre Shatz). In essence, the state, or public realm, is seen as the vehicle of private accumulation.

The historical works cited at the beginning of this chapter, as well as recent studies such as Steven Radelet's *Emerging Africa* and the McKinsey report "Lions on the Move" indicate that black business is clearly not *defined* by such practices. At the same time, however, as I noted in the introduction, there is little to be gained analytically by trying to paint a picture of the African business landscape that does not include crony capitalists, as some globalizationists are wont to do. The problem occurs when analysts, writing through a neopatrimonial prism, err in locating the origins of these behaviors in some real or imagined African "traditions" or "cultural" characteristics and in the degree of permanence they assign to such traits.

It is instructive, therefore, to look at capitalism elsewhere, where successful models emerged despite—even perhaps because of—the linkage between the putatively private sector and the state. Indeed, what this preoccupation with patron-clientelism, (neo)patrimonial capitalism, and crony capitalism (or whatever label one wishes to assign to it), whether black states and black clients or black states and white business (or Asian or Levantine or Chinese, etc.), obscures is that it essentially falls under the same rubric: *doing business*.[38] It may not represent business in its idealized form, but it is business nonetheless.

For minority-owned business, the political stakes may be higher: in return for protection or consideration of some sort (the ability to do business unfettered, favorable regulation/no regulation, side payments, contracts, and so on), minority businessmen frequently must channel patronage to state actors—or the state itself. Paradoxically, this places whites and other minorities at times in the role, effectively, as "patrons" of black state actors. In short, majority businesses receive patronage from the state, whereas minority businesses provide it in return for political protection. While both methods may be considered corrupt, the minority has developed a bona fide going concern, whereas the majority businessperson has created a dependency. Importantly such relationships between public sector and white business may also help foster the development of a private property–respecting, "business friendly" state eventually (although prior to institutional reform, consistency on the part of the state is not assured). The advantage minorities have over their "indigenous" counterparts, at least historically, is that the former are too few in number to represent a political threat.

Toward an Inclusive "African Business"

As a fraction of capital in the Gramscian sense, settler capital may sit uneasily as a component of a larger *class* of capitalists in Africa. Yet this settler fraction cannot be ignored or set apart since it does not exist in total isolation, given its typically favorable relationship with state actors who hail from the majority population and its centrality to the economy of the countries in which it operates. On this point I am very much in agreement with David Himbara, inasmuch as only through a hyperracialized ideological lens can we separate Kenya's Madhvani Group (established in the 1920s) or, for that matter, South Africa's Sanlam (established in 1918) from African business.[39] To be sure, any part, whether real or perceived, played by this fraction in the exclusion and marginalization of black African business interests is subject to exploitation for political purposes. In other words, regardless of their centrality to the health of the national economy, politicians will readily sacrifice the minority business community in the interest of populist political expediency. Thus there is a certain undercurrent of political instability in minority-dominant business communities, as Ugandan Asians and white Zimbabweans and discovered to their peril in the 1970s and 2000s, respectively. But like so many other issues pertaining to business in Africa, this precariousness is hardly unique to Africa either; Chinese business communities in Indonesia and elsewhere in Southeast Asia have been similarly victimized.

Therefore, a private sector dominated by minority businesses is hardly universally good. In Africa prior to widespread political liberalization of the last decade, it could operate "below the radar," engaging in profit-making activities that the majority populace had little ability to affect, because the majority lacked a political voice. Additionally, before economic liberalization, the state sought to provide for the welfare of the black populace, while often allowing minority businesses to continue to operate largely unfettered, as they had throughout the colonial era. However, such capitalist enclaves in polities with persistent labor surpluses, high rates of poverty, and extreme wealth disparities are also suboptimal economically. Because the operations of such enclaves tend to be insular in older and more established sectors and may themselves lack external competitiveness, they could not possibly resolve entrenched economic problems on their own.

A key objective for both groups, therefore, is to identify harmonies between black African (and this would necessarily include micro- and small-scale) enterprises and minority firms through joint ventures, cooperation, subcontracting, and the like. Such linkages serve to extend economic benefits to blacks and mitigate political risk for minorities, both of which are especially critical in light of political liberalization. As average Zimbabweans will attest, Africans would, on the whole, prefer to emulate minority business success rather than employ extralegal, nonmarket methods (e.g., seizures; forced divestment) to undermine and destroy minority businesses. On the other hand, however, significant percentages of African citizens remain ambivalent about the private sector, perhaps because they have yet to see substantial benefits in terms of formal sector jobs and higher wages.[40] This latent discontent can be tapped by elites for nefarious political purposes if necessary in what Amy Chua refers to as an "antimarket backlash." Astute minority business owners have recognized this, among them the more proactive white-owned companies of South Africa, who have structured investment partnerships, training programs, and supplier relationships with their smaller black business counterparts, although admittedly many have done so under pressure from the African National Congress (ANC) government.

In addition to being embedded in the cultural fabric of African business, capital owned by local minorities is essential to the health of a huge cross-section of African economies, from Senegal to Tanzania. "Settler"-owned businesses employ black Africans, after all, and they generally add to the health of the macroeconomy. Moreover, minority businesspeople have class interests; they serve as critical interlocutors of business and capitalism, not only between Africans and some vague understanding of "the market" but between African populations and their skeptical state elites as well. Minority businesses can therefore help acculturate both state and their smaller black counterparts in best practices. This was a critical function at the inauguration of market-friendly economic regimes especially.

BLACK CAPITALISM AND ITS DISCONTENTS

As noted, *black* African capital has long been subordinated to both multinationals and minority business interests, most of which are themselves artifacts of colonialism. In most countries, the state, often in partnership with MNCs, emerged as the leading black business actor, thereby displacing, retarding, or corrupting autonomous business development in the process. The impact of this state centrism was twofold. First, it contributed to the emergence of a political economy in which aspiring black entrepreneurs were often relegated to third or fourth place behind MNCs, the resident minority business class, and the state itself. Black African businesspeople, therefore, were predominant only at the margins of business; though they often outnumber their counterparts, they presided over the smallest, least formal enterprises in terms of contribution to the economy. The scale of autonomous, bona fide black-owned businesses was dwarfed by other business actors, and this generally remains true, as Vijaya Ramachandran, Alan Gelb, and Manju Kedia Shah have thoroughly analyzed in their recent book.

The second important impact of state centrism was that while it marginalized autonomous entrepreneurs and plunged them into a marketplace of cutthroat laissez-faireism, it simultaneously fostered the emergence of a parallel business class of black crony capitalists whose existence was utterly dependent on its relationship with and proximity to the state. This is an important segment of business in sub-Saharan Africa. The bulk of the discussion that follows focuses on the history of these actors, especially the conditions that gave rise to them.

Crony Capitalism

Given the centrality of the state, the prevailing ideological orientation toward welfare in the early independence period, and economic conditions that encouraged rent seeking rather than reproduction, it should not be surprising that the black "capitalists" who emerged following colonialism more often than not owed their continued existence to the state. Scholars from across the ideological spectrum saw them as part of a state-based or "bureaucratic" bourgeoisie.[41] At the forefront of this bureaucratic bourgeoisie were often leading bureaucrats and politicians, including heads of state, who became wealthy as at least nominal businessmen. Although some postcolonial leaders, such as Zambia's Kenneth Kaunda, Tanzania's Julius Nyerere, Burkina Faso's Thomas Sankara, and a few others, enacted leadership codes containing restrictions on business ownership by members of the government or bureaucracy, even these were regularly circumvented using spouses or other relatives as fronts.

Others, such as Mobutu, Felix Houphouet-Boigny, Siaka Stevens, Teodoro Obiang, and Omar Bongo were less circumspect in their use of political power to advance their personal financial positions. Where they were not directly associated with business interests and specific firms, as in the case of Kenya's second president Daniel Arap Moi, leaders often operated through surrogates. Access to rents from illicit activities generated enormous wealth for numerous African presidents and their clients. Many engaged in money laundering, owned commercial property throughout Africa, Europe, and elsewhere, including hotels in the United States, the United Kingdom, and South Africa, established shell companies in the Caribbean, and held ownership of telecommunications firms and banks in Belgium and elsewhere, and maintained known and shaded shareholdings in companies throughout the world.

In sum, this "bureaucratic bourgeoisie" was, in reality, neither bourgeois nor solely bureaucratic. Rather they were compradors and users of capital consisting of politicians, members of the bureaucracy themselves, relatives of elites, and others with access. Although leaders rewarded themselves, clients of the regime were also beneficiaries of no-bid contracts, side payments, and kickbacks. Importantly, their activities can be characterized as, in effect, the privatization of state assets, especially through their using state-owned enterprises for personal gain, starving state-owned enterprises (SOEs) of working capital in the process, and failing to provide public goods. Some elites were genuinely entrepreneurial, but most were more interested in short-term payout rather than productive investment in going concerns. Thus in the most egregious examples, the personal enrichment of the political class contributed directly to the impoverishment of the polity.

Plus ça Change?

Importantly, not all leaders were as rapacious as the veritable rogues' gallery that includes Moi, Mobutu, and Obiang. And many, such as Julius Nyerere, genuinely attempted to spark development by making the state the center of the economy. Regardless, most leaders presided over polities that experienced significant levels of corruption, corruption that was exacerbated by weak, low-capacity postcolonial states. But in a poor, highly centralized but weakly institutionalized postcolonial environment, such as that which prevailed in the 1960s and 1970s, where private wealth may well have been considered anathema to proclaimed national development objectives, the emergence of state-led accumulation is hardly surprising. Nor is it distinctly African. In weak institutional environments, individual elites will act in a more self-interested fashion, motivated by desire for short-term gains because of uncertainty about the future. Such elites will have incentive to cooperate only with entities that yield benefits for the state, and by extension, themselves.[42] In the early years of independence these partners were foreign and/or settler actors rather than local "indigenous" businesses (which did not then exist in substantial numbers, in any event). Rents can be derived from the legitimate business activities of resident minorities or from the extraction of primary commodities by international partners. Such patronage-based relationships can be self-replicating as long as rents can be supplied.

Twenty years or more ago, this was the predominant model. Even among scholars who were mildly sanguine about the prospects for African business and capitalism like Paul Kennedy and Colin Leys, one finds straight-faced claims that African capitalism was *centuries* behind its Euro-American counterpart.[43] Given such a long timeline, the passage of a mere two decades could only be regarded as barely a blip on the calendar. If one's chronological frame of reference is multiple centuries, it is impossible to see changes from year to year or even decade to decade; for all practical purposes, such measures of time are irrelevant. Thus, Africa itself can be dismissively characterized by its critics as *plus ça change, plus c'est la même chose.*

Regrettably, this line of thinking has proved stubbornly resilient. Indeed, far from disappearing, the argument was reinvigorated in the late 1990s as a response to the development failures through that decade. Struck by the apparent lack of development in forty years of African independence, some scholars, famously Patrick Chabal and Jean-Pascal Daloz in *Africa Works: Disorder as Political Instrument*, suggested there was a cultural basis at the root of Africa's relative backwardness; others suggested that what had unfolded represented a cultural adaptation by Africans struggling with systemic corruption. But similar conclusions can likewise be drawn from the arguments by Jean-Francois Bayart and Giorgio Blundo and Jean-Pierre Olivier de Sardan. In this perspective, African capitalism and entrepreneurship were culturally and institutionally, and thus inextricably, moored to a corrupt and disordered state. The continuity in Chabal and Daloz's arguments is plain: they simply reaffirm the views expressed by Thomas Callaghy and others a decade earlier that capitalism cannot "develop a dynamic of its own in the context of patrimonial political systems."[44] Although they reject cultural determinism, comparable currents about the debilitating impact of cronyism and state corruption can be discerned in the more recent and widely read work of writers like George Ayittey and Dambisa Moyo.

Of course, these arguments ultimately consign Africa to an isomorphic world in which a patrimonial state begets a patrimonial business class ad infinitum—or nearly so.[45] This formula presages not only a vicious circle but a constantly shrinking one, characterized by ever-diminishing returns as the state and its malformed offspring engage in an exercise of mutual cannibalization. When patronage resources wane, the state must either be reformed or destroyed altogether. Since the (pessimist) views cannot easily accommodate the former, the latter seems more in line with their predictions. Yet collapse has happened only in the most venal of African polities, of which Mobutu's Zaire is a quintessential example. Even in that case, however, entrepreneurial activity continued. Is it not logical to assume as well that even patrimonial capitalism would be subject to changing environmental conditions—shrinking patronage resources, democratization, the dismantling of statist economic structures, for example— that Kennedy and others could scarcely have predicted from their 1980s vantage point? It has taken far less than centuries to reveal that the theoretical constructs of patrimonial capitalism are outmoded. In the end, the vicious circle remains unclosed—it is a vicious *semi*-circle, perhaps—inasmuch as Chabal and Daloz's thesis is too much Malthus and not enough Marx: business (the de facto bourgeoisie) has a built-in self preservation mechanism. It will not suffer a complete descent into Hobbesian anarchy but will eventually seize and in fact reform the state in own interests.

At bottom, putative *cultures* of corruption and "neopatrimonialism" are not necessarily a brake on the development of what is conventionally accepted as legitimate capitalism or on development itself. Side by side with wholly transparent business transactions and practices, the specter of patrimonial capitalism and its attendant corruption in African business and states will surely continue, just as surely it will continue to be labeled uniquely African by many commentators. But corruption and its attendant maladies have not been insurmountable barriers to business and capitalist development around the world; neither do they pose such an obstacle in Africa.

CONCLUSION

In spite of numerous constraints, Africa has seen the rise of a diverse set of business cultures over the past century. The most visible business entities remain those dominated by minorities and MNCs, which represent an array of business cultures. Importantly, however, the relative success of these groups was not due to any intrinsic cultural superiority but rather to an auspicious combination of favoritism and a high degree of autonomy in their operations. In the contemporary environment, greater cooperation with their black business counterparts is imperative; nevertheless, these communities are part of the economic—and *cultural*—fabric of the societies, notwithstanding the attempt by Robert Mugabe and others to declare them alien. Indeed, perhaps the greater importance of successful minority-owned business is symbolic: they provide evidence that the business environment can be fertile in sub-Saharan Africa.

Black business, of course, has a long and extraordinary, if frequently unappreciated, history in sub-Saharan Africa. Black African or indigenous business development has faced greater constraints over time, and autonomous capitalism was often hampered by states and ideology as much in the postcolonial era as in the era that preceded it. These constraints have engendered diverse business cultures among black Africans as well, both across and within states. A prominent and much-analyzed element is represented by crony capitalists, or the bureaucratic bourgeoisie, which has posed obstacles to the expansion of legitimate capitalism, although not insuperable ones. Importantly, as demonstrated by strictures on black capitalism imposed by colonial and postcolonial regimes alike, the institutional and global context matters. Thus, the cultures of big business that predominated in the 1970s through 1990s are not necessarily the ones that predominate today; analyses of African capitalism in that period thus need to be revisited.

Critiques of Africa's "adjectival capitalism" resounded quite strongly amid the economic crises of the 1980s and 1990s, but these did not turn out to have great predictive capacity. As I have noted, not long ago it was fairly common to equate Africa's capitalism with that found in Europe of the Middle Ages or some other period in the distant past. One might conclude from such analogies that Africa's path would require another four centuries to begin to "catch up" to the West. Although this would today appear self-evidently wrong, the notion that Africa is "behind" remains a prevailing sentiment.[46] Yet let us not ignore the fact that, in many polities a more mature African capitalism has begun to emerge, evidenced by a convergence of economic and political *class* interests of capitalists. Reinvesting profits in the expansion of business enterprises, these actors increasingly identify their interests as commensurate with supposedly Asian, Arab, white, or "settler" class and business interests and with international business and so on rather than with crude precapitalist solidarities steadfastly based on cultural affinities. Importantly, increasingly since the 1990s, "the state" has given them room to do so. Therefore, if conditions can be improved, locally and globally, for African business, there is little reason to conclude that African capitalism, in all its guises, cannot prosper. This changing environment is addressed in the next two chapters.

PART 2
Globalization and Political and Economic Transformation

INSTITUTIONAL CHANGE IN THE 1990s
Economic and Political Reform

INTRODUCTION

Some scholars regard the 1990s as something of a "lost decade" for Africa. In the wake of the calamitous 1980s, it appeared the region was mired in "permanent crisis." Although economies began to show signs of recovery by the mid-1990s, there were genuine questions about sustainability; politically, democratic transitions were faltering. The economic hardship and political oppression suffered between 1979 and 1999 is well documented, and countless observers were properly dismayed at Africa's dismal performance, but what it is less well acknowledged is to extent to which Africa's economic and political institutions and ideologies have also changed dramatically in the past two decades.[1] This chapter explores the origins of those changes in the 1980s and 1990s and examines how various aspects of liberalization affected business in Africa. As we begin the second decade of the twenty-first century—admittedly with the benefit of hindsight—the 1990s in particular look decidedly different; I contend that this period was in fact a critical juncture for the improvement of the political and economic environments for business.

Beginning in the early 1980s, many African states and societies—and the international community—sought to respond to the economic, political, and, indeed, ideological bankruptcy that characterized much of the postcolonial period. Some of the most influential work on African capitalism was written in this era, and coming in the midst of widespread economic decay, their largely cynical assessments of African capitalism and its prospects are perhaps more understandable. As I have been arguing, however, scholars' forecasts to the effect that a genuine African capitalism could only emerge over the course of *centuries* now appear far too dire. Yet inasmuch as they highlighted the importance of time they were surely onto something: both the emergence and entrenchment of capitalism in Africa, as in Europe before it, is an evolutionary, chronological process.

Notwithstanding the predictions, then, the idea that both attitudes toward and the practice of capitalism in Africa could change *over time* is not so altogether outlandish. Essential to changes in capitalism were changes in the environment: a generation ago, few would have predicted that even the most diehard adherents to African socialism and Afro-Marxism would summarily abandon its precepts in favor of economic liberalization. Perhaps even fewer could have envisioned that democracy, however fragile, would be the form of rule in a majority of states in sub-Saharan Africa.

This chapter traces the main economic and political currents of liberalization in the 1990s to illustrate the ways in which they set the stage for later business development. It is not intended to be an exhaustive retrospective analysis of economic decline and attempted reforms that characterized the period, nor of the political transformations that often occurred simultaneously; richly detailed accounts of each can be found elsewhere.[2] More importantly, as pertains to economic issues in particular, my aim is certainly not to rehabilitate structural adjustment programs or the neoliberal agenda they sought to impose. I do suggest, however, that many of the changes—the discarding of outmoded policy frameworks, the initiation of regime transformation, and so forth—were *foundational* and helped establish a more favorable context for subsequent business development. Although the economic and political transformations of the 1990s were clearly linked, not least by the much-maligned donor conditionalities, I treat each separately for the sake of clarity. In the following section I identify the major currents in Africa economies that led to the near universal adoption of adjustment programs before turning analyzing the impact of the programs themselves. The subsequent section addresses political liberalization.

Trends in African Economic Development

Several recent publications have noted that Africa is still one of the slowest places on earth in which to do business.[3] Whether the task requires securing contracts, export licenses, import licenses or hiring and firing, Africa lags far behind the developed OECD countries, as well as other developing regions, and its comparison along these metrics discourages investment and contributes to further declines on the continent. There are simply too many bureaucratic hurdles (even before taking corruption into account) that impede getting *started* in business, let alone *doing* business in Africa. Yet because they offer only a snapshot, these facts tell only part of the story. As virtually anyone who traveled to Zambia, Tanzania, Mozambique, Ethiopia, or Benin before their economies were liberalized will attest, those were environments that were fundamentally *hostile* to commerce and private activity. Private sectors certainly existed, but they faced capricious states, all of which had issued decrees threatening private property at one point or another. The situation among the continent's practitioners of "African capitalism"—namely Kenya, Nigeria, and Cote d'Ivoire, was not as superior as one might expect. They were plagued by currency controls, export controls, tight financial market regulation, and a lack of access to capital that severely constrained business activity, especially for new entrants. Private actors were also crowded out by state-owned enterprises.[4]

In short, across most of the continent, everything from physical and financial infrastructure to business attitudes to supply of goods (both consumer goods and inputs) was considerably worse, say, in 1985 than in 2005. Observers who are discouraged by the contemporary comparisons with OECD countries should consider that a better comparison, at least in terms of "doing business," is that of Africa with its own recent past. Failing to consider how far so many countries on the continent have come—in a relatively short time—with regard to the economic and political context in which business takes place obscures the measurable and, in some countries, downright impressive strides that have been made.

In the 1990s, faced with severe economic declines and growing dependence on donors and international financial institutions (IFIs), African states initiated a genuine, if halting and at times tortuous process of ideological and policy transformation. This, in turn, helped foster the emergence of a more expansive array of business cultures that could accommodate the societal penetration of a deeper and broader form of capitalism than had been practiced previously. This process was hardly linear, however, and it took almost a generation to convince African politicians and publics alike that import substitution, reliance on single commodity export, and heavily statist economic programs were no longer tenable even the face of their failure to produce growth; to be sure, some were never fully convinced. It took longer still to determine what specific economic policy approaches might best fill the void; to varying degrees, this too remains an ongoing process.

Approaching Consensus

African regimes' economic policy and ideological indecision, particularly in the 1980s, was expressed in various fora. Agreements forged in the 1980s to pursue structural adjustment programs were countered by equally untested African international initiatives that attempted to articulate a more autonomous path. Prominent among the latter were the Lagos Plan of Action, drawn up by the Organization of African Unity in 1981 and, a decade later, the Kampala Document, which grew out of a collaboration between the UN Economic Commission of Africa and the Organization for African Unity. At the national level, decades-old commitments to single party regimes crumbled by the dawn of the 1990s, as governments legalized opposition, while Marxist and quasi-Marxist development strategies were abandoned from Angola to Benin to Mozambique and beyond. "Home-grown" adjustment programs sometimes substituted for those of the World Bank and the International Monetary Fund (IMF) in places like Nigeria and Zambia in the 1980s, but these were particularly subject to wavering commitments. In the 1990s, structural adjustment programs (whether home grown or external) became ubiquitous features of the African economic landscape, but countries' adherence to the programs was highly erratic and implementation of key features was frequently partial.

Surely the Janus-faced nature of African leaders' views about development alternatives and economic priorities in this period was a function of contradictory stimuli, including competing pressures from external and domestic actors and events. Domestically, governments had to deal with a reluctance to expose themselves to outside scrutiny and with long-standing ideological commitments as well as fragmenting political constituencies and growing instability. Thus, Zambia adopted structural adjustment in 1986, only to abandon it a year later, Ghana shifted abruptly from economic populism to aggressive liberalization in 1983, and Zimbabwe officially abandoned socialism in 1990 and embraced liberalization, only to have a volatile relationship with both the extant white and embryonic black private sectors thereafter.

What these brief illustrations capture is a system in flux. But what did this mean for business? For many years, donors, IFIs, eager investors, and nascent businesspeople pressured political elites to adopt more business-friendly policies but with only sporadic success. Importantly, however, though the process clearly ebbed and flowed and country experiences varied dramatically, from a pan-African perspective, this period also brought about critical changes that established a foundation for business. What were once tenuous commitments to private sector growth generally began to firm up by the 1990s. Ironically, however, once the policy debate was eventually settled—if, in retrospect, only temporarily—in favor of liberalization and the so-called Washington Consensus, the prevailing conditions were unpropitious if not outrightly hostile to domestic business interests. What is worth noting, therefore, is not that the new policies were ideal for business emergence and development—clearly they were not—but that the old policies they replaced were so much worse. Whereas the previous policy regime often confounded both domestic and foreign business, the new ideological and policy environment at least created *some* space in which business might operate and have an opportunity to expand. Thus by 1999, as the "permanent" crisis began to wane, a new entrant to the private sector enjoyed much better prospects than one in 1979. At bottom, the political and economic and policy changes that took root in the 1980s and 1990s were necessary prerequisites for the establishment of a more hospitable environment for business in Africa.

But this chapter eschews formulas; even if one exists that best enables African business emergence and development, it eludes us. Moreover, clearly no single factor has led ineluctably and inexorably toward a larger role for capitalism and a greater business presence. One simply cannot say with absolute certainty what makes a business thrive in Lusaka or Dar es Salaam, for example, but suffer in Kinshasa, although obviously macroeconomic and political stability, policy coherence, and a viable financial marketplace play at least as important a role as the nature of the enterprise itself. But that is exactly the point. There are indeed certain preconditions—relative stability, security, property rights protections, and adequate infrastructure, for example—which are necessary for capitalism, business, and entrepreneurship to expand on a meaningful scale, but it is difficult to specify the *sufficient* conditions. The larger lesson here is that business and capitalism are not incongruous with contemporary African realities, wherein a market mechanism, whether more or less "governed" and regulated but supported by a coherent state, is widely acknowledged as a critical component of economic development and in which the practice of democracy is increasingly the norm rather than the exception.

ECONOMIC LIBERALIZATION AND AFRICAN BUSINESS

In the mid-1970s, African economies, beset by deteriorating terms of trade, unsustainable debt levels, plummeting socioeconomic conditions, and, often, political strife, went into a deep decline that lasted more than a quarter century. This period also saw Africa's growing dependence on IFIs and the donor community. As early as 1973, the IMF was providing short-term loans to Africa, particularly in the form of the oil facility that provided balance-of-payments support in the wake of the energy crisis that began that year. The World Bank, the IMF, and Western donors began to advocate more encompassing economic structural adjustment following the 1979 oil crisis and the global recession that ensued. By the late 1980s it had become clear that the nearly ubiquitous structural adjustment programs, which had initially been conceived as short-term interventions, had morphed into decidedly long-term undertakings. In fact, African countries on the receiving end of aid, again almost all by 1991, had little choice but to consent to the adoption of these programs as a condition of receiving further support, which by that time was coming from Western sources almost exclusively. The 1980s first witnessed decreased willingness on the part of the Eastern Bloc countries to support Africa economically; the 1982 rejection of Mozambique's request for membership in the Soviet-sponsored Council for Mutual Economic Assistance, for example, was a signal event. Later, the collapse of communism itself precluded the possibility of Eastern Bloc aid altogether and led to the triumph of the "Washington Consensus" and the hegemony of neoliberal policies for the better part of a decade.

Initiated by the World Bank and endorsed by the IMF, whose own loans complemented those of the bank, SAPs imposed a neoliberal orthodoxy on the continent that called for the substantial withdrawal of the state from economic life and its replacement with a market model. The neoliberal formula was designed to accompany stabilization measures and to institute a host of changes, from currency and trade liberalization to privatization, public expenditure reductions, deregulation, and so on, but its application in Africa proved quite problematic. Criticism of SAPs is wide ranging and quite well known. But counterclaims by supporters of adjustment have also been offered; these supporters have accused African governments, often fairly, of showing only sporadic commitment to and partial implementation of reforms.[5] On the other hand, the content of SAPs has drawn widespread and not altogether inappropriate condemnation from left-leaning academics, prominent disaffected staff members from the IFIs, and from the wider African citizenry.[6] Further, even where SAPs were more vigorously adopted, such as in Zimbabwe from 1991–95, results were at best mixed.[7]

It is not necessary to recount here the evidence marshaled by the two sides in this debate, but it is important to note that the criticisms are not entirely mutually exclusive; structural adjustment policies suffered from serious flaws in both design *and* implementation, including the improper sequencing of reforms by their sponsors, their inattention to social issues, and the selective application by states. Moreover, the programs' rigid neoliberal orthodoxy initially represented a gross misreading of the Asian development experience that resulted in misspecified and inappropriate policy instruments.[8] Yet, these substantial shortcomings notwithstanding, *viable* alternatives to SAPs were few, and those proposed, such as the Lagos Plan or the African Alternative Framework of 1989, frequently were based on spurious analysis or just plain wishful thinking regarding the expectations of the continent's donors and creditors. Indeed, they had no financing behind them.[9] In any event, to both critics and champions alike, SAPs' inability to reverse the continent's economic decline was obvious. The 1990s was a decade in which both donors and African countries were searching for a new approach, which eventually resulted in a focus on economic growth and poverty reduction. Although for many countries the economic turning point began around 1995, it was difficult to identify as such at the time; indeed, by 1999, nearly two decades after the first SAPs were tried, Africa's per capita economic *and human* development indicators were worse than at independence forty years prior.[10]

Shifting Roles for State and Business

The widespread adoption of structural adjustment programs fundamentally altered the debate over the role of the state in African development, which was viewed as the principal barrier to private sector development and business emergence. In fact, many scholars and practitioners have long concluded that the African state itself is at the heart of the continent's development problems: irredeemably inefficient, bloated, and corrupt, and, in some cases, "criminal."[11] Throughout the 1980s and 1990s, the international prescriptions for Africa coalesced around the view that a retreat of the state was essential. The practical application of this framework to Africa resulted in a tangle of contradictions, however.

It was widely predicted, mainly by SAPs' architects and proponents, that the programs would benefit businesses, whose growth had long been inhibited by an overly interventionist state. Constrained under the status quo, businesses across a range of sectors were often among the leading societal advocates of adjustment programs, and many existing and aspiring businesspeople celebrated their adoption, especially in the early 1990s. Their enthusiasm can be explained by the fact that SAPs called for better macro management and deregulation that theoretically would allow markets to operate. Although adjustment would exact a painful toll—of which astute business operators should have been aware—significant numbers of businesses, often acting collectively through associations, became part of social coalitions that advocated change. In some countries, such as Zambia, Zimbabwe, and Tanzania, these coalitions helped shape the initial evolution of policy.[12]

Contrary to their lofty expectations, however, the private sector in Africa did not make enormous strides in the early going and, in fact, after the adoption of SAPs, the collective attempts at policy influence on the part of businesses were thereafter largely ignored. In other words, fledgling business communities often proved useful constituencies in the *adoption* of reforms, helping to sell them to a skeptical populace. However, their collective capacity to shape the *implementation* of reforms was limited. As a result, opportunities for them to mitigate some of the more detrimental impacts of the policies were foreclosed. I demonstrate this systematic exclusion of Zambian business groups, for example, in *Business and the State in Southern Africa*.

Of course, mindful mostly of their international audience, African political elites spouted all the right rhetoric about the importance of business and private sector enlargement. Yet few took proactive steps to enlarge or even engage "nontraditional" business actors, largely for four interrelated reasons. First, there was resistance to empowering potential political adversaries in an emergent business-based middle class. Second, productive investment, such as in the infrastructure that would allow business to flourish, was forestalled by corruption and a diversion of resources into other areas. Third, there was a lingering ideological mistrust of capitalism in many countries, especially on the part of elites. Lastly, even if they wished to, states typically lacked both sufficient resources and donor forbearance needed to engage in the kind of "governed-market" state interventionism such as was pursued to great success in Asia. Because weak African states were beholden to donors and the international financial institutions rather than to domestic actors and interests, they lacked the flexibility needed to engage in developmental strategies—they lacked, in other words, the nurturing and partnership that Peter Evans and others have suggested was so essential to East Asian business (and national) development. Unfortunately, such nurturing, or "midwifing" in Evans's terminology, was especially necessary in Africa, where private sectors faced historical disadvantages.[13] Thus, amid the apparent triumph of the Washington Consensus in the early- to mid-1990s, African states encountered a globalized neoliberal environment that was generally hostile to state intervention.

Admittedly, each of these states engages the world economy differently, and in a few countries many businesses were already sufficiently established and internationalized as to not really need much hand holding from the state sphere.[14] Others need only minimal state support, such as limited tariff protection, access to finance, and public-private partnership opportunities. However, a significant number of firms in Africa, both black and minority-owned, and especially those in import-sensitive sectors, needed certain extramarket interventions by the state, such as more extensive protection and subsidization. Yet they failed to get the nurturing that they required. Hence, this first postliberalization generation of business moved from a sheltered but often unsupportive and occasionally hostile domestic environment to a brave new world represented by a competitive internationalized marketplace.

The new reality was "sink or swim," and many businesses, both public and private, indeed sank.[15] But not all actors fared poorly in the initial phase of adjustment, and some were able to respond to certain incentives such as improved access to capital, foreign exchange liberalization, elimination of import and export licensing regimes, and the enshrinement of property rights protections. Among domestic firms, these benefits accrued largely to the resident minority business communities, which already enjoyed structural advantages over their black African counterparts. Nevertheless, even previously successful minority firms in places like Zimbabwe, Kenya, and elsewhere were placed under great strain in the early 1990s, particularly by the rapid and premature trade liberalization that typically accompanied SAPs. After all, these were companies that long operated in protected, closed markets and had faced little in the way of international competition before. They were compelled, therefore, to adapt to the liberalized environment or face closure. For its part, the formal black private sector was largely ill equipped, at least initially, to respond to new opportunities created by this diminished state presence.[16]

The limited capacity of the conventional domestic private sector to respond created a vacuum that was often filled by international firms with their deeper pockets, reigniting old fears about their neocolonial practices, as well as by new and existing crony capitalists, who enjoyed close relations with the state, reinforcing stereotypes about the ubiquity of cronyism in Africa. Yet they were undoubtedly best positioned (given their political linkages to, and protection from, the state) to take advantage of an unsettled political economy. By virtue of their political and bureaucratic roles, these actors gained access to new sources of rents through shares, newly privatized companies, and contracts.

In sum, the economic reform programs exposed business to a number of contradictions. The early 1990s marked the beginning of a drastic shift in African economic regime types, even if this shift was substantially incomplete. The adoption of economic liberalization programs throughout sub-Saharan Africa, however problematic, created at least the credible *prospect* for the emergence and consolidation of a genuine, wholly representative private sector. To a significant degree, the state retreated as prescribed, as evidenced by the privatization of some 40 percent of SOEs by 2001 and a steady flow thereafter.[17] The elimination of most state commodity marketing board and import-export controls and certain other forms of (over) regulation further decreased the level of economic intervention. Government spending was also reduced, although as Nicolas van de Walle argues, these reductions were largely achieved via reduced pressure on budgets as a result of foreign aid.[18] (In addition, despite oft-repeated calls to downsize, governments were not altogether successful on this front.) In any event, African states did withdraw relative to their preliberalization postures, and far fewer states today actively undermine their private sector, *writ large*. This is certainly a consequence of the paradigm shifts begun in the 1990s. Overall, therefore, the reduction in the state's economic role *did* create opportunities for business to emerge and prosper to a degree that simply was not possible in prior eras.

Yet many state-imposed obstacles to business persist, including burdensome and often arbitrary regulations and restrictions on business formation and practice, which continue to impede business investment. For African businesses, therefore, the notion of a truly "enabling state" remains the exception rather than the rule, and this is partly borne out by the contemporary Doing Business project rankings. Nonetheless, if this new environment was not exactly "enabling," at least it offered a context in which autonomous private sector activities were no longer automatically seen as potential threats to the vested interests of the political class, as had been the case in countries such as in Kenya, Nigeria, and Ghana, or as reflexively antithetical to the state's development objectives, as they had been in places like Mozambique, Tanzania, and Zambia. Part of the reason for the changed worldview was the expanded involvement in business of many members of the political class.[19]

At bottom, though, SAPs exacerbated many of the problems they were meant to alleviate, and critics on all sides agree that they largely failed to correct the specific problems they were designed to address. Is it reasonable to insist that "business in Africa" is better off as a result of SAP-inspired changes? Perhaps the benefit was as much indirect as direct. Simply put, it was necessary to change the modus operandi and shatter the old economic and political mindset regarding business writ large; the ideological and policy shifts of the 1990s were instrumental in this regard. Thus, profit emerges (or perhaps *re*emerges) as a legitimate pursuit; a more circumscribed economic role for the state is legitimated; and new opportunities can be created for a more autonomous set of investors and entrepreneurs and long-suffering local business actors. Importantly, however, before these new cultures of business in sub-Saharan Africa could achieve fuller expression, African states required political reforms, which also began to sweep the continent in the 1990s.

BUSINESS AND DEMOCRACY

It is often assumed that business in the developing world favors regime types of an authoritarian bent. Businesses operating under authoritarian regimes are likely spared the vagaries of popular participation and pressures via powerful interest groups or the electorate and they may be subject to fewer regulations and benefit from streamlined decision-making processes. Moreover, most businesses, whether small and local or large and multinational, prefer to maintain a low profile politically rather than clash with authoritarian rulers. Businesses may also benefit considerably from state patronage under a nondemocratic status quo, and these benefits might be threatened in a democratic system, which is typically associated with greater transparency.[20] Consequently, many scholars and practitioners alike have assumed that business actors are at best indifferent to democratic governance and at worst hostile toward it. Examples abound of businesses that supported an authoritarian status quo provided those businesses were able to maintain access to patronage opportunities and/or profit margins, regardless of the broader political and social consequences and irrespective of the incumbent regime's antidemocratic posture and brutality—Royal Dutch Shell's engagement with the notorious Abacha regime in Nigeria in the 1990s perhaps serves as the most extreme example of this phenomenon in Africa, but there are many others in Africa and Latin America and Asia. In short, since private enterprise can thrive in the most nondemocratic of environments, democracy is seldom regarded as a prerequisite for business success.

Indeed, China's experience over the past quarter century demonstrates clearly that democracy is hardly a precondition for the entrenchment of a thriving capitalist system and the exponential expansion of the private sector. Kellee Tsai observes that in 1977 private enterprises were so insignificant in that country that no official statistics on them were even maintained. Yet "by 2005, there were 29.3 million private businesses, employing over 200 million people and accounting for 49.7 percent of GDP."[21] Because "the operational and political environment for private commerce has gradually improved over the course of [China's] reform era" economic and political actors have scant need to dwell on issues of class and democracy; they are too "busy selling products, building networks [and] juggling responsibilities."[22] In other words, China's nominally communist single-party regime has accommodated and integrated capitalism. (The Republic of Korea saw comparable business growth under a military dictatorship from 1961 to 1988, well before it ultimately transitioned to democracy.) Although Tsai refrains from outright prediction, she suggests that a democratic transition in China is unlikely; should such a radical transformation occur, it is even less likely that business will be in its vanguard.

Even if China has managed quite well without, one of the presumed benefits of democratic governance and institutions is a more effective system for stable and efficient transactions. Although political and policy outcomes are not always predictable, democracy allows the expectation that outcomes will be arrived at in accordance with established norms and procedures rather than the whim of an authoritarian. To a far greater degree than in China or Korea—or even in Latin America, where benefits long accrued to business actors from *rightist* authoritarian regimes—most businesses in Africa have been greatly disadvantaged by a long history of excessive and inefficient state economic intervention at the hands of authoritarian, typically left-leaning, regimes. This was compounded by their rank patronage, lack of transparency, and general economic and political illiberality. Ultimately, all firms are vulnerable in conditions of economic instability or decline, and Africa's democratic states (numbering only a handful in the 1980s and early nineties) were not entirely immune to these problems. Nonetheless, it is irrefutable that Africa's authoritarian governments have done little to advance the cause of economic growth. Indeed, as the *Economist* put it so succinctly years ago, "If dictators made countries rich, Africa would be an economic colossus."[23]

Africa's authoritarian regimes made little accommodation for legitimate capitalism or of business—à la China and Korea. Although some firms did well under one-party authoritarianism—multinational oil companies in Nigeria and Angola, Asians in Kenya, and Lebanese in Côte d'Ivoire, for example—such space to operate was ad hoc and individualized rather than based on any broad developmentalist strategy.[24] Structural adjustment and Africa's Western aid dependency, with their emphasis on neoliberal orthodoxy, paradoxically *precluded,* as I have noted, Asian-style strong-state developmentalism. The spread of democracy, however, has introduced a degree of pluralism to the African marketplace that has given greater voice to business. In other words, democratization has been an important contributing factor in creating opportunities for a broader cross-section of business on the African continent, a far more encompassing grouping than that which existed prior to reform. The transformation of the economic landscape that took root in the 1990s represents a critical foundation, without which the broadening of business cultures and development of new enterprises would have proved nearly impossible. Hence the enlargement of the political space, which frequently occurred in tandem with economic liberalization, if equally haltingly, was the other essential piece of the puzzle.

It is those attributes that typically accompany democracy in Africa that are of the greatest utility, including predictability, rule boundedness, security, popular voice, and, in many cases, elite accountability. Inasmuch as business has also contributed to democratization in a few instances, the relationship between business and democracy has been a reciprocal one. In short, the impulse to democratize can emerge from the business community's frustration over its lack of influence on, and access to, the undemocratic state. The cases of Venezuela, Bolivia, Ecuador, and Peru, for example, illustrate that business associations were among the leading institutions advocating democratic rule not because of immediate financial crisis but because they believed that their *long-term* economic self-interest—their property rights and capital accumulation, for example—would be increasingly threatened by the caprices of the authoritarian state structures.[25]

In Africa too, the vision of the singularly corrupt, exploitative, and, indeed, "state-based" business is a caricature. Business does not simply and reflexively mimic the behavior of a corrupt authoritarian state. If such isomorphism were universally the case, business challenges to states would rarely occur; such maneuvering would be tantamount to patricide. Business cannot be viewed solely as an enabler of—or as enabled by—neopatrimonial authoritarian regimes; it can take part in generating positive political externalities, such as political liberalization, as well.

The Role of Business in Democratic Transitions

Only if one were colossally naïve could one aver that all businesspeople are democrats. Nor can we claim that most businesses signed on, whether reluctantly or enthusiastically, as supporters of democratization efforts around the world. Yet it is equally plain, especially in Africa, that a significant percentage of existing and aspiring business actors had ample incentive to do so: prior to the democratization movements of the 1990s, the situation for private sectors in most of Africa was generally dismal. Except for a narrow band of state-based bourgeoisie, some MNCs, particularly in the extractive sectors, and certain minority and residual settler populations, authoritarianism has been none too kind to business in Africa, whether those already in operation or still in the planning stages. Thus, unlike private sectors in Venezuela, Chile, and other onetime right-wing regimes in South America, for example, a reflexively progovernment, reactionary tendency does not exist among a large swath of the business community in Africa. The impulse to support prodemocracy movements, therefore, emerged from the realization by business actors, from Benin to South Africa to Zimbabwe, that the authoritarian state had become a constraint on their ability to accumulate capital. Hence, many firms and business interest associations joined opposition movements in support of political liberalization.[26]

The capriciousness of authoritarian rule can create substantial risk for many businesspeople, even those who are longtime beneficiaries of the status quo. Patron-clientelism often serves as the glue that keeps certain businesses and investors in a favored position, but such relationships are by their very nature ad hoc; lacking institutional architecture, favored "in-groups" and individuals may become unwelcome "out groups" at a moment's notice. Moreover, prior to liberalization, African business typically faced dual challenges: existential threats from the precarious condition of the micro- and macroeconomy, coupled with unresolved frustration over the lack of influence on, and access to, the (undemocratic) state; both can fuel the impulse toward democratization. If firms and associations calculate that their *long-term* economic self interest—including property rights protections and unencumbered capital accumulation—will be increasingly threatened by the vagaries of the authoritarian state, they can be among the leading institutions advocating democratic rule. A state with a history of enmity toward private businesspeople—of which Zambia, Tanzania, or Ethiopia in the 1980s and 1990s are prominent examples—is a major source of uncertainty. Add to that an environment of severe economic contraction, such as that which characterized most African countries in the 1990s, and loyalties to the regime become even more fluid.

In many respects, embattled businesses, at least, would appear to have little to lose by supporting regime change.[27] Indeed, as Bratton and van de Walle argue, "during transitions from neopatrimonial regimes, middle-class elements align with the opposition. . . . The weak national bourgeoisies of Africa are frustrated by state ownership, overregulation, and official corruption. . . . [Further,] businessmen and professionals often take on political leadership roles in the opposition, drawing in other middle-class groups, like public servants, whose downward economic mobility is a powerful impetus to forge an alternative ruling coalition."[28] But the decision to support democratization processes, and often nascent opposition parties, could hardly be taken lightly, especially in the 1990s when all of this was quite novel and outcomes far less certain than today. In order to protect what assets they had, business typically jumped on the democracy bandwagon belatedly rather than get out in front of it. Their approach was pragmatic: "Business support of the democracy movement was usually best understood as an investment decision: businessmen wanted to pick the right horse. For this reason, they were sometimes wary of openly opposing the incumbent until his demise seemed assured."[29]

On occasion, however, business groups may make more direct and explicit demands of the state for democratic change, such as openly supporting opposition movements or demanding equal political rights and the restoration of "normal politics," as happened in Zambia, Benin, and South Africa. In Benin, long-suffering business associations and their leaders distanced themselves from an increasingly delegitimized state, thus contributing to the transition there in 1991.[30] Around the same time, the small and floundering business community in Zambia supported the opposition's ultimately successful bid to unseat a twenty-seven-year incumbent. In South Africa, leading members of the powerful white business community famously recognized the unsustainability of apartheid long before many members of the ruling political class. In fact, as early as 1985, a delegation of businesspeople met with the ANC in exile in Lusaka—an apostasy in the eyes of apartheid's stalwarts.[31] Admittedly, such departures are unusual. Seldom does business *collectively* take a partisan political stance without a history of having been rebuffed by the state on previous attempts at policy advocacy.

Indeed, the risks of challenging an incumbent regime, whether indirectly or explicitly, can be immense. In 1999, Zimbabwe's predominant white business community was seen as a key financial supporter of the then new opposition Movement for Democratic Change. However, that business core, long vital to Zimbabwe's economy, fundamentally miscalculated the susceptibility of the ruling Zimbabwe African National Union-Patriotic Front regime to an opposition challenge and was met with vicious reprisals that ultimately destroyed it. (Of course, the ruling party's response also destroyed the economy in the process and precipitated a dramatic descent into one-party authoritarianism, but the complete erosion of democracy, as in Zimbabwe, is today more exceptional in sub-Saharan Africa.) Not surprisingly, therefore, business support for democracy is probably more often expressed in oblique terms that have more to do with democratic *practices* than with opposition politics and the vagaries of electoral democracy.

Furthermore, business's support for democratization or democracy is certainly conditional. Businesspeople are citizens; they have families; they are members of associations and religious organizations and various bodies within which many opinions are doubtlessly shared. As *individuals,* therefore, businesspeople may be committed democrats. As a business *class,* however, they seldom support democracy solely for democracy's sake. Thus if the new political milieu brings elected governments to power that are ultimately hostile to business interests, business will rethink its commitment to political liberalization. There are multiple examples both within and outside Africa of just such a scenario unfolding, such as following Venezuela's abortive coup in 2002 and President Hugo Chavez's reaction, the unexpected disdain for business interests shown by Zambia's Movement for Multiparty Democracy government after its election in 1991, and in cases, such as those detailed by Amy Chua, where popular backlash against minority businesses is suborned by the state. For the most part, however, where business actors have become proponents of democracy in transitional countries it is because they perceive a positive link between greater democracy and their interests and objectives. This, therefore, is the second and perhaps more critical dimension of business and democracy: the relationship between Africa's increasing levels of democracy and business success. Although there are some exceptions, *in general,* democracy has been good for business and business development in Africa.

Reaping the Democratic Harvest: Democracy's Benefits for Business

We have now witnessed over two decades of democratization in Africa; although this period has seen several alarming setbacks, by and large, democracy has measurably deepened. In 1986, Freedom House (reported, using its designations of "free" and "partly free," that there were fourteen democratic and partially democratic countries in sub-Saharan Africa, By 2007, that figure had risen dramatically to thirty-three of the forty-seven countries in the subregion. This impressive growth in the measurement of political and civil liberties on the continent is affirmed by the Afrobarometer surveys, which find widespread (if somewhat shallow) support for liberal democracy in the Western mold in Africa. Research by Staffan Lindberg reported in his *Democracy and Elections in Africa* indicates that although Africa's young democratic experiments faced severe setbacks by the mid-1990s, they nonetheless established critical precedents; the *practice* of electoral democracy improved in the following decade as a result.

For Africa's business community, this broadened democratic foundation affords political participation and the opportunity to engage with parties and governments, whereas before, access to the state previously was either foreclosed or ad hoc and individualized. It is worth pointing out, however, that a recent study about Mexico suggests that one of the effects of democracy was that the influence of a once powerful segment of the business community declined. Kenneth Shadlen found that small business was marginalized politically in favor of big business and organized labor, which deliver money and voters, respectively. Although Mexico's transition from single-party dominance resembles Africa's, a similar business scenario is unlikely to unfold in African countries. For the most part, African businesses of various scales had such limited access under the ancien régime that there was nowhere to go but up. Moreover, on the whole, Africa's democracies do appear to be creating more favorable conditions for small- and medium-scale business than their nondemocratic counterparts, as the *Doing Business* reports suggest.

Democracy is also more associated with property rights protections enshrined in the rule of law. In many countries, though capricious policies still persist, legal mechanisms are now in place, and increasingly respected. The force of law provides some protection against political interference. A range of various business indicators are better in democratic states and worse in remaining authoritarian ones. Although it is an admittedly rough comparison, of the sixteen countries rated "not free" in Freedom House's 2010 Freedom in the World index, only one, Somalia, is not ranked in the World Bank's Doing Business ranking. Thirteen of the sixteen, however, are in the bottom half of the forty-six sub-Saharan African countries measured for the 2010 Doing Business rankings, and these are also among the lowest in the world. Conversely, Africa's free and partly free countries are in the top half of business climates, albeit with a few notable exceptions.[32]

Transparency, which is also associated with greater democracy, has increased as well. While this may be detrimental to certain business interests close to the regime, it opens up opportunities for new and emergent business actors.[33] Greater transparency may or may not have had the impact of diminishing corruption; in fact, corruption *perceptions* may rise because greater political and civil liberties mean that corruption becomes more visible and therefore susceptible to being more openly criticized than in the past.[34] More importantly, transparency exposes to the light of day the way in which economic and financial decision making is conducted; whereas previously doing business was often clandestine and opaque, the new transparency permits greater information flow, improved awareness, and therefore more strategic decision making on the part of potential new business entrants.

In sum, the political sphere now permits wider participation, including by a broader range of business actors. In addition, democratization has conferred greater accountability, transparency, and regularization in the policy process, along with greater assurance that property rights (such as security from theft and nonconfiscatory taxes, enforcement of contracts, and so forth) will be protected by—and from—the government. This does not mean, however, that democracy is universally good for business, even in Africa. Indeed, stable authoritarian regimes, like those in Rwanda, Swaziland, or the momentarily stable but oil-rich Sudan, may yet be attractive. Further, democratization did not eliminate corruption, especially in the formative 1990s, although it has introduced a measure of transparency and broadened opportunities for those business actors historically outside the scope of the political patronage machine. The benefits that may accrue to business as a result of democratic transitions may be accompanied by the possibility of increased access by other segments of society as well and the very real possibility that fragile *elected* governments will now be more responsive than in the authoritarian past to a wide range of constituencies so as to both maintain popular legitimacy and to retain elected office. This means that, perhaps more than ever before, the threat of economic populism persistently looms large.

These dilemmas aside, I believe a Zambian businessman perhaps put it best. Summing up the relationship between state and business shortly after that country's 1991 transition to multipartyism, he described it as "a bloody mess; but it's better than the previous mess." Indeed, it goes without saying, that virtually no conventional businessperson who is dependent on consistency (of supply, input, regulation) and predictability (of markets, institutions, other rules) would prefer, say, Zimbabwe to Zambia or Congo to Ghana. Greater democracy has, in short, reduced the once daunting political economy barriers to entry for aspiring entrepreneurs. Though Africa's democratization in the 1990s was aptly characterized as occurring in "fits and starts", the first important and tentative steps were made in that decade.[35]

CONCLUSION

The 1990s marked a period of profound institutional change in Africa as a result of the initiation of economic and political reforms. Adjustment programs had a substantially detrimental effect on most existing African businesses, regardless of size. This was despite the fact that, indirectly at least, they were designed to improve the environment in which business was transacted. Yet the much-maligned SAPs were an integral part of a complex of reforms. The SAPs, and the fundamental shift in worldview, as well as other forces that manifested themselves later, including exogenous factors such as international debt relief, a global economic recovery, and record commodity prices, together initiated an important shift in the business environment in Africa.

The early experiments with adjustment changed things for many businesses. For example, in mid-1994, just two years after liberalization, longtime Zambian businessman Theo Bull practically waxed poetic about the newfound ease of accessing and holding foreign exchange and the fact that exports and imports no longer required a cumbersome licensing process. This, he explained, was nothing short of revolutionary for a private sector long under the boot heel of a semisocialist one-party system. Yet, at the same time, the populace at large suffered massive layoffs, mainly as the result of shuttered parastatals, and there was a spike in the number of the poor, who had scant resources to buy the new, plentiful, and newly imported products and services. Such a scenario was repeated across Africa. Additionally, for business itself, it was not as if the magic wand of liberalization suddenly created capital for aspiring—or for that matter, established—entrepreneurs.

On the whole, eventual refinements to the simplistic liberalization templates embodied in the early adjustment programs resulted in reductions in government expenditure on SOEs (as a result of privatization and deindustrialization), reduced interest rates, elimination of currency controls (which allowed access to foreign exchange), and significant opportunities for new private investment, if not necessarily support for existing—and struggling—entrepreneurs by the early 1990s. But above all the macroeconomic stability that began to take root in the 1990s was a significant improvement for business, especially with the onset of lower deficits and lower inflation. This is hardly meant as an apology for SAPs, nor for the unfettered globalization embodied in the Washington Consensus. On the contrary, even by the late 1990s it had become apparent that the near total surrender to the free market was far from the best prescription for Africa—or anywhere else for that matter—and that a new consensus was necessary. The successor programs to SAPs included poverty reduction strategies, for example, which, while not particularly effective with respect to that goal, enabled substantial debt relief for African countries. More recently, the events that precipitated the 2008 global recession only served to reinforce the notion that a new approach was called for, bolstered by a renewed appreciation for Keynesianism and a stronger, not weaker, role for the state; this will continue to impact policies on "development" and within African states themselves in ways that cannot yet be entirely predicted.

Adjustment and subsequent reform in Africa, as carried out by the IFIs and donors and even as proposed by Africans themselves, therefore, has been part of a tortuous learning process. And while this process has been riddled with errors and false starts and overhyped expectations, it is also true that absent the changes wrought by SAPs—not least, the ideational and attitudinal ones—there would be scant foundation for contemporary initiatives that now fall under the rubric of private sector development. These efforts augur positively for the furtherance of a market/business ethos among aspiring business actors and, in some cases, among their state counterparts. The Ghana of 2004, which saw the establishment of a Ministry of Private Sector Development, was a world away even from that under the presidency of Jerry Rawlings, whose government, despite its national embrace of liberalization policies, had a vaguely adversarial relationship with business.

In sum, collectively, the position of business within African economies is remarkably changed from the dire straits of the 1980s. Certainly, informal economic relations continue to characterize many of Africa's expansive rural areas, and informal economies persist in the relatively "ungoverned spaces," such as in the North and South Kivu regions of Eastern Congo and Somalia's hinterland. Yet formal business has certainly moved to the foreground in the majority of countries. Indeed, the concept of private sector development, though coined by the donor community, is now widely disseminated, even if its terminology is not yet part of the universal lexicon.

Admittedly, the commitment to the principle of using the private sector as the leading development tool varies widely. The proliferation of PSD represents, in part, an evolution in thinking about the role of the state and the role of the private sector in national development. My point is not to focus on the "success" or "failure" of PSD as a formal, programmatic strategy (which, given its relative novelty, cannot be adequately determined at this stage). Instead, PSD should be seen as part of a complex, as part of the shift in *mindset* among African political and economic elites from regarding the notions of "profit," "private sector," and "market" as pejoratives to taking them seriously; this was nearly unimaginable less than a generation ago.

In his superbly researched book, *African Economies and the Politics of Permanent Crisis: 1979–1999*, van de Walle characterizes Africans' attitudes toward neoliberal economic reform as ambivalent.[36] These findings, drawn from data collected in the Afrobarometer surveys, could hardly be considered surprising, given that they were recorded in the late 1990s and early 2000s—that is, at the tail end of one of Africa's most tumultuous decades. In light of the foregoing discussion, it is perhaps somewhat surprising that, despite macroeconomic improvement in the 2000s, this ambivalence was recorded in later survey panels. However, poverty and unemployment in most of Africa has remained entrenched at very high levels. Thus, for many ordinary African citizens, visible economic gains, whether during or after SAP programs, have been limited or nonexistent. Political elites, long skeptical of an unadulterated "Washington Consensus" in the first place, have now had their concerns validated by the collapse of this strict neoliberal development agenda.

Among current and aspiring business actors, however, this view is more nuanced. In fact, such grandiose debates about the relative merits of different macroeconomic policies may be out of date, as business seems to have moved on to more directly pressing concerns. Taking off chronologically from where van de Walle left off, the World Bank's Enterprise Surveys conducted between 2001 and 2008 poll the African business community *directly*. Drawing on this data, Vijaya Ramachandran, Alan Gelb, and Manju Kedia Shah find that business reflects much more concern with mundane issues of infrastructure, governance, regulation, and access to finance.[37] For business, the debate about relatively greater liberalization versus statism appears to be long settled, and certainly, little ambivalence is expressed in a host of recent works on the subject from a variety of perspectives.[38]

In contrast, the role of democracy and democratization in sub-Saharan Africa is slightly more ambiguous. The improved political context, which increasingly includes competitive (if ideologically indistinct) parties, widespread popular participation in the electoral process, and free and fair elections (many of which have resulted in government turnover), provides new opportunities for citizens to hold states accountable, including in the form of better service delivery. More and more, states must be responsive to that pressure. To be sure, the newly competitive environment can be messy and violent and can lead to populist reaction by governments or the populace at large that are destructive and threatening to business interests; Zimbabwe, Kenya, and potentially South Africa provide ominous examples. Moreover, decidedly undemocratic states in other regions, notably Asia, have proved effective at managing economic development and the entrenchment of powerful business sectors. This has not been the case in African autocracies, which were rarely if ever predisposed toward the creation of productive business capacity. Instead, Africa's authoritarian elites have traditionally arrogated wealth to themselves, to the exclusion of societal needs. These elites traditionally invested in nonreplicable enterprises or endeavors headed by regime cronies, often funded by natural resource rents wrongly perceived to be inexhaustible and, acutely, during the Cold War, by multi- and bilateral aid.

Thus, in the 1990s, democratization certainly did not eliminate corruption and rent seeking and, like SAPs, has hardly been a panacea in other respects. But the spread of democracy does encourage previously closed regimes to, in effect, "share the wealth" in terms of state resources and attention. Cronies—whether unreconstructed, transformable, or "transformed"—have not disappeared, of course, but they coexist with more conventional capitalist accumulators. Democracy, in short, allows the market to expand, in economic as well as social terms. In the main, political liberalization, like the economic changes that generally occurred in parallel, augurs positively for business in Africa. Extending this discussion chronologically, the next chapter addresses how, during the current century, business in Africa has been able to build on these foundations of economic and political liberalization.

BUSINESS, THE AFRICAN STATE, AND GLOBALIZATION IN THE NEW MILLENNIUM
Transnational Influences and Domestic Responses

INTRODUCTION

In Africa, the 1980s were a period marked by economic and political stagnation and exhausted statism, whereas 1990s ushered in sweeping changes. But if Africa throughout much of the 1990s was characterized by a liberalization and democratization imperative, despite very mixed results, events in the second half of that decade were paradigm-shifting, as both Africa and its international partners alike reacted to the failures of politics and of policy as well as to new exogenous forces. In other words, a high degree of *learning* occurred internationally, as well as at the national and societal levels, including that of business. The Washington Consensus began to unravel, and its decline accelerated in the wake of the 1997 financial crisis in Asia, which eroded confidence in its neoliberal prescriptions. By the start of the new millennium, a number of new developments had begun to transform much of the traditional thinking about African political economies, especially about the role of and prospects for the private sector. Thus, the beginning of the twenty-first century also laid down a significant marker for Africa and particularly for business on the continent.

Neoliberalism's adherents, for example, reconsidered some of its strictures and began to emphasize growth and poverty reduction as a goal. Alterative development strategies saw the creation of an agenda for significant debt relief, enhanced trade relationships, and expanded international assistance. In addition, though it echoed numerous tenets of earlier neoliberal prescriptions, "private sector development" became an increasingly important buzz phrase in development circles. Although "business" had been touted as an important economic actor since the early days of structural adjustment, it was only after 2000 that new African governments and their international partners began to embrace the idea of private sector development as an explicit development objective. The states that have done so most aggressively are, by and large, more democratic, more transparent, and more responsive than their predecessors; indeed, this applies to most of sub-Saharan Africa, where political liberalization has advanced measurably in the past decade.[1]

I situate these international- and domestic-level developments and processes within a larger rubric of globalization, with which Africa remains intertwined. As articulated by in the 1990s by Thomas Friedman, for example, in *The Lexus and the Olive Tree*, "globalization" was generally regarded positively. By the 2000s, however, the concept became tainted, if not discredited, in many circles because of its close association with neoliberalism. And yet, although there is considerable debate about the scholarly utility of the concept, something akin to globalization—regardless of the label assigned to it—continues apace in Africa.[2] It has both economic *and* cultural dimensions. Over a decade into the twenty-first century, the consequences of this new(ish) globalization are decidedly mixed. Economically, Africa appears to be rather poorly served by globalization, but culturally, and particularly in regard to *business cultures,* a more nuanced perspective is called for. Indeed, Africa does not simply passively respond to developments occurring at the international level, even—popular imagery notwithstanding—when it comes to business on the continent. Globalization is not simply "done" to Africa; because endogenous factors also impact both thought and policy, it is necessary to move beyond the idea of globalization, whether economic or cultural, as a set of exclusively international or structural factors. The putatively "global" is internalized and syncretized within African states and societies themselves.

What do contemporary globalization and the changes accompanying it signal for business and business cultures in Africa? More specifically, if the unfettered neoliberalism of structural adjustment failed to reduce poverty or stimulate African development, in what ways is the twenty-first century variant facilitative, especially when it comes to private sector business? In addressing these questions, this chapter first examines how globalization has evolved, particularly in terms of its continuities and discontinuities with neoliberalism. Clearly, globalization continues to be a catchall term that means different things to different audiences; as Susan Strange famously observed, it "can refer to everything from the Internet to a hamburger."[3] Frederick Cooper objects to the concept's imprecision: inasmuch as globalization unites "diverse phenomena into a singular conceptual framework and a singular notion of change, . . . it occlude[s] rather than clarif[ies] historical processes."[4] Notwithstanding such critiques, in general, to critics globalization exemplifies all that is wrong with contemporary international economic and cultural relations, and to its proponents, it connotes peace, mutuality of interests, and shared prosperity.

One can recognize Cooper's critique of the "conceptual apparatus" as "faddish" yet also appreciate the real-world impacts of change wrought partly by processes of increased interconnectedness. In any event, I do not seek to settle debates about the varied interpretations of globalization or whether it is more benign today than it was in the 1990s. Importantly, not all aspects of recent globalization have proved beneficial for Africa; some changes leave Africa even *more* constrained. It is inarguable, however, that the international and domestic policy environment, *as well as the cultural milieu in which business operates,* has changed markedly since 2000–2001; much of this has been affected by changes at the global level. For my purposes, then, what I call globalization can be divided into two essential parts, economic and cultural, and both are aided, in turn, by the global proliferation of technology.

Although economic globalization is seldom consistently defined, perhaps in its most neutral conception it refers to diminished significance of traditional territoriality and a growing interconnectedness.[5] In the 1990s, in the wake of the Cold War and the spread of economic liberalism and democracy, rhetorically, at least, and to many Western eyes that was regarded as a positive outcome. Francis Fukuyama declared in *The End of History* that Western values, particularly democratic capitalism, were in effect the final stage of ideological evolution. Friedman, the award-winning *New York Times* columnist, popularized the notion that this era of globalization, carefully navigated, could prove beneficial for all. Yet, just as some were hailing the virtues of economic globalization, many others were quick to criticize its destructive tendencies in the developing world and especially in sub-Saharan Africa.

In Africa, abstract intellectual arguments about globalization, especially in its economic guise, came to be associated in practice with liberalization and the economic agendas of actors such as the World Bank, the IMF, and the donor countries in the global North, made manifest through structural adjustment. Attacks on the neoliberal agenda and the IMF's preoccupation with stability date to the earliest critiques of SAP programs, but the argument is most famously summarized by Joseph Stiglitz in his 2002 book *Globalization and Its Discontents*. For some Africanists, it seems SAPs are relics of another era. But the global impacts of liberalization and its policy progeny in the debt, aid, and trade regimes continue to the present. Although a negative interpretation of globalization *as liberalization* has clearly gained sway, attitudes toward this "new" variant of globalization are much more forgiving.

Yet Africa's experience with economic globalization remains as contradictory as ever. As scholars like James Ferguson are quick to note, Africa finds itself in the rather paradoxical position of having been both marginalized by globalization and victimized by it at the same time.[6] Economically, African terms of trade have improved, but this is due mainly to the record increases in commodity prices for much of this decade; at the same time, Africa's share of world trade, at about 2 percent, remains below the level it reached in 1980. Africa saw significant new investment in the 2000s, along with a greatly expanded role by nontraditional partners such as India and China, but the bulk of FDI remains concentrated in the extractive sector and has gone overwhelmingly to oil-producing countries and to South Africa; moreover, the continent's share of global FDI remained at an anemic 2–3 percent between 2000 and 2006.

Many of themes discussed in this book pertain to Africa's—and the world's—efforts to deal with this persistent and contradictory set of problems. In recent years, however, some facets of continued globalization offer interesting opportunities for business. Indeed, while economic globalization remains problematic, the cultural variant has helped to buttress the foundation for private sectors in Africa.

There are three principal areas of emphasis in this chapter. The following section revisits the theme of economic globalization with a particular focus on international efforts—and the African response—to redress the many shortcomings of structural adjustment. Second, I turn to the main focus of the chapter: the issue of private sector development. Donors differ in their views on what PSD should entail: some pursue support for microenterprise development; others pursue more "top-down" strategies that endeavor to induce African states to remove regulatory constraints on business.[7] I examine PSD both as a specific range of policies that fall under this rubric and from an ideological and normative standpoint.[8] In my view, private sector development entails "economic globalization" inasmuch as it forms one of the new pillars of economic *policy* prescriptions for Africa and is an explicit acknowledgment that the private sector must both be nurtured and play a significant role. As deliberate policy, PSD may, paradoxically, include elements of statism, given that effective implementation presupposes a measure of state capacity. However, PSD is also an epiphenomenon of *cultural* globalization: Africa's extant entrepreneurial culture is augmented by its increasingly frequent interactions with the world. In this respect, the state is less directly relevant to business growth, though it can play a salutary role.

Thirdly, the chapter offers a series of vignettes that illustrate the ways in which new entrepreneurs and existing businesses—particularly those operating in noncommodity-based sectors—have responded to key stimuli, including changes in the institutional environment (supply-side) and new demand by developing or adjusting their business models in the 2000s. Notwithstanding continued and often severe constraints, many entrepreneurs have been able to seize opportunities to create or expand business in the new century. These cases suggest that the contemporary domestic environment is indeed more promising for business, particularly when contrasted with the incoherence of the 1980s and 1990s.

Finally, the chapter turns this issue around by examining the relationship between the more accommodating contemporary business environment and overall economic performance. Hence, putting an African spin on the old aphorism "What's good for GM is good for the country," I consider whether what's good for business in Africa is also good for Africa. Although causality is difficult to establish, my conclusion is that it is. Indeed, fostering this link between the business environment and favorable economic performance is essential. It is particularly critical in Africa's newly democratic states, which remain weakly institutionalized and face direct or indirect pressure from their electorates over the degree of business-friendly policies pursued.

THE EVOLUTION OF ECONOMIC GLOBALIZATION: FROM NEOLIBERALISM TO THE POST-WASHINGTON CONSENSUS

Critics of neoliberalism argue that its adoption in Africa led to increased poverty, little or no economic growth, deindustrialization, and increased inequality, while rapid financial market liberalization left countries like South Africa, with its sophisticated capital markets, susceptible to "hot-money" flows that can wreak havoc on fragile economies by inducing or exacerbating financial crises.[9] Conversely, the developing countries considered among the most successful economic performers over the past twenty-five years, such as China, India, Malaysia, and Vietnam, actually *eschewed* neoliberalism and pursued heterodox economic policies instead.[10]

At the same time, African political and economic elites are hardly blameless for the economic crisis that reached its nadir in the 1980s and 1990s. Indeed, as noted in chapter 2, scholars like Nicolas van de Walle, who is less reflexively critical of the policies embedded in SAPs, point out that African countries engaged in only partial reforms, rarely if ever completing the full dose of the medication prescribed by their international handlers.[11] One thing is clear: structural adjustment, both as conceived *and* implemented, failed to usher in the positive changes or growth that its designers and leading advocates anticipated in the early 1980s.

Only after more than a decade of failure and a spate of international criticism did leading global institutions, mainly the IFIs and Western donors, begin to incorporate a broader set of reform strategies. Some observers, seeing an emerging synthesis of national developmentalism and the neoliberal policy agenda, have labeled this the "post-Washington Consensus," which displaced the old orthodoxy. In broad strokes, this new consensus calls for a more effective state. However, in so doing it allows for greater state activism, including the preservation of some SOEs (a practice African states never abandoned anyway), greater financial system regulation, more resources for education, and public investment in infrastructure, technology, and agricultural extension.[12] All of these forces are to be marshaled in the cause of growth and poverty alleviation, which SAPs regarded as a positive externality of reform, but is now an explicit goal of international development strategies; indeed, the eradication of extreme poverty now forms the bedrock of aid and development and it is primus inter pares of the eight millennium development goals articulated by the United Nations in 2001 and agreed to by some 191 member nations. But there are important echoes of liberal, market-oriented thinking that remain in these new supposedly more heterodox and more encompassing strategies. Notably, notwithstanding the newfound tolerance of the state, poverty alleviation is perhaps most directly linked to the fostering of growth and jobs through private sector development initiatives, wherein individual (and community) empowerment will emerge through the encouragement of small- and medium-scale enterprises (SMEs).

The post-Washington Consensus can be regarded as part of a complex of views that ushered in a new and important rhetoric about development. That rhetoric entailed the elevation and enshrinement of millennium development goals, with particular emphasis on poverty-related goals, new international commitments to the bilateral and multilateral aid regimes, and the promotion of trade through vehicles like the U.S. African Growth and Opportunities Act (AGOA). This "evolution" away from the strictest neoliberalism was accompanied, fortuitously, by record increases in the prices of primary commodities on which most sub-Saharan African economies depend and contributed to more than 5 percent annual growth in GDP between 2001 and 2008.

More than a decade after the Washington Consensus was supposedly scuttled, the new international development regime remains largely ineffectual itself, and to critics the "new thinking" looks a lot like the "old thinking."[13] They suggest that the post-Washington Consensus is not altogether different in practice and, ultimately, in its impact on African economies: effectively, many aid conditionalities continue and new aid commitments have not been met. Yet despite the fact that rhetoric does not match realities, twenty-first-century-style globalization does appear to have had some mildly positive spillover effects. Furthermore, primary commodity earnings fortunately shielded Africa, albeit temporarily, from the failure of the countries in the global north to meet their new commitments to aid and international development in the period.

Key Elements of the New Model

As noted, the theme of poverty reduction undergirds the post-Washington Consensus. Poverty reduction itself is anchored in the drawing up of a poverty reduction strategy paper (PRSP), a process that was introduced by the IMF and World Bank in 2000. This initiative signified the emergence of poverty alleviation as an explicit concern of these institutions and sought to involve national political and civic actors in developing a national strategy for growth promotion and poverty reduction. The drawing up of PRSPs also became a requisite step for countries to receive debt relief under the highly indebted poor countries (HIPC) initiative and the multilateral debt relief initiative (MDRI).[14]

The PRSP framework has attracted criticism from the left because it imposes demands that are not unlike the "conditionalities" attached to SAPs, including demands for privatization, deregulation, regional integration, and integration with the global economy via expanded trade relations. Yet such conditions notwithstanding, PRSPs are linked to debt reductions from which a number of African countries have already benefited. Indeed, by late 2008, some $51 billion in debt service relief had been approved as part of packages to twenty-seven African countries. Problematically, and to some, predictably, these savings have not been used exclusively on poverty reduction, but on elite consumption and military spending as well. Nonetheless, the debt overhang was seen as a major contributor to entrenched poverty and to constrained social spending altogether. Clearly, PRSPs are flawed instruments, and so the design-implementation tension continues. Yet debt relief is valuable in and of itself, as it affords greater discretion and self-determination to African governments; misuses aside, the reintroduction of free primary education, as in Zambia, or of health care, as in Kenya, indirectly supports entrepreneurship. Moreover, diminished national debt and also makes economies more attractive to investors by lowering perceived investment risk.

The emphasis on poverty reduction also precipitated more forceful rhetoric about assistance to Africa, particularly in the lead-up to and immediate aftermath of the 2005 meeting of the G-8, held in Gleneagles, Scotland. There, the donors agreed to increase foreign aid, doubling it in real terms by 2010, to enact further debt reductions, specifically to cancel all HIPC debt to the International Development Association of the World Bank, the IMF, and the African Development Bank, and to liberalize their own markets by reducing subsidies, especially on agriculture products. The promises, voiced most enthusiastically by Britain's then prime minister Tony Blair, were met with great fanfare and high expectations, but they remain significantly unfulfilled; indeed, the 2009 G-8 meeting returned to a number of the same themes. Many of the promised aid increases—such as the 0.7 percent of GDP that donor countries pledged to devote to aid, for example—have thus far failed to materialize. In addition, and perhaps more damagingly, the agricultural subsidies of countries in the global North have been maintained, meaning that Africa's export potential is stymied indefinitely.

Despite the global North's resistance to agriculture trade liberalization, which is rooted in domestic politics, African development through trade has been a recurring theme. Originally signed in 2000, the U.S.-based AGOA was an attempt to spur African exports through preferential trade with the United States, mainly in the textile sector. Yet the lofty rhetoric of Gleneagles and AGOA notwithstanding, Africa's share of world trade remains minuscule—and it is worse if petroleum is not considered. Preferential trade agreements like AGOA are useful because they may facilitate the growth of certain economic sectors, such as textiles and clothing, and because they explicitly acknowledge the business-international trade-development nexus and its role in poverty reduction, but they are ultimately limited in scope.[15] Further, they are inherently self-serving because they provide reverse incentives for American or other third parties to enter African markets, which ironically renders it difficult for *African* firms to compete. Indeed, AGOA, like Lomé previously, tends to entrench large, mainly minority, and often foreign-owned firms and crowd out small indigenous firms, as Western importers prefer to deal with global contract manufacturers. Thus, preferential trade agreements thus far have had ambiguous impacts on "development" but have tended to preserve the status quo in business and deepen the sociopolitical problem of privileged minorities.[16]

Notwithstanding the risk of such sociopolitical problems stemming from market-dominant minorities, I have argued throughout this book that "minority capital" in Africa is still *capital* and thus that discrimination against it, either analytically or practically, is imprudent; *business in Africa* is often a precursor for *African business*.[17] Thus, AGOA beneficiaries, like the Taiwanese-owned textile manufacturer Shining Century, which is located in Lesotho, have added value to local economies.[18] They provide jobs, contribute to the establishment of an industrial infrastructure, pay taxes, and, in some cases, generate opportunities for upstream and downstream industries as well as demand for businesses engaged in ancillary activities, such as dining, housing, and other services. Nevertheless, if the aim was to markedly expand Africa's industrial development, the predominance of expatriates and multinationals at the expense of domestic firms, especially black African ones, means that the intermediate-term impact of AGOA, at least, is marginal. Furthermore, AGOA in particular has been undermined by the expiration of the Multi Fibre Arrangement, which for more than thirty years imposed a quota system on textiles from developing countries. Since then, even expatriate firms in Africa have found that they are uncompetitive domestically and in U.S. export markets (even with AGOA preferences) with output from China, where production costs have been much lower than elsewhere; numerous factories in Africa therefore have been scaled down or shuttered altogether. Even Shining Century, celebrated in Carol Pineau's film *Africa: Open for Business*, laid off 20 percent of its fifteen-hundred-member workforce just four months after the expiry of the Multi Fibre Arrangement in January 2005.[19] Deborah Brautigam's largely favorable assessment of China in Africa in *The Dragon's Gift* suggests that many African-domiciled firms in the textiles, clothing, and footwear sectors were able to cope with the expiration of agreement and responded competitively. In terms of export markets, this ability to cope was aided, in part, by the imposition of *new* protectionist quotas by both the United States and EU against Chinese textile imports. Paradoxically, however, the inherent unpredictability of such politically motivated protectionism might cause other textile producers in Africa "to be wary of preferences that might seem too good to be true or simply too ephemeral."[20]

Ultimately, trade agreements such as AGOA have not accelerated a "race to the bottom" in Africa, as its early opponents feared, but neither have they spurred the magical transformation of African industrial and wider economic development and poverty reduction, envisioned by its champions. Textiles and clothing are a critical entry point for countries that are attempting to industrialize; hence the challenges faced by African firms, both state-owned and private enterprises, in this sector historically are worrying. In any event, AGOA circumscribes textile imports from Africa, and as Tina Zappile's research demonstrates, despite initial successes in places like Kenya and Lesotho, "there is no evidence that AGOA eligibility translates to increases in AGOA exports to the United States."[21] Perhaps even more distressing than the uncertainties of nonreciprocal trade agreements and their ability to withstand political pressures in the offering countries is the unwillingness of OECD countries to reduce their agricultural subsidies, despite the fact that this would have immediate impact on African economies, which are 70 percent agriculturally based, on average.[22]

The one clear *consensus* reached in the so-called post-Washington consensus is on the poverty reduction imperative. Beyond that, the methods employed by various

international actors on issues of conditionalities, aid commitments, and trade, for example, are often reminiscent of an earlier era. Yet one area in which the climate for
this "new" globalization differed sharply from the old is in commodity prices. Hence,
the various shortcomings of the development agenda embedded in the post-Washington
Consensus arguably mattered less in the 2000s, which saw the strongest global commodity prices in a generation. The price of virtually everything Africa extracts from
the ground, and on which many of its economies are singularly dependent, shot up
dramatically. Much of this increase is attributed to Chinese demand for raw materials—
metals, minerals, timber, and petroleum—to fuel its own double-digit annual growth
rates.

In late 2008 the global economy fell into recession. The Chinese economy was
among the few predicted to remain robust and was estimated to grow at some 7 percent
in 2009, but world prices for primary commodities nevertheless plummeted. Prices
rebounded even by late 2009, and by 2011 some commodities had reached record
prices. Yet African states are notorious for their failure to use windfalls generated by
the previous commodity boom of the 1970s to diversify their economies. Instead, high
commodity prices promoted rent seeking and fueled elite consumption, and revenues
were channeled toward welfarist policies. The contemporary boom and bust is therefore eerily reminiscent of the development dilemma of a generation ago, but with at
least three important differences.

First, a genuine ideological space for business and the private sector now exists,
coupled with more democratic polities—all built on the foundation of the political and
economic institutional change initiated in the 1990s. The post-Washington Consensus
accommodates a measure of statism, but it also seeks explicitly to empower private sectors. Thus, the "orthodox paradox" that stymied liberalization in the 1980s and 1990s
is diminished, if not eliminated altogether. Under the ancien régime, pursuit of liberalization was antithetical to the interests of political and bureaucratic elites. Today,
the incentive structures for elites and private sector interests tend to covary. Second,
although states were laggards, many private firms took advantage of the comparative
boom years to establish or expand operations, especially in the trade and service sectors. (Admittedly, however, prior to the rebound in the extractive sectors that they
served, these firms struggled in the 2008–2009 downturn.) Finally, an emergent private sector lessens the burden on states. In other words, as the private sector grows,
the rationale diminishes for subsidizing floundering sectors once dominated by SOEs,
as employment and tax revenues (seldom contributed by SOEs in any event) are found
elsewhere and demand for goods and services is increasingly satisfied by other means.

At bottom, the post-Washington Consensus rather unprecedentedly acknowledges the structural constraints on African development. Yet despite the range of celebrated and self-congratulatory initiatives ostensibly geared toward poverty reduction,
the *direct* contributions of this new globalization to this goal are, at best, modest: debt

reductions and aid commitments clearly don't hurt, but when they are replaced by new borrowing, new conditionalities, and renewed dependencies, then arguably they don't help much, either. But where the twenty-first-century incarnation of globalization *can* have a substantial impact is in its emphasis on private sector development and specifically in its calls for the promotion of the private sector as one of the critical levers of development and poverty alleviation. Neither the international nor the domestic African environment provided sufficiently fertile soil for private sector growth in the 1980s or 1990s.

PRIVATE SECTOR DEVELOPMENT

Formally, private sector development refers to the specific basket of policies and programs that are aimed at increasing the supply of entrepreneurs. Although such initiatives date to the 1990s, there was not much uniformity among them, and they did not enter the development lexicon until after about 2001. These are, by and large, *externally* influenced, inasmuch as the impetus, funding, nomenclature, and so forth are derived from outside (i.e., the donor community). Thus, like SAPs and the post-Washington Consensus into which it fits, PSD, as a policy, is a manifestation of economic globalization. But private sector development is also an intrinsically cultural phenomenon; to the extent that private sector thinking has permeated sub-Saharan Africa, especially at the governmental level, it reveals a fundamental shift in the ideology and worldview of the African political class that still had not been fully absorbed even as recently as the 1990s—although sections of the populace clearly got the message earlier.

I do not mean to suggest that PSD is entirely externally or "globalization-driven." Indeed, "business" and "Africa" are fully reconcilable concepts. Thus it should come as no surprise that the programs themselves have been endogenized, partly as a result of their finding succor within extant African business cultures.[23]

As SAPs' failures became obvious, Africa's external partners recognized that, given historical constraints, private sectors and business were unlikely to simply *emerge* from a neoliberal policy environment. Insisting that states simply "get out of the way," as prescribed in the 1980s and 1990s, does not facilitate business emergence. In the absence of negative interventions in the market, such retreat of the state can permit some private firms to thrive. Most businesses, however (certainly most of sub-Saharan Africa's historically disadvantaged private sectors), will scarcely get off the ground; they need a proactive state or at least a policy environment that is not adverse to entrepreneurship.

Whether originating from multilateral authorities, donor governments, organizations or foundations, development strategies that emphasize private sectors, empowerment, and the linkages between business and poverty reduction are today de rigueur. Hence although the World Bank's International Finance Corporation has been involved in financing private sector investments in Africa for a quarter century, today such efforts have been enjoined by a host of other entities of vastly differing sizes and capacities. Hence we see everything from the proliferation of think tanks, nongovernmental organizations (NGOs), and donor agencies devoted to "private sector development" to initiatives like the Grameen Bank and the Acumen Fund, which focus on microlending and micro- and small-enterprise development, respectively, and the nonprofit investment facilitator Endeavor or social entrepreneurship promoters like Ashoka. A new coterie of research-oriented groups exists—from large entities like the Private Sector Unit in the World Bank's Africa Region department to small outfits like Enterprise Africa based at George Mason University in the United States—which study and promote African entrepreneurship. Even the UN has gotten into the act, as seen in the functions of the Commission on Private Sector and Development. Business bodies, such as the Corporate Council on Africa (founded in 1992) and the more recent BusinessAction for Africa, seek to promote investment and advance corporate interests while contributing to African development. For-profit consultancies, investment funds, and public and private development agencies also populate this new landscape, including the Whittaker Group, TechnoServe, and boutique firms like the Pan African Capital Group LLC in the United States, to name but a few. Britain's DfID launched a new PSD initiative in January 2009. Japan's JICA established a "one village, one product" approach, and similarly, Denmark's Danida established a business-to-business program geared toward establishing long-term partnerships and mutual commitment between Danish companies and firms in developing countries, as well as a public-private partnership program, both with the aim of deploying the private sector to promote better working and living conditions in host countries.

In the United States, USAID has made African PSD an institutional priority as well. For example, USAID is funding private sector initiatives through two programs: the Africa Global Competitiveness Initiative and the Initiative to End Hunger in Africa. The latter helped create nine hundred local level, public-private partnerships in 2006, which helped some seventy-eight thousand SMEs improve their access to business services and finance. The goal of USAID here is to strengthen the private sector "voice," enhance regional capacities, and, not least, to build alliances between African and U.S. private sectors that will result in trade and investment linkages.[24] Within Africa, country-level initiatives are complemented at the continental level by the pan-African NEPAD business group, which was established in 2005 as a forum for global business organizations whose members seek investment opportunities in Africa.[25]

For its part, the World Bank, including its IFC arm, has been one of the leading players in promoting the African private sector, broadly. The bank has followed its conventional approach, engaging in a mix of research, public outreach, and targeted lending to various initiatives. However, one of its most visible and innovative contributions to the international discourse on PSD is the annual *Doing Business* surveys, which it launched in 2001 to provide a global set of indicators for monitoring microeconomic

and regulatory factors that were based not on business/investor *perceptions* but on actual data. Its goal is "to provide an objective basis for understanding and improving
the regulatory environment for business."[26] Although not limited to sub-Saharan Africa, the surveys establish a new standard by which African states' commitment to private sector development can be measured. The establishment of the Doing Business
indicators reflects the growing awareness in development circles of the intrinsic linkage between business—as a generator of wages, employment, and growth—and poverty reduction; thus, the surveys assess barriers and constraints to entering the formal
sector, where such gains occur. (Although its principal target is the SME sector, obviously the Doing Business initiative speaks to a far larger constituency.) By 2009 the
bank had published its sixth *Doing Business* report; it covered 181 countries and included measures along ten indicators: starting a business; dealing with construction
permits; employing workers; registering property; getting credit; protecting investors;
paying taxes; trading across borders; enforcing contracts; closing a business. Though
geared primarily to small- and medium-sized enterprises, these indicators provide a
good sense of the overall receptivity to business whatever the size.

On the whole, Africa still lags other regions in the Doing Business rankings, but
the adage that "there's nowhere to go but up" seems to apply, as African countries are
regularly included among the world's top reformers, namely those taking steps to ease
business regulations or restrictions. Indeed, "economies in Africa implemented more
reforms in 2007–08 than in any previous year."[27] Although symbolically important,
this has practical significance as well, as "dynamic and growing economies continu-
ally reform and update their regulations and their way of implementing them."[28] In the
2006 report, for example, Rwanda and Nigeria were among the top twenty countries
reforming business policies, and Tanzania, and Ghana were ranked in the top ten. In
2007, Senegal, Burkina Faso, and Botswana were among the top ten reformers.

Lest we get triumphant here, it is important to point out that these reforms are
largely incremental. Even the World Bank itself acknowledges that "there is room to do
more. Entrepreneurs in Africa *still* face greater regulatory and administrative burdens,
and less protection of property and investor rights, than entrepreneurs in any other region."[29] It is tempting, therefore, to dismiss PSD as yet another overzealous, Western-
oriented and ideologically driven donor initiative in sub-Saharan Africa, whose failure
is practically preordained because it is out of step with Africa's presumed entrepreneurial culture and its putative "indigenous value systems."[30] But this temptation should
be resisted.

Culture and Globalization: Endogenizing the PSD Narrative

As the preceding discussion suggests, economic globalization has been a mixed
bag, and states remain constrained by structural and financial considerations as well
as by politics. Although certain African elites enjoy a degree of agency that is often

overlooked (as seen, for example, in their capacity to hoodwink donors via "partial reform syndrome"), it is hard to argue that *Africa* has had much agency within the confines of global political economy. In my interpretation, however, *cultural* dimensions of globalization are a little less one sided. Cultural globalization is more pervasive and absorbed more at the societal than the state level, suggesting that Africa is not merely recipient of globally transmitted norms and influences but a generator as well. The combination results in the dissemination of new norms and modes of thinking.[31] Anthropologist Ulf Hannerz, as James Ferguson notes, called this "'creolization' . . . [,] a dynamic 'cut-and-mix' world of surprising borrowings, ironic reinventions, and dazzling resignifications."[32] In terms of business, African entrepreneurial tendencies—which do exist!—can be reinforced and new identities constructed through various interactions and influences, including via immigration, education, religion, as well as through epistemic communities in which Africans and non-Africans intersect. Technological proliferation makes this ever more possible.

An entrepreneurial culture exists in Africa. Thus, external initiatives (including PSD) are scarcely part of an expression of wishful thinking about business in Africa. Rather, IFIs, donors, NGOs, and others are observing, analyzing, institutionalizing, and investing in a bona fide phenomenon. Indeed, why else would five thousand Kenyan youth energetically enter a national business plan competition to have their ideas judged by national and international experts?[33] These young people can hardly be dismissed as the next generation of compradors or mere stooges of the international community; instead they represent an organic movement but with international linkages. The first-ever Global Entrepreneurship Week, which was celebrated in seventy-five countries in November 2008, is another example of this transnational spirit of entrepreneurialism. "Through numerous events, competitions and websites, including a blog, unleashingideas.org, its goal is to encourage young workers and college students to become more innovative and entrepreneurial."[34] In Africa, participating countries included Burkina Faso, Cameroon, Democratic Republic of Congo, Ghana, Kenya, Madagascar, Mali, Mozambique, Nigeria, Rwanda, South Africa, Uganda, and Zambia.

This dissemination—and reinterpretation—of entrepreneurial values can be observed in other contexts as well. For example, information and ideas flow with people, whose movements are increasingly rapid, complex, and global. Late twentieth-century immigration patterns have helped produce a substantial African diaspora in Europe and the United States, which *officially* numbers about one million. Many of these are educated, middle class Africans—indeed, in the United States, Africans are among the most educated immigrant groups—who remain connected to their home countries through communication, travel, and, increasingly, remittances, which, according to the IMF, reached $25 billion and per the UN's International Fund for Agricultural Development reached $34 billion in 2006; some estimates placed the figure considerably higher still.[35] Moreover, contemporary news accounts and listservs are replete with examples of African entrepreneurs who head home to Nigeria, Ghana, and even Somalia in order to pursue a potentially profitable business venture. Thus, although the brain drain remains a significant problem, Africans abroad represent a critical new constituency for the transfer of business knowledge—and capital—back to their home countries.

David Fick's two books on business in Africa, *African Entrepreneurship: A Study of Successes*, and *Africa: A Continent of Economic Opportunity*, describe myriad cases of businesspeople who were educated formally (through universities) and informally (through observation) abroad, particularly in the United States, who were clearly influenced by its "entrepreneurial culture"—where people driven by good ideas rather than impelled by subsistence needs can put those ideas into practice, and small start ups have the potential to grow quickly into large firms—and who returned to Africa to ply their trades. Formal education is a major vector of entrepreneurialism and business and capitalist values. The education of a new generation of African elites in American, European, and other universities is increasingly important in the transfer of knowledge to both non-Africans, who learn about opportunities and to Africans, who can take what they learn back home. Western business schools are vital, but the current generation of Africans gradually has increasing access to business and financial education within the continent itself. Emergent (and established) African business schools increasingly adhere to a *global* model of business education and have cooperated with one another through the Association of African Business Schools (AABS), a body created only in 2005.[36] The AABS's principal goal is "to promote excellence in business and management education in Africa by supporting graduate business schools through capacity building, collaboration and quality improvement." Its efforts are part of a number of nascent multinational collaborations to develop and/or reinvigorate African higher education. The intrinsic linkages are clear between business school education and *application* of that education in the marketplace as part of a larger PSD strategy. Vijay Ramachandran, Alan Gelb, and Manju Kedia Shah have observed that one of the major deficiencies of black African businesspeople, relative to their minority business owner counterparts, is education. In this vein, the nascent AABS insists that "by training current and future leaders in their home markets, business schools in Africa play a critical role in laying the groundwork for private sector development. Its programmes build effective business schools in order to improve the practice of management in African organisations and to enhance the relevance and contribution of business schools to policy debate on African development research and policy."[37] The AABS effort is in its relative infancy, but it illustrates a cultural shift within Africa that is in part due to international influences and the well-established MBA model in the West and convergence in educational practices.

Another global factor contributing to the inculcation of capitalist norms in Africa is the incredible proliferation of prosperity-gospel Pentecostal and charismatic Christian churches.[38] According to a 2006 Pew Forum on Religion and Public life study, there are now at least 147 million African "renewalists" (which is an umbrella term for both Pentecostals and charismatics).[39] The rise of this brand of evangelical Christianity has numerous causes, of course, but it appears to be expanding far more rapidly than mainline Protestant and Catholic churches, Islam, or certainly traditional practices.

One increasingly important vehicle for imparting their message is through radio and television broadcasts of the same programming offered in American and European media markets. Indeed, leading charismatic preachers appear regularly on state-run television broadcasts across much of Africa. As restrictions on ownership of radio and television transmission have liberalized in Africa, religious broadcast stations, including the California-based Trinity Broadcasting Network and Europe's GOD TV, are an increasingly visible presence.[40] Among the most popular programs are those originating from American so-called megachurches. Although clearly not all charismatics extol a prosperity gospel, which preaches that God wants believers to prosper and celebrates wealth as evidence of divine blessing, Western-based televangelists associated with this line, including pastors Benny Hinn, Creflo Dollar, Joyce Meyer, and Kenneth Copeland host some of the most popular shows on the African airwaves. African ministers have adopted a similar pastoral message and methodology. Zambian megachurch pastor George Mbulo, for example, lauds the idea of "generating wealth using business skills," insisting that "God will show you how to make wealth."[41]

The proliferation of churches that explicitly preach a "health and wealth" gospel hints at a profound change in the relationship between Africans and accumulation. Jean-Philippe Platteau and Yujiro Hayami, among others, have suggested that "indigenous value systems do not always encourage investment, wealth creation, and risk taking."[42] More specifically, in this view, African norms of reciprocity, presumed immutable, serve to hinder entrepreneurship and the accumulation necessary for business success.[43] Citing an argument made by Karla Hoff and Arijit Sen, Ramachandran, Gelb, and Shah suggest that norms related to "wealth sharing may lead to a disincentive to migrate from a village to a town to become an urban worker or entrepreneur," and hence kinship "can be viewed as a poverty trap."[44] Thus, the thinking goes, Africans are not incapable of entrepreneurship; rather they simply lack incentives because any wealth accumulated has to be shared. This argument is belied, however, by the popular reception to prosperity gospel, which accommodates both tithing—itself a form of wealth sharing—and personal wealth. Generations of urban in-migration throughout Africa certainly challenge this thesis as well. It is also belied, self-evidently, by the very existence of successful entrepreneurs.

Whether the medium is television or radio broadcasts of health and wealth gospel, mobile phones, or the Web, technology is an essential vehicle for globalization, both economically and culturally. Arguably, the issue of technology falls somewhat outside the rubric of "globalization," given that it relates to Africa's dire infrastructure needs and meets (presently) largely domestic market demands and given that the communication technology sector has a measurable *African* presence already in companies such as MTN and Econet and, to some extent, Bharti Airtel (formerly Zain and, prior to that, Celtel). Yet Africa's landline infrastructure is the worst in the world, and one of few areas in which Africa has leapfrogged to the twenty-first century is in the proliferation of cellular technology, which now affords millions of Africans access to global information and networks around the world in an unprecedented way, via chat rooms, blogs, internet commerce, and so forth.[45]

Wireless technologies, and specifically cellular phones, have had a substantial impact, and use of cell phones has shot up dramatically. The Afrobarometer regards this as evidence of an emergent cosmopolitanism, finding that 57 percent of Africans surveyed in 2008 reported using mobile phones regularly.[46] Even in 2007, Nigeria had more than thirty million cell phone subscribers, and access is multiplied through sharing.

For business, the advantages of this technological proliferation are abundant. Cell phones facilitate communication, especially for small- and medium-scale business, with minimal infrastructure investment on the part of the firm. Mobile phones can save time, obviate unnecessary travel, or be used to convey pricing or supplier information. Estimates place African current internet users at about sixty-five million. Though well under 10 percent of the continent's population, it nonetheless represents a 1,360 percent increase since 2000. Growing access to the internet in virtually all urban areas has facilitated the role global communication plays in disseminating new norms of business and entrepreneurial (capitalist) values.[47] Improved technology and communication flows mean that African entrepreneurs, extant businesses, and business schools alike can increasingly plug into a global network to locate suppliers, educators, data/market information, and potential partners. The internet has democratized information flows and facilitated the proliferation of global social impact communication networks, many of which are geared toward entrepreneurialism and investment on the African continent. Moreover, this use of technology is decidedly organic—it is not the product of well-worn and top-down strategies of states and their international enablers among the donor and IFI communities; rather it is part of a popular grassroots movement that embraces and amplifies African entrepreneurial culture.

One can find myriad examples of chat rooms, blogs, and websites wholly or partially devoted to business and entrepreneurship, whether sponsored internationally, such as via the British Broadcasting Corporation, or originating within the African continent, with names like AfricanEntrepreneur, Zambian Economist, New Zimbabwean, or Nigeria Village Square. Admittedly, African internet access continues to lag other regions. And, to paraphrase Ferguson, technological globalization, like capital, does not necessarily "flow" across Africa; it "hops," leaving large areas unserved and, in this case, unconnected.[48] At the same time, however, the primary audiences for business chats, entrepreneurial blogs, and the like, are predominantly urban-based, middle-class elites for whom web and wireless connectivity is becoming well entrenched. In this sense, Ferguson's concerns are less relevant for business, at least those above the smallest-scale rural enterprises.

State Roles in Formalizing Private Sector Development Initiatives

In light of these various influences, both structural *and* cultural, and coupled with the institutional changes to the economic and political regimes in Africa, it is little wonder that formal PSD programs have suffered far less resistance at the state level than conventional SAPs. Given the historical capriciousness of numerous African leaders—even some democratically elected ones—however, the apparently warm reception for PSD may yet prove to be the latest incarnation of partial reform syndrome. Yet the readiness of contemporary actors in African private sectors provides an important counterbalance to state capriciousness that did not previously exist. In any event, at the official state level, several countries have demonstrated considerable assertiveness regarding PSD—to be sure, this has been undertaken in conjunction with donors, but it also appears to have been substantially internalized by proactive political and bureaucratic elites.

The two key features of Tanzania's PSD strategy, for example, are "to build a private sector that is "broad-based and pro-poor and which is competitive and can withstand local and global competition."[49] Tanzania established the Tanzania Private Sector Foundation and Tanzania National Business Council\ to facilitate dialogue between the government and the private sector. To be sure, such forums are often dismissed, not inaccurately, as "talk shops" in which business-state dialogue gets so bogged down that it severely limits progress on meaningful reforms.[50] And indeed, the Tanzania Business Council has had problems with "mobilizing resources, follow-up implementation of agreed points, and operationalizing smart partnerships."[51] Yet one measure of progress is the degree of reforms, and Tanzania has instituted a number of them in recent years, such as computerizing business and tax registries and reducing customs inspection delays as well as the number of legal proceedings in 2006, which had been an obstacle to business. Computerization has helped, but the tax regime continues to face a number of challenges, including a "multiplicity of taxes, high tax rates and problems of tax administrations." To address these issues, Tanzania formed a task force on tax reform with both public and private sector membership. These persistent challenges indicate that PSD does not occur instantaneously, nor is it linear; indeed, despite its previous accomplishments, Tanzania dropped several places in the Doing Business survey between 2008 and 2009.

A majority of African countries now have some form of PSD program. Moreover, in most cases, line ministries are directly or partially responsible for PSD activities as well for traditional tasks, although under its previous government Ghana created a ministerial portfolio that was wholly dedicated to private sector development.

In other countries, resources are directed straight to private sector organizations, such as Uganda's Private Sector Foundation, which is essentially a business association umbrella group. The ability of business associations to manage these interactions varies widely by country. In Mozambique since 2008, the Competitive and Private Sector Development Project, supported by the International Development Association, aims to promote an "enabling environment" and to facilitate access to business development services for SMEs and entrepreneurs, particularly in the horticulture and tourism sectors. A second component of the project dovetails with the government's own business environment reform strategy, focusing on the areas of trade, licensing, and public-private dialogue.

Around the continent, private sectors are already thriving. But many of these private sectors are dominated by companies that are minority owned, whether large and long-standing, like the Mehta Group in Uganda and Kenya, or new arrivals, such as Stitch Wise in South Africa. Importantly, however, a foundation for business already exists. In terms of business development and overall contribution to economic growth, the development of big business is more valuable than SMEs.[52] An advantage of SMEs however, is that they coincide with contemporary international development vogue, clearly provide relief at the family and subsistence level and therefore may directly address poverty. In addition, importantly, they signal a growing receptivity of and commitment by states to further improving the business environment.

One country that appears to be ahead of the curve in this respect is Ghana, which has been among the most dedicated adherents to a PSD program. In 2001, only months after John Kufuor, the opposition candidate of the New Patriotic Party, was elected president, he launched the Ministry of Private Sector Development. The new ministry's brief was to coordinate the more than seventy-five private sector-related activities that various ministries oversaw, including mining, forestry, agriculture, trade, and industry. The Ministry of Private Sector Development (which was later combined with the Ministry of Trade and Industry) became the government's vehicle for addressing the problems affecting the private sector, government–private sector coordination, and eliminate institutional bottlenecks created by the previous setup of multiple ministries with contradictory mandates.

Sending a signal that his government would coordinate with the private sector at an unprecedented level, President Kufuor declared a "golden age of business," in which development in Ghana was to be inextricably linked with sustained private sector-led growth.[53] Under Kufuor's government, business-state dialogue increased markedly over that of his predecessor, President Jerry Rawlings of the National Democratic Congress (NDC), who served as Ghana's elected president from 1992 to 2000 (and from 1982 as military ruler). Business was granted access at the highest levels of government. Under the New Patriotic Party, business-friendly officials held prominent positions in the bureaucracy and government. For example, Kwamena Bartels headed the Ministry of Private Sector Development and Yaw Osafo-Maafo, a former banker who also once served as his party's trade and industry spokesman in parliament, was the first minister of finance. President Kufuor himself took an active role, by elevating a private sector liaison to the cabinet level and holding biannual meetings with the Investors Advisory Council, which gave the business community a regular opportunity to provide feedback on the impact of current policies and the existing business climate. Early in his tenure he launched a special initiative that aimed to identify and develop business and explicitly sought to expand nontraditional exports and the private sector role in export markets and to increase capacity through training and credit.[54]

The Kufuor government made important inroads toward addressing several major constraints on the private sector. One outcome was the reduction in corporate tax rate from 32 to 25 percent. In addition, access to long-term credit to facilitate new business development as well as the expansion of existing firms was improved.[55] The National Board for Small-Scale Industries played a central role, providing assistance through capacity-building programs and other activities. Collectively, these initiatives have seen some success, resulting, for example, in "the creation of 767 new businesses in the areas of textile design, bakeries, shoe-making, honey production, bead-making," and so on.[56]

The explicit acknowledgment of a central role for business marks a significant reversal, as historically in Ghana the business sector was permitted little input on economic policy—notwithstanding the existence of a SAP and liberalization policies from 1983 onward that purportedly favored the private sector. Hence, many Kufuor supporters feared that the December 2008 victory of opposition candidate John Atta Mills, Rawlings's former vice president, would undermine the "golden age of business." It is too early to tell whether the influence recently enjoyed by leading private sector actors will be maintained, although it is worth noting that Ghana's rank improved from number 87 out of 181 countries in the World Bank's 2009 *Doing Business* report to 63 of 183 in the 2012 report. This ranking remains a useful metric for the effectiveness of the government's commitment to private sector development.[57] There is a chance that the changes initiated by Kufuor's government were not sufficiently institutionalized by the time he was voted out, though early in his tenure President Mills continued the private sector emphasis.

Yet private sector development faces at least two significant challenges. The first is Ghana's—and Africa's—high degree of informalization. In Ghana, for example, more than 60 percent of private sector activity occurs in the informal sector, similar to the percentage in other sub-Saharan economies.[58] Production of the predominant export crop, cocoa, is carried out mainly by peasant farmers on low-yield landholdings of one to three hectares each, suggesting that transforming subsistence producers into a formal private sector will be a monumental task. Formal sector activity is also dominated by small- and medium-scale enterprises—a good start, but not sufficient to serve as the engine of sustained growth. In the manufacturing sector, 99 percent is small- and medium-scale enterprises, which together employ 66 percent of the industrial work-force. Had these been a focus of national development formulations under Rawlings, many of these might have matured by now into larger enterprises. Rawlings's government instead aggressively pursued private sector investment only in Ghana's dominant gold mining sector. As Jon Kraus observes, this helped "generate its high rates of economic growth and reconstruction."[59] Nonetheless, the economy remains overwhelmingly dependent on primary commodity exports, which account for some 70 percent of foreign exchange earnings. Gold is the leading export, but the country's discovery of oil and the beginning of commercial production in 2011 will surely alter this commodity mix in the coming years.

Ghana's strong economic growth averaged nearly 5 percent annually between 2001 and 2007, although the country's economic performance in the period benefited significantly from the strength of gold prices, as well from as aid and the effects of debt relief.[60] The questionable sustainability of commodity prices, aid, and debt relief aside, a climate of growth is undeniably good for business. Yet more deliberate state interventions can entrench the business sector. Ghana has gone farther than many other African countries, but progress is not necessarily irreversible.

What induces states such as Ghana, Tanzania, Mozambique, or Uganda to formally enact PSD or probusiness policies? Clearly, the IFI, donors, and foreign aid role is important at creating incentives—even negative ones. However, agency on the part of political elites also plays a key role. One hypothesis that emerges from this relationship is that leaders with genuine business experience and background, such as Armando Guebuza, John Kufuor, or even Olusegun Obasanjo and Mwai Kibaki and their ruling cliques tend to produce more business-friendly regimes. It is worth noting, however, that neither Nelson Mandela nor Thabo Mbeki, the successive leaders of Africa's arguably most probusiness state, had such a background.[61] In any event, though there are clearly exceptions, the governments headed by businessmen are decidedly different from the kleptocratic regimes epitomized by Zaire's Mobutu Sese Seko, or the old-style African socialist regimes of Julius Nyerere or Kenneth Kaunda, for example. The apparent expansion of more business-friendly regime types should not, however, be equated with the absence of corruption, as Obasanjo's own administration certainly reveals.

A greater degree of democratization can play an important role in advancing the position of business in the polity, as it did in Ghana in moving from the hostile Rawlings government to the more sympathetic one of Kufuor, whose approach to the private sector's role in development proved considerably more accommodating. It is hard to imagine, for example, the Rawlings government having taken responsibility for constraining the private sector through "poor service," "the imposition of undue costs," and weak and inefficient public service administration.[62] Thus, democracy to some degree, compels incumbents to respond to local demand, should it exist, for more business-friendly policy; currently, majorities favor continuation of economic programs, although these majorities are modest.

Yet, in Ghana, democracy also brought the National Democratic Congress *back* to power under John Atta Mills—previously a member of the government that eschewed meaningful PSD. Elected in 2008, President Mills necessarily had to be sensitive to the needs of a participatory Ghanaian electorate caught up in a global economic recession. In the Afrobarometer survey conducted earlier that year, 59 percent of respondents expressed support for current economic policies, notwithstanding hardship, whereas only a minority (35 percent) favored their abandonment; residents of seventeen other African countries expressed support by considerably narrower margins.[63] Nonetheless, as I have argued, the cultural transformation and entrepreneurial foundation across numerous African polities suggests a greater public receptivity to business, particularly among urban elites, that may also dilute the populist impulse.

Path dependence is also important: the Doing Business rankings, an earned reputation for reforms, and favorable other measures, such as Transparency International's Corruption Perceptions Index, all have an influence on external relations with donors and investors alike and precipitate internal responses. Such "virtuous circles" can become mutually and positively reinforcing. Ultimately, however, the acceptance of PSD programs is a manifestation of a meaningful and important change in worldview about the role of the private sector in development and, implicitly, a recognition that there already exists a foundation for the private sector in Africa, and I believe that that matters more than what the state can and cannot do vis-à-vis PSD programs. Both developments are signs of progress.

BUSINESS IN AFRICA:
ADAPTING TO THE NEW ENVIRONMENT

Thus far, this chapter has addressed how twenty-first-century globalization, broadly conceived, has helped expand the role of the private sector in development and how, unlike the 1990s, deliberate steps beyond rhetoric were taken to inculcate private sector norms and growth strategies. Using a range of illustrations, this section of the chapter seeks to address the impacts of international and domestic efforts at private sector development. Do PSD policies, initiated at the state level and often with international urging, effect change, or is change due to more cultural factors at the societal and firm level? Do more businesses emerge in strong states that have high capacity and that also pursue some form of private sector development strategy? Evidence from various parts of the developing world suggests the answer to these questions is yes, as the cases of China, India, Taiwan, and elsewhere in Asia seem to indicate. In Africa, the evidence is less definitive, but preliminary results of business emergence—as a private sector response to state initiatives—would also seem to indicate a positive link. Ghana's "golden age of business" saw the creation of more than seven hundred new firms, for example.

On the other hand, however, there are also numerous cases of entrepreneurs excelling in weak states, in the absence of PSD, and at times, as in the case of the Democratic Republic of the Congo and Somalia, even without a viable state at all. Though these are probably exceptional, they do suggest that the presence of conventionally strong states, or at least states with the capacity to implement a bona fide PSD strategy, are neither necessary nor sufficient. Economic *policy* changes at the international level and state responses within African countries themselves—what I have referred to in this book broadly as "economic globalization"—helps to explain in part the (new) viability of business. The other explanatory variable, however, is the development, persistence, and adaptability of business cultures in Africa, whether historically latent and only recently stimulated or long-standing, such as those found within minority business communities.

Across sub-Saharan Africa there is evidence that business starts and expansion have taken place commensurate with and in some instances have been facilitated by the changes in the global economic climate, especially since 2000. Although direct data by on the number of business starts by country and firm size are difficult to come by, several proxy measures suggest considerable increases in private sector activity. These include exports of merchandise and services, change in net domestic credit, and change in foreign direct investment. The three tables included in the appendix compare both numerical averages (measured in U.S. dollars) and growth rates in two time periods, 1990–99 and 2000–2009. Table 1 reveals that between 2000 and 2009, sub-Saharan Africa as a whole saw an increase of 148.3 percent in exports of merchandise and services, a marked rise over the period from 1990–99, which measured just 37.3 percent.

Another possible measure of increased business activity is domestic credit in the economy. Net domestic credit is defined as "the sum of net credit to the non-financial public sector, credit to the private sector, and other accounts."[64] Importantly, as noted by Temitope Oshikoya "changes in the volume of bank credit are suggested to have a positive impact on private investment activity among developing countries."[65] As indicated in table 2, there was a sharp difference between the change in domestic credit across the two time periods in each of the nine countries. The period from 2000–2008 shows robust growth in net domestic credit in each of the countries. Among the most substantial increases were seen in Ghana, whose domestic credit rose by 38 percent between 2000 and 2008, after contracting by −48 percent in the 1990–99 period, Tanzania, which grew at 25 percent versus −46 percent in the prior period, and Uganda, which grew at 148 percent after shrinking −60 percent in the prior decade. A third measure, growth in FDI, is shown in table 3. It indicates sharp increases in inward FDI flows in the 2000s as compared to the period from 1990–99. Although it does not measure indigenous business growth per se, the effects of FDI are economically stimulative and illustrate the reformed state attitudes to the private sector in Africa.

Space constraints preclude a detailed set of company and country case studies; however, I highlight several examples here that reveal the opportunities presented by the contemporary business climate in host countries and offer illustrations that clearly challenge the stereotypes about the robustness of business in Africa. Moreover, these cases represent a host of sectors, influenced by deregulation, privatization, and the availability of new technologies. Although these examples are meant to be broadly illustrative rather than fully representative, they nonetheless provide clear evidence that an entrepreneurial culture as well as high impact entrepreneurs exist in Africa.[66]

Adaptive and successful companies are found in the transport, light manufacturing, assembly financial services, and textile sectors. They span the continent, from Tanzania to South Africa to Nigeria. Two cases, Daallo Airlines and Econet Wireless reveal that a business culture can sometimes thrive even in the most unpropitious conditions. The others show the capacity for diversification given changing institutional environments, the ability to capitalize on trends in other sectors, such as mining, and the benefits of connections to global entrepreneurial promotion networks.

Mohammed Enterprises Tanzania Ltd. is the lead company in a group of separately registered companies under the same management group. Owned by Tanzanian Asians, this business was actually founded in early 1980s as an import-export trading company. Taking advantage of changes at the state level, especially privatization of SOEs, it has substantially diversified its business lines, moving into manufacturing, agriculture, and processing, maintaining at the same time its original core trading activities. This expansion has transformed it into a large company that has a significant impact on the Tanzanian economy as well as a regional footprint. As of 2007, it had five thousand employees, some forty sales outlets in the Dar-es-salaam area as well as twenty-seven branches elsewhere in Tanzania and branches throughout the region in Uganda, Burundi, Rwanda and Mozambique. Importantly, the managing director of the company holds a business degree from Georgetown University, an educational background that provides a key strategic advantage, according to Ramachandran, Gelb, and Shah.[67]

Like Mohammed Enterprises, Omatek-Nigeria computers also predates the current epoch of "new" globalization. Omatek was started in 1986, initially as a computer training company and shortly thereafter as a seller of brand-name computers. In 1993, Omatek began assembly of computers under its own brand using semi-knocked down, or incomplete, kits of computer parts. In 2003, Omatek began assembling computers using completely knocked-down parts, mainly or entirely from Asian producers. Both knock downs are useful for labor-intensive production. Continuing this trajectory, by 2003 Omatek had begun manufacturing original computer equipment, aided by a program championed by then president Olusegun Obasanjo that enabled federal civil servants to own Nigerian-made computers at a subsidized rate.[68] In 2008 the company opened a complete knock-down factory in Ghana. What about this case reflects recent trends in globalization? Omatek took advantage of increased global trade in aftermarket computer components and utilized a state program geared toward increasing the reliability of Nigerian capacity and production and localization. It has also followed the classic model from assembly to production utilized so effectively in other industrializing economies.

Another Nigerian company, the International Energy Insurance Co. Plc., has demonstrated similar capacity to adapt to recent changes in the international and domestic marketplace. Founded in 2003 by a group of investors, it occupies a niche market in Nigeria's energy sector, providing nonlife insurance to individuals and companies. The firm now has 150 employees and in 2007 had a return on equity of 11.07 percent. In its audited statements dated 24 April 2008, the company reported 2007 net profit of ₦604 million (approximately $4.1 million). Perhaps most importantly from a national development perspective, the company paid taxes of ₦151.9 million in 2007, four times the amount paid the prior year.

The private sector in South Africa is dominated by a handful of multisectoral conglomerates, which are also concentrated in the mining and financial services sectors. Established in 1997 by a white South African, Stitch Wise is an example of a company that represents an ancillary sector serving the dominant mining industry. As a maker of mine safety gear, Stitch Wise benefited from rapid growth in South Africa's mining sector during the recent boom. It began as a sewing company making protective raingear but later expanded to produce woven polypropylene backfill bags that support overhead rock in the mines that help prevent collapses and thus injuries and fatalities. These are now considered standard safety equipment. Stitch Wise grew to 145 employees and saw revenues of$3.9 million in 2008. Starting in 2004, Stitch Wise business development strategies were advised by the international nonprofit Endeavor. These global entrepreneurship networks are increasingly valuable as epistemic communities and as sources of investment capital for nascent firms in the developing world.

What unites the foregoing companies is that each of them is led by astute entrepreneurs able to identify unmet demand in niche markets, to take advantage of institutional changes such as privatization, and to respond to a range of incentives. The examples of Econet Wireless, which was founded in Zimbabwe in 1994, and Daallo Airlines, established in Somalia in 1991, suggest that successful entrepreneurship is not always a supply-side response and that legitimate businesses can not only emerge without state support but occasionally in the face of state hostility. Each of these firms continued to conduct business in the countries that rank first and second on the 2009 Failed States Index.[69]

Econet founder Strive Masiyiwa exemplifies high-impact entrepreneurship. Yet despite identifying a glaring need for telecommunications, establishing a company, securing investors and suppliers, Masiyiwa was initially blocked in the early 1990s from launching Econet's wireless operation by the Zimbabwe government. Government officials belatedly came to the realization that the apparently lucrative cellular market should be the preserve of the state-owned Posts and Telecommunications Commission—which would control a new licensing regime that would restrict entry by competitors—and government cronies and that it could provide rent-seeking opportunities from tendering. Using Zimbabwe's courts, which were at that time, still largely independent from political interference, Masiyiwa brought two successful legal challenges in 1995, although the government proceeded to ignore these rulings. Eventually, however, Econet began operations in Zimbabwe, although the company is now headquartered in South Africa. This has attendant benefits for the South African economy and for Masiyiwa himself, whose personal safety was at risk in Zimbabwe (despite the fact that the company still does significant business there). Today the company claims eleven million subscribers and has operations and offices in Botswana, Burundi, Kenya, Lesotho, Nigeria, South Africa, and Zimbabwe, as well as New Zealand and the United Kingdom.

Changes in the economic and, to some extent, political environment in Zimbabwe in the 1990s—now a distant memory—including the introduction of competition, privatization, and a property rights regime—created a brief opening for previously latent black entrepreneurship. Masiyiwa's project was threatened ultimately by an aging, politically vulnerable state (and many Zimbabwe businesses subsequently experienced far worse, either in the form of political interference and harassment or by being closed down completely). Conversely, although business in Africa's most robust democratic polities are not invulnerable to state capriciousness, they do enjoy greater insulation from it, which is reflected in their higher Doing Business scores.

It is paradoxical that even states regarded as "failed," such as the Democratic Republic of Congo, play host to successful businesses. The majority of these are doubtless crony operations. However, there also appears to be some space for "legitimate" operations as well. Yet even if strong states may be "good for business," they appear neither necessary nor sufficient. Although the failed state environment clearly is not one to be prescribed, intrepid and otherwise legitimate entrepreneurs can survive, even thrive, in illegitimate, "failed" states. Even in Somalia, where no state exists, robust and competitive businesses have emerged, including five private airlines, satellite companies, and cell phone companies.[70] Thus, even in a place where there is no state to be pressured—or, conversely, to exert pressure—enterprising individuals recognize unmet demand and respond to it.

Founded as a fifty-fifty partnership between Mohammed Ibrahim Yassin and Mohamed Abdillahi Abusita, Daallo Airlines is an excellent example of this phenomenon. Responding to local demand, security conditions, and their own business backgrounds, the two entrepreneurs were able to seize an opportunities in the unregulated, completely laissez-faire vacuum created by state collapse. Daallo, which was based in Somaliland prior to its planned acquisition by a Dubai company, is among a number of thriving businesses in that territory, as well as Somali proper, especially in the construction and telecommunications sectors.

Using their own start-up capital, Yassin and Abdillahi began with just six staff members and a leased Cessna. By 2008 Daallo was operating six aircraft and had 250 employees and was being acquired by the multinational conglomerate Dubai Ports World. The company's financial condition was sound. Daallo reported 2006 net income of $1.88 million on total revenues of $37 million; passenger operations accounted for 75 percent of revenues. Its profit margins of 3.3 percent in 2005 and 5.1 percent in 2006 compare favorably to U.S. carriers in the same period, when low-cost airlines averaged 3.6 percent and all U.S. airlines averaged 5.5 percent. At year end 2006, the company had net worth of $4.5 million and total assets of $11.4 million.[71]

Importantly, Daallo Airlines contributes to the regional economy in several important ways. First, it provides employment, albeit modest, in a region with formal sector unemployment as high as 90 percent. Secondly, as part of a transportation network, it represents a lifeline to parts of the Horn otherwise cut off from international commerce. Lastly, Daallo pays taxes within Somaliland and in Djibouti, although "no taxes are paid in other parts of Somalia and Dubai. In Somalia we deal with what ever authority there and pay them some service charges to ensure security [i.e., side payments to warlords and Union of Islamic Courts types]."[72]

In the main, these are "good news out of Africa" stories, like those Carol Pineau and David Fick tell with nearly unbridled enthusiasm.[73] But where I part company with them is over the implication that a firm that appears to have achieved some success is therefore unequivocally a "success story." Any analysis of firm strength, even with multiyear data, is necessarily a snapshot and is frequently incomplete. Certainly, some firms are in far worse shape than depicted in interviews with eager cheerleaders and in their published annual reports, business plans, or websites; to the extent that any of these media exist, they may be complicated by sometimes dubious auditing and an often lax regulatory environment.[74] Further, some firms appear "autonomous" but in fact enjoy deep ties to the regime; all certainly continue to face the challenges of doing business in Africa of infrastructure, especially unreliability of the power supply and transport, the inconsistent regulatory environment, and limited access to regional and other export markets, as well as potential political interference. The businesses highlighted here have performed, at times impressively, despite these entrenched challenges.

What these brief anecdotes show, however, is the ability of certain firms and entrepreneurs to take advantage of changes in the "global" context as well as the local. Businesses in Africa availed themselves of the growing environment that characterized much of the 2000s—and with it, more consumers, a strengthened marketplace, and corresponding benefits to state economic flexibility; in other words, on the whole, economic reform and growth have been good for business. And where data exist, there are strong suggestions that the converse is also true, that is, that these successful firms make *national* contributions in terms of expanding employment, paying taxes, and generating return for shareholders. This helps African economies.

BUSINESS AND THE ECONOMY

This chapter has shown that many of the developments of the past decade have been good for business in Africa. But has business been good for Africa? A comprehensive analysis of the linkage between business and economic growth is beyond the scope of this chapter, but it is the next logical area of inquiry. Sub-Saharan Africa remains intensely poor on nearly all indicators. The continent is famously short of all of the millennium development goals. Within the narrower human development indicators (HDI), Africa still lags markedly, with a 2005 HDI value 0.514 (on a scale of 0 to 1) and average life expectancy of fifty-four years. Per capita income lags behind other regions, and Africa's 2007 GNI per capita of $1,071 even obscures the impact of a handful of oil economies and growing wealth disparities throughout the continent. Moreover, adult combined male and female illiteracy of 33.3 percent in 2007 continues to pose a massive barrier to development.[75]

On the positive side, certain indicators, such as infant mortality and under-five mortality have both improved measurably in a generation, and as William Easterly has observed, though Africa will fall short on the millennium development goals, there have been noteworthy, and usually unheralded, improvements on seven of the eight indicators over time.[76] In addition, significantly, though some debt relief has been used for nefarious or at least economically unproductive ends, debt relief has, as noted, provided governments like Zambia's with management flexibility to address certain poverty, education, healthcare, and macroeconomic needs in a way that has not seen in more than three decades. The most noteworthy change, of course, is that African economic performance, *overall,* improved in the 2000s; the decade witnessed GDP growth averaging nearly 5 percent annually, rates not seen since the 1960s.

How much of this improved economic performance is attributable to improved private sector performance and a better climate for business overall? Establishing a causal link is admittedly difficult. The formal private sector represents only about 22 percent of GDP in Africa, whereas the informal and public sectors represent 52 and 26 percent, respectively. Yet growth is dependent on numerous factors, including, in the first decade of the twenty-first century, some restoration of fiscal discipline and more realistic exchange rates that have aided essential macroeconomic stability, as well as greater political and economic space for private sector activity. In the 2000s, the substantial increase in global prices of primary commodities have been a critical element of Africa's newfound economic growth.

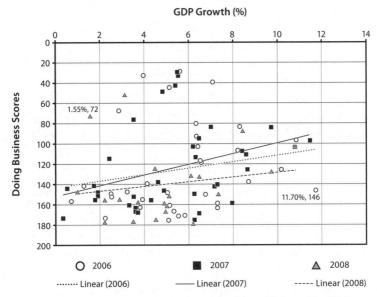

Figure 3.1. Sources: http://databank.worldbank.org/ddp/home.do (GDP growth); http://doingbusiness.org (Doing Business scores).

Drilling down further, Steven Radelet insists that commodity prices were not the sole reason for the turnaround in the seventeen countries he deems part of "emerging Africa." He argues that commodity prices did not begin their upward climb until 2001, but he pegs the mid-1990s as the start of the economic turnaround in these countries, a time when commodity prices were actually *falling*.[77] Although Radelet does not assert that commodity prices have not helped, he attributes economic progress more to more democracy, sensible economic policies, the end of the debt crisis, new technologies, and new African leadership.

Figure 3.1 provides some support for Radelet's position that growth is not all reducible to commodity prices. Specifically, it indicates that more sensible economic policies, in the form of a better business environment, have had a salutary impact on growth; this suggests that business *has* been good for Africa in the twenty-first century. The figure provides a scatter plot showing the relationship between the World Bank's Doing Business scores and real GDP growth for thirty-five African countries (nonoil majors) between 2006 and 2008. I excluded the year 2009 because the effects of the global recession depressed growth rates in Africa, despite its lack of connection to the crisis. Oil economies, some of which grew at rates far exceeding the norm in the period (more than 10 percent per year average in some cases), were also excluded. In all three years, we see a positive correlation between low Doing Business average (i.e., more business-friendly environments) and high growth. The reverse is particularly evident for countries placing in the lower left corner of the diagram, where we see a strong concentration of African countries with low Doing Business ranks (in the 140–60 range globally) and GDP growth of just 0–4 percent per year. Although individual countries are not identified in the diagram, there are some outliers, such as Kenya, which recorded very low GDP growth in 2008 despite its credible Doing Business rank of 72. Similarly, Mauritania, in 2006, had a GDP growth of 11.7 percent with a Doing Business score of 146. The Kenyan result, however, is largely attributable to the aftereffects of the ethnic and regional violence that struck the country following the controversial 2007 election.

These patterns shown in the scatter plot are confirmed by Simoen Djankov, Caralee McLeish, and Rita Maria Ramlho, who posit that a relationship exists between business regulations and growth.[78] Using the Doing Business indicators from the 135 countries that were included at the time, in the then seven regulatory areas (starting a business, hiring and firing, registering property, getting credit, protecting investors, enforcing contracts, closing a business), Djankov, McLeish, and Ramlho's. multivariate regression model finds that countries with better regulations do in fact grow faster. Specifically, "improving from the worst quartile of business regulations to the best implies a 2.3 percentage point increase in annual growth."[79]

Nonetheless, the risk of continued primary commodity dependence, despite the currently favorable prices, remains significant. Indeed, one of the foremost environments for business on the continent did not provide a bulwark against economic decline in South Africa, which saw in 2009 its first economic contraction since the democratic transition of 1994. South Africa's formal business sector, which remains highly dependent on the mining sector as well as SOEs, lost nearly 180,000 jobs in the first quarter of 2009. And though it almost goes without saying, the slumping global economy had a direct and negative impact on business. Ironically, it is because South Africa is more deeply linked to the world economy—via greater globalization, if you will—than other African countries that it felt the effects of the recession more severely than most.

By definition, developing economies have scant influence over exogenous shocks such as global recession, and even well-managed economies like South Africa's are subject to contagion effects beyond their control. But caveats about exogenous factors notwithstanding, significant numbers of South African firms and, as noted, those based elsewhere have been employers, tax and duty payers, and providers of important product and services that support potential and existing upstream and downstream industries. Given Africa's high formal sector unemployment, high poverty, and high levels of subsistence, the presumption is that growth in the number and size of formal sector businesses will result in salutary benefits for the economy as a whole. There is ample evidence in the development literature of a connection between private sector performance and economic growth.[80] If the champions of private sector development in sub-Saharan Africa are correct, then the improvement of firms and the business environment, in turn, will lay the foundation for further economic growth.

CONCLUSION: CONSTRAINTS AND OPPORTUNITIES

This chapter has argued that new businesses emerged or expanded in part through the modestly positive aspects of economic globalization and via cultural globalization, broadly conceived. New economic patterns reveal the various changes wrought by the so-called post-Washington Consensus (and increasingly by the equally misnamed Beijing Consensus), which portends further opportunities for African countries, including reduced debt loads and the promise, at least, of additional aid and trade relations. Culturally, it includes the (re)construction of new and newly articulated African entrepreneurial identities as a result of numerous factors, such as a burgeoning global diaspora, the spread of prosperity gospel churches, business education abroad and increasingly within Africa as well, and the role of the internet and global communication networks in transmitting and disseminating new norms of business and entrepreneurial (capitalist) values. At the same time, all values are not simply "imports" to Africa; Ramachandran, Gelb, and Shah's condemnation of "indigenous value systems" for their purportedly detrimental impact on entrepreneurship is both overbroad and anachronistic.[81] "Indigenous value systems"—already, I argue, receptive to capitalism—are neither static nor monolithic in any event.

The 2000s have witnessed a genuine sea change in the form and frequency of and the prospects for Africa-domiciled business, as well as the milieu in which they operate, both "indigenous" and "minority." But it is important not to oversell the potential of "private sector development," writ large, or for that matter, other approaches. Yet a host of recent works appear to do just that, as they set out to offer a picture of African business and consumers that often borders on boosterism.[82] These presentations have a certain refreshing quality about them, inasmuch as they differ radically from the largely negative popular perception about Africa and certainly business in Africa that prevails in Western capitals.[83] As someone who objects strenuously to the knee-jerk Afropessimism that pervades so much popular and academic discourse on Africa, I applaud the efforts to portray an "Africa rising."

Yet this book is as much a critique as it is a celebration of works in this genre. These types of "good news out of Africa" stories, however gratifying, are sometimes as guilty of misinforming readers (or viewers, as the case may be) as their counterparts. On the other hand, the Afropessimists have long drowned out the voices of the "Africa good news" crowd, so perhaps turnabout is, at last, fair play. I endeavored to accommodate the happier stories in this chapter, but of course these must be juxtaposed against others, such as the experience of telecoms entrepreneur Strive Masiyiwa in Zimbabwe at the hands of a vengeful state or of other businesspeople or firms that have encountered both financial and political hardship, such as the Lesotho-based textile firm Shining Century, which featured prominently in Pineau's film but later faced existential threats.[84] These examples, and of course countless others, reveal the challenges that persist, even amid great progress.

Sub-Saharan African businesses face serious deficits, some of which defy quick fixes, even by the most business-friendly policies. The UN Development Program notes that for many countries, the playing field is not level, and thus that for the private sector to flourish, predictable and fair rules (on tax, employment, business registration, and so on) need to be enacted.[85] Africa's labor costs are severely hampered by low productivity, raising the costs of production considerably relative to China and much of Southeast Asia, for example. Moreover, as the *Doing Business* studies indicate, Africa's labor regulations are also unfavorable, especially to outsiders considering investment in nontraditional sectors on the African continent. The UN Development Program also cites inadequate knowledge and skills development, as well as meager financing that is currently unable to meet the demand of many existing enterprises, let alone aspiring entrepreneurs.[86]

For reasons laid out elsewhere in the book, I do not believe that corruption in and of itself is an insuperable barrier to business emergence and growth in Africa. Furthermore, a credible case can be made that African corruption is not qualitatively different than that elsewhere. Yet it would be naïve to insist that corruption or at least the *perception* of it have not had adverse impacts on African development. In this respect, it is difficult to be heard above the Afropessimist din. Africa undoubtedly suffers from what marketing people would call a "branding problem." It is perhaps uniquely subject to regional spillover/contagion effects, resulting in tendency to neglect to differentiate between countries. Thus, everything from the AIDS pandemic to the Corruption Perceptions Index to regional food shortages promote the image of a generalized "Africa" that then becomes the domain of Bono and "charity brands" rather than of business and entrepreneurship.[87]

Perhaps the most glaring and possibly most long-term constraint on business, as noted by Ramachandran, Gelb, and Shah, is Africa's poor infrastructure. The principal infrastructure deficiency is power generation—the lifeblood of business—but the continent is also plagued by a still inadequate telecommunications sector (notwithstanding the remarkable progress in wireless communication), as well as a poorly integrated and maintained road and transportation network.[88] Nigeria, for example, has operating capacity of just 3,500MW but has a demand more in the range of 7,600MW. In 2007, fewer than twenty of seventy-nine power stations were working. Nigeria's predicament is connected, of course, to its renowned levels of corruption, but the pervasiveness of power generation problems in Africa, including in South Africa, demonstrates that power shortages are also explained by structural factors, miscalculated public policy choices, and national poverty as well. At bottom, though, given the various challenges to entrepreneurship—everywhere but perhaps especially in Africa, the performance of some of the businesses highlighted in this chapter is even more remarkable.

However, the point of this chapter is not to demonstrate unbridled heroism or "miracle worker" capabilities among businesspeople in twenty-first century Africa. Rather, my objective has been to illustrate the role and efforts of entrepreneurial agents who took advantage of a new climate. It is important to remember that the intrinsic risk of doing business in certain sectors (for example, textiles, airlines) does not disappear just because the business is being done in a new place; these are exceedingly volatile sectors anywhere, subject to crippling exogenous shocks, and their challenges are exacerbated in sub-Saharan Africa. This chapter simply reveals both the diverse, underappreciated possibilities available to aspiring businesspeople, many of whom *have* seen tremendous success, and the breadth of business cultures at work in contemporary Africa.

The principal obstacle to business in Africa is no longer the state per se, nor is it an absence of entrepreneurial culture but instead inadequate physical and financial infrastructure on which to sustain entrepreneurs. In providing this foundation, strong, capable states still matter. The following chapter turns to the role contemporary FDI can play in developing linkages between states and international and domestic businesses that promote virtuous circles.

PART 3
The Diversity of African Business: Problems and Prospects

FOREIGN INVESTMENT BEYOND COMPRADORISM AND PRIMARY COMMODITIES
The Role of the Global South

INTRODUCTION

If Africa had a dollar for every time a scholar, policymaker, journalist, or casual observer noted that "Africa is rich," the statement might actually be true. Or at least it might have some validity beyond the geologically based wealth to which that expression almost universally refers. Without question, Africa does have stunning natural resource wealth. The continent boasts the world's highest reserves of platinum and diamonds. Africa is home to approximately 10 percent of the world's proven oil reserves, 8 percent of its natural gas, and 40 percent of its gold deposits. Uranium, copper, cobalt, columbite tantalum, chromite, coal, asbestos, and gemstones are found in abundance, not to mention plentiful timber, fisheries, and forestry resources. And hydrologic resources in the Congo Basin alone could supply 150,000 megawatts of power, far more than the entire continent's present consumption. These abundant natural resources have attracted outsiders for millennia, but it was not until the colonial period that the extraction of these resources was truly transformed into a modus vivendi for Africa's unequal entry into the global economy.

It is not necessary to recount here the tortured history of economic exploitation in Africa, whether via slavery, "legitimate trade," colonialism, or neocolonialism, other than to note that each of these epochs involved the extraction of primary resources. Following independence, very little changed. Primary commodities were given such pride of place that even where African governments claimed control of their economies through nationalization, these resources were inextricably bound up in the assertion of sovereignty. Only around 1999, after a quarter century during which primary commodity prices were flat or falling, and African economies lost their principal sources of foreign exchange earnings, did global demand for Africa's metals and minerals again begin to rise. This spurred renewed interest by foreign investors keen to access African resources directly, and revitalization of the extractive sectors has been a major driver of Africa's economic recovery.

Yet Africa's current dependence on primary commodities evokes a feeling of déjà vu: its economies remain substantially undiversified and vast majority of its primary products are exported as raw materials. Thus, even modest value addition—whether it is refining petroleum, fabricating metals, cutting gemstones, or processing agricultural goods—tends to be done elsewhere and largely for the benefit of non-Africans. In the wake of privatization, investment in the extractive sectors is led by North American, European, and, increasingly, Asian firms, although governments typically maintain some ownership stake. Given the vicissitudes of the marketplace, foreign companies will routinely curtail or cease production at a moment's notice if prevailing conditions change, as was briefly the case in the 2008 global recession. Several of Zambia's foreign-owned mines, for example, found it cheaper to suspend production. Africa's vulnerability to price shocks, a major factor in the economic collapse that befell the continent in the 1980s, therefore continues. In short, the familiar historical model that privileges foreign investors—particularly in the mining, petroleum, and other extractive sectors—and finds local political elites and putative businesspeople in the role of servile compradors has not been sufficient to foster Africa's economic development. Certainly, that approach has done little to engender the growth of a genuine business class. Foreign direct investment must diverge considerably from its historical pattern in Africa if it is to contribute to genuine technology and knowledge transfer as well as to measurable *and sustainable* employment gains for African business.

One of the main arguments of this book, however, is that business in Africa can transcend the narrow historical confines resulting from commodity-driven economies. As chapter 3 indicates, many African-based companies are indeed investing in nontraditional sectors, albeit on a smaller scale and often without the game-changing impact that large-scale international investment can have. A critical question, therefore, is whether and to what degree *international* investors are contributing, directly or indirectly, to diversification and value addition or merely entrenching the status quo. Investment that leads to the former generates not only formal sector employment but greater prospects for local firms through joint ventures, partnerships, and technological transfer. This chapter considers the prospects for FDI to be channeled in such beneficial directions.

Champions of FDI suggest that it can be harnessed for development purposes if it is oriented toward international markets and integrated into the parent company's supply chain; thus, the national origin of the investing company should matter little.[1] It is worth noting, however, that FDI emanating from the global North, which is still the largest source of FDI in Africa, has not played this transformative role, despite its presence in Africa for fifty years of independence, and in many cases, for many years prior to that. (Of course, it is unfair to lay the continued dependence on unrefined primary commodities and its association with a more exploitative form of investment solely at the feet of Northern investors. Clearly, as previous chapters have noted, African government policies, persistent corruption, and disinvestment by Africans themselves have all contributed to the current dilemma.)[2] Whereas skepticism of Northern

FDI remains high, especially among Africans, many observers believe that so-called South-South investment holds far greater promise. Companies and countries representing the global South, particularly China and India, are thus regarded by many as "kindred spirits" that can enable Africa to reduce its dependence.

This chapter first considers the attractiveness of primary commodities, elucidating some of the familiar reasons why foreign investment in Africa continues to be directed overwhelmingly toward raw materials, mainly the extractive sectors and, to a lesser degree, agricultural products, as well as the services sector and, to a lesser degree still, manufacturing. Second, the chapter aims to illuminate the basis for the claims that Africa's new ostensible Chinese and Indian partners will be investors in business activities that can generate positive externalities in nontraditional sectors. As demonstrated by decades of frequently sincere development rhetoric, however, this may be somewhat easier said than done for at least three reasons. One, although FDI has increased around the world, Africa is getting a diminishing share of it. While the dollar value of investment has risen sharply in the early twenty-first century, Africa's *share* of world FDI remains stagnant. Hovering around 2–3 percent between 2000 and 2006, it is about the same as a generation ago. New FDI to the developing world has gone overwhelmingly to Asia, and this competition continues to redound to Africa's detriment. Two, notwithstanding the new hopes placed in Southern investors, the bulk of FDI inflows to sub-Saharan as well as North Africa still originate in Northern countries, mainly the United States, the UK, and France. In the 1996–2000 period, these accounted for as much as 90 percent of flows to African countries. Although the developed country share of FDI flows has since fallen to around 60 percent, these age-old patterns are hard to break; the largest investments remain in the extractive sectors. Three, although the interests of China, India and other investors from the global South are diverse and present certain opportunities for new directions, their large-scale investments are substantially oriented toward the same resource-seeking ends as their Western/Northern counterparts. Hence, Southern investors' ability to help generate positive externalities for Africa, including the development of nontraditional sectors, rests on their capacity and willingness to access and interact with Africa and Africans in ways that differ from the historical norm.

The results thus far are mixed. Yet it is abundantly clear that China and India are two of the largest and most celebrated and aggressive practitioners of "South-South" FDI in contemporary Africa. As of 2004–5, Singapore's FDI stocks in Africa (North Africa as well as sub-Saharan Africa) actually exceeded both India and China's, but nearly all represented previous investment in one country, Mauritius.[3] Brazil (which together with Russia, India, and China and, increasingly, South Africa form the bloc of so-called BRICs, countries that are positioning themselves as an economic counterweight to the G-7) is another country that is touted by some as a new player in Africa. Like Singapore, however, Brazilian companies' investments in Africa are concentrated in just two countries.

Brazilian FDI has been directed mainly to projects in Portuguese-speaking Mozambique and Angola, including coal mining in the former and oil exploration in the latter. But Brazilian firms are partnering in hydropower projects in Nigeria, and therefore reach in Africa will likely expand in the future.

In addition, firms of South African origin (typically identified with the white minority) are also among the most visible and assertive investors throughout the continent, as are Africa-domiciled companies that are owned or controlled by other minorities, albeit to a lesser extent. Certain sections of resident "minority capital" may be a critical interlocutor for new FDI from developing Asia. In the main, however, because the former is tied to Africa in fundamentally different ways, the phenomenon is considered more fully in chapter 6.

AN "ATTRACTIVE NUISANCE":
AFRICA'S PRIMARY COMMODITIES

In legal parlance, an attractive nuisance is a hazardous or dangerous condition that is irresistible or attractive, in this case, to children, such as an unfenced swimming pool. Under the law, even though the injured are guilty of trespassing, the person who created or permitted the condition is the liable party. Like attractive nuisances, Africa's bountiful resources are an irresistible temptation, not only to outsiders but to Africa as well. And like attractive nuisances, these resources have become liabilities, in a way, for their African owners. Although it would be senseless for Africa to reject its riches—to continue the metaphor, to fill in their own pool—countries must utilize them differently and leverage the interests and investments of international suitors in a way that promotes sustainable *African* development and business, as well as diversification.

It all started so promisingly. In the 1960s, when the bulk of sub-Saharan African countries gained their independence, primary commodities were in high demand and commanded strong global prices. In the main, foreign corporations predominated in these sectors, as local private and public sector firms in the newly independent African countries lacked both the technical capacity and the capital to play a role as owners. Even after many states increased their ownership stakes, such as through Africanization programs and nationalist-inspired restrictions on foreign capital, MNCs typically remained as minority shareholders. In fact, they were often anxious to do so, even if the new arrangement was on the host country's terms. The 1973 oil crisis precipitated a global decline in many other (nonpetroleum) commodity prices, and with remarkable consistency, these prices scarcely recovered until the late 1990s. Simultaneously, production declines and slack demand fomented vicious circles: Africa's own economic and in some cases political decline left it incapable of reinvestment in its mining and mineral infrastructures, and as foreign exchange earnings dried up, other sectors collapsed for want of investment as well; faced with unattractive returns and low global prices and put off by the cost of reestablishing or maintaining interests in Africa, many MNCs withdrew.

For states, a shrinking GDP provides an added incentive for diversification. Yet a context of precipitous economic decline, such as that Africa faced in the 1970s, 1980s, and much of 1990s, marked by high debt burdens and unavailability of credit, a climate of deindustrialization, and ideological ambivalence toward business is not an auspicious one in which to embark on a program of diversification and investment in nontraditional sectors. In short, at a time when African states most needed to expand into nontraditional sectors, they were least able to do so.

Paradoxically, the return of high global prices for Africa's primary commodities helped once again to fill the continent's treasuries with foreign exchange, thereby *reducing* the incentive for economic diversification. Zambia, which depends on copper for well over 60 percent of its foreign exchange earnings, provides a clear example of this problem. Global demand increased copper prices from $1,500 a ton in 2002 to around $7,700 a ton in 2006. The value reached nearly $9,000 per ton in August 2008. Although prices subsequently plummeted with the onset of the recession to just $2,520 per ton (or $1.26 per pound) in December 2008, by September 2009 they had rebounded to $2.37 per pound in September 2009, continuing upward thereafter. Mining companies doing business in Zambia now hail from all over the world—Switzerland, Australia, Canada, India, as well as China—but the country's moribund economy was reinvigorated in large part by Chinese demand for industrial metals, which continued despite the recession. Indeed, not only copper producers like Zambia benefited: by 2009 China was the leading global consumer of base metals, including nearly 35 percent of copper, 38 percent of zinc, 28 percent of nickel, and over 38 percent of aluminum. Notwithstanding the scare in late 2008, therefore, China's sustained demand ensured that commodity price declines were far shorter and shallower than in typical recessions. Moreover, industrial metals are forecast to continue to increase *for the next decade*. Though this certainly bodes well for GDP growth, it again promotes complacency among governments. Few concerns are aroused as long as revenues are rising but, as we saw in the 1970s, it reveals tragically short-term thinking—a failure to properly secure the "attractive nuisance." When contemporary African governments revert to such bad habits, they fail to leverage FDI toward bolstering domestic business sectors and domestic capacity, which lies at the heart of successful diversification.

Empty Rhetoric

African nationalist rhetoric long hailed the virtue of broadening beyond primary products; hence most economies pursued a measure of import substitution industrialization (ISI) and developed at least fledgling manufacturing sectors. Some, such as Nigeria, Kenya, and Cote d'Ivoire, developed a relatively extensive industrial footprint, although none except the settler states of Zimbabwe and South Africa truly had the capacity to generate substantial foreign exchange earnings from such activities. Even producers in Zimbabwe and South Africa were mainly confined to regional export markets and chiefly for light manufactures such as processed foods or relatively low value-added processed metals.[4] Otherwise, given small postcolonial private sectors, manufacturing was largely led by MNCs' local affiliates and state enterprises and by local, mainly minority-dominated, private sectors. Countries that followed a more self-consciously state-led development path, such as Tanzania and Zambia, also used ISI to "diversify" their economies but only in a superficial sense. Their industrial base, fueled by state-owned enterprises—often white elephants—and/or captive markets for local affiliates of international companies (typically barred from repatriating profits) was incapable of generating exports; indeed, exports were not part of Africa's ISI calculus. What all of these manufacturing sector experiments had in common was that only domestic markets (which were mostly small) were targeted and that they were viable only to the extent that the economies were closed to competition. Once policies of trade liberalization in particular were enacted in the 1990s—far too rapidly, it is now widely agreed—these previously protected industries almost universally collapsed. Of course, there is considerable space between industrial manufactures and raw material export, such as a modest effort to add value, though African states failed to fill it.

The export base for these countries, that is, their principal linkage to the global economy, remained substantially unchanged throughout the postcolonial era. During the 1960s and 1970s, sentiments in favor of meaningful diversification into nontraditional exports were subverted to nationalist, largely *political*, projects rather than made part of a comprehensive economic strategy—one that might also reasonably have included services, export-competitive light manufacturing, and commercial agriculture, *as well as* extraction. In short, any early incentive to diversify exports or to increase the competitiveness of local products was displaced by ISI, whose exhaustion was inevitable, and diminished by the naïve belief that high global commodity prices would prevail forever.

At the same time that they contributed to Africa's deindustrialization, the liberalization programs of the 1990s also revived the rhetoric about nontraditional exports. Often at the behest of the donors, who apparently lacked appreciation for irony, countries that were wedded to one or two primary commodities spoke of diversifying— at the very least of adding, say, agricultural exports to their mineral exports and vice versa. By and large, however, this was not very successful, and the failure drew out the familiar critics: neoliberals who assailed governments for corruption and partial implementation and structuralists who insisted that the international trade regime, one aspect of which was protectionism in OECD countries, foreclosed new export strategies from Africa. A few states such as Kenya and Ghana made inroads in specialized products, such as floriculture and horticulture, but this has not been sufficient to appreciably alter the structure of these economies. Moreover, with the arrival of the 2000s, pressure for diversification again took a back seat, as global commodity prices reached record highs, economic growth boomed, and political elites lapsed once more into complacency.

A diversified pool of investors adhering to market-seeking and efficiency-seeking investment strategies is a proven way for economies to transcend primary commodity dependence. But there is more to MNCs' historic avoidance of Africa's noncommodity markets than can be explained by archaic references to dependency theory, patterns of multinational exploitation and the purposeful underdevelopment of Africa: African markets simply have not been that attractive except for the resource sectors. Especially in the wake of liberalization—which opened African economies to trade and removed the barriers to entry that once gave both staid MNC affiliates and local proto-industrialists protected monopoly access to local markets—companies have had little incentive to invest. Certainly this is the case with large firms. Markets are too small, absent regional integration, which has not yet yielded the expected results despite efforts at various configurations throughout the continent.[5] Foreign producers can now accomplish through trade what states once offered them via local production monopolies. Evidence exists of an emergent consumerism and newfound wealth in all economies (and corresponding inequality), but those with purchasing power are overwhelmingly buying imports rather than locally produced goods even where local alternatives are available. Regardless, oftentimes imports are either cheaper (which pleases the poor) or have cachet (which the wealthy prefer). Moreover, the vulnerability to economic downturn of all African consumers adds another disincentive to would-be foreign investors in these sectors. Even local companies that are potentially viable on a regional scale have sometimes scant incentive to pursue a market-seeking strategy when domestic markets are small and impoverished. Additionally, the surprisingly high cost and low productivity of African labor renders efficiency-seeking investment problematic as well, notwithstanding export incentive programs such as AGOA.

In sum, it is generally cheaper to import than to produce locally in Africa, whether for export or domestic consumption. Consequently, FDI still tends to gravitate toward precisely those sectors that made Africa attractive 150 years ago, namely gold, platinum, copper, cobalt, diamonds, palm oil, coffee, cocoa, tobacco, timber, and a few relative newcomers like natural gas, oil, and coltan. Indeed, the United Nation's World Investment Report 2007 reveals that "the top ten destinations for FDI in Africa in 2006, in descending order, were Egypt, Nigeria, Sudan, Tunisia, Morocco, Algeria, Libya, Equatorial Guinea, Chad, and Ghana. The first nine countries in this list are either North African states that are benefiting from ever closer trading links with the EU, or oil and gas producers, or both." These 10 countries received an astonishing 90 percent of the $35.6 billion FDI in 2006.[6]

FDI Past and Present: Commodities Still Rule

Investments made in Africa by Western corporations are certainly not limited to extraction. And though financial return is the raison d'être of the modern corporation, neither nefarious intent nor tragic outcome is universal. Yet Northern-domiciled corporations, due partly to the predominance of resource-seeking investment and partly to their historical association with unpopular African governments, have a difficult legacy to overcome in Africa.

Western firms gained a foothold in Africa during colonialism, a position that few surrendered at independence. Faced with neocolonial domination, a few African states such as Zambia and Tanzania responded with widespread nationalizations, although virtually all countries enacted policies to constrain international investment to some degree, as discussed in chapter 1. The colonial legacy common to most countries, however, was an insubstantial or nonexistent indigenous capitalist class. Hence, notwithstanding increases in state ownership via Africanization, particularly in the extractive sectors, Western MNCs typically retained at least a minority shareholding or managerial role and often continued to dominate manufacturing sectors in countries like Nigeria, Cote d'Ivoire, Gabon, and Kenya. Regardless of official regime ideology, a few firms that had local affiliates were granted monopolies in local markets but, on the whole, limits on repatriation of profits, high tariffs, corruption, and inadequate infrastructure made Africa less attractive for a significant expansion of FDI during this period, which lasted until the late 1990s.

Nor did states utilize existing FDI effectively, that is, to coerce or cajole investors into, for example, partnerships and upstream and downstream linkages with local entities. There are various explanations for this, including that relations between foreign firms and local elites encouraged rent seeking and corruption rather than investment, that in many countries "local entities" did not exist, and that a misplaced belief that favorable commodity prices would continue indefinitely (thereby providing a steady stream of revenues for a fledgling state) led to poor policy decision making.

Notwithstanding this rather abysmal history, a combination of factors seemed to offer Africa another opportunity to attract FDI: privatization in the early 1990s and, later in the decade, the return of favorable commodity prices. Western mining firms, including companies such as Rio Tinto, Glencore, and BHP-Billiton, are among the leading contemporary investors. Similarly, Western oil companies such as TotalFinaElf, Exxon-Mobil, Chevron, and Shell have expanded their long-standing operations in traditional oil-producing countries such as Nigeria, Equatorial Guinea, and Angola and extended their reach into new oil states like Sudan and Chad and emergent oil producers such as Ghana. Importantly, international investors in the service and financial sectors are also present in Africa after a long absence. In 2011, Walmart, the world's largest retailer, purchased a controlling interest in Massmart Holdings, a South African company with 288 retail stores in several African countries. Certainly, Western corporations have begun to take note of Africa's consumers as well as its natural resources.

Yet this new or renewed activity by Western MNCs, while noteworthy, is still in its early stages. Up to now, Africa has only returned to the status quo ante as far as FDI is concerned: vigorous activity in the extractive sectors, complemented by a smattering of private financial institutions and retailers, and a diminutive presence in the manufacturing sector. At first blush it almost looks like 1964 in Africa—but for the detritus of five decades of frustrated development.

South-South Investment: Beyond Primary Commodities?

A key element in avoiding a replay of the postcolonial experience is South-South investment. Some research suggests that firms from the global South enjoy familiarity with the technological and business practices in their counterparts' economies. Consequently, they are more likely to be knowledgeable about local consumer demands, to employ appropriate intermediate technologies, to utilize local inputs, and to engage in more labor-intensive production. For Southern firms engaging in market-seeking strategies (especially with its presumed benefits for recipient countries) elsewhere in the global South, arguably more incentive exists to provide accessible goods and services, make use of local distribution networks, and promote forward and backward linkages locally.[7] They are also less risk averse and more realistic about negotiating bureaucratic entanglements; whether this entails corrupt interactions depends on the context. Regardless, Southern investors may be more politically savvy in a familiar environment and therefore better able to understand and manage political and economic risks in the host country; such competencies aid *sustainable* investment.[8]

As noted, the flurry of investment activity in Africa in recent years is partly a reflection of the rise of China and, to a lesser extent, India, as each searches to provide both raw materials *and markets* for their red-hot economies. Many of those who have celebrated the emergence of India, China, and other Southern countries such as Malaysia and even South Africa, as new investors in sub-Saharan Africa, have suggested that these relationships represent a potentially critical contribution to the globalization of African business by enabling those actors to develop international linkages in their own right. China in particular began to be regarded by advocates of these emergent partnerships, such as economist Harry Broadman and many African leaders, as the vehicle through which African states and resident private sectors could acquire the capital, information, and technological advances necessary to become competitive, at least in their own economies, if not globally. Political scientist Deborah Brautigam suggests this is beginning to happen in special economic zones China has established in Mauritius, Zambia and Nigeria, but so far only limited data are available.

In contrast, we have more than a century's worth of data to examine the role of Western MNCs in Africa; by and large, the picture is not pretty, notwithstanding measurable progress in international corporate behavior in the developing world through initiatives of corporate social responsibility, the U.S. Foreign Corrupt Practices Act of 1977, changes in France and Germany that ended tax deductions for foreign business bribery, and the Extractive Industries Transparency Initiative, for example.[9] Corporations from the South, by contrast, lack such a long track record, good or bad, in Africa, so their behavior is not fully known. Although Asian FDI remains a minority of investment in Africa, significant growth is expected in coming years. FDI that originates in the global South has been on the rise in Africa. A recent study found that while Northern firms unsurprisingly dominated investment in the immediate postcolonial era, representing 79 percent of new investment in Africa prior to 1981. However, they represented only 37 percent of those starting operations after 2000.[10]

The relative novelty of Southern investment thus presents both real world opportunities and analytical challenges. The extent to which investors from the global South can engage African states and business—in new partnerships that facilitate a move beyond primary commodity dependence and its attendant compradorism and *toward* genuine business development—therefore begs examination.

A SOUTHERN ADVANTAGE?

In general, FDI can be assigned to one of three categories, market seeking, resource seeking, and efficiency seeking. According to Stephen Gelb, most Indian investment and South African investment in Africa is market seeking, whereas Chinese (and Taiwanese) investment tends to be resource seeking.[11] (Although resources can be both natural and human, labor has *not* been a major attractor of FDI to Africa.) Such rigid categorizations should be treated cautiously, however, as they obscure both the complexity and diversity of FDI, perhaps especially that from China.[12] Furthermore, both forms have their advantages and disadvantages for recipient countries. Market-seeking investment

> offers much more potential in terms of promoting forward and backward linkages and in terms of impacting on competition in the domestic market, though the latter effect might be negative. Market-seeking FDI is likely to increase the scope and quality of goods and services that are available to domestic firms and households as inputs into production and consumption. In contrast, resource-seeking investment . . . is more likely to have some impact on employment promotion and exports, with some possible impact on the transfer into the host economy of technology and new business models and on establishing or improving productive infrastructure.[13]

Theoretically, resource-seeking FDI is more commonly associated with technological transfer between firms and/or sectors that can possibly expedite productivity growth, technological capacity, and service delivery for African host-country firms.

These can be shared through formal institutions as well as through partnerships or regularized transactions between firms, such as those that introduce new skills or materials that can then be adopted within the host country. *Historically,* however, while resource-seeking investment has delivered a measure of employment and certainly periodic export growth, there has been limited success in transferring technology, creating business models worthy of emulation, and establishing multi-use infrastructure. Botswana's experience with diamonds is one of few obvious exceptions. Yet South-South FDI, regardless of whether it is primarily market seeking or resource seeking, "enhances the possibility of technological spillovers via FDI" because a smaller technology gap exists between domestic firms and their foreign investor counterparts than is typically the case between host-country firms and Northern-based investors.[14]

Nonetheless, the ability of Chinese- or Indian-originating FDI to foster a rapid structural transformation in African business and in African economies more broadly remains open to question. First, even with the most benign of international partners, we should not expect that technology transfer, should it occur, will lead to a burgeoning of upstream or downstream industries in most countries. For example, although high-volume manufacturing, such as in textiles, clothing, and footwear, has been the route to development taken by many developing countries, this path now substantially foreclosed for Africa given deindustrialization in the 1980s and 1990s and China's own insurmountable dominance in these industrial sectors, which was entrenched by the expiration of the Multi Fibre Arrangement in 2005. Consequently, a "combination of natural resource exploitation, agricultural self-sufficiency and high-value agro-exports, and the expansion of its unique range of service industries, including tourism, would seem to be the most likely and rewarding growth path for many African states."[15] This is not necessarily a bad thing, and private sectors *can* respond adequately, but it will require the right mix of incentives and political will.

Second, it is necessary to question the willingness of the Asia-based firms, or indeed any business, to consciously play a developmental role. There are legitimate concerns about the political and economic objectives of both China and India and their companies, and Western-style corporate social responsibility is a novel practice, particularly among Chinese firms. It is unrealistic in the extreme for Africans to expect Indian and Chinese firms, whether private or state owned, to play a self-regulating, benign role in sub-Saharan Africa. Both politically and economically, bilaterally and at the firm level, China and India are necessarily self-interested. Thus, African states (and firms) will need to maximize the presence of these foreign actors in a manner they proved almost singularly incapable of —whether out of willfulness, incompetence, or structural constraints imposed by the international system—with Northern MNCs in previous eras. Given their own capacity constraints, states must employ a combination of regulations and incentives to engage in greater levels of corporate social responsibility. The evidence suggests, however, that absent social or political pressure, state elites will have limited incentive to alter the status quo; this is most unlikely in nondemocratic regimes.[16]

Nonetheless, as argued in chapter 3, this is a decidedly *new* era, with a more auspicious combination of political and economic conditions for Africa and African business. Although it is impossible to predict precise future behavior, it is especially important to examine the track records thus far and the likely trajectories they suggest.

The following discussion examines China's path first. As the spate of recent analyses reveals, there exists an undeniable preoccupation with China among nearly all contemporary observers of Africa. The factors driving this interest vary but certainly include the implied strategic competition between China and the West, especially the United States, and the sheer visibility of the Chinese in Africa. But perhaps no factor is more significant than the breakneck pace at which China has expanded its investment and trade in sub-Saharan Africa. In contrast, despite the depth and breadth of the relationship between *Indians*—that is, people, including members of the diaspora, whose roots lie in the subcontinent—and Africa, there is surprisingly little attention paid to the role of Indian businesses in Africa. By comparison with the ubiquitous, if preliminary, analyses of "China in Africa," both public and scholarly treatments of "India in Africa" are relatively muted.[17] To be fair, this is a function of the scale of India's economic activity in Africa and its geostrategic role, both of which are currently dwarfed by China. Yet like China and its firms, India and Indian firms unquestionably inject a new and invaluable vigor into discourses about African development, multinational investment, and the continent's own business prospects.

CHINA AND AFRICA: NEW PARTNERSHIPS OR NEOCOLONIALISM REDUX?

China's Promise

Western critics of China's expanding global investments argue that Chinese companies have little regard for democracy, human rights, labor, or environmental regulation and therefore insist on vigilance. Such critics—and certainly they are found among Africans as well—fear that the net effect of Chinese FDI in Africa will be detrimental, as the continent falls prey to a twenty-first-century variant of neocolonialism. Most contemporary African leaders, however, regard such claims as disingenuous at best. They need merely point to the generally dismal history of Western corporations in Africa—from their support for apartheid to their ignominious role in sustaining the brutal rule of Nigeria's Sani Abacha to toxic waste dumping in West Africa—in order to highlight the fact that Western FDI in Africa has seldom fulfilled a development function. In contrast, a bullish sentiment accompanied China's growing presence in Africa, initially from the wider populace as well as the political class.

Indeed, as late as 2005, African countries from the Cape to Cairo were abuzz with talk of possibility of China's having an enormous positive impact in Africa. Many longtime Africa observers imagined that China, because of ideological links to Africa historically and its own status as a "developing country," would play a unique role in Africa: as an investor, partner, donor, and kindred spirit. The combination of China's growing wealth and development experience, exported via the overseas business arms of the Chinese state and a host of smaller-scale private Chinese investors, would lead, many assumed, to technology transfer, joint-venture opportunities, and a raft of Sino-African businesses—precisely the kind of cooperative entrepreneurship that might enable diversification.

The preponderance of initial evidence, drawn from the surfeit of analyses, editorializing, and policy recommendations on the subject of China in Africa, seemed to suggest a more negative view: the growing Sinoization of business in Africa has not been accompanied by an enhancement of African business. Certainly, Chinese investment has been significant, but its impact on employment levels was disappointingly limited, and the prospects for technology transfer remain largely unrealized at this point. Moreover, within Africa, the carefully cultivated image of the Chinese economic machine has been tarnished by labor disputes, anti-Chinese demonstrations, and increasingly frequent popular rejections of cheap Chinese consumer goods.

As Chinese companies have become a regular feature of the African business landscape, in certain ways they are no longer altogether different from other primary commodity investors. China's leading trade partners are Angola, Equatorial Guinea, Nigeria, Congo Republic, and Sudan, and its principal investment targets include Sudan, Algeria, and Zambia. Arguably these countries, save Zambia, have dubious records with respect to stamping out corruption, promoting democracy, protecting the environment, protecting human rights, and ensuring fair labor practices. In these states and many others in Africa, Chinese firms are primarily engaged in resource seeking, which has garnered the widest attention. China is preoccupied with the same resources that have so long appealed to Western nations: oil, industrial minerals and metals, and other primary commodities, which the country needs desperately to fuel its own industrialization. Indeed, were the eminent leftist scholar Walter Rodney alive today, he might note the irony of nominally communist China supplanting Europe as the agent of African underdevelopment.

This caricature of China's role in Africa is decidedly unhelpful, however. While the optimism in which many shrouded the Chinese was premature, the record prices of global commodities, in large part due to accelerated Chinese demand for these goods, has had a salutary impact on African GDP growth rates. Moreover, popular perceptions notwithstanding, China's investment in Africa is actually surprisingly diverse. Approximately one-third of Chinese firms are engaged in manufacturing, mainly in textiles and garment production. These firms together have an average book value of $5.4 million and annual sales of $7 million.[18] Chinese companies are far smaller than the state-run behemoths that capture the international imagination. In short, China's investment in services and manufacturing and the variety of Chinese investors, as well as the China's appetite for primary commodities, all have important implications for the future of *African* business.

An exhaustive analysis of China's role in Africa is well beyond the scope of this chapter, though it is worth noting that Deborah Brautigam's 2009 book *The Dragon's Gift: The Real Story of China in Africa* is largely unmatched in its comprehensiveness. She deals with China's economic engagement with Africa in its entirety, exploring the interconnections between business, aid, and trade and international politics. With a far more modest aim in mind, the following discussion highlights four key dimensions of China's multifaceted relationship with Africa but only insofar as they impact business in Africa. First, though the Chinese government is no longer the sole link, it is at the pinnacle of relations, providing much of the loan capital and resources for development projects that enable both Chinese and African business interests. Thus, the role played by Chinese political leadership is instructive. Second, I turn to the leading role China has taken in the construction of infrastructure. Although often an adjunct to core Chinese industrial activity, it can act as a critical multiplier for African business. A third area of emphasis is labor, which has become one of the most controversial aspects of the Chinese presence because it involves an increasingly participatory African citizenry. Employment, which is vital to skills and knowledge acquisition, is a critical lever to catalyzing local industry in Africa, as Brautigam points out.[19] Yet employment of Africans has been one of the most controversial aspects of the relationship. A fourth and related dimension pertains to the tensions between the growing presence of Chinese—as laborers, managers, and entrepreneurs—and the African populations among whom they reside. A Chinese "diaspora" remains quite small and is present in only a handful of countries, yet its growth and integration will be critical to long-term harmony with African states and societies, including business. All of these factors affect the prospects for Chinese actors to help their African counterparts to go beyond primary commodities.

The Politics of China's Africa Strategy

China, of course, has had bilateral relationships with a broad range of African states since their independence. In the three decades that followed, these ties produced diplomatic exchanges, low-level trade, and some important cultural and economic infrastructure projects, such as the construction of national sports stadiums and the Tazara Railway linking Tanzania and Zambia. Historically, Chinese FDI in Africa was limited and generally connected to aid projects, albeit not in the Western mold. As recently as the 1998–2002 period, investment was a negligible $120 million.[20] By the late 1990s, however, this relationship began to change as China's geopolitical stature and economy began to rise markedly.

The Forum on China-Africa Cooperation was launched in Beijing with a relatively small meeting in 2000 and followed up with another meeting in 2003; both were attended by African and Chinese ministers, but only a handful of African presidents participated. The signal event in recent Chinese diplomatic overtures to Africa that lent official imprimatur to this burgeoning relationship was the China-Africa Summit, held in Beijing in November 2006. It was followed by another in 2009, which pledged even greater Chinese support for Africa. The 2006 summit, which was attended by forty-eight African heads of state, espoused a range of measures to improve relations between China and Africa, such as the provision of additional economic assistance and personnel training and a reduction of tariff barriers. At that time, Chinese president Hu Jintao promised $5 billion in loans and credit, as well as a doubling of aid. The pledges made in Beijing were followed a few months later by a twelve-day Africa trip by President Hu himself, who traveled to Cameroon, Liberia, Sudan, Zambia, Namibia, South Africa, Mozambique, and Seychelles in January and February 2007. Hu declared that China would lend Africa $3 billion in preferential credit over three years.

The 2006 summit came in the midst of a ballooning economic relationship between China and Africa. In 2006, two-way trade totaled $55 billion. By 2008, this figure had nearly doubled, climbing to $107 billion—a staggering sum considering the global recession that decimated commodity prices in the fourth quarter of that year. This was a reflection of China's continued growth—and policy of stockpiling inputs at a time of low prices—despite the global slowdown. By 2007, Chinese foreign direct investment in Africa totaled nearly $7 billion and was averaging about $1.5 billion per year. Thus, the first summit merely reinforced a trend already well under way in 2006. By the time of the second summit in November 2009, when China pledged an additional $10 billion in new low-interest development loans for the next three years, additional debt forgiveness, and a $1 billion program for SME development, the relationship had expanded significantly.

The Nature of Chinese Investment in Africa

Critics of the Chinese presence in Africa perceive a rapacious state eagerly devouring Africa's primary commodities. Yet, as noted, the country's economic interests in Africa are quite diverse. It is also important to disaggregate "China" itself and differentiate among Chinese in Africa. Some seven hundred Chinese enterprises, including state-owned, partly state-owned, provincial and municipal government-owned, and private companies are doing business in Africa. Hundreds of thousands of Chinese now reside in Africa, as medium-term laborers, managers, and proprietors of small businesses. The figures are unreliable, but most estimates place the number between 750,000 and 1,000,000.

The bulk of large Chinese enterprises have some basis in or connection to the state; they are usually regionally based and owned by various public institutions or the Communist Party. As a result, these firms enjoy access to subsidized capital, which enables them to take economic risks purely private firms cannot afford to take. Certain investments therefore serve as loss leaders for subsequent Chinese investment or, more often, ensure access to key natural resources. Thus, a common transaction enables the Chinese firm to acquire African assets, whether fisheries, forests, or mines, in return for a pledge to develop infrastructure, generally using loans provided by China's export-import bank (EXIM).

A prominent example of such transactions is those China has engaged in with the Democratic Republic of Congo. In 2009, the Chinese entered a joint venture with Gecamines, the struggling state-owned Congolese mining giant. Sinohydro and China Railway Engineering Corporation acquired a 67 percent controlling interest in the company, and in exchange China's export-import bank pledged the financing to restore the copper and cobalt mines to productivity and rebuild vital infrastructure. This $9 billion transaction mirrors ones China has carried out in its acquisition of dilapidated state-owned resources in other countries, wherein loans to governments are then utilized to fund rehabilitation projects, as well as road, rail, water, and power development, and also at times investment in health and education infrastructure, in return for a substantial ownership stake. The loans are then repaid with mineral, petroleum, or other resource revenues and with fees that have been collected, such as road tolls.

Frequently in conjunction with its mining interests, China is also investing in construction, manufacturing, retail, and the service sectors. Some noteworthy business partnerships have been developed, but the tendency for large-scale Chinese firms to partner with African SOEs does little to directly advance Africa's private sector interests. Brautigam highlights several cases—principally in Mauritius, Kenya, and Nigeria—where Chinese investment has promoted joint-venture activity with private African firms and fostered further innovation by Africans who have been able to capitalize on the Chinese presence, but even she is hard pressed to enumerate more than a few examples thus far. On the whole, Chinese FDI (and trade) thus far has scarcely undergirded an African private sector. Yet in more indirect fashion, Chinese investment has impacted GDP growth, and it has resulted in the establishment or rehabilitation of critical infrastructure on which nascent African businesses can build. In addition, the 2009 Forum on China-Africa Cooperation explicitly set aside resources for private sector development, and thus the possibility remains that such direct linkages to African business promotion will emerge.

Employment Generation: Both African and Chinese

One recent study determined that Chinese companies in Africa employ an average of 660 people.[21] This is hardly an insignificant number, yet Chinese firms get little credit for their labor impact, not least because many of these large companies, whether in the construction, mining, energy, or engineering sectors, employ large numbers of Chinese nationals, both at managerial *and staff* levels. The perception that Chinese FDI has failed to facilitate African formal sector employment growth is both widespread and highly problematic. Although reality is somewhere in the middle, the view of Chinese as only employing "their own" has fostered severe tensions with African civil societies, especially organized labor, and these poor relations can have dire sociopolitical consequences. But it is also indicative of the inability of Africans to maximize China's presence in a way that would enable Africans to gain entrepreneurial and business management experience.[22]

One of the reasons that Chinese investment has had a mixed impact on employment at the staff and management levels is the propensity of Chinese companies to import Chinese labor. Chinese businesspeople, who are active in manufacturing, mining, retail, commercial trades, construction, and petroleum sectors, hail from all over China. However, the more numerous workers come from that country's poorest regions and travel to Africa to earn wages in Chinese-owned factories that far exceed what they might collect back home. Indeed, a state factory worker from central China may earn $90 per month, but in many parts of Africa, he can earn $550 or more a month, plus room and board. Although they endure notoriously spartan living conditions and separation from their families, prevailing labor migration patterns indicate that most of these workers return to China upon project completion.

For Chinese investors, this predilection for employing their own makes economic sense. Chinese workers offer quicker results and help to surmount language barriers (and their recruitment also frequently companies them to circumvent local labor laws and wages). This preference for fellow Chinese is reflected at the managerial level as well, where some 37 percent of university graduates employed by Chinese-owed companies are themselves Chinese.[23] Surprisingly, Chinese managers have made little effort to mask their preference for Chinese labor. A manager in Zambia, for example, noted that "Chinese people can stand very hard work. This is a cultural difference. Chinese people work until they finish and then rest. Here they are like the British, they work according to a plan. They have tea breaks and a lot of days off. For our construction company that means it costs a lot more."[24] Such claims not only demonstrate the glaring cultural insensitivity that occasionally prevails between Chinese firms and African host countries but also provides grist for populist backlash, especially within Africa's more participatory polities. To add insult to injury, Africa's fragile industrial sectors in clothing and textiles, for example, cannot compete with China's imported trade and manufactured goods, thereby forcing closures and layoffs of African laborers. Although FDI offsets this, it adds to the view that the Chinese are taking *African* jobs.

This dichotomy between development and cooperative potential and perceived exploitation and labor discrimination is perhaps nowhere more apparent than in Zambia, where tensions between Chinese firms and African labor, as well as the larger population, have repeatedly boiled over into conflict. One of the leading Chinese investors in Zambia, the China NonFerrous Metal Mining Group, operating under the name NFC Africa Mining Plc., has been at the center of several controversies. NFC bought the shuttered state-owned Chambishi mine in 1998 for $20 million, invested $100 million, and restarted production in 2001.[25] While bringing much-needed investment to Zambia's Copperbelt, NFC has been accused of ignoring Zambian labor law by initially banning union activity and threatening potential organizers and of paying its Zambian workers less than the $67 per month minimum wage. In April 2005, an accident at the company's explosives factory claimed nearly fifty Zambian lives, triggering mass protests and clashes between management and the Zambian staff. Michael Sata of the Patriotic Front, then a leading opposition party politician, was able to both capitalize on and further inflame public resentment of the Chinese, claiming that Zambia had become a "dumping ground" for Chinese "slave labor," which he numbered at eighty thousand—an obviously exaggerated number.[26] An anti-Chinese riot in Lusaka in 2006 was partly fomented by such rhetoric, and Sata rode these sentiments to a close second-place finish in the October 2006 presidential election, in which he garnered 30 percent of the vote.

The conflict appeared to peak with the 2006 election. Sata himself later claimed to welcome the Chinese, and after he finally won the presidency in 2011 with 42 percent of the vote, his very first official meeting was with the Chinese ambassador. Nonetheless, certain tensions persist, and few of the underlying issues have been resolved, particularly in the area of labor relations. Zambians well remember, for example, that in January 2008 five hundred employees of Chambishi were suspended for demonstrating in protest of low wages and poor working conditions at the facility, and in March 2008 a Chinese manager was attacked. Yet NFC has actually *expanded* its presence and now has five subsidiaries in Zambia. Including its $50 million acquisition of an 80 percent stake in Luanshya Copper Mine, which it bought in October 2009, the company has made a total investment of some $700 million.

While clashes like those in Zambia have been rare thus far, a similar ambivalence toward Chinese investment exists across the African continent. State elites clearly welcome the Chinese combination of loans, trade guarantees, and investment and the rents they generate, increasingly as an alternative to Western aid. At the popular level, however, deep suspicions remain, and to the extent that the Chinese presence is perceived to be detrimental to African workers, this can only serve to embolden populist demagoguery, like that which propelled Zambia's Michael Sata to national and international prominence. Notwithstanding their (self-)depiction as "fellow travelers" from the global South, the Chinese clearly inhabit a culture of business that is not as yet in harmony with contemporary practices in Africa. The integration and acculturation of businesses of Chinese provenance can be aided, over time, by a growing community on the African continent. Although as the Chinese community expands and puts down roots in Africa, the likelihood of clashes with the majority probably *escalates* in the immediate term, if they are to be consequential players in Africa's political economy over the long term, a well-established but also well-integrated diaspora will play a vital role.

The Prospects for a Chinese Diaspora in Africa

Before the 2000s and the immigration of hundreds of thousands of company workers, officials, and entrepreneurs, the Chinese could have been referred to as Africa's "invisible minority." Indeed, most popular and social science discourse pegs the Chinese as recent arrivals. Yet, some Chinese families came to Africa as early as the 1820s, and countries such as South Africa and Mauritius, for example, have Chinese diaspora communities whose roots extend back more than a century.[27] Despite these longer-term residents, however, it is true that *most* Chinese are fairly recent arrivals, and they are usually transient ones at that. When asked, Chinese laborers generally say that they plan to return to China after a few years of working in Africa, and tens of thousands did so in late 2008 and early 2009, as the global recession struck. In contrast, most members of Africa's ethnically Indian population call Africa their home. Consequently, the Chinese thus far tend to be far less embedded in the local business and economy (or occasionally politics) than those minority groups that arrived in significantly higher numbers prior to independence, such as Indians, white Europeans, and others.

Inevitably, as Chinese increasingly invest in sub-Saharan Africa, their presence will deepen, thereby creating opportunities for new large-scale investment to encounter a culturally acclimated Chinese population; this could benefit both Chinese and African popular and business interests. While the existence of a diaspora clearly cannot insulate minority investors from every contingency, the cultural facility they provide through their longevity, experience, and established networks can significantly advance the interests of foreign minority entrepreneurs and, importantly, generate positive externalities for local businesspeople. There are examples of Chinese communities outside of the long-standing Chinese presence in places like Mauritius and South Africa. In Lagos, Nigeria, for example, a small Chinatown has long been a fixture; its residents own restaurants, and engage in textile trade and other commercial activities. Lagos is also home to an association of Chinese entrepreneurs—an explicitly ethnic formulation that is not altogether unknown among other minority groups. Senegal, too, has a growing Chinese community comprised of shopkeepers and others. Indeed, from poor-resource economies like Senegal to resource-rich environments like Nigeria and Zambia, Chinese people and firms of varying sizes are an increasingly visible presence.

New arrivals might do well to emulate Nigeria's Jacob Wood, who is embedded in the culture of business in Africa rather than, like many other of his erstwhile countrymen, detached from it. Born Hu Jieguo in Shanghai in 1948, Wood came to Nigeria in the late 1970s. Wood's Golden Gate Group, which claims $100 million in assets, has interests ranging from tourism, construction, interior design, building materials, and wood processing to real estate, restaurants, and hotels. His enterprises employ hundreds of Nigerians, and he apparently has the status of an honorary chief. Moreover, he was named by former president Olusegun Obasanjo as liaison to the Chinese. As Chinese investment, official and smaller scale, expanded rapidly in Nigeria, Wood has acted as an intermediary. A pattern of utilizing the Chinese "diaspora," such as it is— especially individuals and firms with as much local credibility as Wood—to make inroads in African countries, however, is still the exception rather than the rule.

Yet in sub-Saharan Africa's increasingly participatory regimes, as the Zambian case illustrates, *publics matter*. Whereas in authoritarian environments, foreign firms usually need only cultivate the state as their primary constituency, in more democratic circumstances a measure of social and cultural fluency is essential. Evaluations of the Chinese record on this front vary. Scholars like Brautigam urge a more nuanced appreciation of the complex role of "China" in Africa, and argue that the Chinese have already moved substantially in a positive direction. At the same time, Chinese investors have been particularly tone deaf in Zambia and Senegal, where their presence has fostered noteworthy resentments.[28] Special economic zones in Zambia and Tanzania, tariff-free zones designed to facilitate value-added exports, have been slow to materialize and in any event have generally served to further *Chinese* business interests rather than facilitate the technological spillover to African firms that was anticipated by proponents. The resentments such maneuvers generate should give Chinese business and state actors pause.

At bottom, China's relationship with Africa is part of a tale that remains substantially unfinished. It cannot simply be caricatured as neocolonial exploiter of Africa any more than it can be seen as the continent's savior. Missteps on labor, the environment, and politics are striking. And many of the transactions appear at first blush unbalanced. Nonetheless, the infrastructure creation brought about through these transactions is valuable for Africa. Though partnerships between Chinese and African business interests remain elusive, African and other businesspeople can quite literally *build* on this infrastructure. That said, part of the negative visceral reaction to "China" is the size of its collective footprint. In this sense, China still lacks an advantage enjoyed by its smaller Indian competitors: a better understanding of and access to the *other* cultures of business in sub-Saharan Africa.

INDIA IN AFRICA: NEW DIRECTIONS AND OLD RELATIONSHIPS

A History of Indian Economic Relations with Africa

China's historical contact with the African littoral actually dates back more than a millennium; India's trade with Africa (including, apparently, trade in slaves), with coastal Africa, and with the Indian Ocean islands dates back perhaps centuries prior to that, although few South Asians penetrated East Africa and southern African interior until the European colonial period began in the nineteenth century.[29] At that time, Indians began to play an important intermediary role between Africans and the colonial state, as indentured laborers in South Africa and as workers and later entrepreneurs in East Africa and elsewhere. The prominence of this population in the last century means that the historical connections between Africans and people of Indian descent run far deeper than do those between Africans and Chinese.

This history has not been without conflict, of course. Certainly, any moderately informed reader—or anyone familiar with the 1991 Hollywood film *Mississippi Masala*—could reasonably question the validity of an argument that suggests that the Asian diaspora is better placed than other minority communities to advance a new cooperative culture of business, especially one that enhances the mutual interests of Indians and Africans.

Indeed, *Mississippi Masala* dramatized the severe persecution of Indians at the hands Idi Amin, the Ugandan dictator who infamously expropriated Asian-owned businesses and properties in 1972 and expelled the country's eighty-thousand resident Indians, most of whom never returned. Although many of these people held citizenship elsewhere, at least a quarter were Ugandan citizens. Tensions between Asian business owners and black Africans have also been observed in Zambia, Kenya, Tanzania, and South Africa. Though none have been nearly as dramatic as those in Amin's Uganda, such clashes cannot simply be dismissed as insignificant events. In the context of Africa's fragile economies and amid real and perceived inequalities, economic and political populism may be wielded by demagogic political leaders to scapegoat relatively privileged minority groups. Yet people of Indian origin (PIOs) have been particularly resilient, less transient and arguably more keen to seek sociopolitical solutions that involve both states and majority communities than have their Chinese counterparts.[30] These qualities augur positively for the integration of new Indian FDI as well.

In the past decade a new migration of capital has complemented the Indian presence in Africa. It is smaller than China's collective investment and trade relationship, although its FDI stocks from 1996–2004 actually exceeded those of China.[31] The profile of Indian firms differs in both focus and size from that of the Chinese: one survey found that one-third of the Indian companies are in the chemical, plastics, and rubber manufacturing subsectors and that they invested an average of $780,000 from 2003 to 2005, whereas the average Chinese firm invested $1.24 million.[32] Certainly, India has not garnered the international popular or scholarly interest that attends China's role in Africa. Yet I argue that it is at least as important as China to the future of African business and that it can precipitate the kind of business development that will allow Africa finally to move beyond its singular reliance on primary commodities. Indeed, while India's more extensive history in Africa does not automatically confer greater advantage on newly arriving Indian investors representing corporate interests, I contend that the potential for links with the Indian diaspora, born of their long and deep history in Africa, confers one genuine advantage on Indian firms vis-à-vis their Chinese counterparts. Second, although Indian investors are pursuing many of the same resources as the Chinese, they are also more amply engaged in more market-seeking investment, a relatively less invasive and intrusive approach that can facilitate African business development.

Potential Linkages with the Resident South Asian Diaspora

The Indian diaspora provides a potential resource for Indian FDI. Estimates of the size of the Indian community in Africa vary, but it is concentrated in Anglophone eastern and southern Africa. Approximately 1,000,000 PIO lived in South Africa as of 2001 (according to official estimates provided in the Report of the High Level Committee on the Indian Diaspora), some 715,756 in Mauritius, 100,000 in Kenya, and 90,000 in Tanzania. Mozambique, Zambia, Zimbabwe, and Uganda had far smaller concentrations, numbering between 12,000 and 20,000 people, but these populations have nevertheless been quite influential in the political economies of these countries. In contrast, in West Africa, the only country with an appreciable South Asian population is Nigeria, whose Indian population numbered 25,000 in 2001, and in Francophone countries, where Levantine communities predominate, Indians are few.

Certainly in East Africa, however, their presence provides both an established business architecture and a functioning network that better enables *new* investors access on the ground; the Indian diaspora is well positioned to help Indian corporate investors understand readily the prevailing cultures of business in Africa better than newly arriving Chinese. But even where such networks are not utilized to their potential, India's advantage in eastern and southern Africa arises from the fact that people of Indian descent are a familiar presence. Further, as a result of their shared British colonial heritage, Indians face less of a language barrier than Chinese; although many long-term Indian residents of Africa reside in ethnic enclaves, they commonly speak Swahili or other local languages as well.

Indian MNCs: Accessing the Network

Certainly, the Indian government anticipates that its cultural links in Africa lend it an advantage in business. But because Indian diaspora communities in Africa are often one hundred or more years old, that may be wishful thinking. Indeed, while their permanent domicile serves to cement their African identity, it also makes it less likely that PIOs will think of India as "motherland," in contrast to recent Chinese immigrants who do think of China as their true homeland, as Gijsbert Oonk points out. In fact, even more so than their African country of residence, Indians may identify first with kith and kin in the United Kingdom, Canada, the United States, and elsewhere before they identify with family and friends in India. Hence, the Indian High Level Commission may have overestimated the degree to which these PIO communities can serve as a reservoir or network for new Indian investors from their ancestral homeland.[33] Another complicating factor is that India, to an even greater degree than China, is not a monolith. Indians in Africa may differ in caste and social standing and represent a diversity of faiths including Hinduism, Sikhism, Islam and Christianity. Moreover, they speak a range of languages and hail from all over the subcontinent. Those who migrated in the 1860s to South Africa, initially as indentured servants and to Mauritius later in the nineteenth century as plantation workers, for instance, were largely unskilled laborers, whom mainly came from north-central India (Haryana, Uttar Pradesh, and Bihar) and Tamil Nadu. The first large wave of Indians to East Africa were Punjabis, who built the East African Railway; however, as much as 90 percent of them returned to India after its completion in the early twentieth century.[34] Indians who settled in the East African region, on the other hand, were largely petty traders and artisans who were mainly Gujerati speakers.[35] Lastly, recent Indian emigrants, who in any event mainly head to Western destinations, are primarily skilled laborers, predominantly from Punjab, Gujarat, Kerala, and Andhra Pradesh. These differences illustrate some intrinsic challenges that can complicate cooperation between new Indian investors and PIO networks.

The Indian State and Africa

The Indian state and India-based corporations have only recently begun to follow PIOs to sub-Saharan Africa. In this sense, they are relative latecomers, even in comparison to the Chinese. India's more outward-looking strategy began in the late 1990s, as it has become a more global player in key sectors such as pharmaceuticals, metals, and technology and in response to the recent growth and relative prosperity of the Indian economy. In fact, although SME investors have a history, very few Indian MNCs have been in Africa for more than a decade or so, with rare exceptions such as the Tata Group, which has had operations on the continent for over thirty years.[36] A key difference from the Chinese case, however, is that state-owned firms are not the leading or largest Indian investors in Africa. The contemporary Indian model is *more* private sector/Indian conglomerate-driven, which has potential implications for investment and development trajectories. Arguably, while Chinese state-connected firms will invest in Sudan or Zimbabwe with scant concern for how the public may react, Indian companies are more preoccupied with marketing and image and with taking on a *measure* of corporate social responsibility.[37]

Importantly, however, whereas the diaspora gives both the Indian state and private corporations an enviable foothold in Africa, at both the business and bilateral levels, "India" lags "China" by a significant margin. The country is behind China, whose Forum on China-Africa Cooperation is in full gear, in terms of its diplomatic outreach to Africa as a means of boosting its trade and investment relationship. At the political level, for example, India hosted its first summit in April 2008—two years after

Beijing—to far less global fanfare and with less robust African attendance. Meanwhile, China used its second summit in November 2009 as a platform to announce an additional $10 billion worth of transactions. The next multilateral meeting between India and Africa—which, like China's second forum, was held in Africa—did not occur until 2011 and was attended by fifteen African heads of state.

At its 2008 summit, India offered $5 billion in new credit as well as additional aid. The Indian government expected two-way trade to grow to $50 billion by 2012, but even this impressive growth would, if it were to transpire, be far behind China's, whose trade with Africa had already reached $107 billion in 2008. Importantly, India's outreach is driven by the same economic forces propelling China: demand for petroleum, agricultural products, and metals, *as well as markets,* to support the country's own energy and development needs. Like China, which long sought to isolate Taiwan diplomatically, India's official overtures to sub-Saharan Africa are similarly geostrategic, inasmuch as India requires the support of African states in the UN to fulfill its Security Council aspirations. Thus, in addition to nurturing a growing economic relationship, India has also engaged in peacekeeping, food relief, and other forms of humanitarian aid.[38]

Geographically speaking, the diaspora in eastern and southern Africa gives India's state-based and private investors a leg up in those regions. In West Africa, however, Indian FDI faces the same cultural and historical barriers as its Chinese competitors, especially in the Francophone countries. In fact, at the state level, India has probably had far less exposure than China, which has long had cooperation agreements with the governments of the region. India, by contrast, has but four diplomatic missions responsible for *twenty-one* states in the subregion.[39] Thus, one of the ways in which the Indian government has sought to make inroads in West Africa is through its Techno-Economic Approach for Africa-India Movement (TEAM-9). TEAM-9, which is comprised of Burkina Faso, Chad, Cote d'Ivoire, Equatorial Guinea, Ghana, Guinea Bissau, Mali, and Senegal, as well as India, is an initiative created in 2004 to provide concessional loans for technology transfers to Africa. The specific project areas include agriculture, small-scale industries, rural development, pharmaceuticals, telecoms, and energy. The size of the TEAM-9 credit facility was $500 million, on concessional terms, though by 2007 not all of the funds had been disbursed. Some had been used to fund such initiatives as a $30 million rural electrification project in Ghana and a $15 million tractor assembly plant in Mali.

Similarly, the India-Africa Partnership Conference, which was spearheaded by the Indian Ministry of External Affairs with the support of the Confederation of Indian Industries, provided another venue for fostering economic linkages. At its October 2005 conference some $5 billion worth of joint projects was discussed. A subsequent meeting held in Delhi a year later was attended by 300 African businesspeople and some 375 Indian businesspeople who discussed a reported three hundred current and potential projects valued at $17 billion.[40] Importantly, the Indian engagement with Africa goes beyond bilateral, governmental ties and increasingly takes the form of business-to-business relations.

The Dimensions of Indian Investment in Africa

I have already indicated that Indian activities in sub-Saharan Africa have been broadly characterized as market seeking whereas China's have largely been described as resource seeking, although neither of these classifications is entirely accurate. Indeed, some observers point out that "energy is at the forefront of India's strategy in Africa," suggesting an investment imperative much like China's; currently, 30 percent of India's energy needs are provided by oil, of which 70 percent is imported; imports are expected to comprise more than 90 percent of India's oil by 2025.[41] In 2007, India's industrial output measured only about 15 percent of its GDP versus 27 percent for China. But as India grows, its demand for industrial inputs, not least petroleum resources, will rise sharply as well. Indeed, one of the most important companies seeking investment in Africa is India's largest, the state-owned Oil and Natural Gas Corporation (ONGC). Its overseas investment arm, ONGC Videsh Ltd. (OVL), has acquired shares in oil exploration firms in Libya and Nigeria. Perhaps even more controversially, OVL invested in a 45 percent stake in the Greater Nile Petroleum Oil Company in Sudan in 2003 (which, ironically, it acquired from Talisman Energy, the Canadian firm for whom investment in Sudan became a political and public relations nightmare). Although OVL has not attracted as much criticism as China National Petroleum Corporation and its partners, OVL's presence does raise questions about the virtuous nature of Indian FDI relative to Chinese.

Resource-Seeking FDI

India's foray into resource-seeking investment thus stems from its own industrial growth. Yet while the acquisition of natural resources is essential for India's continued economic growth, the movement toward a resource-seeking FDI profile also poses familiar risks for the promise of India's relationship with African business—and the wider African populace. India may find itself inhibited by the same type of critiques leveled at the Chinese, as well as those often directed at Western MNCs, such as Royal Dutch Shell. The political economy problems posed by India's oil demand will likely worsen given its forecast demand for imported oil.

Although India appears to be attempting to navigate this potentially explosive political terrain, it may only appear more virtuous in contrast to China because it has been less successful. OVL, for example, famously lost out to the Chinese on new oil production facilities in Angola, where India was near to closing a deal with Shell for a 50 percent share of an oil exploration project in 2004. OVL's offer of $200 million in aid as part of a railway construction proposal was bested by China's of $2.3 *billion,* and hence the Chinese won the deal (Angola's state-owned oil company, Sonangol, had pre-emption rights in the transaction). On the other hand, the Indian government refused to sanction a deal to buy a 45 percent stake worth $2 billion in Nigeria's offshore Akpo Field, because it thought it too risky; China eventually secured this contract as well.

Yet OVL and India as a whole are hardly perpetual bridesmaids. Indeed, OVL it-self is active in number of deals including an offshore project in Cote d'Ivoire and on-shore in Libya and in oil and gas ventures in Gabon. It is also engaged in exploration in Egypt in the Gulf of Suez. (Notably, there is nary a democracy in the lot.) Further, OVL entered into a joint venture in 2005 with the private corporation, Mittal Steel, to form ONGC Mittal Energy Ltd., which won two oil blocks in Nigeria in 2006.[42] This transaction generates some positive spillover benefits for Nigeria, as it called for an investment of $6 billion to build a refinery, a power plant, and railway lines. Beyond petroleum, Indian mining firms such as Hyderabad-based Nava Bharat Ventures Ltd., Vedanta Resources Plc., Sande Sara Mining Group and Mittal, among others, are en-gaged in extraction of other resources in Africa, including coal, copper, cobalt and iron ore. Importantly, as in Chinese-led transactions, Indian company bids regularly include agreements to invest in ports, railways, and computer networks as sweeteners.[43] Like in the Chinese case, such infrastructure creation is essential for the development and functioning of African business, and, as in the China example, the *direct* linkages to and partnerships with private sector African firms are less immediately visible.

Market-Seeking Investment

India, however, has made measurable inroads in Africa's nonresource sectors as well and with nontraditional partners, even as India and its firms maintain relation-ships with traditional partners in the Indian Ocean littoral. Indian greenfield invest-ment and cross-border mergers and acquisitions between 1987 and 2005 were targeted chiefly toward those African countries in which Indian firms are already well estab-lished, namely South Africa, Mauritius, and Kenya. Indian firms in Zambia and Nige-ria made smaller investments. The major sectors for India's greenfield investment in these countries has included metals and mining, but it also made new investments in textiles, plastics and rubber manufacturing, financial services, telecoms, and vehicle assembly. Moreover, Indian companies are also making inroads in places like Ethiopia and Ghana.[44]

In Ethiopia, some 351 different Indian companies had invested a total of $1.8 bil-lion as of mid-2008 in areas such as rural electrification and the sugar industry. Ac-cording to Indian Embassy in Addis, India was the fifth largest overall investor in Ethio-pia by FDI stock in 2008 and had the highest investment inflows in 2007–2008. In Ghana, new and prospective Indian investors seek to emulate the success of the Poly Group, whose companies produce a range of plastic products, including bags, tanks, boxes, and polythene sheeting, exporting about 28 percent of their output and selling the remainder within Ghana. Poly Group employs Ghanaians in both production and management positions and has forward linkages with local affiliates of MNCs such as Nestle, Unilever, and Heinz, and it also has factories in Nigeria, as well as in Hong Kong and India. A number of other Indian-linked firms are entering Ghana's export sectors, including plastics (e.g., Top Industries Co., Ltd., and Letap Plastics), automobile spare parts (e.g., Automotive Springs), and jewelry (e.g., the British-Indian La Mode de l'Afrique). Although these are relatively small potatoes thus far, they illustrate India's newfound appreciation for opportunities in West Africa.

The Indian conglomerate Tata Group, as I noted, now operates in a number of African countries (Zimbabwe, South Africa, Tanzania, Namibia, Uganda, Mozambique, Malawi, and Ghana, in addition to Zambia, where it started in Africa) across a range of productive sectors and employs seven hundred people. One of the world's largest companies, with interests in steel, automobiles, information technology, and services sectors, in its Africa operations Tata currently produces vehicles and has interests in hospitality, telecommunications, steel, and software, many of which were acquired through privatization. Around 2007 Tata Steel, the company's steel-making arm, constructed a ferrochrome plant in Richard's Bay, South Africa, worth $108 million, reflecting the company's thirty years of bullishness on Africa. Tata Group also had plans to invest in an instant coffee processing plant worth $12 million in Uganda in 2007.

With the rapid spread of wireless phones described in chapter 3, the telecommunications sector has provided lucrative new market opportunities for investors. Tata owns a 26 percent stake in Neotel, a fixed-line telecoms company in South Africa. Another Indian company, Bharti Airtel, made a major push into Africa with its 2010 acquisition of Zain (the company originally started by the Sudanese businessman Mohammed Ibrahim as Celtel). Bharti Airtel, one of the largest cellular service providers in the world, gained fifteen new markets in the transaction valued at over $9 billion.

The automotive sector is a particularly low-margin business in sub-Saharan Africa owing to the comparatively high labor and transportation costs. Yet since 2000 the Tata Group's Tata Motors subsidiary has built trucks, buses, and cars for the South Africa market, which it first entered in 1994. Vijay Mahajan reports that Tata's commercial vehicle business grew sixfold in just four years.[45] In Senegal, which has become emblematic of India's efforts to expand its relationship with Francophone Africa, Tata partnered with the Senegalese government in 2003 to form Senbus Industries. This joint venture, which is 40 percent owned by Tata, assembles Tata buses. The contract was announced by President Wade and made possible by $15 million from the World Bank. The initial contract called for 500 buses, with a planned run of 10,000 buses for the regional market.[46] In a transaction reminiscent of the Chinese approach, the Senegalese government bought 350 of the buses—effectively from itself—with the purchase financed in part by a loan from the government of India of $18 million.[47] Plans were also developed to establish a plant to manufacture three-wheel vehicles. Other Indian companies such as Mahindra Group are also profiting from investments in the automotive sector.

Two final observations about India in Africa pertain to infrastructure and employment, issues for which the Chinese have garnered far more headlines. Like the Chinese, the Indian state and Indian firms have engaged in infrastructure projects, some with project loans provided by Indian state institutions. The sampling of projects listed here are dwarfed by many of China's; consider the $6 billion allocated to infrastructure as part of the Gecamines transaction, for example. Nonetheless, Indian-led initiatives provide a modest platform for African economic expansion that otherwise would be unfeasible, given the continent's badly degraded economic foundations. Mark Sorbara identifies several broad initiatives taken in recent years. Overseas Infrastructure Alliance, Pvt. Ltd., reached a $65 million deal with Ethiopia to supply electrical equipment, while KEC International won a $40 million contract to build a power plant in that country. IRCON International agreed to construct 120 kilometers of roads in Ethiopia and to rehabilitate the critical Beira Railway in Mozambique. Similarly, RITES International began rehabilitating the railway in Angola's Huila Province, devastated by that country's four-decade war. In neighboring Zambia and Namibia, Kamani Engineering Corporation was engaged to build an $11 million transmission line between Zambia and Namibia.[48]

Finally, although Indian firms doing business in Africa have not been immune to criticism about their labor practices, Indian companies also boast of hiring locally and emphasizing training for their African employees, especially on maintenance of plant and equipment. It is nearly impossible, for example, to imagine an Indian entrepreneur or manager publicly denigrating his African workers, as the Chinese boss I cited did. To be fair, Indian firms' proclaimed labor sensitivity clearly differs from the historical *perception* of Indian firms in East Africa, especially those run by PIOs. The frictions and controversies that have arisen are discussed more fully in chapter 6. Nevertheless, Indian companies old and new are more fully integrated into the African political economy than their Chinese counterparts. This is by dint of their association with more benign investment, the longevity of their networks on the continent, and their more adroit approach to human resource and public relations management.[49]

CONCLUSION

South-South FDI notwithstanding, African countries have generally failed to diversify their economies, unless we count the short-lived experiments with ISI that ended in the 1980s and effectively reversed in the 1990s. Indeed, in some places, notably the oil producers, African countries have actually become *less* diversified, as the effects of Dutch disease have crippled other areas of the economy. This remains an obvious danger, and 2008–2009, widely regarded as the world's worst economic slowdown since the Great Depression, provided a stark reminder of that fact. At the same time, however, there is a very modest measure of diversification and clearer signs of economic revival at the subnational level in a number of countries. New entrepreneurs have emerged, shrewd cronies have seized opportunities, and ancillary businesses have sprung up alongside new projects, including multinational mining operations especially, availing themselves of revitalized physical and technological infrastructure that has accompanied these projects. Much of this new infrastructure is courtesy of Chinese loans, construction companies, and an army of imported semiskilled labor.

Yet the investment from China, particularly in Africa's large scale extractive sectors, while critically important for economic growth in recent years (as well as the future), has proved rather disappointing for those who anticipated that Chinese investment would facilitate rapid sectoral diversification, that Chinese entities would unambiguously partner with local African counterparts, and that China would precipitate some form of business (re)naissance on the African continent. Irrespective of national origin, investors are, after all, in Africa not for altruism but for profit; in the case of both Chinese and Indian firms, their principal objective is to continue their own exponential growth (at the micro- and macroeconomic levels), not, in the first instance, to spur Africa's development. Yet notwithstanding the need to temper the enthusiasm many scholars and observers initially expressed for China—or the substantial optimism still echoed by many African leaders—African states and businesses have no more to fear from China's expanding presence in Africa than from any other international source. Neither do they have *less* to fear, however.

I will not impute vice to Chinese companies nor virtue to Indian (or, for that matter, African). Such a Manichean perspective is a far too simplistic and belied by the complex and sometimes contradictory behaviors of actors on the ground. Indeed, although I believe they are better positioned to spread benefits more quickly to African business, it is equally inappropriate to hold out Indian corporations—in Africa or from the subcontinent—as virtuous. They are implicated in corruption in domestic African politics and within India.[50] In the end, they are self-interested, utility maximizers whose behaviors include practices that are both corrupt and malign. In fact, Indian companies topped the list in the 2006 Bribe Payers' Index produced by Transparency International, which suggested that Indian companies have a higher propensity to pay bribes than any other, including those from China.[51]

Ceteris paribus, neither the Chinese and Indian investors nor African political leaders can be blindly trusted to preserve the public good; the history of imperialism and neocolonialism in Africa is a stark reminder that, whatever their national origin, corporate capitalist foxes should not be placed in charge of Africa's resource rich henhouses. However, self-restraint on the part of the Chinese—whether it exists or not is irrelevant, though we should assume it does not—cannot provide the main check on Sino-imperialism (or Indo-, for that matter). Rather that must come from Africans *themselves.* Indeed, as discussed in chapters 2 and 3, it is the *political* changes in sub-Saharan Africa that must serve as the chief constraint on a return to the neocolonial policies of the past. In this sense, the aftermath of the 2005 explosion at the Chinese-run Chambishi mine site in Zambia marks a small step forward, as it served as a catalyst for popular mobilization and new legislation—even if it did not prove very durable this time. The events in Zambia thus served as a potential harbinger for China and its allies among the members of the African ruling class, should they fail to heed its lessons: greater democracy yields a public increasingly able and willing to express its discontent, in the streets and at the polls.

A further observation emerging from this chapter is that diasporas can have tremendous value. "Diasporas stimulate international entrepreneurship by creating cross-border social networks that serve an important role in helping entrepreneurs to circumvent the barriers to business relations and trade arising from imperfect local institutions in developing countries."[52] Raphael Kaplinsky portrays this interaction with diaspora communities as a "channel of impact" that magnifies India's—and perhaps eventually China's—capacity in Africa.[53] Thus, Nigeria's Jacob Wood provides perhaps the new exemplar, an "Indian-style" model, for China to follow in Africa. Members of the Chinese diaspora, embedded and acculturated in African countries like Nigeria, may be the least disruptive route to long-term success in Africa—and it increases the likelihood of success *for* Africa as well. In short, China might seek to emulate India in this sense, that is, try to partner with members of its own diaspora in Africa in order to benefit from their cultural, political, and economic connections.

As the anti-Chinese sentiment in Zambia reached its apex, Dr. Guy Scott, the white former government minister and, as of 2011, national vice president, made this observation: "People are saying: 'We've had bad people before. The whites were bad, the Indians were worse, but the Chinese are worst of all.'"[54] Setting aside the irony of a white Zambian quoting "people" on this subject, Scott was quite correct. At present, the methods adopted by both Chinese small traders and Chinese MNCs are more discriminating against African labor and more exclusive—by race, language, housing, and so forth—thereby making Chinese a more "foreign" target. However ironically, this accrues to the advantage of Indian MNCs and their local Indian counterparts, who are also aided by their seemingly more accommodating labor practices and propensity for market-seeking FDI. Yet, what Scott's statement also reveals is that, over time, the assessment of particular groups as "other" can and does shift, as it did for the whites in Zambia and as is happening increasingly for long-established Indian and Levantine groups. The Chinese, as the ubiquitous newcomers, are the new "foreigners" and thus more "legitimate" targets. Africa's political and economic maturity, and of course its sovereignty, means that the Chinese are incapable of imitating the worst characteristics of the white European imperialism, even if they wished to (and evidence suggests they do not). Yet actual or potential clashes induced by differing cultures, traditions, and languages or by the sheer size of their operations would seem to argue for greater circumspection. Otherwise, they risk inviting both political backlash on themselves and economic cost to putative partners in Africa's private sector. A fair number of the latter remain optimistic about the prospects for partnership across a diverse set of industries, the mixed results of Chinese and Indian forays into Africa notwithstanding.

FROM PATRIMONIALISM TO PROFIT? THE TRANSFORMATION OF CRONY CAPITALISTS AND BUREAUCRATIC BOURGEOISIES

INTRODUCTION

The prevalence of crony capitalism in sub-Saharan African polities, from neopatrimonial regimes to stable political economies, has formed part of the subtext of each of the preceding chapters. In effect, the pervasive analytical frame of neopatrimonialism suggests that "modern" state institutions in Africa are but a façade, and this extends to thinking about markets as well. Those who consider African politics to be defined by neopatrimonialism assume that African business, at least business as conventionally understood in the West, is a highly dubious proposition because of the endemic corruption found in such environments.[1] To them, an autonomous private sector, at least one with any clout or capacity to transform the economy and the state, faces impossible odds; it will be constantly penetrated by neopatrimonial state elites and therefore has no hope of playing a transformative role in the political economy.

But this effort to tar all of Africa with one neopatrimonial brush is misleading at best and disingenuous at worst, although it makes for analytical convenience and parsimony, it scarcely represents the diverse realities of contemporary African business on the ground. Previous chapters have called attention to the existence of business ownership and activities and polities that simply do not fit within the confines of the neopatrimonial paradigm. Yet it is of little utility to commit the opposite sin by denying that neopatrimonialism—or something like it—exists *at all* in sub-Saharan Africa or by admitting it exists but insisting that it does not affect business. Admittedly, there are many examples of the politics—and economics—of "the big man" in Africa, wherein elites systematically utilize public resources for private gain and power and position are based on personal loyalty to "big men" rather than adherence to the rule of law and patron-client relations predominate.

It is tempting, therefore, to argue that Africa is going in two directions at once, that one set of countries toward is heading "normal capitalism," while the rest remain mired in "patrimonial capitalism." But this strikes me as too simplistic. A less parsimonious but more accurate assessment is that "Africa" is going in *multiple* directions at once: the view across countries thus more closely resembles a continuum; the view within countries is equally varied, inasmuch as each country contains examples of both patrimonial and "normal" capitalism, as well as considerable activity between these extremes. Places along this continuum are not necessarily *fixed*, however. Hence, we must also avoid the temptation to simply write off so-called neopatrimonial polities and their resident business communities and interests as irredeemable; the prospects for transformation exist in Africa, as they do elsewhere. Indeed, numerous countries that are both geographically and culturally distant from Africa display neopatrimonialism or something remarkably similar to it, yet they have developed robust business sectors and, ultimately, impressive national development as well. But by holding sub-Saharan Africa to a more exacting standard than elsewhere in the developing world, we must ultimately resort to culturalist explanations that sound persuasive but cannot be falsified and thus are ill suited as hypotheses.

Certainly, some forms of cronyism—those which lie toward the far end of the continuum—are less likely to lead to beneficial development outcomes than others. There is a distinction, for example, between economic predators and kleptocrats who hew closely to ever more rapacious tendencies, scrupulously avoid reinvestment, and degrade economies beyond redemption and political-economic cronies who receive certain favors that facilitate acquisition or protection of their business interests. Indeed, many of the latter can be found among the successful and conventionally legitimate businesspeople featured in chapter 3, whereas those that have reached the pinnacle of success are among those addressed in chapter 6's discussion of Africa's "giants." It is naïve to assert that even these flourishing businesspeople achieved that status all alone. (It is worth noting for example that the provenance and essential legitimacy of minority- and settler-owned firms in Africa is seldom questioned. They are erroneously believed to resort to the state last rather than first. Yet examples of such "cronyism" abound, not only in Africa but in Indonesia, the Philippines, and countless other regions, as discussed in chapter 1.) At bottom, as long as there are businesspeople, cronyism will persist, regardless of the geographic or cultural political context or what label we decide to assign to it. It is a mistake, therefore, to assume that patrimonial capitalism, and its attendant cronyism, pose insuperable barriers to business success.

Hence, this chapter does not deny the existence of neopatrimonialism, patron-clientelism, corruption, crony capitalism, and variants thereof. Moreover, I do not argue that these forms of economic relations are ipso facto debilitating, whether to capitalist development, political liberalization, or perhaps even commerce altogether.[2] Indeed, there are other countries in which neopatrimonialism can actually play an important role in the evolution of business—and potentially *of capitalism* as well. In polities where patrimonial capitalism is prevalent, fertile ground for the creation of legitimate business is not laid by the eradication of corruption—or even the neopatrimonial tendencies that presumably give rise to it—but via a transformation in the calculations of existing crony capitalists. In other words, erstwhile cronies, members of the so-called bureaucratic bourgeoisie, and others, are hardly incapable of formulating medium- and longer-term interest horizons, of reinvesting in business and creating *going concerns*. The changes in the economic and political institutional environments discussed in previous chapters provide just such a catalyst for altering perspectives and reformulating objectives in response to new incentives. Certainly, the neopatrimonial argument held great sway in the 1980s and 1990s, but its scope is less encompassing today as a result of those environmental changes. This, in turn, has contributed to lower returns to kleptocracy and the zero sum form of corruption for which Africa has been widely, if unfairly, known.

This chapter examines first the corrupt origins of Africa's crony-derived businesses. For analytical purposes, I propose that there are essentially three paths to this corruption: a conventional path, through privatization, and by means of contemporary indigenization programs. Although these categories are not mutually exclusive in practice, they do tend to be associated with distinct phases in recent history. What I call the "conventional" route to crony capitalism is also the most long-standing and encompassing. These cronies were borne of proximity to the political leadership and/or the state bureaucracy, through various family connections, or via extended kinship. This form of cronyism also includes reciprocal relations of protection, such as between wealthy minority business owners and the state. Almost by definition, the conventional path involves a degree of opacity if not outright corruption. This path gave rise to the crony capitalists and "bureaucratic bourgeoisie"—the focus of so much scholarship in the early years of the postcolonial era. Yet since nepotism, favoritism, and other illicit connections between state and business obviously persist in the contemporary era, this traditional route to cronyism, although diminished in many countries, continues as well.

Two other developments helped cultivate crony capitalists in Africa: privatization and indigenization. Privatization was a strategy accorded international legitimacy. And while this central component of liberalization programs was intended to provide the grist for new market-oriented economies, it also created myriad opportunities for cronyism. Finally, indigenization programs, which were a staple of postcolonial political economies across Africa beginning in the 1960s, experienced a resurgence in the 1990s. For more than a generation, the practice was mainly a *state* project falling under the rubric of Africanization, which gave birth to a host of state-owned enterprises. Since the 1990s, however, indigenization has generally been perceived as a mechanism for empowering Africans in and through the *private* sector; it is also seen a vehicle for the empowerment of a new generation of crony capitalists.

Following this review, the chapter then turns to the ways in which cronies, however they originated, can transform from mere appendages of the state into credible business actors. While there is no "one size fits all" mechanism that can be applied across cases, cronies tend to undergo a similar process of legitimation, both at the level of the individual entrepreneur as well as the firm. Moreover, simply because some cronies transform into bona fide businesspeople is not to say that they are reborn as pillars of society—only that their businesses become more sustainable. Thus, transformed cronies may generate positive spillover effects and can begin to benefit national political economies in terms of employment and taxes and as a stimulator of ancillary businesses and the like.

The chapter concludes with an assessment of the prospects for reforming the state. Whereas degeneration of the state and state capacity help foster a political and economic environment for patrimonial capitalism in the first place, when such actors engage in economic pursuits of profit—and, admittedly, of power—they can transition from transgressing to stabilizing to ultimately validating the market, thereby initiating an alternative route to economic development and, paradoxically, to the restoration of state institutions.

CORRUPT ORIGINS

The Conventional Path to Cronyism

The "first generation" of cronies that emerged after independence were the recipients of largesse from bloated states, whether Afrocapitalist or nominally socialist. These actors, like the "briefcase businessmen" they came to personify, would come and go—receiving state contracts, acting as international compradors, and surviving off rents—and, since they seldom invested in brick and mortar enterprises, had an almost ephemeral quality. Although some certainly succeeded in channeling patronage into productive enterprise, it is difficult to argue that such was the objective for most. Save for the acquisition of luxury goods (to the extent they could get away with it), wealth was routinely exported, typically to Swiss bank accounts or coastal Mediterranean real property. Political ideology posed another constraint to genuine business investment, as did the declining fortunes of most African countries beginning in the 1970s. The former meant that would-be businesspeople, in an African socialist or heavily statist environment, would run smack into strictures against business ownership or capitalist behavior. Given the historical record, it is hard to argue that such official strictures did much to discourage corruption, but they did discourage any incentive for transformation: as long as the illicit flows of patronage were maintained, reinvestment in or profitability of the enterprise was largely unnecessary. Such protobusinessmen often literally grew up with the states themselves, as political elites in a one-party system in which patronage was seen as an entitlement. Since many in this traditional category were from political families, they had even less incentive to develop a "going concern" logic. Arguably, having direct access to the state and assuming that its patronage flows were virtually inexhaustible, there was scant need to prepare business plans, follow best practices, and so on.

Of course, African socialist and economic nationalist ideology no longer carries the weight it once did, notwithstanding the fairly recent demise of the Washington Consensus. But the conventional path to crony capitalist accumulation via political connections remains an important one. In fact, in spite of changes in the domestic and international climate that should have made traditional crony accumulation more difficult in recent years, there are numerous examples of politically connected elites exploiting their power or proximity to power in order to channel resources to their personal businesses, viable or not. One prominent example is Bakili Muluzi, the former president of Malawi. Prior to becoming president in 1994, Muluzi was a businessman who had accumulated significant wealth, according to John Lwanda's 1997 book on Malawi's democratic transition.[3] Yet some more recent accounts suggest that Muluzi's "companies were largely struggling to remain afloat."[4] Certainly, Muluzi's ascension to the presidency not only provided him with a lifeline for his company holdings but enabled him to entrench a business empire that included operations in property management, financial services, sugar distribution, and transportation.

Yet Muluzi—like others in this vein who failed to transition business holdings from their dependence on patronage to reliable profit—failed to sufficiently plan for his postpolitical future via going concerns. Muluzi's business interests were particularly threatened once he became alienated from, and subsequently targeted by, his successor Bingu wa Mutharika. Thus, by 2006, two years after Muluzi left the presidency, one observer wrote, "It appears as if the centre of both his economic and political bases can no longer hold and things are falling apart for a man who in his hey days could have people of all shades of colors and status mingling around him whenever he coughed to signal attention."[5] Muluzi saw his assets shrink once he left office and suffered legal judgments against some of his businesses (including a $700,000-plus judgment against his Atupele Properties in February 2006 for nonpayment of rent). It is little wonder that 2007 and 2008 saw Muluzi renew his quest for the presidency and attempt to get back into power, although his bid was ultimately unsuccessful.

Other contemporary illustrations of this phenomenon include Leo Mugabe, the nephew of Zimbabwe's president Robert Mugabe, and Zacky Nujoma, the son of former Namibian president Sam Nujoma. Leo Mugabe has significant shareholdings in a number of Zimbabwe's (erstwhile) blue chip companies, owns at least three large-scale commercial farms, illicitly acquired, and is famed for attaching his name to projects in order to enhance bidding prospects such as the Harare International Airport, which opened in 1999. Likewise, since his father was Nambia's founding president, Zacky Nujoma was *born* to power and used his proximity to power and the family name to acquire considerable wealth. Nujoma fils also shares with the younger Mugabe a lack of proven business acumen or even a demonstrable interest in actually running a business. Unlike Muluzi, for example, Zacky Nujoma apparently did not use his position to shore up shaky businesses. On the contrary, the bulk of Nujoma's business endeavors are widely believed to be merely shell operations rather than bona fide enterprises.

The younger Nujoma was also alleged by some investigative reporters to have connections to a host of other unsavory characters. Moreover, various individuals and organizations, both illicit and more legitimate, proved keen to enter transactions with Nujoma, who in turn was willing to trade quite explicitly on his familial and political connections. Through a series of holding companies, Nujoma also appears to be a major player in the Namibian black empowerment enterprises. Yet while his attractiveness to such business partners is obviously rooted in having a famous and powerful relative, Zacky Nujoma also has some roots of his own in the state hierarchy, having previously served as an intelligence operative for the state intelligence agency. Ultimately, Nujoma operates largely in the orbit of business rather than being invested in it on the ground; his main roles have been as "business consultant" through several different investment firms, for which he collects fees and occasionally acquires company stakes.[6] He is particularly active in the extractive industry sector, which tends to attract international investors and is renowned for accommodating rent-seeking behavior.

At bottom, individuals such as Nujoma and Muluzi provide recent illustrations of traditional crony capitalism, thus revealing that the practice continues to the present. Their position in or proximity to the state can produce impressive rents. Unlike more astute cronies-cum-entrepreneurs, however, they appear to have neglected to utilize their positions or the rents collected to attempt to establish viable going concerns. With scant regard for even the thinnest veneer of business legitimacy, other characters appear more in the mold of some of Africa's most infamous kleptocrats, including Zaire's Mobutu Sese Seko or, perhaps less notoriously, the inner circle of former Kenyan president Daniel arap Moi.[7] Mobutu mainly engaged in conspicuous consumption and rent seeking while "investing" proceeds abroad; one of the Moi government's most infamous "business" transgressions was the so-called Goldenberg scandal, in which real cash, more than $600 million, was paid for phantom gold exports. This is "business" as barely concealed thuggery.

In contrast, Nigerian elites have done it better—or at least more artfully. Nigeria is widely regarded as one of sub-Saharan Africa's most corrupt countries; certainly, it has a generous share of cronies in the "traditional" style, that is, who are linked, often in name, to virtually all of the country's former leaders, military as well as civilian. Indeed, Nigeria's recent history is littered with examples of corruption both grand and petty, and many of its political elites, both from its many years of military rule and since the instauration of civilian rule in 1999, have been implicated in acts ranging from diversion of resources, procurement fraud, diversion of contracts, and outright theft. A complete accounting of the linkage between state, business, and corruption and its role in fomenting crony capitalism in Nigeria would take volumes; in fact, volumes have already been written on the subject.[8] In Nigeria, it starts at the top: civilian and military leaders alike, at the national and state levels, enjoy enormous wealth and control vast business empires.

Olesugun Obasanjo, the one-time military head of state who later won two terms as the elected president of Nigeria, is one of the wealthiest people in the country. Once hailed as a leading figure in the restoration of democracy in Africa, Obasanjo is now widely believed to have profited handsomely from his tenure in office, which lasted from 1999 to 2007. Allegations of corrupt involvement in various business ventures have amplified, especially since his leaving office in 2007. Many of the accusations of business-related corruption center around Obasanjo Farms Ltd., the former president's commercial farming operation in his home state of Ogun.

The most vocal criticism of Obasanjo comes from Nigeria itself, as well as Nigerians in the diaspora, who demand to know the provenance of the president's wealth. Obasanjo Farms was actually started in 1973, but it is worth noting that Obasanjo was then a senior officer in the military government of Yakubu Gowon; Obasanjo himself became head of state in 1976 before ceding power in 1979. In 1979, Obasanjo Farms began its commercial operations, although some reports suggest it remained a small operation until more recently—coinciding with Obansanjo's term in office.[9] Today the 150-acre facility engages in poultry and pig farming and employs as many as three thousand people, which generated—according to the president himself—an estimated ₦30 million per month in 2004 (then about $250,000); Obasanjo Farms has done business with the government, though reports vary as to the extent of these transactions.[10] Nigeria's ubiquitous bloggers suggest instead that Obasanjo Farms was corrupt from its inception, its raison d'être being to divert resources, including cash, machinery and other materials, from Operation Feed the Nation (1976–79) to Obasanjo's farm.[11]

Privatization and Crony Capitalists

Although the conventional method has a long and sordid history, privatization offers a unique and newer opportunity for business via corruption. Indeed, even where seemingly transparent, the privatization process presents insiders, with their privileged access to financial information and competing bids, with a chance to extract a side payment from would-be investors; such sweeteners can be the difference between successful and unsuccessful bids. Aside from enabling mere rent seeking, however, privatization also offers a singular opportunity for the political class to invest directly in business enterprises by acquiring former state-owned assets for their own private portfolios. In an environment of weak or nonexistent financial disclosure laws, government and bureaucratic officials may have better knowledge of real asset values, cash flows, and so on, and they may be able to engineer sweetheart deals for themselves and their associates or cronies. Even in cases where oversight of the privatization process was deemed transparent, such as in Zambia—where international investment bankers were appointed to prominent roles to ensure the validity of the process, websites were created, and bidding was publicly announced—numerous cases of this kind of abuse nonetheless occurred.

Interestingly enough, in the early stages of Zambia's privatization, the involvement of state officials was even celebrated, despite the obvious conflicts of interest. For example, in a 1996 article entitled "Politicians Buy," a Zambian business journal approvingly argued that the acquisition of former SOEs by politicians was evidence of their commitment to the success of privatization.[12] In fact, in some cases politicians "bought" for nothing or they stole state funds to facilitate their purchase.

Ultimately, however, privatization can be a double-edged sword. It is not automatically the ticket to sustained riches that politicians may anticipate— those without business expertise or a reliable source of working capital (whether licit or illicit) in particular may flounder. Many of Zambia's illicitly privatized businesses, for example, failed for a range of reasons common to other African countries: the new owners lacked the requisite expertise to run the companies; they had insufficient capital to manage the enterprises without a continued lifeline from the state; and businesses were simply too eroded after years of neglect and asset stripping to be revived following their "sale." This would appear to have been the case, for example, with Bennie Mwiinga, who, as Zambia's minister of Local Government and Social Welfare in 1996, acquired the formerly state-owned Manchinchi Bay Lodge in 1996 under highly dubious terms that Mwiinga, on the face of it, could scarcely afford. The facility, like many in Zambia and elsewhere, was already faltering under state control; its new private ownership ran it into the ground.

Even politicians with business backgrounds can find the "easy riches" promised by privatization elusive. Zambia's former defense minister, Ben Mwila, was a business owner since the mid-1970s. Taking advantage of his proximity to the president and his own ministerial positions while in government, Mwila expanded his business empire, Investment Holdings, enormously through privatization. However, the companies fell on hard times after 2001, when Mwila lost many of his assets in a series of repossessions and unpaid loans. Not surprisingly, this corresponded with his departure from office in 2001.

Like Zambia, privatization in Uganda has been rife with insider deals. Although, also like Zambia, many transactions raised public criticism, in the press as well as in parliament, they greatly enriched the participants and dramatically expanded their business holdings. A case that is illustrative of this phenomenon involved the privatization of passenger and cargo handling services at Uganda's Entebbe Airport, which was effected by regime insiders.[13] In 1993, the Uganda's Civil Aviation Authority (CAA) announced that it would privatize these services, which had been administered by the parastatal Uganda Airlines Corporation (UAC, the national-flag carrier); handling services represented some 60 percent of UAC revenue. The CAA based its decision to privatize air handling on a review that discovered that UAC was improperly financing its failing transport business with revenue from handling charges. Despite these concerns, however, no bids were submitted for handling services for two years. Finally in

1995, Sam Kutesa, a former attorney general and close associate of Ugandan president Yoweri Museveni, submitted a bid for the privatization.[14] The success of Kutesa's application became a foregone conclusion when a subsequent rival bid was disallowed, reportedly for "arriving too late."[15] Kutesa was asked to meet with Salim Saleh (aka Caleb Akandwanaho), President Museveni's brother and the head of the CAA, to discuss privatization plans. At the meeting it was agreed, without any formal proposal being submitted, that the airport handling would be spun off as Entebbe Handling Services Ltd., or ENHAS.

This initial accord also established that ownership of the new company was to be held 50 percent by UAC and 50 percent by private investors but that UAC would control only two out of six seats on the board of directors. The sale of private shares went to a partnership of two Ugandan companies: Efforte Aviation, which also had ties to an Israeli businessman but was linked as well to Salim Saleh, and Global Airlinks, owned by Sam Kutesa, as well as Sabena, the former Belgian national carrier airline. A small amount of stock was set aside for employees of the CAA.[16]

Sam Kutesa took an aggressive approach following the ENHAS privatization. He systematically sidelined the UAC leadership from ENHAS management, for example, by switching the signatories to all company bank accounts into his own name and the executives of Efforte and Global Airlinks, without notifying UAC. This prompted complaints from his putative partners at both UAC and Sabena that funds were being diverted and angry exchanges between Kutesa and Dick Turanwe, the chairman of UAC. Turanwe was subsequently removed. He was replaced by Agad Didi, who also served as managing director of Calebs International, another of Salim Saleh's companies.

In 1998, Global Airlinks and Efforte, the two companies controlled by Kutesa and Saleh, respectively, consolidated their ownership of ENHAS by purchasing those shares still owned by UAC. Officially, UAC decided to sell its ENHAS shares in order to offset other debts. As revealed in parliamentary testimony in 1999, however, the shares were sold substantially below their market value. Although two auditing firms had estimated the value of the UAC shares in ENHAS at between $5–8 million, the local office of Delloitte and Touche valued the shares at just $3.38 million. Global Airlinks and Efforte ultimately purchased the UAC shares for $3.75 million, although there was no evidence of actual payment for the shares.[17] Without the revenue provided from ENHAS, UAC itself collapsed in 1999; it was privatized under the name AfricaOne, which collapsed itself soon thereafter. In the wake of the UAC demise, East African Airlines, another company controlled by Sam Kutesa, lobbied President Museveni to be designated Uganda's new "national flag carrier," which would mean it would inherit all of the routes that had been allotted to UAC.

In 1999, Kutesa, who returned to the cabinet two years later as Museveni's minister of state for investment, was censured by parliament for misconduct related to

ENHAS. The offenses included concealing financial information on the company from the government, overinvoicing, threatening a government official, and other misconduct.[18] For his part, Kutesa did not refute the substance of the allegations. Instead he insisted that as a private citizen when he initially bid for ENHAS, he should be exempt for censure for anything related to the transaction; he was censured anyway, although he continued to cycle in and out of government thereafter.

Sam Kutesa's political fortunes were uncertain, especially around the time of the ENHAS investigation by parliament. Museveni dropped him in 1999, though in 2001 he returned, equally inexplicably, to a cabinet position. And from January 2005 Kutesa served as Uganda's foreign minister. Salim Saleh, the president's brother, rode a similar roller coaster. He amassed an impressive portfolio of companies and apparently wealth. His insiderism facilitated numerous abuses—profiteering from conflict diamonds and coltan in the Democratic Republic of Congo and the illicit acquisition of other former SOEs, like the Uganda Commercial Bank and the Uganda Grain Milling Corporation— all of which were widely publicized, and regularly condemned, by Ugandan media, its parliament, and the United Nations. Although ultimately censured by his own brother, whose involvement in the various transactions is suspected, Saleh's marginalization was only temporary. Importantly, despite their dubious origins, both Saleh's and Kutesa's business interests continued, if less controversially.

Uganda, like much of contemporary Africa, is a peculiar admixture of electoral politics, erratic governance, and fragile institutions. Thus, although abuses of authority take place, impunity is nonetheless bounded to some extent by the vagaries of elections and constituent demands. In a way, this situation is far more volatile and gives rise to far more capricious leadership than would be the case in stable authoritarianisms. In the current environment, today's cronies can be tomorrow's scapegoats, sacrificed in the interests of political expediency. In and of itself, therefore, crony capitalism is an unreliable source of sustained income. "Smart cronies" diversify.

Indigenization Schemes

To critics, indigenization is tantamount to a socialist redistribution of wealth. Yet to its proponents, it is a complement to privatization policies and economic liberalization of the 1990s. Indigenization recognizes that in an increasingly private sector-driven economy, the need to include more black Africans in that process becomes an economic, and even political, necessity.

"Indigenization," which also encompasses African attempts at affirmative action and black economic empowerment, is increasingly popular across the continent. Theoretically, such policies are an attempt to reverse the discrimination against black business and entrepreneurship and foster the middle-class growth denied as a result of vestiges of colonialism and neocolonialism. Somewhat surprisingly, perhaps, such policies are not limited to former settler colonies but are also found in such places as Zambia in its Citizens Empowerment Act (2006), in Nigeria's preferential procurement programs, and in Cote d'Ivoire's controversial policy of Ivoirité.

The argument that some type of African advancement or affirmative action policies are needed in these polities is not invalid; indeed, it is a sad testament to the lack of socioeconomic progress, despite nearly five decades of independence, a lack of progress that owes to discrimination, racism, and (neo)colonialism, to be sure, but certainly also to failed statist policies that attempted indigenization *on behalf* of the African people. Thus, consistent with the more liberal context of the present, contemporary initiatives attempt to empower black Africans by enhancing their *private* sector access: as managers, investors, and owners of firms.

Surely, to the extent that affirmative action fosters expansion of overall wealth and creation of a middle class rather than merely redistributes wealth, it can be a useful tool in societies from South Africa to Malaysia to the United States (where it was first introduced more than four decades ago). At the same time, however, as practiced in Africa, indigenization is rife with potential for abuse by politically connected elites.

The basic concept of indigenization is hardly new. Yet I wish to differentiate between old-style "Africanization" and contemporary indigenization. The former is rooted in the African nationalism that undergirded independence movements throughout the continent; these had an economic as well as a political component. Economic nationalism, typically manifesting itself as Africanization, was the attempt to increase the African presence in business and the economy writ large after nearly a century of colonial control. Since very few countries, including famously those adhering to an "African capitalist" development path such as Kenya and Nigeria, could claim a measurable black investor class at independence, the state itself became the leading vehicle for Africanization. To wit: the Nigerianization Decree of 1971, Zaireanization in the 1970s, Uganda's seizure of Asian properties in 1972; Zambianization via the Mulungushi reforms of 1968; Tanzania's Ujamaa after 1967, and so on. In Afrocapitalist systems, however, the promotion of Africanization policies did help create space for the emergence of some black African private business owners as well. And in virtually all cases in the 1960s and 1970s, Africanization came at the expense of multi-national ownership, colonial and settler interests, or resident ethnic intermediaries such as East Africa's South Asian population. In Kenya, for example, Africanization meant displacing the local Indian population from much of the trade sector, which was seen as having the lowest barriers to entry for the nascent black business class.[19]

The contemporary equivalent of the old Africanization policies calls for the economic empowerment of "indigenous" peoples but recognizes the intrinsic importance of *private* accumulation. In theory, such empowerment strategies are a thoughtful attempt to use legislation to compensate for structural disadvantages among black Africans, who have been historically excluded from market participation. Like earlier policies of Africanization, however, even the most well-meaning indigenization initiative is potentially vulnerable to abuse. Existing firms that are owned and controlled by nonblacks may feel significant pressure, in the form of thinly veiled threats, on the one end of the spectrum to extortion, on the other, to open their doors to black politically connected elites, who then acquire deeply discounted or even cost-free shareholdings or managerial positions. Conversely, it is hardly uncommon for nonblack owned companies, which typically have far greater business experience and access to capital, to bribe state officials in order to avoid having to comply with indigenization legislation in any meaningful way.

In my view, indigenization programs that in practice focus only on a narrow elite are imperfect and perhaps even objectionable. There are definite signs of this in South Africa's black economic empowerment program, despite the fact that the issue was the subject of years of study and debate in the country.[20] Indeed, widespread frustration of the perceived narrow beneficiaries of the program led to the enactment of a new "broad-based" black economic empowerment program in 2003, although many of the problems continue. In Namibia too, with its similar demographic profile, Henning Melber argues that black economic empowerment policies facilitated the emergence of a "crypto-capitalist, petty-minded, self-enriching new black elite, which expends its energy of exploiting the public purse."[21]

Yet despite its ill-gotten gain, even this narrow elite is capable, nonetheless, of generating positive externalities. Indeed, the potential for indigenization efforts to be corrupted, resulting in a mere replacement of a few white or Asian business elites by an equally small number of black ones, should not lead us to conclude that the beneficiaries of indigenization are simply cardboard cutouts—engaging solely in rent seeking and ultimately leave everybody worse off—rather than potentially viable businesspeople, regardless of their origins. Certainly, indigenization facilitates opportunism by well-placed regime cronies, yet even if that process is hijacked by self-interested elites, it need not preclude opportunities for value-added investment, wage labor expansion, and the generation of surplus and wealth creation in historically disadvantaged communities.

For all the country's problems, Zimbabwe's indigenization program provides several illustrations of this phenomenon. As in other countries, Africanization of the public sector began shortly after independence, although the modern private sector-oriented program, employing the nomenclature of "indigenization," did not take hold until the early 1990s. In recent years, indigenization has come to be associated most closely with the seizures of white-owned agricultural land by regime loyalists; in the main, therefore, indigenization has been an economic disaster. Yet a few actors have navigated this terrain adroitly, blending political access, and the patronage that flows from it, with genuine business acumen.

One-time music producer Philip Chiyangwa is a prominent example of a crony capitalist-turned-business magnate. Politically and economically savvy, Chiyangwa was able to parlay his proximity to the political class, including a familial relationship to Robert Mugabe, into a business conglomerate. In 1993, Chiyangwa, then a thirty-four-year-old music producer, founded the Affirmative Action Group, together with his partner, the late Peter Pamire. This entity served as the personal vehicle through which Chiyangwa acquired both wealth and a national reputation. The ostensible goal of the body was black empowerment, but the method was intimidation and extortion: firms would be certified "affirmative-action compliant" in return for contracting an agreement, an ownership stake, and, it was alleged, outright side payments. Chiyangwa led the "group," which was never able to document actual members, until 1998. Having enabled Chiyangwa's ascent but lacking institutional continuity, it petered out not long thereafter.

Although he was not initially taken very seriously, with the tacit and at times explicit support of Mugabe behind him, Chiyangwa became feared by many, both white and black, among Zimbabwe's more conventional business class. Significantly, in 1996, Chiyangwa served as chairman of President Mugabe's reelection campaign. Though a largely ceremonial role, it not only cemented Chiyangwa's position as a national figure but gave him the invaluable imprimatur of the president. Chiyangwa's own foray into electoral politics began about the same time, and in the controversial 2000 election he was even elected as a member of parliament from the Zimbabwe African National Union–Patriotic Front for Chinoyi and became party chairman for the Mashonaland West province. Chiyangwa leveraged ruling party politics and elected office to his significant advantage, at least for several years.

In 2000, Chiyangwa, together with businessman Mutumwa Mawere, became head of the National Economic Consultative Forum's anticorruption subcommittee. However ironically, Chiyangwa's role, according to one well-placed observer, was "to harass successful private companies. Mawere provides Chiyangwa with the financial analysis and strategies he needs to attack successful companies that ZANU-PF wants an interest in. Their first targets [were] Econet Wireless and Kingdom Holdings," which were then dubiously charged with corrupt stock transactions. There was "a slow but steady transfer in Kingdom stock staring about the time the assault began."[22]

Econet and Kingdom Securities were, famously, firms started and skillfully expanded by black Zimbabwean entrepreneurs Strive Masiyiwa and Nigel Chanakira, respectively. Thus, it is evident that although the rhetoric of "indigenization" remained part of the Zimbabwe African National Union–Patriotic Front's approach, it was supplanted in practice by a semiofficial policy of targeting real and perceived enemies of the state. Chiyangwa clearly benefited from this as well, though he himself fell out of political favor beginning about 2005 and was victimized by political interference by political and economic rivals. Although the adage "Live by the sword, die by the sword" has a certain poignancy here, Chiyangwa undeniably created one of Zimbabwe's most formidable business empires in this decade, represented by his holding company, New Africa Investments Ltd. Political interference aside, not all of the companies he controlled thrived—a once prominent footwear company, G and D shoes, for example, collapsed owing to larger economic conditions—but Chiyangwa is undeniably a gifted, if mercenary, entrepreneur. By acquiring controlling stakes in legitimate companies, he turned kinship into capital.

THE PROCESS OF TRANSFORMATION

In those places where patronage resources are increasingly limited, particularly in the absence of oil or another high-value commodity, once-favored groups cannot rely on state generated largesse ad infinitum. Admittedly, many reform processes, like privatization, generate additional rents, however, these are finite sources: once the bulk of SOEs are privatized, the ability of elites to profit on their sale is gone. On the whole, economic reforms contribute to a diminished *supply* of patronage, while political reforms, even if initially modest, render kickbacks, extortion, and other illicit means ever more costly. Other aspects of the liberalization regime, such as currency market liberalization or increased transparency—demanded, if not always achieved, by both domestic and international constituencies—have also engendered opportunities for business that may have been foreclosed under the ancien régime. This is not to suggest that erstwhile crony capitalists and their ilk become personally virtuous; indeed, their personal attributes are essentially irrelevant. Rather, since at least 2000, African crony capitalists have found themselves confronting the colossal changes in the institutional environment detailed in chapters 2 and 3 of this book.

Where crony businesses can longer depend on a reliable supply of patronage, they become more dependent on predictable access to capital, markets, and labor and on more predictable behavior by governments. (Many governments have also been compelled to respond, gradually moving away from confiscatory taxes, capricious policies, and inadequate legal protections.) Those crony capitalists who are incapable of adapting to the new conditions may continue to benefit in the short term, but over time they will find patronage resources constricted, along with opportunities. Conversely, those who make this transition are able to identify new opportunities—for diversification of production and markets, for profit, and for growth—in a changed landscape. As suggested elsewhere in this book, this phenomenon of transformation is not unknown; rather, it is just rarely associated with Africa.

The Mechanism of Transformation

Cronyism and corruption plague all polities. They are the seemingly ineradicable consequences of economic systems that, in the view of most theorists, inhibit economic growth and development. Some scholars tell us that self-interest may lead to willingness to engage in corrupt pursuits but, as Mushtaq Khan argues, it is greed *plus* discretion to act on it that enables corruption to occur. In environments where mature political and economic institutions and regulations are lacking, such malfeasance in business, as well between political and economic actors, becomes more pervasive. Nonexistent or unenforced oversight mechanisms present opportunities for corrupt politicians, their cronies, and criminal networks to advance private agendas at the expense of the public interest. As Susan Rose-Ackerman and others demonstrate, corruption is nearly always economically suboptimal.

I am not advocating corruption and certainly not prescribing it as a development strategy; to do so would be foolhardy. But crony capitalism is neither culturally determined, nor is it path dependent. Indeed, examples of the transformation of crony capitalists are found throughout the globe, including in Russia of the late 1990s. According to Vadim Volkov, the somewhat experimental capitalism, Russian-style, of that period frequently saw business as a site of "violent entrepreneurship," promulgated by groups, often mafia-affiliated, who built enforcement partnerships and protection rackets with fledgling enterprises.[23] Given the disorder that characterized the transitional Russian polity at the time, this system instilled a degree of regularization and stability in an otherwise unpredictable environment for business. Perhaps paradoxically, violent entrepreneurs were institution builders, providing a framework for security, contract enforcement, dispute settlement, and provision of information as well as a bridge to state agencies that the Yeltsin-led state was simply unable to provide.[24] Thus, an environment was fostered in which an entrepreneurial class, although not wholly unconstrained, could begin to expand.

Protection fees were high, reaching 20–30 percent of some businesses' revenues, and drawn by this successful and profitable enterprise, criminal groups took substantial ownership stakes in businesses as well.[25] Yet the more deeply involved in business violent entrepreneurs became, they more they began to take part in management and decision making. It was as owners of business rather than as merely extortionists and providers of "protection" that erstwhile criminal syndicates moved to both legitimize and consolidate their holdings. Although not all mafiosi in Russia followed this path, Volkov suggests that those who did demonstrated significant business savvy. In addition, they became increasingly concerned with both access to and exercise of political and economic power.

Essentially, these actors went as far as they could using violent entrepreneurship; business expansion, on the other hand, required a different set of tools, and they pursued a range of policies that supported reasonable taxation and property rights protections.[26] "Criminal businesses . . . abandon less legitimate activities once they have sufficient ability to maintain wealth and once they have achieved social respectability in a legitimate society."[27] Transitional Russia's particular brand of capitalist big men, therefore, helped to shore up a fragile political economy in a state that was noticeably deficient in the provision of protection of business interests and, indeed, of law and order.

Of course, not all crony capitalists are cast in the mold of the Russian violent entrepreneur, whose nearest African equivalent might be the warlord capitalist. Notwithstanding an international media preoccupied with images of atrocities and chaos, most contemporary African polities are not as lawless as Yeltsin-era Russia. Moreover, unlike Russia, most African countries had some experience, albeit limited, with business and capitalism, and many cronies who expanded into "legitimate capitalism" began with a modest business background. Thus, Africans may have held some advantage over their Russian counterparts. Ceteris paribus, experienced businesspeople, even if corrupted, arguably have a greater chance of success than do opportunistic neophytes. To be sure, although many African cronies were enriched by their newfound proximity to the state, not all used their positions and business acumen (or lack thereof), to develop *sustainable* business empires; Malawi's President Muluzi and Zambia's former defense minister Ben Mwila are examples of this failure.[28]

Yet there is no reason that a viable, or potentially viable, enterprise should fail merely because its origins are illicit. Instead, we must look for explanations of success and failure in the motivations of and the resources available to the crony capitalist; his prior experience in business, if any; the nature of the enterprise; the patronage resources in the political economy and, not least, the prevailing macroeconomic conditions.

Evidence of Redemption and Legitimation

That cronies can be redeemed and rehabilitated as credible business actors is not to suggest that they undergo some kind of spiritual transformation—from rapacious cronies to diehard adherents of corporate social responsibility. In fact, such a change of heart is hardly necessary, and herein lie the problems inherent in neopatrimonial-style critiques. Neopatrimonialism is regularly associated with personal and often cultural depravity, yet for all the unreserved self-interest assigned to neopatrimonial elites, we disregard self-interest when it comes to their businesses! I do not doubt that, with the exception of those possessing entrepreneurial spirit bordering on zealotry, most businesspeople would prefer a guaranteed annuity from a political sponsor and ally to the rough and tumble of the marketplace. But annuities in the form of patronage are hardly immutable from year to year. Although political connections are the lifeblood of contemporary corporate existence the world over, a given business recipient of state largesse, regardless of geography, cannot assume he or she will continue to have access to patronage, especially in the context of regime change. Africa's businesspeople are, ultimately, as much motivated by the desire to accumulate wealth—in a word, *profit*—as businesspeople elsewhere. Thus, to suggest that they are capable only of pursuing the short-term and often nonrenewable gratification of patronage, as suggested by neopatrimonialism's adherents, while eschewing longer-term (and investment) horizons is as racist as it is exaggerated.

Many examples of "cronies gone good" can be found in American history. Rockefeller, Gould, Huntington, and others were widely regarded as the robber barons of nineteenth-century America. Often vilified in their day, more contemporary analyses take a much more nuanced, even favorable, view. The example of Colis P. Huntington and his colleague Leland Stanford, the California governor and university founder, is illustrative. Like African businessmen-cum-politicians and their dubious privatizations, the pair secured public assets at virtually no cost for their own private interests. Although Huntington and Stanford did not always win favorable votes in Congress, they built the Central Pacific Railroad, a $25 million project, on just a $50,000 investment. They employed a range of methods, some legitimate but many unethical and probably illegal, in pursuit of their corporate objectives. In the end, they built a formidable business empire and great personal wealth. However, the spillover effects were noteworthy: they also contributed to the establishment of the national railroad infrastructure in the United States and furthered the nation's economic expansion.

Admittedly, Africa as yet has few Huntingtons and Stanfords, though their emergence is not unthinkable in the contemporary climate. Those potentially in this class of tycoons include Strive Masiyiwa, South Africa's Reul Khoza, and Sudanese-born Mohammed Ibrahim (importantly, these and Africa's other magnates have not been associated with any crony capitalist origins, so I discuss them in chapter 6). On the other hand, those I highlight here, whose crony capitalist origins are not obscure, tend to be as yet smaller economic players. What their stories reveal, however, is that these actors have remade their companies as credible, even upstanding, commercial enterprises. Personal transformation, from predator to plutocrat is also characteristic.

One example of both business and personal reform, albeit on a small scale, is the Burkina Faso businessman and one-time civil servant Seydou Idani. He attracted allegations of corruption in his business activities, yet it remains unclear whether Idani profited *directly* from his position in the Burkinabé state. Idani has served as a government appointee, including as head of the government's public works and job creation agency, although he was implicated in a corruption scandal involving bogus World Bank consulting contracts.[29] In 2004, the World Bank blacklisted both Idani and one of his companies, Alpha Training and Consulting, as part of an investigation into kickbacks going back a decade. Its investigation alleged that Idani, who had received several no-bid technology-related contracts, served as a middleman between the corrupt World Bank staff economist Leslie Jean-Robert Pean and companies seeking bank contracts for public works and employment projects.[30] The World Bank found that the theft and corruption were widespread in these projects in Senegal, Burkina Faso, and elsewhere. Yet the corruption involved in Idani's dealings both with Pean and others was potentially much larger than the investigation revealed publicly, given Idani's role as head of the corresponding government agency in Burkina Faso.[31]

Despite the naming and shaming that attends international blacklisting and his association with one of the most notorious incidents of corruption by bank personnel, a history of conflicts of interest (in roles as a bureaucrat with oversight responsibilities and a private businessperson) and his apparent predilection for rent seeking rather than genuine entrepreneurship, Seydou Idani fashioned at least one of his companies, Nouvelle Espace Technologies (NET), into a viable and *respected* enterprise. In 2000, Idani established NET as a technology company specializing in the sale of computers and related hardware and software, as well as network installation and computer training.[32] The Burkina Faso firm is hardly a giant, but it appears to have successfully overcome an inauspicious heritage, counting among its clients the U.S. Peace Corps and the NGO Save the Children, as well as government agencies and local nonprofits.[33] In fact, the company attracted a host of high-profile international business, including a $100,000 contract for logistics and network support on a good governance project, and was designated by Dell Computers as a premium service partner in the region.[34]

Idani himself emerged as an establishment businessman. Following his founding of NET he became vice treasurer of the Association of Import-Exporters, vice president of the President's Economic and Social Advisory Council's Economic and Finance Committee, and an active member in the Lion's Club, the quintessential bastion of corporate social responsibility and respectability.[35] His transformation complete, Idani was named IT manager of the year in Burkina Faso for 2005.[36]

At bottom, though NET certainly appears to be a more modest-sized operation than those undertaken by other members of the "bureaucratic bourgeoisie," it also appears to have found a key business niche in which to operate, apparently both legitimately and profitably. In some respects, the relatively small size of such firms may allow their politico-entrepreneur founders to engage in business activities under the radar and largely unfettered by a prying international or domestic public. They may also be more resistant to scrutiny by both international community watchdogs and potential domestic rivals.

Uganda's ENHAS also underwent a transformation, overcoming the company's murky origins via Uganda's equally opaque privatization process in the 1990s. In fact, ENHAS emerged as a respected player in a competitive marketplace. As Salim Saleh and Sam Kutesa receded into the background, the principal public face of ENHAS became Georges Tytens, a European who was brought in as managing director in 1998 (after UAC sold its shares). Tytens himself has been recognized by the International

Labour Organisation for his management skills and by the French government for service, honors that not only bolstered his own reputation but redounded positively to that of the company.[37]

We see a different kind of transformation in Zimbabwe's Philip Chiyangwa, whose business holdings eventually came to include some of Zimbabwe's most well established companies. Brash and outspoken, Chiyangwa relished women, gaudy houses, expensive suits, and fast cars. Yet he was also an adroit political operator, as well as a savvy businessman and investor, even if the origins of his investments or his methods of acquisition raised eyebrows.

Chiyangwa amassed a vast, multisectoral business empire in real estate, metals, and manufacturing, employing a network of politically influential and interconnected holding companies, such as Native Africa Investments Ltd., and Midiron Investments. Through Midiron, one of Chiyangwa's highest-profile acquisitions was G and D Shoes, a once profitable firm that was in fact undone by the competitive effects of trade liberalization. His Native Africa amassed also a trove of companies, including ZECO, one of Zimbabwe's largest steel fabrication and metals engineering companies. ZECO Holdings, the result of a 2007 merger with Crittal-Hope, reportedly had a value in excess of US $300 million; the combined firm fell under Chiyangwa's control. Chiyangwa's Pinnacle Property Holdings acquired a vast portfolio, including some of Zimbabwe's most prized real estate, and the Phillip Chiyangwa Family Trust held significant ownership positions in several of Zimbabwe's other leading companies. Although some of these enterprises struggled in the 2000s, their difficulties can be traced more to the conditions of the Zimbabwean economy as a whole than to Chiyangwa's now renowned business acumen.

Faustian Bargains

Like Uganda's Salim Saleh and Sam Kutesa, Philip Chiyangwa discovered that "insiderism" is not a license to permanent privilege and sinecure on the state's dole. Cronies who do not move to put their businesses on a stable, and more legitimate, footing remain more vulnerable to continued interference from their often capricious (erstwhile) benefactors—even if that benefactor is one's own kin. Indeed, the emergence of ENHAS is a quintessential case of regime insiders advancing their economic interests as a result of their positions in or proximity to government. Yet the firm and its principals became regular targets for criticism by the very regime to which ENHAS owed its existence.

Upon taking over the air cargo business in Uganda, ENHAS quickly became an example of an uncompetitive private monopoly that replaced the equally uncompetitive public monopoly. Between 1999 and 2003 ENHAS drew criticism from both domestic and international actors for mismanagement and inefficiency and was accused of being a drag on the country's resource export markets. In fact, by July 2000, the Ministry of Finance was suggesting that the ENHAS monopoly was impeding development: the absence of competition meant inadequate technical and management expertise in the sector, as well as a lack of efficiency in refrigeration and cold storage. Many of the Uganda government's strategic plans therefore stressed the importance of opening ENHAS to competition, and the government ultimately determined that ENHAS's monopoly would be abolished and new entrants would be introduced through a competitive bidding process. ENHAS was not simply criticized for its monopolistic inefficiency; the firm was also taken to task by no less than President Museveni himself, who admonished the firm for being insufficiently patriotic.[38]

The government criticism directed at ENHAS is, at first blush, puzzling, not least because President Museveni's own brother, Salim Saleh, was a prominent participant in the ENHAS transaction, as was Sam Kutesa, a government minister. In Uganda, part of the criticism directed at ENHAS was itself a response to domestic and international pressure on the Museveni government—long a darling of the donor community— which needed to appear to be acting against favoritism and corruption.

In Zimbabwe, Philip Chiyangwa discovered that some of his sponsors in the ruling party found his access threatening to their own interests, despite or perhaps because of his family connection with President Mugabe. Certainly, not all of Chiyangwa's business ventures bore fruit, but he also faced substantial challenges of an unambiguously *political* nature from various rivals. After a meteoric political rise—including stints as chair of President Mugabe's 1996 reelection committee and as a member of parliament—which in many ways mirrored his business growth, Chiyangwa left politics. No longer the golden boy of Mugabe, he retreated to a lower profile—certainly relative to jet-setting image he aggressively promoted between 1994 and 2004.

Interestingly, Chiyangwa's fall from grace appears to have had more to do with political missteps than with business ones. Beginning about 2004, Chiyangwa ran afoul of the Zimbabwe African National Union–Patriotic Front and his erstwhile benefactor Mugabe. He was arrested on multiple occasions in 2004 and 2005.[39]

Chiyangwa was pressured to give up ownership of Pinnacle, and he was undoubtedly pressured to sell the lucrative Midiron Enterprises to Sonanke Holdings, an entity controlled by the family of then attorney general Sobusa Gula-Ndebele, whose office pursued Chiyangwa in a case of alleged espionage; the sale was transacted eerily close to the legal proceedings—providing more evidence of the "live by the sword, die by the sword" ethos of patrimonial capitalism. Two of Midiron's key assets, G and D Shoes, which supplied footwear to the South African market prior to its closure and liquidation, and Belmont Leather, which exported leather to France, were valuable earners of foreign exchange.[40]

Ultimately, the flamboyance with which Chiyangwa approached his business activities and his wealth, cars, playboy lifestyle, and political life turned off many and created rivalries among powerful political counterparts. Having found himself on more than one occasion on the bad side of the Zimbabwe African National Union–Patriotic Front, the fact that by the 2000s he became decidedly less flamboyant and significantly less visible in his activities suggests that there are limits to even cronies playing the political game. In Zimbabwe, they must be mindful of what happened to their counterparts, and indeed, Chiyangwa is fairly lucky by that standard; Mutumwa Mawere was also deprived of his assets, and businessman James Makamba, for instance, lost control of his corporate interests and nearly lost his life. Others were harassed by the regime.

Of course, there is no guarantee that state actors will leave reformed cronies alone and respect their desire to recede into the apolitical background—the occasional harassment of Chiyangwa, Salim Saleh, and, for that matter, the Russian oligarchs under then president Vladimir Putin, indicates this. Ultimately, like Chiyangwa, these actors would rather quietly retain their interests and continue to acquire wealth than maintain a high profile, where they remain more visible targets. Certainly, this is individualistic, perhaps even isolating, behavior considering the elite company they formerly kept; the opportunities for the amalgamation of interests—economic *and* political—as a class presupposes a critical mass of actors with whom to align.

Certainly, nondemocratic regimes make political interference in the affairs of business more likely, whether those businesses are illegitimate, legitimate, or somewhere in between. The rule of law is capriciously applied, weak state and societal institutions may not adequately protect individuals and firms, and there is a regular need to score cheap political points in order to maintain at least a veneer of popular legitimacy (hence scapegoating and show trials are commonplace). Cronies may find it expedient to distance themselves, at least publicly, from their business holdings as a means of protecting their investments.

ECONOMIC SPILLOVER EFFECTS

In the first instance, firms based on cronyism wish to maintain ties to their political and state benefactors. Firms generally seek little to no taxation, flexible employment laws or at least few restrictions on employment, and limited competition. Businesses founded in the crony capitalist tradition, especially those in an authoritarian or semiauthoritarian environment, enjoy such latitude almost by definition, and they typically have the added benefit of operating in an environment in which they are protected from domestic and international competition. Yet these perquisites are of limited benefit to *national* wealth and development, however much they may aid individuals. The transformation of such businesses thus makes contributions possible in the areas of taxation, meaningful employment, and even competition, which can in turn foster higher efficiencies and value added.

To the extent that these linkages become a liability, however, erstwhile cronies may not become devotees of Milton Friedman, but they do develop a newfound appreciation for the market. The experience of the Ugandan company ENHAS again provides a useful illustration. As noted, crony capitalists are often monopolists, or would like to be, and as long as they curry favor with the regime (or hold political power themselves), they may be protected from competition. As dwindling patronage leads erstwhile cronies to begin to wean themselves from the state, private competitors emerge. Importantly, however, potential competitors may come not only from the market but from other bureaucrats and politicians who want in on the business.

Prior to the privatization of ENHAS, the London-based cargo company Dairo Air Services (DAS) operated as an independent cargo carrier in Uganda. During the privatization of ENHAS, DAS was exempted from having to use ENHAS to handle its cargo and was allowed to set up its own handling services instead. Licensed to compete with ENHAS for handling contracts in 2001, DAS made significant inroads in the Ugandan market, including winning a $200,000 contract from Kenya Airways in 2005 that had previously been awarded to ENHAS.[41] Perhaps not surprisingly, DAS is not without government ties itself; the company was reported to have close ties with CAA officials. In fact, a scandal erupted when DAS received a USh2.2 billion tax waiver from the CAA, without the requisite approval from business and finance minister John Nasasira. It is worth noting that Nasasira was himself investigated for his involvement in the ENHAS privatization, although he was not officially censured, as was Sam Kutesa. Clearly, ENHAS and DAS had different godfathers in the Ugandan state, but the rivalry appears to have played out in a way that actually *enhances* rather than diminishes competition; this is beneficial for the sector, as well as consumers. Indeed, a third company, Fresh Handling Ltd., which specializes in floriculture exports, also received a license to handle cargo at Entebbe. Each company established its own warehouse facilities at the airport.

The transformation of ENHAS produced a very favorable outlook, notwithstanding the company's inauspicious beginnings.[42] Within a decade of its privatization, ENHAS's business was growing at a very rapid rate. The volume of passengers and produce increased markedly between 2002 and 2005. For example, fish products grew by over 400 percent between 2002 and 2005, and the handling of fruits and vegetables increased by 30 percent in the same period. To meet rising demand, the company doubled its employees from 150 to 300 and began an aggressive investment in infrastructure and capital equipment. ENHAS invested in major refrigeration and warehousing facility at Entebbe, at a cost of $800,000, in order to meet EU export standards. Moreover, between 1998 and 2003, the company purchased $6 million worth of equipment at Entebbe and planned to invest an additional $3 million upcountry between 2003 and 2005 in order to expand its operation to additional airports in Uganda.

Thus, by 2006, ENHAS appeared to be on solid footing, and its expansion to new upcountry airports and operations was under way. In addition, the company won a three-year contract to operate ten UN-operated airports in the Democratic Republic of

Congo and negotiated to manage an additional ten air facilities in Sudan. In the transaction with the Democratic Republic of Congo, ENHAS successfully beat out three international handling companies (firms from the United States, Australia, and South Africa), and its bid had the support of Congolese, French, and Ugandan diplomats. In awarding the contract to ENHAS, the United Nations cited the company's commitment to employee development as the primary reason for its selection.

Indeed, the company's role and responsibility as an employer appears to have emerged as one of its strong suits. Although still a relatively small employer, ENHAS has earned a reputation for high labor standards on a continent not often known for them. In fact, the firm has won several awards as one of Uganda's best employers, which managing director Georges Tytens attributes to ENHAS's commitment to employee development. ENHAS provides opportunities for promotion, demonstrating a preference for internal hiring, thereby allowing baggage workers to move up to office jobs, and awards bonuses to outstanding employees. It also budgets some $25,000 annually for employee training and emphasizes occupational safety. Tytens also insists that ENHAS has emerged as a valued corporate citizen in Uganda by, for example, providing malaria treatment and bed nets to all of its workers. Although these claims appear slightly self-congratulatory, the firm's favorable labor practices were subsequently corroborated by none other than the International Labour Organisation.[43] ENHAS was also recognized in 2005 by International Air Transport Association for its excellent service.

CONCLUSION: TRANSFORMING MARKET AND STATE?

The examples highlighted in this chapter illustrate that crony capitalists can transform themselves from mere appendages of the state to independent capitalists. The factors that precipitate these changes are patronage declines, changes in the macroeconomic environment, or political changes that alter their role in the system—or a combination of all three. "Virtue"—even though some of these actors may acquire it and go on to be great philanthropists or seemingly selfless magnates of some kind (à la Huntington of nineteenth century America)—is not required. In the process of transforming themselves, these actors can also change the markets in which they operate. These impacts include providing employment and a more reliable tax base, spurring their own (and state) investment in infrastructure, helping to provide impetus for emergence of ancillary businesses or the development of upstream and downstream firms, and even generating competition. They can help precipitate a transition from more closed markets to more open ones. But what about the state?

Can erstwhile cronies transform the state itself? At best, revisiting some of the themes introduced in chapter 2, perhaps we can only say that with more entrepreneurs, both legitimate and otherwise, economic and/or political regime transformation is more likely. But "business," broadly conceived, is only one of the factors influencing such transformation. Business alone cannot be the sole cause of change in Africa; other endogenous forces, as well as externally derived ones, such as the aid regime, political leadership and ideology, economic resources, and so on, are also critical factors.

Clearly, there are limits to the transformative power of crony capitalists, even if they themselves have been transformed into captains of more legitimate pursuits. The experiences of Chiyangwa, Kutesa, Idani, even Salim Saleh, and the like suggest that in more restrictive political climates, at least, the capacity of these nouveaux riches entrepreneurs to effect change in the state, à la Marx's bourgeoisie, is limited. Even if they have abandoned state largesse—whether willingly or as a result of being cut off from it—and are no longer dependent on political benefactors, there are seldom sufficient numbers of former cronies to press for change, save at the margins and at the level of their own firms. Thus, Zimbabwe and Uganda, two nominally democratic states, can have legitimate businesses operating for profit—and trying, notwithstanding political constraints and the economic blight, to reinvest in their operations—amid a capricious clientelist state.

The Value of Cronies

This chapter should not be read as an apology for crony capitalism in Africa or anywhere else, for that matter. Social science and popular literature are replete with analyses of the danger of cronyism and corruption, which impose social and political as well as economic costs on populations.

Certainly, we must take care not to "advocate" cronyism as a *substitute* for or satisfactory alternative to "traditional" capitalism (notwithstanding its own varied definitions and interpretations) in Africa. Rather, considering the expropriation and externalization of Zimbabwean monies during the last decade, we should ask what it is that makes cronies reinvest rather than export their "surplus." It is the presence of a local market, that is, demand, and opportunity for profit. If cronies can recirculate their monies—however ill gotten—in the domestic economy, an opportunity exists for genuine transformation. Moreover, although Patrick Bond rightly assails the Zimbabwe situation—in which by his estimate $24 billion in capital flight (much of it crony capital) has departed the country in recent years—one is left to wonder whether such of exporting of "dividends" by Zimbabwe's corrupt political elite is altogether different from MNCs in Africa's mining sector, with their tax holidays, labor exemptions, and repatriation of profits.[44]

Susan Rose-Ackerman rejects the notion that corruption might have "developmental value," stating that "because criminals are as interested in getting rich as anyone, optimists might contend that if criminals actually control the government they will modify their ways. But this seems utopian."[45] She further claims that the net result of this criminally controlled state is an interest in "quick profits" rather than an industrial base and, ultimately, the undermining of capitalist institutions. Colin Leys and

Nicolas van de Walle are also among the skeptics.[46] I would respond by emphasizing that it is important to distinguish between mere corruption and so-called ghost companies, such as Kenya's Goldenberg International and Anglo-Leasing, or Zambia's Carlington Sales, to name a few, and bona fide going concerns. The former are examples of outright theft and were never remotely viable *as businesses*. Moreover, I am hardly suggesting that reforming cronies is a preferred route, only that it is one that has some validity and therefore cannot be dismissed out of hand.

That Africa would be better off without corruption is self-evident. But this chapter is not about things as we *wish* them to be. Instead this chapter has emphasized how Africa can and does make use over the corruption and cronyism it *has,* thereby aiming to present a much more realistic look at political economy on the continent. Moreover, although the chapter does not allow for extensive interregional comparisons, it strenuously rejects the notion that cronyism and corruption are sui generis in Africa. Others have overcome the limitations and constraints imposed by cronyism and corruption without undermining the very essence of capitalism, and so will Africa. However, as the rest of this book indicates, the path described in this chapter is scarcely the only route to business development—or indeed, development writ large—in contemporary Africa.

GOING CONTINENTAL, GOING GLOBAL
Africa's Corporate "Giants"

INTRODUCTION

The champions of the view that Africa is "open for business" display an almost unbridled enthusiasm for Africa's private sector development prospects. Even those who insist that business in Africa is an exercise in intrepidity, such as the producers of the preposterously titled 2009 CNBC series "Dollars and Danger: Africa, the Final Investing Frontier," wish to convey that there are great opportunities for entrepreneurship in Africa.[1] Notwithstanding the enthusiasm of this crowd for business on the continent, their interest is mainly in the potential of small- and medium-scale enterprises, which tends to be the focus of most policy initiatives as well as academic research. Indeed, the principal target of private sector development programs, as described in chapter 3, is expansion of SMEs. Likewise, though their aim is analytical rather than promotional, Ramachandran, Gelb and Shah similarly focus on medium-sized firms, analyzing the constraints faced by entities of this size.

This preoccupation with micro-, small-, and medium-scale enterprises stands in stark contrast to the level of attention given to large-scale enterprises on the continent. Indeed, when the subject is big business in Africa, the discussion nearly always refers to *foreign* companies. In short, because Africa is hardly known as a haven for big business, that is, transnational firms *domiciled in Africa,* popular media, policy analyses, and scholarship alike tend to disregard them. As Leslie Sklair and Peter Robbins point out, this tendency is not confined to discussions about Africa—outside of the Asian newly industrialized countries and China, corporations from the Third World are widely overlooked or assumed to be confined to extractive sectors—but it is particularly acute in commentary on Africa.[2] Indeed, the idea of big business in *and from* Africa simply does not comport with conventional understandings of the business climate.

Such assessments are misguided. Contrary to popular perceptions, Africa has its own corporate giants, many of which have a regional, continental and, increasingly, global footprint. Recognition of this scope must necessarily impact the way in which "business" is conventionally perceived on the continent. Therefore, as with other themes and issues highlighted in this book, the existence of giants, especially those most visibly engaged in regionalization and internationalization, demands that we both discard the crude assumptions about "Africa as basket case" and revisit the equally anachronistic assumption that Africa is inhospitable to business—whether domestic or foreign, "indigenous" or "minority," in origin. Indeed, much of popular—and, distressingly, scholarly—understanding of Africa is based on perception—or more appropriately misperception. While regrettable, it also reminds us of the importance of image: Africa's negative reputation thus becomes self-perpetuating and certainly destructive once it manifests itself everywhere from the Corruption Perceptions Index to the millennium development goals to the representation of all of Africa as a Conradian "heart of darkness."

One way to rethink and reorder those misplaced perceptions is to render African businesses of significant size visible, especially those with capacity to invest abroad. In short, the emerging global presence of certain African companies, regardless of ownership, benefits all firms from the continent. But the visibility of these giants is more than merely of symbolic value to their counterparts among emergent medium- to large-scale enterprises from sub-Saharan Africa. Indeed, it actually enhances the capacity of Africa *writ large* to market the very idea of African business by establishing precedents and partnerships and portraying sub-Saharan Africa as a site of entrepreneurial activity. Such developments, by promoting virtuous circles, should decisively put to rest any residual notions of "African business"—and certainly the broader "business in Africa"—as oxymoron.

Clearly, what constitutes a "giant" is, to some extent, in the eye of the beholder; there are numerous ways of measuring the size of firms for the purpose of comparison, and each method has its drawbacks. Moreover, most of the sub-Saharan Africa's giant firms are big only in relation to typical companies on the continent, and few rank on global indices that are not limited to developing countries, for example. Importantly, however, despite the fact that African corporations are smaller than their global counterparts, they nonetheless qualify as *big* across a range of conventional indicators, whether defined by asset values, number of employees, output, domestic or international market share, or some combination of these factors.[3] Rankings of the top African businesses now appear on several indices, and the variety of firms may surprise naysayers.

Geographically, the leading sources of Africa's big businesses are the Anglophone countries of eastern and southern Africa, with their more established history of large-scale private sector activity, itself owing partly to settler origins. This legacy affects the demographic profile of Africa's giants in important ways. Indeed, one factor that becomes apparent almost immediately is that among the giants, even those with a mainly domestic profile (i.e., whose business operations are limited primarily to one country), firms owned by black Africans are still relatively rare. Although increasingly there are examples of black firms transcending SME status—either through natural growth or initial emergence as a larger entity—by and large, because of their scale and capital limitations, it is more difficult, however, for black or so-called indigenous African firms to export themselves or translocate than it is for minority-owned or minority-controlled firms. Nonetheless, a number of authentic magnates have emerged that presage the arrival of a new grouping of black big business.

More numerous among large companies are those owned by Africans of Indian and South Asian descent, especially in certain East African markets. Since colonial times, these entrepreneurs have occupied a prominent economic niche, which they have often skillfully expanded. As noted by Vijaya Ramachandran, Manu Kedia Shah, and Stephen Gelb in *Africa's Private Sector,* these companies enjoy nearly as much longevity as their white-owned counterparts and generally greater access to business networks and capital than smaller black-run enterprises. Although not "indigenous," resident Asian-owned firms especially have deep roots in Africa, portray themselves as African in literature, on websites, and in interviews, and often pride themselves, at least publicly, on their ability to relate to and interact with the majority population.[4] Among the leaders are minority companies from Tanzania and Kenya, many of which now have operations throughout the subregion.

On the opposite end of the spectrum, firms long associated with white South Africans—as founders, owners, executives, and leading investors—have had more than a century's head start, and they dominate the rankings of Africa's largest companies. In fact, their presence dates back to the 1652 arrival of the Dutch East India Company in what is today South Africa's Western Cape. Of course, the level of African big business activity—whether primarily domestic-oriented or transnational in scope and whether of "indigenous" or especially minority origin—is nowhere equal to South Africa. Not surprisingly, then, the bulk of the discussion in this chapter focuses on big business in that country. The South African firms that feature prominently here have perfected South-South investment, especially since 1994, and particularly in continental Africa; from the late 1990s, several also began to invest in companies in the global North with great effectiveness. Hence, numerous South African firms now enjoy a global profile.

At bottom, the presence of large corporations both within and from Africa carries practical as well as symbolic significance—a theme that is revisited in the conclusion to this chapter. Indeed, as much as any of the phenomena discussed in this book, the existence of a cohort of big business—*Africa's giants*—compels us to reexamine common assumptions about the cultures of and prospects for business on the continent. A proliferation of big business across a range of sectors can be advantageous for job creation, fostering upstream and downstream linkages and spurring additional investment and jobs. It may also help Africa secure a better place in the world. In this vein, the following sections examine a cross-section of large Africa-based firms. This investigation is not meant to be exhaustive but rather illustrative of the types of firms that have risen to prominence nationally and regionally in Africa. I begin with a sample of non-South African companies before turning to the more plentiful representatives of Africa's wealthiest economy.

AFRICAN'S LARGE CORPORATIONS: NOT JUST A SOUTH AFRICAN PHENOMENON

Even on a brief visit to an African capital, it is fairly easy to ascertain which are the giants of the local economy; most urban residents, at least, will know who the leading captains of industry are and the firms with which they are associated. As I have suggested, however, measuring "bigness" objectively, especially for the purpose of employing a comparative metric, is a more challenging process, as consistent data can be notoriously difficult to acquire. Several indices have ranked global businesses by size, albeit using differing scales. For example, *BusinessWeek's* Global 1200 Index used market value until 2005, whereas the *Fortune* Global 500 ranks companies by revenue. Forbes Global 2000 ranks the world's biggest companies using a composite measure that equally weights sales, profits, assets and market value. Although firms from Africa routinely make these lists, what such Western—and predominantly American— financial magazine rankings have in common is their inevitable exclusion of the relatively less giant African firms.

Two indexes that focus exclusively on Africa provide a far clearer sense of the continent's biggest firms, although each also has its shortcomings. The first, the Dow Jones Africa Titans 50 Index, measures "the stock performance of 50 leading companies that are headquartered or generate the majority of their revenues in Africa." Because the Titans 50 caps the number of stocks from any given country at fifteen, it allows for some diversity in the countries. "Stocks are selected to the index by float-adjusted market capitalization, subject to screens for size and liquidity. . . . The index is modified capitalization weighted, adjusting for free float and to meet diversification requirements." As a result, among the November 2011 rankings, just 25 percent of the companies were South African, 19 percent were Nigerian, 16 percent were Egyptian, and 13 percent were Moroccan.[5] Unfortunately, the only other country with more than one company on the list is Kenya, so we cannot get a clear sense of the identity of big firms operating within other economies. Moreover, since stocks eligible for the Titans 50 are traded on domestic African bourses as well as *international* exchanges, some 10 percent of the companies represented are formally based in the United Kingdom. Again, a fuller *African* list would be more illuminating.

The magazine *African Business* provides a partial corrective. It produces an annual list of the continent's top two hundred firms, ranked by market value. Perhaps predictably, South African firms, followed by Egyptian and, to a lesser extent, Moroccan firms, overwhelmingly dominate this list as well. But the *African Business* ranking has slightly more country variation than the Titans 50 Index: Nigeria has had a number of companies listed, principally in banking and financial services, and multiple companies from Kenya as well as firms from a host of other countries including Botswana, Mauritius, Cote d'Ivoire, and others have also appeared. Like the Dow Jones Titans 50, "Africa's Top 200" also includes local affiliates of multinational firms conducting significant business in Africa, such as the British-based Barclays Bank and Standard Chartered Bank, Guinness (part of UK-based Diageo), and Switzerland's Nestle Corporation. Further, although it lists the country of operation, it does not indicate the provenance of less familiar companies in the ranking. Thus, the casual observer would not know, for example, that Ilovo Sugar Malawi (ranked 136 in 2007) is in fact owned by the South African firm Illovo Sugar, which is itself now a subsidiary of Associated British Foods Plc.[6] Although such is the nature of the modern transnational corporation, establishing the *African* identity of contemporary giant firms objectively remains a challenge.

Nevertheless, the rankings provided by both Dow Jones Titans 50 and *African Business*, as well as another index utilized by an entity called African Investor, provide a useful set of benchmarks or metrics that give us a sense of the sizes and positions of African businesses. Yet my intention here is neither to rely upon these problematic devices nor to devise some sort of new ranking of Africa's biggest businesses. Rather, both worldwide and Africa-only indexes, like the other phenomena described in this book, further illuminate the fact that there is far more to African business than the stereotype. Indeed, notwithstanding the inclusion of certain European subsidiaries and affiliate companies, the indexes show, for example, that Africa is home to a wide variety of big businesses with market values that have ranged from a low of $375 million to a high of $73 billion in early 2007.[7] They demonstrate that, using the lexicon of international finance and investment, African companies can be measured according to the same standards; although admittedly, most are not big enough to rank on indices of the world's biggest firms, a number of them are in fact competitive in the global marketplace.[8] Thus, these indexes are useful innovations inasmuch as they not only fulfill the Western business media-driven desire to rank, but also challenge widespread popular misperceptions about the size of African business, and size is one recognized measure of business power.

But indexing alone is, at best, an imperfect means for gauging the true breadth and national or regional presence of Africa's giants. In addition to the shortcomings already identified, another problem is that such indexes fail to capture many large companies based in Africa, including those that are privately or closely held and those are small internationally and comparatively but that may be big players in small domestic markets. For example, revenue data may not be public. Or equities are not traded because firms may be privately held. Further, even ownership structures may be concealed for political purposes. In short, using many of the common metrics, the bigness of some of Kenya's, Uganda's, and Tanzania's most prominent and well-established companies, for instance, is difficult to "measure."

Thus, to come full circle, it seems that to some extent it is also necessary to utilize at least some subjective measures, such as popular perceptions, to assess the identity of "the giants" after all. To go beyond the international rankings approach, therefore, one must draw also on local knowledge—the impressions of urban denizens, media coverage, a given firm's national and regional visibility—as well as existing scholarship. Hence, I focus here on a limited sample of companies that illuminate a broader understanding of African big business and of business generally. Proceeding in order of general firm size and number, in the following section I first discuss black-identified firms regarded as giants and then turn to more numerous Asian-linked firms before considering giants in South Africa, which, while publicly traded, are historically identified as "white."

Africa's New Tycoons and Black Business Giants

As explained in chapter 1, under colonialism, Africans were permitted to operate ventures only in a tightly circumscribed set of economic sectors and in some cases prohibited from owning businesses altogether. Thus, today it is unsurprising firms owned or controlled by blacks or even publicly associated with black Africans are seldom among the larger or older entities on the continent. Despite increases in the number of big firms closely identified with blacks, the aggregate number of black African entities remains quite small. Several magnates, however, have overcome these structural and historical constraints and established impressive, internationally oriented companies.

The list of such firms is certainly longer than those discussed here; there are "black" firms of formidable size and economic clout in virtually every African country. It is worth considering the full spectrum of companies addressed in chapter 3 and chapter 5 as part of a continuum, of sorts, on which the firms discussed in this chapter also can be located. Some of the emergent companies discussed in chapter 3, like Zimbabwe-born Econet Wireless, are poised to become "giants" in their own right. The viable firms discussed in chapter 5, whose origins lie in political connections and cronyism, may also be giants and vice versa; clearly, the categories are not necessarily mutually exclusive.[9]

The categorization of many companies is less ambiguous, however. A glance at *African Business's* Top 200 Companies list reveals a number of Nigeria-based firms. Although a smattering of nonfinancial sector entities appears—for example, the oil and gas distributor and retailer African Petroleum Plc. and beverage manufacturer Nigerian Breweries, Plc.—most of Nigeria's largest corporations are banks. The Dangote Group, whose publicly-traded Dangote Sugar Refinery Plc. appears on the *African Business* ranking, is noteworthy because it is a multisectoral, conglomerate owned by black Africans. Additionally, its operations span sectors that include light manufacturing, such as sugar refining, flour milling, cement manufacturing, and textiles (a sector long regarded as essential for value-added manufacturing and national development), as well as real estate, oil, and gas. Founded in 1977 by Aliko Dangote, a northern Nigerian businessman from Kano, Dangote Group was employing more than thirteen thousand people by 2009. It is now the country's leading manufacturing-based conglomerate, although considerable portions of its operations remain trade-based. Aliko Dangote himself has been listed for several years among *Forbes* Global Billionaires list, with an estimated net worth of $13.8 billion. The 2008 recession impacted the eponymous firms as well as their founder, forcing, for example, the closure of textile firms in Kano and Lagos. However, Dangote Group's diversity, plus a more conducive economic climate in 2009, continued to create business opportunities for it beginning that year; in October 2009, for example, subsidiaries Dangote Industries Senegal and Dangote Industries Zambia entered into cement procurement and production contracts worth some $228 million with China's Sinoma International Engineering.[10] This is an example of cooperation and partnership with Chinese investors that has generally been elusive in Africa. It is also an excellent example of African business's transnationalization, which has been largely limited to South African companies historically, although Dangote has clearly replicated this pattern; by 2011 the company had additional plants under construction in Tanzania, Congo, and Ethiopia.

Unlike other Nigerian giants, such as African Petroleum and the Dangote Group, Transnational Corporation of Nigeria, Plc. (Transcorp) warrants attention because of its *lack* of success. Indeed, it highlights the difficulties aspiring African giants have as they attempt to replicate an Asian-style "national champions" model of business and economic development; there are few opportunities for shortcuts in contemporary Africa. Transcorp was launched in 2004 as a Nigerian megacompany and effectively designated as a national champion by the administration of then president Olusegun Obasanjo. It aimed to be an industrial company owned and controlled by Nigerians and to be a competitor in Nigeria and internationally in a number of key sectors. Supporters believed that as a private company, Transcorp could achieve efficiencies that have been nonexistent among Nigeria's SOEs, help reduce the country's legendary corruption, and even foster the emergence of a transnational capitalist class that would serve as an effective counterpoise to the rent-seeking compradors that predominate Nigeria's oil-based economy. When the corporation began doing business in 2005, it got off to an auspicious start. Indeed, the company was positioned to acquire stakes in privatized state-owned companies; perhaps it was even established for that purpose, as the company rapidly pursued ownership stakes in the telecommunications, hospitality, and energy sectors. Transcorp bought controlling stakes in the Hilton Hotel in Abuja and Nigerian Telecommunications Ltd. for approximately $105 million and $750 million, respectively.

Though poised to assume a role as a giant, Transcorp suffered an Icarus-like fall. Several questionable dealings raised suspicions about Transcorp's political independence and thus raises questions as to whether the company is more accurately labeled a "crony" than a "giant." Professor Ndi Okereke-Onyuike, the chairperson of Transcorp, served simultaneously as the director general of the Nigerian Stock Exchange, a role that would seem to suggest a conflict of interest, as the exchange listed the Transcorp IPO. An ardent Transcorp supporter, President Obasanjo himself purchased some two hundred million shares of the company—another clear conflict of interest. After the transaction was revealed publicly, he moved the shares into a blind trust that housed his business interests, Obasanjo Holdings Ltd. Yet despite being close to President Obasanjo, Transcorp's demise apparently did not stem from corruption or political meddling, at least not directly.

Transcorp's IPO in August 2007 raised only one-third of the expected capital (₦22 billion vs. ₦60 billion), which was unrelated to concerns about Transcorp's viability, according to Chairman Okereke-Onyuike. Instead, she attributed it to "political risk associated with the change of government and uncertainties about potential actions by the new government [and] institutional investors."[11] In all likelihood, these were not mutually exclusive concerns. Yet whatever the reasons, the undersubscription left the firm with severe liquidity problems, not least because of the massive debt it had assumed to acquire Nigerian Telecommunications Limited, which is popularly known as NITEL. Transcorp failed to fulfill its promise to invest an additional ₦8.9 billion in NITEL within a hundred days, which had been a condition of the acquisition. Many employees went unpaid for months, and the firm suffered a severe contraction in market share from 15 percent to less than 1 percent. In June 2009, the sale of NITEL was reversed, and ownership reverted to the government, which began to seek new buyers. Meanwhile, Transcorp remained with only the Hilton as its principal asset while simultaneously facing low revenues and debts of at least ₦31 billion to Nigerian banks.

Transcorp's experience illustrates at least three things about big business in contemporary Africa. First, moral and rhetorical support from the state and society is not enough; effective business models remain essential. Transcorp's highly leveraged approach to bigness proved unviable, particularly in an environment of immature capital markets. Second, the vagaries of the business and political environment are sometimes difficult to discern, and this is especially true in Nigeria. However, trite as it may seem to say, some enterprises will succeed, whereas others will fail. It remains unclear at the time of writing whether Transcorp will eventually thrive or fold altogether. Third, any business or entrepreneurial venture can prove transient. Indeed, the near failure of Transcorp is no more a reflection on Africa's inhospitable environment for big business than the failure of General Motors (which was later resuscitated with government assistance) or of AOL are indicative of hostility to big business in the United States.

Importantly, a wider view of the field reveals that there is little danger that Transcorp's collapse is symbolic of the direction of big business by black Africans. Indeed, even the other Nigerian cases cited here, African Petroleum and Dangote Group, give lie to that assessment. Moreover, astute international investors are not only aware of a different dimension of African big business but have identified opportunities these firms present for grabbing an immediate market presence through takeovers. Thus, several giants associated with black African magnates have become so prominent in their sectors and internationally that they have become attractive targets for acquisition by non-African suitors. As noted in chapter 4, global multinationals have long done business in Africa either by investing in African companies (especially in natural resource sectors) or by opening their own local affiliates, which enjoyed protected markets. Historically, nearly all of these large-scale transactions were structured as investment partnerships in which African *governments* had a significant shareholding. The acquisition of black, *privately owned* firms of any size by international investors, however, is a novel phenomenon in Africa, but then, so is the emergence of cohort of viable, efficiently managed black companies of sufficient scale to attract the world's attention.

Two prominent examples of this phenomenon are the Ghanaian mining company Ashanti Goldfields, the gold mining company the government of Ghana had maintained a controlling interest in since 1972, and Celtel, the firm founded by Sudanese businessman-cum-philanthropist Mohammad Ibrahim. In 1994, the Ghanaian government began privatizing a significant portion of its shareholding in Ashanti Goldfields, listing shares on the Ghana and London stock exchanges. In 1995, it became the first African company to be listed on the New York Stock Exchange. Under then CEO Ghanaian Sam Jonah, Ashanti increased its gold production by nearly 700 percent, which helped precipitate its 2004 merger with the South Africa–based Anglogold, itself a part of the Anglo American Plc. group. The new company, initially led by Jonah and AngloGold's chief Bobby Godsell, became known as AngloGold Ashanti. With headquarters in South Africa, the combined company is one of the largest gold producers in the world.

Celtel International began operating in 1998 as MSI Cellular Investments. Although domiciled in Europe, Celtel was identified with its founder-executive Ibrahim and with Africa. Ibrahim provides a superb example of African entrepreneurship—he was able to identify a key niche, mobile telecommunications, which today is one of the fastest growing sectors in Africa. Communications infrastructure has long been lacking in Africa; thus Ibrahim's company and other cellular providers such as Kenya's Safaricom and South Africa's MTN and Vodacom have facilitated commercial activities in other sectors as well. In 2005, however, Ibrahim sold the firm to the Kuwaiti company MTC (later known as Zain) for $3.4 billion. Doing business in fifteen African countries, Celtel, which subsequently began to operate under the Zain name, employed more than 8,000 people and indirectly supported an estimated 170,000 more as sellers of prepaid phone cards.[12] The company reached 29.4 million subscribers in sub-Saharan Africa in 2008. Zain reported 2008 net income of $1.2 billion on consolidated revenues of $7.4 billion in its African and Middle East operations. In 2010, Mohammad Ibrahim's onetime startup was again sold, this time to the Indian company Bharti Airtel Limited in a deal worth $10.7 billion.

There is a temptation to regard this emerging appetite for Africa's black business negatively. Beginning in the 1990s, privatization disproportionately benefited non-Africans; the acquisition of Celtel, Ashanti Goldfields, and Somaliland's Diallo Airlines might be interpreted as *de-Africanizing* African private business: just as they rise to a certain stature, the African private sector firms lose their identity by being swallowed by non-African MNCs. In a way, this was precisely the scenario that the "national champions" model enshrined in Transcorp sought to avoid. Wearing its African identity on its sleeve, Transcorp proudly sought "to serve global markets with premier products and services from world-class facilities *sited in Nigeria, owned by Nigerians and managed by Nigerians.*"[13] Given widespread perceptions of African business, such reimaging is imperative. Yet that vision may be imperiled by the reality and imagery of global MNCs' voracious appetites for acquisition, which perpetuates centuries-old notions that Africans *themselves* are for sale rather than advancing the idea that Africans are, at long last, doing the selling.

On the other hand, the acquisitions suggest that *there is something worth buying in Africa.* Thus, such transactions help to enhance the position of black African businesspeople by increasing private wealth and injecting new capital for additional entrepreneurial activities.[14] Furthermore, although still novel (in part because of market structures and the fact that Africa still has relatively few publicly traded firms), acquisitions of African-linked private firms by non-African buyers also serve to improve global perceptions of current and future African big business.

Giants with a Low Profile: Asian Minority Big Business in Africa

The vast majority of sub-Saharan Africa's large businesses that are more than a few decades old have no connection to black owner-entrepreneurs. In addition to companies associated still with Europeans who arrived during the colonial period, other "nonblack" companies, no less firmly rooted in Africa, include those linked to other minority groups such as the Levantine populace of West Africa and the South Asian population of eastern and southern Africa. Since space limitations preclude an extensive examination of all of these communities, I concentrate here on the more populous and arguably more economically formidable (in terms of business scale and penetration) Indian ("Asian") firms of East Africa.[15]

Chapter 1 revisited the legitimate debate among Africanist scholars about the "Africanness" of minority/non-African business classes. Some authors such as Roger

Tangri contend that these actors must be considered distinct from the wider and invariably poorer black populace. Many others have noted the incendiary potential of a racial division of wealth and business, a phenomenon well captured by Amy Chua in her popular and aptly titled book *World on Fire*. Zimbabwe in recent years, Idi Amin's expulsion of Ugandan Asians in 1972, and the periodic tensions between blacks and Asians in Tanzania all attest to the vulnerability of those Chua labels "market-dominant minorities" (or MDMs); such victimization surely indicates their "otherness."

Conversely, scholars like David Himbara, argue that enterprises owned by East Africans of Indian descent are "simply transferred to the foreign category by sheer force of ideology," rather than through analytical rigor.[16] And this debate *is,* significantly, an ideological one, since it is impossible to determine scientifically when, if ever, a nonindigenous person "becomes" African. Via prolonged residency? Citizenship? Cultural assimilation? Achievement of a percentage—some "critical mass"—of the population? Obviously, nonblacks cannot change their skin color, their ethnicity, or heritage. Yet there is scant reason people cannot naturalize formally and psychologically even while preserving their cultural heritage; these elements—essential to multiculturalism—are not necessarily mutually exclusive. (For another example, consider Korean immigrant shopkeepers in putatively "black" Los Angeles neighborhoods, who remain vulnerable, even though both groups are effectively American.) At the same time, however, we must also acknowledge that resident MDMs' "identity" as Africans is often highly contextual. To their political allies, as well as to American researchers, the refrain is voiced in the first person plural ("we Africans") and the possessive ("our country" and "our president"). In less guarded moments, MDMs themselves cast their African counterparts as alien "other." Arguably, this too is no different from *any* in- or out-group in a multicultural society.

Ultimately, while noting the problematic nature of minority business domination, historically and presently and acknowledging that there are times when racial differences *are* important to highlight, I am persuaded by Himbara's argument that minorities—whites, Lebanese, South Asians and other long-term populations who are African by citizenship or established residency—should be included under the rubric of "African business." In fact, it is rather absurd to treat some of Africa's most long-standing firms, with deep roots in the region—and often *solely* in the region—as "foreign" or "settler" capital. The preponderance of these firms typically have no external ties— or at best limited ones—to their ancestral homeland. Describing that alienation, an Ivoirian businessman of Lebanese descent noted, "Nous sommes etrangers ici, nous sommes etrangers au Liban—gens sans pays."[17] Although their relationship with their adoptive countries can be equally strained, it is worth noting that, inasmuch as they are vital to the economic foundations of the country and are often key sources of rents/ patronage in support of the ruling political elites, these groups are *already* assimilated economically—and assimilated within Africa's cultures of business.

The recent experience of Uganda's Mehta Group is instructive. The company was founded in Uganda in the 1930s and soon began operating in Kenya. Today, with interests spanning multiple sectors in trade and industry, including building materials, packaging, horticulture, sugar and steel production, and plastics, Mehta Group employs more than fifteen thousand people in Africa and elsewhere. By global standards, it is of modest size with assets of approximately $350 million. Despite its deep footprint in the region, as recently as April 2007, for example, a controversy arose over the Group's negotiations to expand the company's sugar cane cultivation by utilizing a seven-thousand-hectare tract in the Mabira Forest Reserve. In addition to being a major water catchment area, Mabira Forest is also of cultural significance to Ugandans in the area.[18] Despite the government of Uganda's blessing, protests broke out in Kampala against the proposal, a Hindu temple was attacked, and three people were killed, including a non-resident Indian.

This episode reveals a number of important themes. First, despite official declarations by governments, Asian businesses and Asian people are still foreigners—*étrangers*—in many respects. Fearing backlash, many in the Ugandan Indian population actually denounced Mehta Group's Mabira Forest transaction and suggested that the initiative risked discrediting all Indians in Uganda.[19] "Mabira has made all of us suffer from some Ugandans' anger. The earlier he [Mahendra Mehta] gives up on Mabira the better for all of us,' said Sign Pravel, coordinator of the Association of Asian Community in Uganda."[20]

Second, despite the display of violence, how Asians perceive themselves and how others perceive them differs markedly from a generation ago. Some weeks after the incident, Kenya's *East African Standard* published an essay that sought to raise awareness of continued xenophobia toward Asians that gave rise to the hostilities, as well as to emphasize the *Ugandan* identity of the South Asian community, especially the Mehtas.[21] This was consistent with an earlier article published by Uganda's *New Vision* that emphasized Mahendra Mehta's background and identity as a Ugandan and the deep roots of the Mehta Group in Uganda, including the company's corporate social responsibility initiatives within the local community. Notably, it also praised the Mabira Forest transaction for its economic benefits and its pledge to preserve the environment of the watershed.[22] Although this episode highlights the potential frailty of the Afro-Indian relationship, a similar defense would not easily be offered in favor of Chinese firms in Africa, notwithstanding the occasional praise emanating from African political leaders. With few exceptions, most observers would be hard pressed to cite a record of corporate social responsibility or community engagement or the intrinsic *Africanness* of any major Chinese company at this point. The Mehta Group is emblematic of Indian-African firms that are more astutely attuned to local politics and culture.

Regardless, such challenges are not uncommon, as the Indian business community has had to contend with occasionally difficult sociopolitical conditions throughout

East Africa. Yet many "Asian-run" businesses have expanded in size and scope in spite of the barriers. Most still dominate the economies of East Africa, for example. Like the Mehta group, other local Indian companies began as trading companies and later diversified to become multisectoral conglomerate groups engaging in trade, manufacturing, distribution, and finance.

Ironically, in Kenya, for example, this Indian predominance vis-à-vis blacks in the manufacturing sector was actually *enhanced* by political interference in business development in postcolonial Kenya. Although most contemporary Indian firms got their start in the interwar period, they were largely concentrated in the commercial trading sector. It was only the promulgation of Kenya's indigenization policies of the early 1970s that essentially pushed Indians out of the commercial trading sector, with its low barriers to entry, in favor of blacks. Although this may have offered black Kenyans a foothold in the business economy, it also gave Asians a platform to expand.

Asian-owned firms have tended toward multisectoral conglomeration throughout East Africa, nearly all centered around families who arrived during the colonial era. Uganda-based Madhvani Group, for example, followed a familiar model by availing itself of economic "space" in sectors unattractive to whites and foreclosed to blacks. The group started in Uganda in 1914 but has Kenyan operations dating to the 1920s. With 2009 assets of about $200 million, this conglomerate is today a regional powerhouse as well as a fixture of the East African private sector. It has investments in Rwanda, Sudan, and Tanzania as well as outside Africa and employs some ten thousand people. Its companies engage in sugar, steel, glass and plastics manufacturing, as well as packaging, tourism, horticulture, and energy. Within Uganda, Madhvani is one of Uganda's leading employers and taxpayers, contributing approximately 8 percent of the total tax revenues collected in the country, a role that has earned praise from President Museveni.[23]

In contrast, the Chandaria Group of Companies and the Sunflag Group, both domiciled in Kenya, are relative latecomers. Chandaria, which was founded in Mombasa in 1947, made early investments in paper and packaging in the 1950s, later expanding to recycled paper, real estate, and banking. It remains a family-owned enterprise, employing some about twelve hundred in Kenya and nearly three hundred in Tanzania, with self-reported turnover of $72.5 million. Likewise, Sunflag started in 1937 but really began expanding with the establishment of Sunflag Textile Mills in the 1950s. Of its ten thousand employees, 25 percent are based in Kenya, whereas the remainder work in Sunflag operations in Tanzania, Nigeria, and Cameroon, as well as in Asia and other regions.

Importantly, South Asian-owned companies such as Mehta, Madhvani, Sunflag, and the Chandaria Group have risen to become pillars of African economies. Few could be easily separated from these economies without disastrous consequences for labor, the tax base, and the economy as a whole. Certainly, racial tensions persist, but Asian firms are far more than simply colonial or neocolonial holdovers. Indeed, a number of individuals from leading businesses have played senior roles in African governments.[24] Moreover, although Asians' political status is often precarious and they sometimes are socially cut off, they are firmly embedded in the business cultures of Africa. Although they are members of a diaspora and have the potential for "extra-African" (i.e., international) economic relationships, a point emphasized in chapter 4, their orientation is essentially African; that is, Asian-identified firms domiciled in Africa are focused on local and, increasingly, regional economies.

SOUTH AFRICAN FIRMS IN AFRICA AND THE WORLD

South Africa's large firms, which tend to be identified with whites, are both more international than their Indian counterparts and, at the same time, extremely conscious of their *African* surroundings. This combination gives rise to a cultural dualism that is increasingly acute, as South Africa's largest companies seek to compete in the global sphere while simultaneously attempting to reach out to other African countries. They often ground their appeal to African countries in the idea of South Africans' inherent *Africanness* and ability to understand "African culture" in a way that counterparts, say, from India and China or the United States, for that matter, cannot.

Nonetheless, transnational South African firms admittedly have a certain Janus-faced quality about them. These and other South African companies increasingly have to reconcile global aspirations with their noteworthy expansion into the rest of Africa. Because of its peculiar history, its racialized political economy, and the inherent tensions between the diplomatic interests of South Africa's black government and the investment imperatives of its overwhelmingly white big business community, South African firms are in a somewhat precarious position when it comes to their business activities on the continent. Surely African-domiciled firms have an advantage over their counterparts in the global North when investing elsewhere in Africa because they are more likely to have cultural fluency and can refer to shared, if somewhat mythologized, experiences. On the other hand, as South African firms endeavor to become truly global companies, their forays into Africa risk looking less like investment by firms that can relate to Africa *as fellow Africans* and more like a resurgence of the phenomenon of "settler capital" described in earlier chapters (albeit now transnationalized), which can prove sociopolitically incendiary if disconnected from host economies. Only when properly managed and integrated (racially and economically) can South African investment in Africa facilitate diversified production chains, ownership, and management structures, thereby aiding private sector development in a host of countries.

I briefly examine South Africa's giants as *domestic* players before turning to their regional and increasingly global footprint. Inarguably, the prominence and power of big business in South Africa stands out; other countries have big businesses, but only South Africa has so many of global stature.

Big Business in South Africa

In most sectors, "large" firms are those with more than two hundred employees, and these represent only about one percent of the more than nine hundred thousand private enterprises in South Africa. Nonetheless, big business in South Africa enjoys important structural advantages; it is the major source of government tax revenues and a resource for technical and market expertise, particularly about export markets. Big business also represents the leading providers of employment; by the late 1990s, such firms employed 3.2 million workers—or 43 percent of all 7.4 million private sector employees.[25] Despite the relatively high number of large firms, however, within South Africa, only one hundred or so companies are considered truly giants, some of which represent local affiliates of MNCs. Among those whose origins are South African, literally a handful of conglomerate companies predominate.

The multisectoral interests of these conglomerates means they are deeply embedded in the national economy. Companies such as Anglo American, for example, have been a dominating influence with South African governments for a century, whether under apartheid after 1948 or under the prior governments linked to Anglo-British interests. Apartheid was highly beneficial to business, in fact, particularly in the early decades following its establishment in 1948. The economy grew at almost 6 percent per year from 1960 to 1969, and FDI inflows increased substantially, especially to the manufacturing sector, which itself grew at nearly 12 percent annually during that period while becoming increasingly capital intensive.[26]

The leading beneficiaries of South Africa's flourishing business environment were the country's six largest conglomerates: Liberty Life (which became Stanbic), Sanlam, and Old Mutual (later SA Mutual), engaged primarily in financial services; Anglovaal and Anglo American, principally in the mining and manufacturing sectors; and the Rembrandt Group (later Remgro), whose lead business was tobacco products. By the mid-1970s, the top 5 percent of companies dominated these respective sectors, accounting for some 63 percent of manufacturing turnover, 69 percent of turnover in the wholesale and retail trades, 76 percent of turnover in the transport sector, and 63 percent in the construction sector.[27] By the 1980s, the six largest companies controlled some 80 percent of the shares traded on the Johannesburg Stock Exchange, and Anglo American alone controlled 60.1 percent of the exchange's market capitalization in 1987.[28] Even by 1994, the year majority rule was established, Anglo's collective activities still represented more than 43 percent of the exchange's market capitalization.

Conglomeration and concentration remain key features of contemporary South African business, despite measurable unbundling under African National Congress rule since 1994. Historically, these companies were characterized by a series of interlocking and confusing pyramid ownership structures. In recent years, share listings on foreign bourses, unbundling, and the impact of South Africa's program of black economic empowerment have reduced somewhat the domination of the conglomerates. Yet even in this context these entities face scant domestic competition. Moreover, in the postapartheid era, nonvoting shares became a tool to widely diffuse ownership while keeping control tightly held.[29] Hence, the benefits of unbundling are fewer than anticipated, leading Neo Chabane, Andrea Goldstein, and Simon Roberts to argue that the conglomerates are "if anything even more entrenched, especially in industrial and mining sectors, with important vertical acquisitions extending their reach" further.[30] In spite of these considerable shortcomings, prominent, often politically connected black elites have been among the leading beneficiaries of the process.

The New Black Big Business in South Africa

The new class of black business tycoons that has emerged in South Africa fits surprisingly well into this still white-dominated and conglomerated business environment. South Africa inaugurated an aggressive program of black economic empowerment intended to provide blacks with a range of opportunities that had been foreclosed to them for more than four and a half centuries. Although the scope of this program and its most recent incarnation, "broad-based black economic empowerment," includes everything from management, to employment, access to financial and land resources, and human resources and skills development, arguably the most visible outcome is the ascendance of certain black South Africans to highly prominent business positions. Despite its promise, therefore, on the whole the results of empowerment programs have been decidedly mixed. An investigation of its manifold social and economic development shortcomings is beyond the scope of this book; in terms of its business impact, the vast majority of the so-called BEE companies that fall under the rubric of "big business" continue to be white owned and/or controlled.

Initially, it appeared that a number of such companies, such as Real Africa, NAIL, Johnic, and HCI, had genuinely joined the ranks of big business, but several never reached their lofty expectations due to excessive debt levels and under-capitalization.[31] Inevitably, black economic empowerment companies lacked the deep financial roots of their white counterparts, and as the program progressed, it became clear that many were essentially shells. The legislation required that to be considered "black owned," a company had to have at least 50 percent black ownership. Since this was orchestrated through the creation of *holding companies* for the purpose of acquiring shares, however, it created a loophole in which underlying operating companies remained mostly white. Thus, the underlying structures in South Africa have proved extremely slow to change.

As its name implies, broad-based black economic empowerment, which was phased in over a more than four-year transition period ending in 2008, attempts to broaden the scope of black empowerment while redressing the shortcomings of the previous framework. It introduced a complex new scoring and evaluation system to measure both obligations and compliance. It and related legislation like the 2002 Mining Charter call for both the expansion of blacks in management and in ownership and institute requirements for procurement and contracting from black-owned suppliers to help develop upstream industries. The Mining Charter, for example, required that nearly 40 percent of management positions in the sector be filled by blacks within five years of signing; empowerment laws also call for certain historically white companies to procure as much as 40 percent of supplies from black economic empowerment companies. Yet one persistent problem in the administration of the program has been its circumvention by those historically white companies whose monopoly the laws are intended to dislodge. Grand gestures, if not always precise compliance, by South Africa's largest firms have been commonplace, but midsized companies felt especially squeezed. From the beginning, they complained that the laws discriminated against them and substantially raised costs. Larger firms, meanwhile, argued that there was an insufficient supply of qualified blacks to fill the managerial ranks as demanded by the laws, though many now have programs in place designed to boost these numbers.

Violating the spirit of black empowerment was not solely the preserve of South Africa's whites. Indeed, though one can hardly fault their entrepreneurial, if somewhat mercenary, savvy or their sociopolitical legerdemain, many members of the new black economic elite were able to leverage the exigency for black empowerment with enormous success. Thus emerged a class of the black "superrich," including Cyril Ramaphosa, Nthatho Motlana, Mzee Kumahlo, and Tokyo Sexwale. Many in this class emerged in the postapartheid period not as owner/entrepreneurs of productive, operational, enterprises but as large shareholders.

Yet, although black empowerment has not had the transformative impact anticipated by some of its more fervent architects and supporters, it has helped to foster a cross-racial, and to some extent multiracial, business culture in South Africa. Indeed, having joined the ranks of the superrich, black business elites now participate fully in leading business organizations like the South Africa Foundation (now Business Leadership South Africa), an elite association of the nation's corporate titans, in philanthropic activities such as the Business Trust and are invited to sit with their white counterparts in government-sponsored forums, such as the Big Business Working Groups initiated by former South African president Thabo Mbeki. Many of these black elites, who are ironically comprised of erstwhile African National Congress stalwarts and former leftists, increasingly identify *as a class* with the white senior executives with whom they regularly interact.[32] Perhaps a majority of South Africa's new black business elite are scarcely "entrepreneurs" in the strictest sense; most of those enriched under the first phase of black economic empowerment especially are more akin to portfolio managers. Nevertheless, the accumulated wealth of this grouping and its formidable stature and visibility, within South Africa as well as outside, is a boon to business in Africa more broadly. These are *dealmakers*. No less than those engaged in more conventional manufacturing or service industries—Aliko Dangote and Mohammad Ibrahim, for example—South Africa's black business titans are part of the new *black* African face of an increasingly globalized African business.

In Search of New Markets

The size of South Africa's middle class was recently estimated at just under ten million people, which includes a small but rapidly growing black middle class. Although "the material middle class standard of living" is admittedly modest—"residing in formal housing with following facilities: water tap in the residence, flush toilet, electricity or gas as main cooking source, telephone landline or cell phone"—the nascent black middle class has considerable purchasing power.[33] Indeed, South Africa has one of the continent's most formidable consumer markets. This domestic buying power is supplemented by the country's vast resources, which include precious metals and minerals. As a result of import substitution, especially under apartheid, and South Africa's long-held role as the regional economic hegemon, the country is home to Africa's largest and most established businesses. Moreover, the contemporary size and vitality of South Africa's domestic marketplace means that its most prominent companies, such as SAB-Miller, Old Mutual, SASOL, Shoprite, MTN, Massmart, and Anglo American, continue to do a substantial percentage of their business *inside* the country.

Yet several forces are driving these firms to increasingly invest in activities outside as well. Despite a total population approaching fifty million, the South African market is growing too saturated for the country's business giants, especially those in the services sectors. In addition, the country's pervasive security concerns, persistent real (by the "broad definition") unemployment of more than 35 percent, HIV/AIDS, and entrenched poverty pose genuine challenges, not just for society but for business; expansion abroad thus allows big business to capture new markets as well as mitigate risks of overexposure.

It is a truism that African countries need investment; chapter 4 is devoted entirely to this subject. What that chapter alludes to but does not discuss in detail is that South African firms today are among the most visible and numerous of these investors. Not only as representatives of the global South but of Africa itself, South African firms enjoy greater familiarity with the technical constraints, consumer demands, and business practices elsewhere on the continent. South African corporations have become more sensitized to the use and promotion of backward and forward linkages with local companies. And, racial differences aside, they are generally better versed in the bureaucratic politics of Africa and are often more effective politically than outsiders.[34]

These advantages accrue to South African firms, whether their interests lie primarily in market-seeking or resource-seeking activities, and contemporary South African firms engage in both forms (as well as substantial portfolio investment). Those involved in the former have expanded out of their home market in order to offer products or services to a greater number of buyers or consumers, mainly in the retail, services, or financial sectors. FDI emanating from South Africa is also significantly focused on resource-seeking activities on the continent, principally in the mining and other extractive industries sectors—sectors that form a critical pillar of South Africa's national economy. As resource-seeking investors, their objectives, if not their methods, are little different from those of traditional extractive industries in the West.

The discussion that follows elaborates first on South Africa's increasing role *in Africa*, where South African firms are today a ubiquitous presence, literally from the Cape to Cairo. Thereafter I turn to analysis of the expanding *worldwide* footprint of those corporations whose roots lie in South Africa. In fact, several of South Africa's giants are investing not only elsewhere on the continent but have now become truly global entities. This is a significant milestone for Africa's leading corporations, and their global expansion has important implications, both for the perceptions of "African business" around the world and for evolving cultures of business within Africa itself.

Going Continental: Corporate Manifest Destiny

South African business's strongest sustained push into Africa began following the collapse of apartheid. Although big business was clearly a beneficiary of the apartheid system, it was also instrumental in hastening the end of the racist regime beginning in the 1980s, after the policies had begun to severely constrain private enterprise. With the government's encouragement and favorable policies, investment on the part of South African companies in the rest of Africa has expanded such that today South Africa remains the largest single source of FDI into sub-Saharan Africa; South Africa had contributed $93 billion as of the end of 2007, nearly one-quarter of the $393 billion total FDI stock. Africa accounts for more than 50 percent of South Africa's FDI outflows, and leading recent recipients have included long-standing partners among the Southern African Development Community countries, including the Democratic Republic of Congo, as well as countries like Nigeria and Mauritius. As of 2005, there were some 122 South African investors in Africa, 18 of which were parastatals.[35] These South African giants have embraced the continent at a dizzying pace and across a wide range of sectors. The top five sectors were telecoms, mining, electricity, steel, and energy, oil and gas, whereas food, leisure, banking, transport, and general retail together accounted for 7 percent of outgoing FDI.[36]

Mobile telecommunications represents one of Africa's fastest-growing industries, and South Africa is the launching point for some of the continent's leading mobile phone providers. MTN, which was established in 1994, provides service to twenty-one countries in Africa and the Middle East. By year end 2008, it had ninety-one million subscribers, and posttax profits reached R17.1 billion, a 44 percent increase over the previous year. In the mining sector, South African firms were party to six of the thirty largest cross-border mergers and acquisitions *in the entire developing world* between 1987 and 2004. Although firms from the United States, the United Kingdom, France, and Canada were included, no other country was as well represented as South Africa, whose firms completed some $661 billion of transactions in that period. All of the targets were in Africa, although since that time South African mining firms have invested heavily outside of Africa as well.[37]

A similar, if smaller, picture is evident in the energy sector, for example, where the integrated energy and chemical company Sasol currently produces gas in Mozambique and oil in Gabon (and engages in chemical manufacturing in Europe and the United States, the Middle East, and Asia as well). Within South Africa Sasol continues its original business of converting coal and natural gas into synthetic fuels and chemicals—which had been a critical function during ISI and apartheid—as well as maintains its coal mining and chemical operations, refinement of imported crude oil, and retail distribution network.

In the financial sphere, South Africa's four large banking groups, Nedbank, FirstRand, Standard Bank, and Absa have also spread rapidly into other African markets since the end of apartheid. Of these, Standard Bank has been the most aggressive, expanding first into neighboring Namibia and Swaziland, then moving into Zimbabwe, Nigeria, Kenya and later into Uganda, Tanzania, Malawi, Mozambique, and Mauritius. According to Dianna Games, South African banks generate a more than 30 percent return on equity in foreign markets versus 20–23 percent domestically.[38] Although they engage in retail business as well, the banks have been instrumental in facilitating the foreign business transactions—both inflows and outflows—of *South African* corporations; such transnational banking operations help to lower barriers to entry for South African investors.

Finally, one of the most ubiquitous, if often concealed, players in Africa is SAB-Miller, the beverage giant whose origins as South African Breweries date from the 1890s. Developing first a regional presence in southern Africa, SAB began aggressively expanding it beer brands throughout Africa by the early 1990s, particularly through the acquisition of former state-owned breweries. Its approach is to buy local breweries, upgrade operations, and continue under locally established popular brands—whether Laurentina, Kilimanjaro, Mosi, or Star—and hence many local consumers are scarcely aware of the South African presence. Today, SAB is the market leader in thirteen African countries in which it operates, including Swaziland, Botswana, Tanzania, Zambia, Lesotho, Mozambique, Ghana, Uganda, and Ethiopia and has the capacity for significant further expansion. Finally, South African firms have also been prominent in the retail sector, and companies such as Shoprite Holdings and Massmart have opened stores throughout the region. Following Walmart's purchase of a 51 percent stake in Massmart in 2011, that company gained significant new resources to fuel its expansion push.

Reconciling Business Cultures

Although South African companies are now a near-ubiquitous presence in the liberalized, postprivatization but still investment-hungry economies of Africa, their "cultural literacy" in the rest of Africa cannot be taken for granted. Conflicts inevitably emerge as a result of competition with local firms or particular South African management styles as well as various ethical challenges, such as host-country corruption.[39] The fact that most of the expatriate managers tend to be white South Africans—although for a typical investor however, this may be fewer than a handful of people—introduces a racial dimension that can also contribute to resentments toward South African investors, especially in the former frontline states of southern Africa.

Like any researcher on private sectors in Africa, I have been exposed to countless reports of slights, both real and perceived, against black staff and even patrons by white South African business owners and managers. Importantly, however, as with similar grievances against South Asians, Arabs, and more recently, Chinese, such sentiments have seldom evoked lasting boycotts, nor have they measurably dampened consumer traffic at these enterprises; both governments and the wider populace typically have vested interest in seeing the investment maintained. Moreover, to the extent that white South Africans display racial insensitivity or hostility to locals in host countries, scant evidence exists to show that it is any worse than that displayed by other minorities.[40] Consequently, although racial difference can precipitate friction, its impact on the prospects for, as well as the reception and influence of, South African FDI in Africa appear limited.

In any event, the racial dimension is just one of several factors that complicate South Africa's business relations with the rest of Africa, which can be characterized best as *ambivalent*. South Africa plays the role of both competitor (for global FDI) and peer (that is, as part of Africa, a view especially championed by Thabo Mbeki), as well as continental hegemon with all that leadership position entails. These roles are often in tension with one another, especially since some speak to South African geopolitical aspirations, whereas others pertain to macroeconomic or even firm-level concerns. Efforts at balancing inevitably impact business operations, as firms must deal with competing and contradictory identities as "corporate citizens, corporate activists, corporate tourists, or corporate colonialists."[41]

In a 2004 interview, SAB-Miller chief executive Graham Mackay insisted that his firm is essentially trying to be a good corporate—and indeed, African—citizen, noting that "we have something of an advantage in that South Africa doesn't have a cultural hegemony it's trying to establish. It's not a world power. There was less resistance against South Africans coming in. It's hard to imagine a country in Eastern Europe being South Africanized, whereas it's easy for locals to believe they're being Americanized."[42] This suggests that—at least from a cultural, and perhaps economic, globalization standpoint—South African firms certainly prefer to portray themselves as more benign and less threatening (than American firms especially) and perhaps as more sensitive to host-country values. Many Africans would undoubtedly question whether they really are more benign. Many in fact regard South African FDI as a form of "corporate colonialism."

Occasional racial and other frictions aside, however, South African firms nevertheless enjoy a leg up on global competitors in Africa as a result of their affinity with and connection to "African culture." Owing to many factors, including geographic proximity, politics, history, and just good business sense, South African companies, *in general,* have shown a greater willingness than other investors to engage favorably with host countries in terms of labor relations and lexicology and in the creation of supplier linkages along the value chain. Numerous companies *voluntarily* adhere to the same principles of black economic empowerment, its shortcomings notwithstanding, that they are legally required to uphold in their domestic South African operations. Thus, it is not uncommon to see a range of programs such as management training schemes or initiatives in the mold of corporate social responsibility. Yet even where South African companies are appreciably less exploitative of host countries than others, it is nonetheless important not to deny South African firms the same profit motive that motivates FDI in Africa that originates from anywhere else in the world: they are in Africa to make money, and the results speak for themselves.

The experience of the grocery-chain giant Shoprite offers useful case study on the ways in which South African firms juxtapose these profit-seeking and community-building imperatives. As Shoprite has discovered in its development of local supply chains, economic and sociopolitical rationales are not mutually exclusive. Moreover, Shoprite's successful expansion has helped project an image of commercial vitality in once moribund communities and a corresponding view that associates African business with achievement rather than decay.

South African chains such as Shoprite and its brands, Massmart, with its brands Makro, Game, and other stores, as well as Pic 'n' Pay, PEP, and a host of restaurant chains and other retail outlets, are now a ubiquitous presence around the African continent. Founded in 1979, Shoprite is an excellent example of market-seeking investment. It began to expand out of South Africa with the acquisition of a Namibian chain in 1990 and invested in Zambia and Mozambique shortly thereafter. Rapidly expanding through acquisition of defunct state-owned chains as well as through greenfield investment, by 2002 Shoprite was present in a dozen sub-Saharan countries. By decades' end, Shoprite had opened more than 70 supermarkets in sixteen Sub-Saharan and North African countries, as well as at least 20 USave stores, which retail mainly "no frills" discount consumables. In all, Shoprite Holdings, the parent company, has over 1,000 outlets, including 309 Shoprite stores, as well as its Hungry Lion, Checkers, USave, and other chains, though the vast majority of stores are still in South Africa itself.

In Zambia, for example, Shoprite acquired the state-owned Mwaiseni Stores, whose holding company was dissolved and whose operating units were privatized in 1996. The first store opened on Cairo Road in downtown Lusaka, replacing the bare shelves that characterized Mwaiseni and the other state-owned chain, the Zambia Consumers' Buying Corporation, with overflowing produce and consumables, from regular groceries to household items in a near-"superstore"-type environment. In many locales Shoprite has constructed new, warehouse-sized stores that rival any of the largest grocery chains worldwide. Goods are now regularly available to consumers in these countries where previously scarcity reigned.

Unsurprisingly, most manufactured goods sold at retail are imported from South Africa. Yet the company had a long history of supplying produce from South Africa as well, thus bypassing local producers and dampening prospects for upstream linkages. Indeed, Shoprite has been roundly criticized for excluding local producers, even medium- and large-scale farmers, by claiming that their prices were uncompetitive and that their produce failed to meet supply quality standards.[43] Several interventions in the last decade, however, have begun to foster supplier linkages *within* the countries in which Shoprite does business. Aided by agricultural development programs supported by the United Nations, the World Bank, and other donors, Shoprite stores in Mozambique, Tanzania, and Nigeria, for example, now source much more of their vegetables from local small farmers. In some countries, Shoprite also sources sugar, flour, cooking oil, bottled water, coffee, tea, and fruit juices from local suppliers as well. In Zambia, Shoprite asserts that it now buys more than 90 percent of its fresh produce from local farmers, leading to increased incomes and greater access to health and educational resources; development agencies in fact hailed Shoprite's progress. Zambia is Shoprite's largest market outside South Africa, so the corporation has an added incentive to facilitate local supplier relationships.

While the Shoprite brand targets a lower-middle income tier in South Africa, most of its shops are scarcely "down market" in other countries. Hence, the prices of many goods continue to exceed the capacity of most citizens outside urban, largely middle-class strata, although there are also indications that Shoprite is rapidly gaining market share among lower-income customers as well.[44] That market share is expanding at the expense of traditional markets in Africa, which Shoprite is gradually displacing; however, the impact on livelihoods and access to foodstuffs is at least partly offset by the development of sustainable outgrower schemes and (increasingly) competitive prices.

All of this suggests that entities like Shoprite and its South African competitors are increasingly important players on the business and economic landscape. Unsettled questions remain, particularly about local linkages and reinvestment—challenges that bedevil virtually all FDI. Shoprite's detractors, such as those from the Benchmarks Foundation, have offered salient criticisms in this regard, although the expectation that FDI should have a direct, immediate, and unmistakable impact on poverty levels is misguided.[45] Nonetheless, FDI can have a transformative impact on economies. To expect investment by a giant multinational grocery chain to be a vessel for development is perhaps somewhat naïve, but it can be a harbinger of a new business investment.

Indeed, South African FDI can benefit the development of other African economies by demonstrating that there is more to "business in Africa" than generally perceived; re*branding* Africa is essential, and South African firms like Massmart and Shoprite can and often *do* play a role in that reimaging. The presence of Shoprite in Zambia, for instance, is one more positive factor that makes to local market more appealing and attractive. Few people, whether individual investors, large multinational firms, or tourists, for that matter, want to come to a market deemed to be stagnant or dying, insecure and lacking conveniences; in this sense, perhaps, *BusinessWeek's* allusion to "fearless investors" is oddly apropos. Success breeds success, however, and the recognition of a market opportunity by Shoprite spurs the revitalization of shopping areas (e.g., Lusaka's Cairo Road), inspires others to come, and facilitates the rebranding of Zambia. In other markets, Pep, Spar, Pic 'n' Pay, and Kenya's Uchumi are also playing this role. Over the *long term,* does Zambia—or any other country for that matter—want its image to be tied to a failing, empty Mwaiseni store? The positive, flourishing, bountiful Shoprite is far more desirable. In fact, stores like Shoprite are a critical if incremental step in the process of rebranding Africa as a place of flourishing investment—and full shelves—rather than mud huts and kwashiorkor.

The Challenge of Becoming Global ("Globalization or De-Africanization?")

South Africa's giants like to assert their familiarity with and affinity for the rest of Africa—their backyard. Yet fitting in with the rest of Africa requires that South Africa–based firms must overcome residual distrust in order to establish legitimacy and credibility *as fellow Africans.* Those South African companies with global operations or aspirations face a doubly difficult and perhaps irreconcilable challenge: while they need to be *more* African in Africa, they often strive to appear *less* African as they endeavor to further their investments at the global level. The wider, non-African context requires both the establishment and projection of a wholly different kind of legitimacy: excellence on the *global* stage. Arguably, it is the nature of the modern transnational corporation to be something of a Rorschach test on which individuals impress whatever identity—or nationality—they chose; in fact, it may be essential. Although South African firms have begun to master this global dualism, paradoxically it may come at the expense of the promotion of African business. If the firms downplay their Africanity, their origins scarcely provide a symbolic advantage for business from/in Africa writ large.

Writing on India, Timothy de Waal Malefyt and Brian Moeran observe that advertisers seek to translate global brands for local markets so that they resonate with local consumers (by giving products a certain "Indianness," for example); "advertising agencies [thus] act as cultural brokers as they tell their clients what is and is not 'Indian' and thereby legitimate their existence."[46] South African companies face the opposite problem. That is, when investing outside of the African continent, they must translate their *local* brands for *global* markets. Paradoxically, to the extent that they are successful in "globalizing" their wares, the *African* dimension of the company is necessarily diminished; thus "going global" and conveying a worldwide image of a successful African corporation may be a zero-sum game. Clearly, this is not the case in all circumstances. While it is comparatively easy to see how a Nandos might want to play up its Africanness when operating abroad because that Luso-African theme has cachet in the restaurant business, it is quite another to do that with mining, or retail, or breweries, for example, which have legitimate reasons to downplay any residual Africanness and perhaps de-Africanize altogether.

Another discernible trend in the internationalization of South African business is the increasing willingness to shift share listings to European or American stock exchanges—a path followed by a number of South Africa's largest and best-known companies. It is not beyond the pale to label this *de-Africanization* of a sort, but the motives of various corporate actors differ, as do their impacts. Paradoxically, however, listing on international exchanges is perhaps the ultimate indication of the globalization of African business. Regardless of where one stands on the issue, the numbers, thus far, are modest. There were more than four thousand companies listed on African exchanges in 2008, for example, but only seventeen African (origin) companies, nearly all of them South African, listed on the New York Stock Exchange's European exchange, Euronext.[47]

Among the South African giants that have taken this step are Telkom, the partially private communications company (39 percent state owned). Now enjoying a global profile, Telkom, which has been listed on the New York Stock Exchange since 2003, had revenues of $6.9 billion in 2005. It continues to employ over twenty-six thousand in thirty-one African countries. Similarly, AngloGold Ashanti is also listed on the exchange. Sasol Ltd. (Sasol) the integrated energy and chemical company has been listed on Euronext since 2003. The Johannesburg Stock Exchange could not support the company's ambition to be a global energy player.[48] It listed at $10.43, reached a high of $49 a share and was trading in the high $30s in late 2009, which gave the company a market cap of $25 billion. By definition, international listings attract new investors, and Sasol's U.S. shareholders held some 24 percent of the company by September 2008. These companies have a clear rationale for changing their listing and/or country of domicile. Valuations in hard currency help insulate against negative rand swings, and improved access to Western capital markets help fund potential expansion. In addition, overseas listings also diminish the companies' vulnerability to state and/or political pressure.[49]

On one hand, this apparent departure of firms and the diminution, if not de-coupling, of their connection to Africa has a familiar and unsettling feel. Indeed—and perhaps this dilemma is particularly acute in the case of South African mining companies—such changes are eerily reminiscent of colonial and neocolonial practices: Africa serves as supplier of raw material resources, but profits are repatriated to the metropole and European (and other) investors rather than plowed back into Africa. Although market-seeking firms in the services sector are not diluting or taking the continent's resources per se, the contemporary climate may nevertheless foretell of a corporate flight from Africa that robs the continent of its claim to some of its most well-known firms at precisely the time that their international legitimacy, business savvy, and capital are most needed to help shape new business expansion.

It is not unreasonable to ask whether, for example, we can even continue to call certain companies "African" at all. One such giant is the very un-African sounding SAB-Miller, which is the name adopted by the former South African Breweries fol-lowing its unprecedented combination with American beer maker Miller in 2002. The combined company, now the world's second largest beer brewer, is headquartered in the United Kingdom and maintains operations that span the globe, including in Latin America and China. SAB-Miller "is British-registered, with dual listing in London and Johannesburg; its management is overwhelmingly of South African nationality, although it is unclear where the managers reside; its major shareholder (Altria) is American and the second largest (the Santo Domingo family) is Colombian."[50] Again, this is perhaps a dilemma posed by all contemporary transnational corporations.[51]

On the other hand, however, listing on American and European exchanges and relocating corporate headquarters does not signal the death knell for African busi-ness and must be seen in the context of growing global capacity of African corporate entities. Indeed, listing on leading Euro-American exchanges provides new sources of capital; coupled with the increasing internationalization of African business, such as through investment abroad of actual firms, however tentative at this point, this augurs positively. Their increasingly *trans*national character in fact makes African corpora-tions less exceptional and more like their global counterparts; the key for the former lies in maintaining the African link.

And, apparent de-Africanizing notwithstanding, most remain firmly rooted in Africa; even the giants continue to conduct the bulk of their operations in Africa. In-deed, South Africa remains SAB-Miller's most important market, for example, and the company has a market presence in thirty-one African countries. Some 41 percent of the group's pretax 2008 earnings were generated in Africa. Similarly, although London-listed (since 1999) Anglo American engages in exploration in Brazil, Canada, China, and Russia, it remains a familiar presence throughout the African continent, including in Zimbabwe, Namibia, Botswana, Tanzania, the Democratic Republic of Congo, and Angola. It is also a critical business actor within South Africa, where it has been one of the country's leading mining houses/conglomerates for the better part of a century. Anglo's shift to London in 1999 generated considerable protest. Critics felt the move was an attempt to deemphasize Anglo's African identity—which arguably it was— though the firm claimed it mainly sought better access to London's/Europe's larger capital markets. Yet to date the combined company's principal business operations, as well as its platinum, coal, base metals, and diamond mining activity, remain in South Africa and Africa, as do the majority of its 105,000 employees. The company's operating profit in 2008 was $10.1 billion on total group revenue of $23.6 billion. Moreover, Anglo American has made a commitment to South African society—from the Lusaka meetings with the exiled African National Congress in 1986 to its more contemporary commitment to black economic empowerment in the form of partnerships with companies such as Exxaro Resources and Ponahalo Holdings—that clearly earns it a degree of credibility. Anglo boasts that its procurement from historically disadvantaged South African –owned companies amounted to R17.6 billion ($2.1billion), or 37 percent of its 2008 procurement spending.[52]

These steps suggest that South Africa's newly transnationalized corporate giants have managed, thus far at least, to preserve this delicate balance between Africanness and globalization.

CONCLUSION

The presence and prominence of a coterie of large multinational corporations *from* Africa carries both immense symbolic and practical significance. Indeed, the existence of diverse and profitable "conventional" businesses such as those touched on in this chapter compels us to revisit the "Africa as neopatrimonial basket case" trope that would have us believe that such fanciful notions as "profit" and "(re)investment" and "shareholder value" are completely alien concepts in an African landscape falsely characterized as driven solely by rents, greed, corruption and inevitably, decay.

This misreading of the African business scene leads to misplaced prescriptions and sometimes almost singular emphasis on M/SMEs as the hope for Africa. Practitioners and academics alike contribute to these myths, and thus Western foundations, nongovernmental organizations, and Western-based bilateral and multilateral development agencies are consistently oriented toward M/SMEs. Our imagery is inundated with pictures or the sole proprietor, the lonely outpost, the women's microenterprise/microcredit and credit-sharing schemes. Even Carol Pineau, with her cheery portrait in *Africa: Open for Business,* is overwhelmingly focused on SMEs and an effort to demonstrate "the entrepreneurial spirit" or culture among Africans (and others residing on the continent). Although Pineau's promotion of business in Africa is a welcome corrective to pervasive Afropessimism, it inadvertently obscures an altogether different picture of a more robust private sector in Africa that is regionally and globally savvy. In reality, Africa is a place of multimillion dollar transactions and billion-dollar companies, too.

The practical importance for African economies of these entities is readily apparent. Indeed, large corporate operations at the national and regional levels provide vital goods, services, and investment that African countries must have. Moreover, they can promote upstream and downstream linkages, especially when encouraged by states, using such measures as carefully calibrated indigenization legislation, national champions strategies, and so on. Such strategies, in turn, can compel the giants to help foster the development of local black businesses—as suppliers, distributors, subcontractors.

A symbolic but equally important perspective can be gained, especially for those international observers inclined to subscribe to the *BusinessWeek* or CNBC hyperbole, by taking a hard look at the breadth of African business and by recognizing that it also comprises globally renowned and competitive firms. Indeed, to the extent that the world identifies these firms *as African* and associates them with Africa, reciprocal effects and virtuous circles become far more achievable.

CONCLUSION
Prospects for Business
in Africa and African Business

THE RELEVANCE OF HISTORY

Much of the modern history of Africa is grim, featuring as it does slavery and co-lonialism and dictatorship and decline. Africa's present-day conflicts in places such as Sudan, the Democratic Republic of Congo, and Somalia figure prominently in Western and other accounts of the continent, perhaps eclipsed in coverage only by the devas-tation of HIV/AIDS. The sense of a "continent in crisis" is never far away from most people's imaginings—or from the next magazine cover to feature Africa. In the midst of this apparently pervasive despair, the idea that there might be a thriving private sector and bona fide business class emerging is practically unimaginable for most ob-servers. The prevailing popular view of business in Africa is commensurate with the dominant narrative of the African continent: a vicious circle of abiding pessimism re-inforced by unrelenting chaos.

This grim history is relevant, even important, in considering the terrain of African political economy and, indeed, the place of business within it. Yet as this book has ar-gued, it is equally critical that we not allow ourselves to get too enmeshed in Afropessi-mism, lest we miss both the diversity and dynamism that also characterize in modern sub-Saharan Africa. Thus, in many respects, I admire the efforts of the Africa business boosters; this valiant minority, perhaps best represented recently by David Fick and Carol Pineau, seeks to redeem Africa in the face of an onslaught of Afropessimism that has become the reductio ad absurdum of too much contemporary "analysis" of the Af-rican continent. The cases highlighted by Pineau in her film *Africa: Open for Business* are undeniably authentic—and therefore illustrative of genuine business development and progress throughout the continent. However refreshing I find such perspectives, there is nonetheless a hint of unreality about them; their optimism is overgeneralized and their accounts insufficiently critical and analytical. I have attempted to hew to a middle path in this book, between such untempered optimism on one hand, and the maladroit attempts to tar all of Africa with one neopatrimonial brush, on the other.

REVISITING ASSUMPTIONS

This book began with questions about the source and veracity of Africa's reputa-tion as devoid of a strong business culture and asked whether it was possible to move

African business beyond its association with primary commodity dependence. It asked about the capacity of various countries to develop business sectors and cultures that are consistent with "modern" business and suited toward national development and that possibly could have global impact. As we conclude, one thing that should be clear from the arguments presented is that in many respects African business, in its various permutations, has *already* moved beyond these constraints. Thus, to paraphrase the words Glinda the Good Witch imparted to an incredulous Dorothy in the climactic scene of *The Wizard of Oz*, this capacity was there all along. Indeed, Dorothy-like, we have become so preoccupied with reaching the mythical "Oz" of "development"—that magical destination where all needs are met and all problems resolved—that we fail to notice that Africa already *has* robust business and "entrepreneurial cultures" that have been in evidence for generations. The examples range from the unconventional and the sinister to the inventive and the visionary, from the infamous "419" email scammers of Nigeria's corrupt underbelly to the denizens of Eastern Congo profiting from patronage, informal networks, and the quasi-state environment captured in Janet MacGaffey's scholarship to, more positively, the panoply of small-scale enterprises described in Anita Spring and Barbara E. McDade's *African Entrepreneurship* and the vibrant entrepreneurial business plan competitions in Kenya and elsewhere that can attract thousands of aspiring businesspeople. These examples, and many others of larger scale emphasized throughout this book, should leave little doubt as to the reservoir of entrepreneurialism in African societies.

This is not to say, however, that African businesses are now fully realized entities throughout the continent. In other words, the expression of business or entrepreneurial culture was long proscribed by colonial edict, postcolonial ideology, and a long hostile institutional environment, factors that have had a lasting impact; the easing of some of these constraints has not exactly brought about utopia. They have not succeeded in transforming African economies some fifty years after independence. Although the pessimists go too far, it is clear that Africa as a whole continues to face structural constraints of global marginality and dependence, exacerbated by climatological unpredictability and demographic pressures. Further, the majority of countries must also contend with a legacy of political malfeasance and a host of policy blunders whose origins are both internal and external. Yet while constraints certainly persist, the presence of bona fide businesses that embody Africa's *intrinsic* entrepreneurialism is increasingly apparent. The institutional changes discussed in chapter 3 indicate that the environment is appreciably different as a result of international and domestic changes, the bulk of which have occurred in the past decade or two.

Evolving slowly in the 1990s, a more stable institutional environment—a system of rules, regulations, and laws, undergirded by discernible democratization—today is an increasingly visible part of the African political-economic landscape. This is not to suggest, however, that "rational legal" forms of authority now everywhere predominate, nor that gains are irreversible where they have been made. After all, rational legal authority and the meritorious bureaucracies and governance that purportedly accompany it are *ideal types* that still remain aspirational in many parts of the world (see David Kang's treatment of South Korea in *Crony Capitalism,* for example). Nonetheless, awareness of the changes in sub-Saharan Africa and appreciation for their implications compels us to fundamentally alter the way we conceive of the prospects for business and private sector development broadly (and formal PSD programs more narrowly) in Africa today.

In addition, international investment, led by multinational corporations from the global North and, increasingly, the global South (chapter 4), a coterie of "reformed cronies" (chapter 5), and Africa's extant big business (chapter 6) together paint a much fuller picture of the cultures of big business in contemporary Africa. These actors and enterprises help facilitate movement beyond primary commodity dependence through such mechanisms as market-seeking investment and networking with local diasporas. But more than that, the breadth of their activities reveals that there is already a great deal of nuance to business in Africa: it is more diverse, more successful even by conventional measures, more sustainable, and more international than depicted—if one is willing to look beyond the neopatrimonial, "dark continent" stereotypes.

TAKING ON THE BOOSTERS

In many ways, this book can be read as a rejoinder to reactionary Afropessimism in its various guises. But the critique should not be taken as an apology for the triumphalist claims occasionally voiced on the other side. In no way am I asserting that the African business boosters or their "globalizationist" peers in the development community are measurably more persuasive in their own arguments. Much of their enthusiasm is vested in the hopes that micro- and small-scale African entrepreneurs as well as those from elsewhere can sow the seeds of a nascent business class on the continent, thereby prompting economic growth, poverty reduction, and, ultimately, development.

The preoccupation with micro-, small- and medium-scale enterprises that one finds in both academic and practical writing is proper inasmuch as it entails and explicit recognition of Africa's historically underutilized and frequently untapped entrepreneurialism. But as a barometer of the current business climate, or indeed, as a policy objective, the focus on these kinds of operations is ultimately too narrow if not altogether misplaced. Indeed, if we are thinking teleologically (as the development community does by definition), then "our" goal should not be SMEs; yet too often, rather than being considered simply one possible component of the means to the end of business development, they become the end themselves. I find such thinking reflective of an archaic paternalism that consigns African business to the quaint idyll of the typical Western stereotype: the roadside stall, the two-cow dairy operation, or the bicycle repairman ready with his tools under a village tree. This brand of optimism, though deeply and no doubt sincerely felt, will neither alter mindsets nor shift paradigms.

I contend that the symbolism conveyed by this "face" of Africa, as well as to some degree the PSD initiatives that aim to promote such enterprises, is in fact a constraint, at least in the near and intermediate term. Generating sustainable business enterprise through SMEs is both a difficult and extremely long-term undertaking. Of course, SMEs can be an important route to business development on a case by case basis, but it is wishful thinking to expect that programs focused *solely* on SME development will lead inexorably to successful business sectors. Many such enterprises, especially at the micro level, perform what is, at bottom, a subsistence function; absent marked success early on, states, aspiring entrepreneurs, and the donors who purport to support them will abandon the effort. This suggests that more emphasis and support, in terms of finance, infrastructural development, and policies could be more profitably directed at bigger players because of their potential impact on diversification, transformation, employment generation, and growth. Still, the prospects for a large cohort of diverse, international competitive African firms are certainly modest.

That at least part of the answer to Africa's development conundrum, in the near term, lies more in bigger business (both foreign and domestic) than in smaller ones and as much in reformed cronies as conventional entrepreneurship is certainly not uncontroversial. But given the opportunities and constraints presented by economic and political reforms, Africa's erstwhile cronies and its own international players are often best able to avail themselves of this dynamic, if still unsettled, environment. The access these actors enjoy to resources and often to government can overcome shortages of electrical power, infrastructure, inputs, and credit far better than an SME whose financial health is entirely dependent on much more erratic supply chains, whether what is being supplied is industrial inputs or political patronage.

*   *   *

Not very long ago, Nicolas van de Walle wrote of a "permanent crisis" afflicting African economies, but he astutely delimited that "permanence" to the years 1979–1999 in his book's often overlooked subtitle. In fact, van de Walle's bracketing of the dates appeared particularly prescient when less than three years into the new century Africa saw some of its greatest growth rates in a decade. We now know, of course, that this economic boom abated somewhat in the 2008–2009 period, and though growth resumed thereafter, it may again prove transient. For while many countries in Africa— perhaps starting with the seventeen Steven Radelet describes currently as "emerging"— demonstrate markedly improved economic and political fundamentals, they remain vulnerable.[1] Indeed, given the vagaries of African economies, it would be tempting when faced with the next downturn to proclaim anew that the African predicament *is* in fact ineradicable: *plus ça change, plus c'est la même chose.*

And yet the *cultural* fabric of business in Africa at the end of the inaugural decade of the twenty-first century is much richer than at any time in the past. For one thing, it is more diverse. Western MNCs are still there, joined by those from India, China, and elsewhere, as well as a host of new portfolio and private equity investors. Minority capital and local entrepreneurs of varied origins and African big business are also prominent. Politically and economically, these actors have a stake and a vested interest in self-preservation and, increasingly, the capacity to defend that interest. In addition, more and more, they coexist with civil societies, plural political parties, and a moderately more vigilant international and to a lesser extent continental community. These factors hardly preclude the recurrence of crisis, but they do bode well for its being geographically and temporally circumscribed.

THE CULTURES OF BUSINESS IN AFRICA

If locally, and in some spheres globally, competitive African business already exists, if business and entrepreneurial cultures are already abundant, and if Africa has already seen some success beyond primary commodities, perhaps we need to revisit and restate our fundamental questions and ask instead what will it take to *further* develop African business. First, we should not underestimate the value of time and patience. I have assailed the notion promulgated by numerous, largely Western, Africa watchers and development experts that "Africa is just like we were a century ago"— or two, or three, or even more, depending on the issue under discussion. While ideas of this kind have a certain dramatic flair, such facile comparisons are of little utility. Nevertheless, the notion of chronological *time* is, in fact, critical, and its passage will surely see the achievement of solutions to many of the development problems now presumed to be intractable. Some of these changes are not easily predicted, although recently we have seen sub-Saharan Africa effectively leapfrog many of these obstacles, such as communication technology, and with Chinese, Indian, and other technology and investment, it may have the opportunity to leapfrog further. Recent structural and institutional changes in its political economy, namely widespread democratization, economic reform, and demonstration effects, augur positively as well. Future research must pay keen attention to these trends and show new attention to the diversity of business cultures in Africa and how they can be sufficiently and appropriately marshaled for optimal development.

At bottom, both the neopatrimonial adherents and their optimistic counterparts offer us many useful insights, though they are ultimately incomplete. Most previous studies are overly pessimistic (e.g., Chabal and Daloz; Callaghy), overly optimistic

(Fick; Pineau; Mahajan), or necessarily circumscribed in their focus on predominantly on one end of the scale (e.g., Ramachandran, Gelb, and Shah). Many pessimists and optimists alike are also generally "presentist" inasmuch as they are fixated on one particular *moment* in time and thereby fail or otherwise neglect to account for trajectories, thus missing the myriad changes over time. In the past generation these have included altered global conditions and an environment of globalization, a search for higher growth rates that can accelerate poverty reduction, and a new national receptiveness and positive attitudes toward business—influenced by democracy and capitalism. We have also witnessed a surprising ability of new and existing entrepreneurs to adapt to these new realities, such as by establishing linkages at home with political actors and minorities or internationally with investors such as the Chinese, Indians, and others.

I have assigned a variety of labels to the characters in this book: promising newcomers, traditional and nontraditional investors, transformed cronies, and a new generation of giants. Yet whatever the label, the categories are perhaps *more* fluid and richly varied than my treatment here allowed. More importantly, perhaps, is that all of Africa's cultural varieties have comparable counterparts among business communities throughout the world. Indeed, it is this final observation that leaves the most durable impression: the "cultures of business in Africa" are in fact a fair representation of a broad cross-section of *global* business cultures rather than merely a feeble reflection of them.

Table 1. Exports of Merchandise and Services

	Average (Millions of $)*			Growth Rates	
	1980–89	1990–99	2000–2009	1990–99	2000–2009
World	2,709,229.08	5,779,649.36	12,610,810.14	113.33%	118.19%
Developing economies	656,241.43	1,521,979.25	4,257,212.76	131.92%	179.72%
Developing economies: Africa	102,313.67	137,335.50	350,233.12	34.23%	155.02%
Eastern Africa	8,136.20	13,575.47	26,301.38	66.85%	93.74%
Middle Africa	9,099.90	12,526.58	50,105.29	37.66%	299.99%
Northern Africa	38,965.20	49,786.89	136,638.26	27.77%	174.45%
Southern Africa	25,628.74	36,480.59	72,227.70	42.34%	97.99%
Western Africa	20,483.63	24,965.97	64,960.49	21.88%	160.20%
Africa excluding South Africa	79,429.17	105,808.23	287,460.69	33.21%	171.68%
Northern Africa excluding Sudan	38,137.91	49,194.93	131,422.79	28.99%	167.15%
Sub-Saharan Africa	64,175.76	88,140.57	218,810.32	37.34%	148.25%
Sub-Saharan Africa excluding South Africa	41,291.26	56,613.30	156,037.89	37.11%	175.62%

*Measured in USD at current prices and current exchange rates.
Source: UN Conference on Trade and Development Statistical Database, http://unctadstat.unctad.org

Table 2. Net Domestic Credit

Country	Average ($)*			Growth Rates	
	1980–89	1990–99	2000–2008	1990–99	2000–2008
Ghana	2,777,276,718	1,430,959,357	1,972,647,061	–48%	38%
Kenya	2,389,079,859	3,632,208,365	7,101,546,955	52%	96%
Mauritius	721,615,596	2,321,961,255	5,994,408,716	222%	158%
Nigeria	23,910,569,581	14,296,813,239	17,216,909,646	–40%	20%
Senegal	1,515,210,373	1,368,789,243	1,841,628,480	–10%	35%
South Africa	43,757,353,332	77,009,147,887	160,506,217,659	76%	108%
Tanzania	2,262,484,333	1,224,401,015	1,532,345,824	–46%	25%
Uganda	779,190,490	309,384,800	767,966,939	–60%	148%
Zambia	2,082,400,823	1,820,233,087	1,943,912,402	–13%	7%

*Adjusted for exchange rate fluctuations. Data reported in LCU. Average exchange rate per year used for conversion to USD.

Source: World Bank Development Indicators and Global Development Finance, http://databank.worldbank.org/ddp/home.do

Table 3. Foreign Direct Investment in Reporting Economy (FDI Inward)

	Average (Millions of $)*			Growth Rates	
	1980–89	1990–99	2000–2009	1990–99	2000–2009
World	1,080,865.87	3,634,710.07	11,988,420.11	236.28%	229.83%
Developing economies	381,604.53	893,908.85	2,922,668.77	134.25%	226.95%
Developing economies: Africa	45,151.27	89,746.44	286,512.13	98.77%	219.25%
Eastern Africa	3,796.78	7,376.87	25,168.98	94.29%	241.19%
Middle Africa	3,691.57	7,170.27	28,829.09	94.23%	302.06%
Northern Africa	14,963.46	32,456.00	100,676.75	116.90%	210.19%
Southern Africa	14,713.00	20,117.09	73,706.81	36.73%	266.39%
Western Africa	7,986.45	22,626.20	58,130.50	183.31%	156.92%
Major petroleum exporters: Developing Africa	8,590.02	23,492.44	85,023.76	173.49%	261.92%
Africa excluding South Africa	33,575.02	73,167.38	217,892.01	117.92%	197.80%
Northern Africa excluding Sudan	14,894.34	32,195.04	92,333.50	116.16%	186.79%
Sub-Saharan Africa	30,256.92	57,551.40	194,178.62	90.21%	237.40%
Sub-Saharan Africa excluding South Africa	18,680.68	40,972.34	125,558.50	119.33%	206.45%

*Measured in USD at current prices and current exchange rates.
Source: World Bank Development Indicators and Global Development Finance, http://databank.worldbank.org/ddp/home.do.

NOTES

PREFACE

1. Curtis Keim, Mistaking Africa: Curiosities and Inventions of the American Mind, 2nd ed. (Boulder, CO: Westview, 2010), 8.

2. It is perhaps a further irony that he apparently made the same error of judgment—a rush to judgment—based on preconceived notions.

3. John R. Heilbrunn, "Commerce, Politics, and Business Associations in Benin and Togo," Comparative Politics 29. 4 (1997), 473–92; Janet MacGaffey and Rémy Bazenguissa-Ganga, Congo-Paris: Transnational Traders on the Margins of the Law (Bloomington: Indiana University Press, 2000); Karen Tranberg Hansen, Salaula: The World of Second Hand Clothing and Zambia (Chicago: University of Chicago Press, 2000); Gareth Austin, "African Business in Nineteenth Century West Africa," in Black Business and Economic Power, edited by Alusine Jalloh and Toyin Falola, 114–44 (Rochester, NY: University of Rochester Press, 2002); Michael O. West, The Rise of an African Middle Class: Colonial Zimbabwe, 1898–1965 (Bloomington: Indiana University Press, 2002); John Iliffe, The Emergence of African Capitalism (Minneapolis: University of Minnesota Press, 1983).

4. Gareth Austin, "African Business in Nineteenth-Century West Africa," 119–20.

5. Rogers Brubaker qtd. in Thomas Callaghy, "The State and the Development of Capitalism in Africa: Theoretical, Historical, and Comparative Reflections," in The Precarious Balance, ed. Donald Rothschild (Boulder, CO: Westview, 1988), 70.

6. David Stark and László Bruszt, "One Way or Multiple Paths: For a Comparative Sociology of East European Capitalism," American Journal of Sociology 106.4 (2001): 1131.

7. Ruth McVey, Southeast Asian Capitalists (Ithaca, NY: Cornell Southeast Asia Program Publications, 1992), 8.

8. Ibid., emphasis added.

9. There is some variation between the IFC and the European Union: the EU defines large-scale enterprises as those with more than 250 employees. In any event, both measurements include a second criterion, either a revenue or asset minimum, which few African firms meet: $15 million and $15 million (IFC) and €50 million and €43 million in assets and turnover, respectively.

10. For industry-specific analysis see, for example, Pádraig Carmody, Tearing the Social Fabric: Neoliberalism, Deindustrialization, and the Crisis of Governance in Zimbabwe (Westport, CT: Greenwood, 2001), or Farhad Noorbakhsh and Alberto Paloni, "Structural Adjustment Programs and Industry in Sub-Saharan Africa: Restructuring or De-Industrialization?," Journal of Developing Areas 33.4 (1999), 549–80.

11. Roger Tangri, The Politics of Patronage in Africa: Parastatals, Privatization and Private Enterprise (Trenton, NJ: Africa Word Press, 1999). See also George B. N. Ayittey, Africa Betrayed (New York: St. Martin's, 1993), and Giorgio Blundo and Jean-Pierre Olivier de Sardan, Everyday Corruption and the State (London: Zed, 2006).

12. Pádraig Carmody, Globalization in Africa: Recolonization or Renaissance (Boulder, CO: Lynne Rienner, 2010), 3.

INTRODUCTION

1. Although many of the arguments in this book also pertain to the countries of North Africa, "Africa" as used herein refers to sub-Saharan Africa unless otherwise specified.

2. Of the forty-four developing world companies on the 2006 Fortune Global 500.

3. This is most vividly represented in Transparency International's annual Corruption Perceptions Index.

4. Leslie Sklair and Peter Robbins, "Global Capitalism and Major Corporations from the Third World," Third World Quarterly 23.1 (2002): 81–100.

5. In this book, "African business" refers to business and investment activity of firms resident in or principally identified with Africa, regardless of their ethnic, racial, or cultural origins. Where noted, this more inclusive definition is distinguished from "black African business." A broader characterization, "business in Africa," refers to business activity by all firms and entities doing business on the continent, including multinational corporations. My book thus addresses all three categories: black African, minority, and multinational.

6. Mark Casson, Entrepreneurship and Business Culture (Aldershot, UK: Edward Elgar 1995), esp. 79 and 91.

7. Expressions of Afropessimism are found in everything from film (see Martha Evans and Ian Glenn, "'TIA—This is Africa': Afropessimism in Twenty-First Century Narrative Film" Black Camera 2, n.s., 1 [2010]: 14–35) to the African university (see Paul T. Zeleza, "Beyond Afropessimism: Historical Accounting of African Universities" Pambazuka News [Cape Town, South Africa], 30 August 2006, http://www.pambazuka .org/en/category/features/35832 [accessed 24 October 2011]), to the prevalence of HIV/ AIDS (see Pádraig Carmody, Globalization and Africa: Recolonization or Renaissance [Boulder, CO: Lynne Rienner, 2010]).

8. Zeleza, "Beyond Afropessimism."

9. Afropessimism is more than simply a convenient straw man or an unfair lumping together of Africa's critics. What unites perspectives under the banner of Afropessimism is a resounding belief that positive outcomes are unlikely. Afropessimists consign Africa to a trajectory of a vicious circle that has real-world implications.

10. "The market landscape that is Africa is every bit as marvelous and surprising as its geographic landscape" (Vijay Mahajan, Africa Rising: How 900 Million African Consumers Offer More Than You Think [Upper Saddle River, NJ: Prentice Hall, 2009], xii).

11. Thomas Callaghy, "The State and the Development of Capitalism in Africa: Theoretical, Historical and Comparative Reflections," in The Precarious Balance, ed. Donald Rothchild (Boulder, CO: Westview, 1988), 67–99. See also Karla Hoff and Arijit Sen, "The Kin System as a Poverty Trap?," Policy Research Paper 3575, World Bank, 2006.

12. Ruth McVey, *Southeast Asian Capitalists* (Ithaca, NY: Cornell Southeast Asia Program Publications, 1992), 9.

13. Ibid., 10, emphasis added.

14. Lately, the scholarly tradition of neopatrimonialism has been under fire, not least because it has been conceptually overstretched (see Anne Pitcher, Mary H. Moran, and Michael Johnston, "Rethinking Patrimonialism and Neopatrimonialism in Africa," *African Studies Review* 52.1 [2009]: 125–56, Gero Erdmann and Ulf Engel, "Neopatrimonialism Reconsidered: Critical Review and Elaboration of an Elusive Concept," *Commonwealth and Comparative Politics* 45.1 [2007]: 95–119, Aaron DeGrassi, "'Neopatrimonialism' and Agricultural Development in Africa: Contributions and Limitations of a Contested Concept," *African Studies Review* 51. 3 [2008]: 107–33 2008). Pitcher, Moran, and Johnston, like McVey, argue for a return to Weber's original conception of patrimonial authority and its relationship to legitimacy.

15. Callaghy, "The State and the Development of Capitalism in Africa," 69–70. In fairness, authors like Michael Bratton and Nicolas van de Walle do allow for the possibility of political transitions *from* neopatrimonial rule, however difficult. See their *Democratic Experiments in Africa: Regime Transitions in Comparative Perspective* (Cambridge: Cambridge University Press, 1997), 83–96.

16. McVey, *Southeast Asian Capitalists*, 8. See also Pitcher, Moran, and Johnston, "Rethinking Patrimonialism."

17. A reading of David Kang's *Crony Capitalism: Corruption and Development in South Korea and the Philippines* (Cambridge: University Press, 2002), for example, conveys an impression of a level of malfeasance and business-state corruption that outstrips many countries in Africa

18. See Vadim Volkov, *Violent Entrepreneurs: The Use of Force in the Making of Russian Capitalism* (Ithaca, NY: Cornell University Press, 2002), Kang, *Crony Capitalism,* and Kenneth Ackerman, *Boss Tweed: The Rise and Fall of the Corrupt Pol Who Conceived the Soul of Modern New York* (New York: Carroll and Graf, 2005).

19. Kang, *Crony Capitalism;* Volkov, *Violent Entrepreneurs.*

20. Susan Rose-Ackerman, *Corruption and Government: Causes, Consequences, and Reform* (Cambridge: Cambridge University Press, 1999), 122.

21. Indeed, Johnston's " primary focus is... upon systemic corruption problems: uses of and connections between wealth and power that significantly weaken open competitive participation and/or economic and political institutions, or delay or prevent their development" (*Syndromes of Corruption: Wealth, Power, and Democracy* [Cambridge: Cambridge University Press, 2006], 12). Although such an approach has intrinsic value, I argue that capitalist accumulation even through corruption can lead to long-term institutional strengthening and perhaps even to democratic change eventually.

22. Ian Birrell, "It's Time the World Listened to New Stories out of Africa," *Guardian* (Manchester, UK), 20 February 2011.

23. See Carmody, *Globalization in Africa,* and Cooper, "What Is the Concept of Globalization Good For? An African Historian's Perspective," *African Affairs* 100.399 (2001): 192, on the problems with this conceptualization.

24. Carmody, *Globalization,* 6.

25. For damning critiques of the impact of globalization in Africa and elsewhere,

see James Ferguson, *Global Shadows: Africa in the Neoliberal World Order.* (Durham, NC: Duke University Press, 2006), David C. Korten, *When Corporations Ruled the World,* rev. ed. (Bloomfield, CT: Kumarian Press, 2001), and Cooper, "What Is the Concept of Globalization Good For?"

26. World Bank, "Economy Rankings," 2009, Doing Business Project, http://www .doingbusiness.org/EconomyRankings (accessed 18 May 2010).

27. Daniel Kaufman, speech, "Governance Matters: Debunking the Afropessimism Myth" conference, 28 November 2007, Washington, DC, http://www.cgdev.org/doc/events/11.28.07/Governance_Matters_Transcript_2007.pdf (accessed 23 October 2011).

28. Of course, "minority-owned" capital can also refer to the economic interests of a given country's *ethnic* minority as well, all of which have been characterized by Amy Chua as "market-dominant minorities" (*World on Fire: How Exporting Free Market Democracy Breeds Ethnic Hatred and Global Instability* [New York: Random House, 2003]). It is impossible to deny the role of African ethnic groups that have been relatively privileged historically in terms of business: Kenya's Kikuyu, Igbo in Nigeria, and Amhara in Ethiopia, for example. Yet whereas members of these groups were often privileged, nowhere do they enjoy as much dominance, *as a group,* as their European or Asian counterparts. Thus, I focus mainly on the racial cleavages rather than the ethnolinguistic ones.

29. See Carmody, *Globalization in Africa,* for a summary of the views.

1. AFRICAN BUSINESS AND CAPITALISM IN HISTORICAL PERSPECTIVE

1. See, for example, Curtis Keim, *Mistaking Africa: Curiosities and Inventions of the American Mind,* 2nd ed. (Boulder, CO: Westview, 2010).

2. Perhaps the foremost example of this was Marxist Angola's relationship with the American corporation Gulf Oil. Elsewhere, multinational corporations utilized local affiliates. Though these were seldom geared to export markets and were often proscribed from exporting (due to lack of price competitiveness or deliberate political policy or both) and faced restrictions on repatriation of profits as well, their operations enabled them to acquire—or, more often, maintain—a toehold in various African domestic markets. For host governments, these affiliates were a key part of the effort to meet national demand as part of import substitution strategies.

3. Uganda in the 1970s and Zimbabwe in the 2000s are the two most prominent exceptions. It is important to note, however, that Zimbabwe's expropriation of white-owned farms and other assets was not ideological but political, and it came two decades after independence in 1980. Idi Amin's disastrous expulsion of Asian businesspeople from Uganda in 1972 was ultimately reversed twenty years later.

4. A. G. Hopkins, "Big Business in African Studies," *Journal of African History* 28.1 (1987): 126.

5. Abner Cohen, *Custom and Politics in Urban Africa: A Study of Hausa Migrants in Yoruba Towns* (Berkeley: University of California Press, 1967), 5–6.

6. See Cohen, *Custom and Politics in Urban Africa,* and Alusine Jalloh, *African Entrepreneurship: Muslim Fula Merchants in Sierra Leone* (Athens: Ohio University Center for International Studies, 1999).

7. Ralph Austen, *African Economic History* (Berkeley: University of California Press, 1987), 22–24.

8. Cited in C. Magbaily Fyle, "Indigenous Values and the Organization of Informal Sector Business in West Africa," in *Black Business and Economic Power,* edited by Alusine Jalloh and Toyin Falola (Rochester, NY: University of Rochester Press, 2002), 31–32.

9. Austen, *African Economic History,* 24.

10. Cited in Fyle, "Indigenous Values and the Organization of Informal Sector Business in West Africa," 30.

11. Ibid.; Austen, *African Economic History.*

12. See Joseph E. Inikori, "The Development of Entrepreneurship in Africa: Southeastern Nigeria during the Era of the Trans-Atlantic Slave Trade," in *Black Business and Economic Power,* edited by Alusine Jalloh and Toyin Falola (Rochester, NY: University of Rochester Press, 2002), 67.

13. Gareth Austin, "African Business in Nineteenth-Century West Africa," in *Black Business and Economic Power,* 17.

14. Austin, "African Business in Nineteenth-Century West Africa," 119–120.

15. Ibid., 122.

16. Ibid., 117.

17. Cohen, *Custom and Politics in Urban Africa,* 7.

18. A superb cataloging of the multinational firms that invested in Africa throughout the colonial period can be found in A. G. Hopkins's "Imperial Business in Africa: Part I, Sources," *Journal of African History* 17.1 (1976): 29–48.

19. Thomas Callaghy, "The State and the Development of Capitalism in Africa: Theoretical, Historical, and Comparative Reflections," in *The Precarious Balance,* ed. Donald Rothschild (Boulder, CO: Westview, 1988), 67–99.

20. The British South Africa Company and the Imperial British East Africa Company, among others, were essentially bailed out by the British Colonial Office.

21. For an analysis of the development and performance of black entrepreneurs in urban South Africa, for example, see Sipho Sibusiso Maseko, "From Pavement Entrepreneurs to Stock Exchange Capitalists: the Case of the South African Black Business Class" (DPhil thesis, University of the Western Cape, Bellville, 2000).

22. Mac Dixon-Fyle, "Agricultural Improvement and Political Protest on the Tonga Plateau, Northern Rhodesia," *Journal of African History* 18.4 (1977): 579–96.

23. Colin Bundy reveals how black South African peasant farmers were systematically crushed by their white counterparts in an attempt to both prevent potential competition and provide an urban labor reserve (*The Rise and Fall of the South African Peasantry* [Berkeley: University of California Press, 1979]).

24. Gracia Clark, "Gender Fictions and Gender Tensions Involving 'Traditional' Asante Market Women," *African Studies Quarterly* 11.2/3 (2010): 50.

25. Marjorie McIntosh, *Yoruba Women, Work, and Social Change* (Bloomington: Indiana University Press, 2009).

26. David Himbara, "Domestic Capitalists and the State in Kenya," in *African Capitalists in African Development,* ed. Bruce Berman and Colin Leys (Boulder, CO: Lynne Rienner, 1994), 80. See, for example, E. A. Brett, *Colonialism and Underdevelopment in East Africa* (New York: NOK Publishers, 1973), 294, and Nicola Swainson, "Indigenous

Capitalism in Postcolonial Kenya," in *The African Bourgeoisie: Capitalist Development in Nigeria, Kenya, and the Ivory Coast*, ed. Paul Lubeck (Boulder, CO: Lynne Rienner, 1987), 140. Michael Chege offers an argument supportive of Himbara in "Introducing Race as a Variable into the Political Economy of Kenya Debate: An Incendiary Idea," *African Affairs*, 97.387 (1998): 209–30.

27. See Paul Lubeck, "The African Bourgeoisie: Debates, Methods, and Units of Analysis," in *The African Bourgeoisie*, 19. Here Lubeck clearly echoes Karl Marx ("On Imperialism in India") in finding virtue in imperialist exploitation.

28. Austen, *African Economic History*, 236–40.

29. Evans argues that the sustained interaction of state and society facilitates the emergence of a state that is "embedded" in its societal institutions. The "developmental state" is one that displays the characteristics of embedded autonomy: it is strong state that is characterized by a meritorious Weberian bureaucracy and that possesses a substantial degree of autonomy to carry out policy, yet it is simultaneously "embedded" in societal institutions. However, "developmentalism" is an essential part of embedded autonomy, and absent developmentalism, states will not develop (*Embedded Autonomy* [Princeton, NJ: Princeton University Press, 1995], 243–50). By implication, a *strong state* is required to promote developmentalism, leaving us with a circular and ultimately unsatisfactory *statist* theory of little help where states are weak, as in Africa.

In Evans's framework, the state bureaucracy plays a nurturing role in developing business. There are certain similarities between Evan's model and apartheid-era South Africa, although it was a racially exclusive model that instead created a system of "socialism for the whites" while denying opportunities to black businesses and the citizenry at large (see Jeffrey Herbst, *State Politics in Zimbabwe* [Berkeley: California, 1990], 22).

30. See Thandika Mkandawire and Charles Soludo, *Our Continent, Our Future* (Trenton, NJ: Africa World Press, 1998).

31. East Asian import substitution industrialization was aided by the region's different factor endowments and comparative advantage (labor versus Africa's land), as well as by established bureaucracies, a favorable geostrategic position under the blanket of American hegemony, and a transition to an export-led growth model as an outlet for its industrial production. Importantly, corruption was not a constraint on development, as the South Korea case illustrates (see Kang, *Crony Capitalism: Corruption and Development in South Korea and the Philippines* [Cambridge: University Press, 2002]).

32. This prospect is discussed in the context of black economic empowerment schemes in chapter 6.

33. Although the private sector development programs discussed in subsequent chapters of this book focus on small-and medium-size enterprises and thus implicitly target black Africans, very few states have explicit black or "indigenous" empowerment programs that necessarily exclude whites and others. South Africa and Namibia are among the noteworthy exceptions.

34. Vijaya Ramachandran, Alan Gelb, and Manju Kedia Shah, *Africa's Private Sector: What's Wrong with the Business Environment and What to Do about It?* (Washington, DC: Center for Global Development, 2009).

35. Ibid.

36. See, for example, Barry Seargent, "Zimbabwe's Pale Barons," *Moneyweb*, 30 June

2008, http://www.moneyweb.co.za/mw/view/mw/en/page292676?oid=212866&sn=2009 +Detail&pid=292676 (accessed 18 May 2010).

37. Amy Chua, author of *World on Fire: How Exporting Free Market Democracy Breeds Ethnic Hatred and Global Instability* (New York: Random House, 2003), is among the rare exceptions. See also Kang's analysis of Chinese business community in the Philippines in *Crony Capitalism.*

38. For illustrations of Asian cases, see Andrew MacIntyre, ed., *Business and Government in Industrialising Asia* (Ithaca, NY: Cornell University Press, 1994). An interesting examination of comparative public policy is supplied by Ian Emsley, *The Malaysian Experience of Affirmative Action: Lessons for South Africa* (Johannesburg, South Africa: Tafelberg, 1995). See also Scott Taylor, "Race, Class, and Neopatrimonial Politics," in *State, Conflict, and Democracy in Africa,* ed. Richard A. Joseph (Boulder, CO: Lynne Rienner, 1998), 239–66, Tor Skalnes, *The Politics of Economic Reform in Zimbabwe: Continuity and Change in Development* (Basingstoke, UK: Macmillan Press, 1995), and Tom Ostergaard, "The Role of the 'National' Bourgeoisie in National Development: The Case of the Textile and Clothing Industries in Zimbabwe," in *African Capitalists in African Development,* 115–38.

39. Himbara, "Domestic Capitalists and the State in Kenya," 84.

40. Michael Bratton and Peter Lolojih, "Rationality, Cosmopolitanism, and Adjustment Fatigue: Public Attitudes to Economic Reform in Zambia," Afrobarometer Working Paper 105, April 2009.

41. See Taylor, "Race, Class, and Neopatrimonial Politics" for a review. The term "bureaucratic bourgeoisie" was coined by Issa Shivji in 1976.

42. This scenario bears some resemblance to three of four corruption "syndromes" described by Michael Johnston in his *Syndromes of Corruption: Wealth, Power, and Democracy* (Cambridge: Cambridge University Press, 2006).

43. Kennedy *optimistically* volunteered that African capitalism is two hundred years behind Europe (cited in Colin Leys, "African Capitalists and Development: Theoretical Questions," in *African Capitalists in African Development,* 23).

44. Callaghy, "The State and the Development of Capitalism in Africa," 72.

45. In the view of Ayittey and Moyo, the pattern can only be broken by a major rupture, such as the removal of African leaders or the immediate cessation of foreign aid. See George B. N. Ayittey, *Africa Betrayed* (New York: St. Martin's, 1993), and Dambisa Moyo, *Dead Aid: Why Aid Is Not Working and How There Is a Better Way for Africa* (New York: Farrar, Straus, and Giroux, 2009).

46. Although today the comparisons are more likely to be made by way of reference to Europe of the early nineteenth century (is this progress?) or the metrics of the Millennium Development Goals. But the point is the same: Africa is *behind.* This entire logic suggests a teleology that is not necessarily advantageous to Africa or particularly helpful for analysis.

2. INSTITUTIONAL CHANGE IN THE 1990s

1. Nicolas van de Walle, *African Economies and the Politics of Permanent Crisis, 1979–1999* (Cambridge: Cambridge University Press).

2. See Adebayo O. Olukoshi, ed., *The Politics of Structural Adjustment in Nigeria* (London: James Currey, 1993). On politics, see Michael Bratton and Nicolas van de Walle, *Democratic Experiments in Africa: Regime Transitions in Comparative Perspective* (Cambridge: Cambridge University Press, 1997), and Richard A. Joseph, ed., *State, Conflict, and Democracy in Africa* (Boulder, CO: Lynne Rienner, 1998), and Leonardo A. Villalón and Peter VonDoepp, *The Fate of Africa's Democratic Experiments* (Bloomington: Indiana University Press, 2008).

3. Todd Moss, *African Development: Making Sense of the Actors and Issues* (Boulder, CO: Lynne Rienner, 2007), 234–36; Vijaya Ramachandran, Alan Gelb, and Manju Kedia Shah, *Africa's Private Sector: What's Wrong with the Business Environment and What to Do about It?* (Washington, DC: Center for Global Development, 2009); World Bank, *Doing Business 2009: Comparing Regulation in 181 Economies,* September 2008, Doing Business Project, http://www.doingbusiness.org/~/media/fpdkm/doing %20business/documents/annual-reports/english/db09-fullreport.pdf (accessed 23 October 2011).

4. For a time in the 1980s, for example, Cote d'Ivoire was still regarded as one of Africa's foremost practitioner of bourgeois capitalism, boasting a vibrant manufacturing sector as well as robust private business activity in commercial trade and plantation agriculture. But closer investigation reveals the fairly precarious architecture common to these supposed exemplars of African capitalism. The private sector was dominated by Asians and largely expatriate Europeans, while most Africans, outside a small, politically connected elite, faced high barriers to entry. In addition, state-owned enterprises represented 10.5 percent of GDP, 39.5 percent of investment measured by gross fixed capital formation, and 29 percent of domestic credit in 1984—all rates higher than in Tanzania. See John Nellis, "Public Enterprises in Sub-Saharan Africa," in *State-Owned Enterprises in Africa,* ed. Barbara Grosh and Rwekaza Mukandala (Boulder, CO: Lynne Rienner, 1994), 5–8.

5. SAPs have been defended most effectively by Nicolas van de Walle in *African Economics and the Politics of Permanent Crisis* and by Lise Rakner, Nicolas van de Walle, and Dominic Mulaisho in "Aid and Reform in Zambia," in *Aid and Reform in Africa: Lessons From Ten Case Studies,* ed. Shantayanan Devarajan, David R. Dollar, and Torgny Holmgren (Washington, DC: World Bank), 533–626.

6. See Patrick Bond, *Uneven Zimbabwe: A Study of Finance, Development, and Underdevelopment* (Trenton, NJ: Africa World Press, 1998), Thandika Mkandawire and Charles Soludo, *Our Continent, Our Future* (Trenton, NJ: Africa World Press, 1998), Joseph Stiglitz, *Globalization and its Discontents* (New York: Norton, 2002), and Michael Bratton, Robert Mattes, and Emmanuel Gyimah-Boadi, *Public Opinion, Democracy, and Reform* (New York: Cambridge University Press, 2005).

7. Bond, *Uneven Zimbabwe.*

8. For a thorough critique of the failings of structural adjustment programs, see, for example, Olukoshi, *The Politics of Structural Adjustment in Nigeria.* On the misreading of Asia, see Howard Stein, ed., *Asian Industrialization and Africa* (New York: St. Martin's, 1996), although eventually the bank showed some capacity for learning. See Reginald Herbold Green, "The IMF and World Bank in Africa: How Much Learning," in *Hemmed In: Responses to Africa's Economic Decline,* ed. Thomas Callaghy and John Ravenhill (New York: Columbia University Press, 1993), 54–89. See also Mkandawire

and Soludo, *Our Continent, Our Future*. For an alternative view, see van de Walle, *African Economics and the Politics of Permanent Crisis*.

9. See Carol Lancaster, "The Lagos Three," in *Africa in World Politics: Post–Cold War Challenges*, 2nd ed., ed. John Harbeson and Donald Rothchild (Boulder, CO: Westview, 1995), 189--206, and Nicolas van de Walle, "Adjustment Alternatives and Alternatives to Adjustment," *African Studies Review* 37.3 (1994): 103–17.

10. I am grateful to Callisto Madavo for pointing this out.

11. See Jean-François Bayart, *The State in Africa: The Politics of the Belly* (New York: Longman, 1993), Thomas Callaghy, "The State and the Development of Capitalism in Africa: Theoretical, Historical, and Comparative Reflections," in *The Precarious Balance*, ed. Donald Rothchild (Boulder, CO: Westview, 1988), 67–99, Jean-François Bayart, Stephen Ellis, and Béatrice Hibou, *The Criminalization of the State in Africa* (Bloomington: Indiana University Press, 1999), and Patrick Chabal and Jean-Pascal Daloz, *Africa Works: Disorder as Political Instrument* (Bloomington: Indiana University Press, 1999).

12. Scott D. Taylor, *Business and the State in Southern Africa: The Politics of Economic Reform* (Boulder, CO: Lynne Rienner, 2007); Tor Skalnes, *The Politics of Economic Reform in Zimbabwe: Continuity and Change in Development* (Basingstoke, UK: Macmillan, 1995); Bruce Heilman and John Lucas, "A Social Movement for African Capitalism? A Comparison of Business Associations in Two African Cities, *African Studies Review* 40.2 (1997): 141–71.

13. See Peter Evans, "Indian Informatics in the 1980s: The Changing Character of State Involvement," *World Development* 201 (1992): 1–18, Peter Evans, *Embedded Autonomy* (Princeton, NJ: Princeton University Press), and Meredith Woo-Cumings, ed., *The Developmental State* (Ithaca, NY: Cornell University Press, 1999).

14. Prominent among these was South Africa, which adopted a "home-grown" structural adjustment program and whose white-dominated big-business, private-sector conglomerates were advanced, internationalized entities with little need for state "intervention" by the time significant liberalization began in the 1990s. They possessed intrinsic capacity and thus had only limited need of the greater state support or "husbandry" characteristic of a developmental state. Ironically, however, state intervention was the hallmark of South African economic policy under the apartheid regime of the national party: businesses, particularly those associated with Afrikaners, were afforded massive support from the state, thereby enabling many of these giants to emerge.

15. Pádraig Carmody details the substantial degree of deindustrialization in Zimbabwe, for example, in *Tearing the Social Fabric: Neoliberalism, Deindustrialization, and the Crisis of Governance in Zimbabwe* (Westport, CT: Greenwood, 2001). See also Farhad Noorbakhsh and Alberto Paloni, "Structural Adjustment Programs and Industry in Sub-Saharan Africa: Restructuring or De-Industrialization?," *Journal of Developing Areas* 33.4 (1999): 549–80.

16. Note that small-scale actors in informal markets did not necessarily face the same constraints. In Zambia, for instance, informal vendors of used clothing thrived in this period. See Karen Tranberg Hansen, *Salaula: The World of Secondhand Clothing and Zambia* (Chicago: University of Chicago Press, 2000). See also Janet MacGaffey and Rémy Bazenguissa-Ganga, *Congo-Paris: Transnational Traders on the Margins of the Law* (Bloomington: Indiana University Press, 2000).

17. Nellis, "Privatization in Africa," 7. Privatizations diminished after 1997 but re-

bounded sharply in the 2000s, especially in the financial, telecoms and energy sectors; see World Bank Privatization Database, http://rru.worldbank.org/Privatization/Default.aspx (accessed 24 October 2011).

18. van de Walle, *African Economies and the Politics of Permanent Crisis*, 71.

19. See Anne Pitcher, *Transforming Mozambique: The Politics of Privatization, 1975–2000* (Cambridge: University of Cambridge Press, 2002).

20. Michael Bratton, "Micro-Democracy? The Merger of Farmer Unions in Zimbabwe," *African Studies Review* 37.1 (1994): 9–37.

21. Kellee Tsai, *Capitalism without Democracy: The Private Sector in Contemporary China* (Ithaca, NY: Cornell University Press, 2007), 3.

22. Ibid., 16.

23. "Why Voting is Good for You," *Economist*, 27 August 27 1994, 15.

24. Gregory White and Scott D. Taylor, "Well-Oiled Regimes," *Review of African Political Economy* 28.89 (2001): 323–44; Tony Hodges, *Angola: Anatomy of an Oil Economy*, 2nd ed. (Bloomington: Indiana University Press, 2003).

25. Catherine Conaghan, "Capitalists, Technocrats and Politicians: Economic Policy Making and Democracy in the Central Andes," in *Issues in Democratic Consolidation: The New South American Democracies in Comparative Perspective*, ed. Scott Mainwaring, Guillermo O'Donnell, and Samuel J. Valenzuela (Notre Dame, IN: University of Notre Dame Press), 199–42. See also David Becker, "Business Associations in Latin America: The Venezuelan Case," *Comparative Political Studies* 23.1 (1990): 114–38, and Eduardo Silva, "From Dictatorship to Democracy: The Business-State Nexus in Chile's Economic Transformation, 1975–1994," *Comparative Politics* 28.3 (1996): 299–320.

26. See Bratton and van de Walle, *Democratic Experiments in Africa*, 467–68, and Carolyn Baylies and Morris Szeftel, "The Fall and Rise of Multiparty Politics in Zambia," *Review of African Political Economy* 54 (1992): 75–91.

27. In Zimbabwe, the era of liberalization and competitive parties arrived only in 1999, nearly a decade after most countries' experiments with democracy had begun. Certainly, in cases such as Zimbabwe, the business community would have been better served, in retrospect, by heeding the adage "better the devil you know." Its decision to throw its weight behind the new political opposition proved disastrous, contributing to an authoritarian backlash by the regime and the subsequent decimation of the economy.

28. Bratton and van de Walle, *Democratic Experiments in Africa*, 467–68.

29. Ibid., 167.

30. John R. Heilbrunn, "Commerce, Politics, and Business Associations in Benin and Togo," *Comparative Politics* 29.4 (1997): 473–92.

31. Dan O'Meara, *Forty Lost Years: The Apartheid State and the Politics of the National Party, 1948–94* (Randberg, South Africa: Ravan Press, 1995): 365.

32. A handful of Africa's most politically "free" countries, Benin, Cape Verde, Mali and Sao Tome, and Principe, have doing business rankings of just 36, 20, 25 and 43, respectively, out of the forty-six countries evaluated.

33. The Extractive Industries Transparency Initiative, for example, imposes new costs of compliance on firms in extractive sectors, principally petroleum.

34. See Charles Sampord, Arthur Shacklock, Carmel Connors, and Fredrik Galtung, eds., *Measuring Corruption* (Aldershot, UK: Ashgate, 2006).

35. Christopher Fomunyoh, "Democratization in Fits and Starts," *Journal of Democracy* 12.3 (2001): 37–50.

36. van de Walle, *African Economies and the Politics of Permanent Crisis,* 146.

37. Ramachandran, Gelb, and Shah, *Africa's Private Sector,* 21–24.

38. See Taylor, *Business and the State in Southern Africa,* David S. Fick, *Entrepreneurship in Africa: A Study of Successes* (Westport, CT: Quorum Books, 2002), Carol Pineau's 2006 documentary film *Africa: Open for Business*; Vijay Mahajan, *Africa Rising: How 900 Million African Consumers Offer More Than You Think* (Upper Saddle River, NJ: Prentice Hall, 2009), 179, and the World Bank Enterprise Surveys that can be found at http://www.enterprisesurveys.org.

3. BUSINESS, THE AFRICAN STATE, AND GLOBALIZATION IN THE
NEW MILLENNIUM

1. Although favorable commodity prices also clearly affected African trajectories in the period, this chapter restricts itself to exploration of the multilateral, policy-oriented aspects of evolving globalization, as well as the African responses thereto, at the country level and at the level of the firm.

2. Frederick Cooper, "What Is the Concept of Globalization Good For? An African Historian's Perspective," *African Affairs* 100.399 (2001): 189–213.

3. Susan Strange, *The Retreat of the State: The Diffusion of Power in the World Economy* (Cambridge: Cambridge University Press, 1996), xiii.

4. Cooper, "What Is the Concept of Globalization Good For?," 112.

5. I share this rather bare-bones interpretation with Carmody (*Globalization in Africa: Recolonization or Renaissance* [Boulder, CO: Lynne Rienner, 2010]), which would seem to avoid the teleology derided by Cooper that sees globalization as movement "toward the progressive integration of different parts of the world into a singular whole" ("What Is the Concept of Globalization Good For?," 211).

6. James Ferguson, *Global Shadows: Africa in the Neoliberal World Order* (Durham, NC: Duke University Press, 2006).

7. Kiyoto Kurokawa, Fletcher Tembo, and Dirk Willem te Velde, "Donor Support to Private Sector Development in Sub-Saharan Africa: Understanding the Japanese OVOP Programme," ODI/JICA Working Paper 290, April 2008, http://www.odi.org.uk/resources/download/1116.pdf (accessed 26 October 2011).

8. My interest is in the relationship between private sector development, broadly conceived, and formal business—*not* micro—and small enterprises that have unproven impact on economic development.

9. Such investment is particularly vulnerable to contagion effects; even South Africa, with its generally sound fiscal and monetary policies, has seen its currency dramatically impacted by capital outflows precipitated by events elsewhere in Africa and the developing world (Ziya Öniş and Fikret Şenses, "Rethinking the Emerging Post-Washington Consensus," *Development and Change* 36.2 [2005]: 268).

10. Öniş and Şenses, "Rethinking the Emerging Post-Washington Consensus," 270–71.

11. Nicolas van de Walle, *African Economies and the Politics of Permanent Crisis, 1979–1999* (Cambridge: Cambridge University Press, 2001).

12. Öniş and Şenses, "Rethinking the Emerging Post-Washington Consensus," 276.

13. These would include scholars such as Moeletsi Mbeki, James Mittleman, and Patrick Bond, among many others.

14. Debt relief under the HIPC initiative actually began, albeit modestly, in 1996. This was followed by the enhanced HIPC in 1999 and the MDRI in 2005.

15. The EU-based Lomé Accord was disallowed by World Trade Organization rules in 1994 because it discriminated against non-African Caribbean and Pacific countries and was nonreciprocal.

16. Peter Gibbon, "Present-day Capitalism, the New International Trade Regime and Africa," *Review of African Political Economy* 29.91 (2002): 101, 108, 111.

17. Amy Chua, *World on Fire: How Exporting Free Market Democracy Breeds Ethnic Hatred and Global Instability* (New York: Random House, 2003).

18. See Carol Pineau's film *Africa: Open for Business*.

19. Basildon Peta, "Lesotho Textile Workers Left in Rags," *Star* (Johannesburg, South Africa), 28 April 2005.

20. Tina M. Zappile, "Nonreciprocal Trade Agreements and Trade: Does the African Growth and Opportunity Act (AGOA) Increase Trade?," *International Studies Perspectives* 12.1 (2011): 56.

21. Zappile, "Nonreciprocal Trade Agreements and Trade?," 62.

22. According to the OECD, agricultural subsidies to its member states amounted to approximately $365 billion in 2007, of which some $100 billion came from the United States. Further, African agricultural exports are discriminated against via escalating tariffs in the global North of up to 500 percent. Despite lofty rhetoric about poverty, trade representatives from the United States and the European Union alike did not budge on the common agricultural policy or agricultural subsidies, leading to the collapse of the Doha Round of the World Trade Organization. For their part, African countries sought greater protectionism through import restrictions, especially following the devastation of both the industrial and agricultural sectors in the 1990s.

23. In fact, it is possible that the programs themselves, or many of them, are actually *failures*, but that the entrepreneurial spirit prevails in spite of those failures.

24. Henrietta Fore, opening remarks, Partnerships for Promoting the African Entrepreneur panel discussion, 19 October 2007, Washington, DC.

25. Participants in the Nepad Business Group are mainly themselves relatively new business umbrella organizations in the global North and include the African Business Roundtable (established in 1990 by the Africa Development Bank); the International Chamber of Commerce; Commonwealth Business Council (established 1997), comprising 150 corporate members, 2000 small-and medium-size enterprise associates; Forum Francophone des Affaires (not just Africa); Business Humanitarian Forum (Kofi Annan-inspired); Conseil Français des Investisseurs en Afrique, which itself represents some 100 companies or about 80 percent of French firms in Africa; Corporate Council on Africa (established 1992), which has 180 U.S. corporate members; British Africa Business Association (established 1995) through which UK business associations facilitate foreign direct investment and trade in Africa; International Business Leaders' Forum; Business Council Europe Africa Mediterranean, comprising 1,500 EU-based companies with in-

terests in Africa; Pan African Employers Confederation; and the Canadian Council on Africa (established 2002).

26. World Bank, *Doing Business 2009: Comparing Regulation in 181 Economies,* September 2008, 1, Doing Business Project, http://www.doingbusiness.org/~/media/fpdkm/ doing%20business/documents/annual-reports/english/db09-fullreport.pdf (accessed 23 October 2011).

27. Ibid., 8. Forty-six Africa countries appear in the survey.

28. Ibid., 3.

29. Ibid., 9.

30. Vijaya Ramachandran, Alan Gelb, and Manju Kedia Shah, *Africa's Private Sector: What's Wrong with the Business Environment and What to Do about It* (Washington DC: Center for Global Development, 2009), 55.

31. Clearly, Africa is not merely "recipient": globalization also means that I can now buy Nandos in Washington, DC, or Castle Lager throughout the African continent.

32. Ferguson, *Global Shadows,* 30.

33. The competition was initiated by the Youth Ministry and managed by TechnoServe. One hundred finalists were then selected to attend a workshop in late 2007 where they pitched their ideas and received feedback to determine the award winners ("Begin, Believe, Become: Kenya's National Business Plan Competition," 12 November 2007, http:// www.believe-begin-become.com/Kenya/morenews.asp?NewsID=97 [accessed 21 November 2011]).

34. "Start-Ups and Slow-Downs: What Impact Will Recession Have on Entrepreneurship," *Economist.com,* 18 November 2008, http://www.economist.com/displaystory .cfm?story_id=12625763 (accessed 3 November 2011).

35. The highest estimate was $74 billion (Adolfo Barajas, Ralph Chami, Connel Fullenkamp, and Anjali Garg, "The Global Financial Crisis and Workers' Remittances to Africa: What's the Damage?," IMF Working Paper 10/24, January 2010).

36. Members as of 2009 include Catholic University of Eastern Africa (Kenya); School for Human Resource and Development (Kenya); Strathmore Business School (Kenya); United States International University (Kenya); the University of Nairobi School of Business (Kenya); Gordon Institute of Business Science (South Africa); Nelson Mandela Metropolitan University Business School (South Africa); Turfloop Graduate School of Leadership (South Africa); University of South Africa Graduate School of Business Leadership; University of Cape Town, Graduate School of Business (South Africa); University of Stellenbosch Business School (South Africa); Wits Business School (South Africa); Lagos Business School—Pan African University (Nigeria); Obafemi Awolowo University—Ile Ife (Nigeria); Institut Africain de Management and the Senegal Institut Superieur de Management; Ghana Institute of Management and Public Administration; University of Botswana; University of Dar es Salaam, Faculty of Commerce and Management (Tanzania).

37. See http://www.aabschools.com/page/about_us/overview.html.

38. Allan Anderson, "The Pentecostal Gospel, Religion, and Culture in African Perspective," paper, history of religion seminar, University of Oxford, 29 May 2000, http:// artsweb.bham.ac.uk/aanderson/Publications/pentecostal_gospel.htm (accessed 24 Octo-

ber 2011); see also Paul Gifford, *Ghana's New Christianity: Pentecostalism in a Globalizing African Economy* (Bloomington: Indiana University Press, 2004).

39. Pew Research Center, *Spirit and Power: A 10-Country Survey of Pentecostalists*, Pew Research Center/Pew Forum on Religion and Public Life, October 2006.

40. Isaac Phiri and Joe Maxwell, "Gospel Riches: Africa's Rapid Embrace of Prosperity Pentecostalism Provokes Concern—and Hope," *Christianity Today*, July 2007, http://www .christianitytoday.com/ct/2007/july/12.22.html?start=3 (accessed 24 October 2011).

41. Phiri and Maxwell, "Gospel Riches."

42. See Ramachandran, Gelb, and Shah, *Africa's Private Sector*, 67.

43. Daniel J. Smith, *A Culture of Corruption: Everyday Corruption and Popular Discontent in Nigeria* (Princeton, NJ: Princeton University Press, 2007).

44. Ramachandran, Gelb, and Shah, *Africa's Private Sector*, 68.

45. Indeed, as Jeffery Sachs notes, "The cell phone is the single most transformative technology for development" (qtd. in Jack Ewing, "Upwardly Mobile in Africa: How Basic Cell Phones Are Sparking Economic Hope and Growth in Emerging and Even Non-Emerging Nations," *Businessweek*, 24 September, 2007).

46. Eric Little and Carolyn Logan, comps., "The Quality of Democracy and Governance in Africa: New Results from Afrobarometer Round 4," Afrobarometer Working Paper 108, May 2009.

47. In terms of technology and globalization, see Afrobarometer, "Citizens of the World? Africans, Media and Telecommunications," Briefing Paper 69, May 2009. Their findings suggest Africans remain more locally rather than globally oriented, but the study reports that this is changing.

48. Ferguson, *Global Shadows*, 37–38.

49. World Bank, "Economy Rankings," 2009, Doing Business Project, http://www .doingbusiness.org/EconomyRankings (accessed 18 May 2010).

50. Scott D. Taylor, *Business and the State in Southern Africa: The Politics of Economic Reform* (Boulder, CO: Lynne Rienner, 2007).

51. Theo Mushi, "How the Private Sector Fares in Tanzania," *Guardian* (Manchester, UK), 7 March 2007.

52. In "Donor Support to Private Sector Development," Kurokawa, Tembo, and te Velde note that the purported link between small-and medium-size enterprises and economic development is at best inconclusive.

53. Peter Arthur, "'The State, Private Sector Development, and Ghana's 'Golden Age of Business,'" *African Studies Review* 49.1 (2006): 31–50.

54. Gaddiel Baah, "Minister Says The Future of the Private Sector in Ghana is 'Beautiful,'" www.AllAfrica.com, 3 February 2006.

55. Arthur, "The State, Private Sector Development, and Ghana's 'Golden Age of Business,'" 40.

56. Ibid., 40–41.

57. World Bank, "Economy Rankings."

58. Osei Boeh-Ocansey, "Private Sector Development in Ghana: The Challenges and the Lessons," PowerPoint presentation, roundtable meeting on promoting private sector development, 17 July 2005, Accra, Ghana, http://web.idrc.ca/en/ev-85356-201-1-DO _TOPIC.html (accessed 26 October 2011).

59. Jon Kraus, "Capital, Power and Business Associations in the African Political Economy: A Tale of Two Countries, Ghana and Nigeria," *Journal of Modern African Studies* 40.3 (2002): 395–436.

60. Aid funded approximately 32 percent of the 2005 budget and provided support for related programs through the enhanced HIPC/PRSP process, known locally as the Ghana poverty reduction strategy; see "Ghana Moves Ahead," *Business in Africa Online*, 3 March 2005.

61. Many of their associates did, however. Moreover, these leaders inherited a powerful business community, whose support they required to grow the postapartheid economy.

62. Note that although this criticism certainly targets the Rawlings regime, coming as it did three years after the New Patriotic Party victory, it also implicates the Kufuor government. See government of Ghana, *National Medium-Term Private Sector Development Strategy, 2004–2008*, December 2003.

63. "The costs of reforming the economy are too high; the government should therefore abandon its current economic policies" versus "In order for the economy to get better in the future, it is necessary for us to accept some hardships now" (Afrobarometer, "Citizens of the World?," 37).

64. See http://search.worldbank.org/data?qterm=%22net+domestic+credit%22&language=&format= (accessed 3 November 2011).

65. Temitope W. Oshikoya, "Macroeconomic Determinants of Domestic Private Investment in Africa: An Empirical Analysis, *Economic Development and Cultural Change* 42.3 (1994): 584.

66. *The Economist* characterizes "high-impact entrepreneurs" as those who have already proven they have a working business model but grapple with the challenge of achieving the larger scale, for which they tend to need access to experienced business mentors and powerful networks. High-impact entrepreneurs do well at producing start-ups that rapidly grow from small firms into big ones ("Start-Ups and Slow-Downs: What Impact Will Recession Have on Entrepreneurship," *Economist.com*, 18 November 2008). http://www.economist.com/displaystory.cfm?story_id=12625763 (accessed 21 May 2010).

67. Ramachandran, Gelb, and Shah, *Africa's Private Sector*.

68. Perhaps surprisingly, there appears to be no direct evidence linking Omatek to the government. Indeed, it continued to pay a 5–7 percent duty on its imported parts, the same as foreign-brand imports. Since this was expected to draw a zero-rate duty, it seems to suggest an *absence* of government favoritism.

69. See http://www.fundforpeace.org.

70. Carol Pineau, "A Changing Continent: The Africa You Never See," *Washington Post*, 17 April 2005; David S. Fick, *Entrepreneurship in Africa: A Study of Successes* (Westport, CT: Quorum Books, 2002), 287–91.

71. Morten Beyer and Agnew, "Daallo Airlines: Transformation of an African Airline," PowerPoint presentation, 16–17, 17 March 2007.

72. Mohammed Ibrahim Yassin, telephone interview conducted by Ramah Dualeh, March 2008.

73. See also Mahajan, *Africa Rising: How 900 Million African Consumers Offer More Than You Think* (Upper Saddle River, NJ: Prentice Hall, 2009), and Luyton Driman, *Go-*

ing the Extra Mile: A Guide to Trading in Africa (East London, South Africa: Bradmanton Trading and Publishing, 2005).

74. Indeed, consider the recent American examples of Enron, Fannie Mae, AIG, Merrill Lynch, or Bernard Madoff: these corporate transgressions took years to expose, despite America's "advanced" system. In the infamous Enron case, even the auditors, Arthur Andersen, were complicit.

75. Africa Development Bank, *Selected Statistics on African Countries*, vol. 27 (Tunis: African Development Bank, 2008).

76. William Easterly, "How the Millennium Development Goals are Unfair to Africa," Brookings Institution Working Paper 14, November 2007.

77. Steven C. Radelet, *Emerging Africa: How 17 Countries Are Leading the Way* (Washington, DC: Center for Global Development, 2010), 43.

78. Simeon Djankov, Caralee McLeish, and Rita Maria Ramlho, "Regulation and Growth," *Economics Letters* 92.3 (2006): 395–401.

79. Ibid., 400.

80. Ben Schneider and Sylvia Maxfield, eds., *Business and the State in Developing Countries* (Ithaca, NY: Cornell University Press, 1997); Kellee Tsai, *Capitalism without Democracy: The Private Sector in Contemporary China* (Ithaca, NY: Cornell University Press, 2007).

81. Ramachandran, Gelb, and Shah, *Africa's Private Sector,* 67.

82. See Carol Pineau's films *Africa: Open for Business"* and *A Changing Continent,* David S. Fick, *Africa: A Continent of Economic Opportunity* (Johannesburg, South Africa: STE Publishers, 2007), and Mahajan, *Africa Rising,* and Driman, *Going the Extra Mile.*

83. In a recent series broadcast on the business channel CNBC, the producers managed to both overhype the opportunities and portray Africa in caricatured pessimistic terms at the same time. No easy feat.

84. Similarly, Andrew Sardanis offers a personal narrative of the potential pitfalls of doing business on the continent, providing a damning counterpoint to Fick and a partial corrective to the triumphalism that characterizes some analyses. See his *A Venture in Africa: The Challenges of African Business* (New York: I. B. Tauris, 2007).

85. United Nations Development Program, *Unleashing Entrepreneurship: Making Business Work for the Poor,* Commission on Private Sector and Development, report to the secretary general, 1 March 2004, 17.

86. United Nations Development Program, *Unleashing Entrepreneurship,* 17.

87. Melissa Davis, "Is Africa Misbranded?," *Brand Channel,* 13 August 2007, http://www.brandchannel.com/features_effect.asp?pf_id=381 (accessed 26 October 2011).

88. Ramachandran, Gelb, and Shah, *Africa's Private Sector.*

4. FOREIGN INVESTMENT BEYOND COMPRADORISM AND PRIMARY COMMODITIES

1. Theodore H. Moran, *Harnessing Foreign Direct Investment for Development* (Washington, DC: Center for Global Development, 2006), 3.

2. It is also worth noting that Botswana's experience reveals that it is not impossible for states to utilize primary commodities as a basis for development. Yet few states share Botswana's unique combination of a shallow colonial footprint, low population size

and density, a small and efficient state characterized by effective institutions, and low levels of ethno-political tension. Also, Botswana's main commodity is unique. Diamonds are traded in an international market that is 75 percent controlled by DeBeers, thereby smoothing price fluctuations. These factors contribute to low levels of rent seeking and corruption in Botswana. Historically, Africans have been "significant divestors in their own countries (around 40 percent of African capital has fled the continent)" (Brenthurst Foundation, Chinese Academy of Social Sciences, Council on Foreign Relations, and the Leon Sullivan Foundation, *Africa-China-U.S. Trilateral Dialogue: Summary Report* [Washington, DC: Council on Foreign Relations, 2007], 31). This indicates that it's not only foreigners who have eschewed investment in Africa beyond the profitable and expedient commodities. *Africa Confidential* reported that Africa lost more than $850 billion between 1970 and 2008 as a result of illicit financial flows, including "corporate tax evasion [65 percent of the losses], trade mispricing and overpriced supply contracts." These "could total as much as $1.8 trillion if transfer pricing schemes and mispricing of trade in services with Africa are taken into account." The leading offenders are Nigeria ($89.5 billion), North Africa, then South Africa (at $24.9 billion). See "Blue Lines," *Africa Confidential* 51.7 (2010): 1.

3. Although Mauritius was also home to nearly 50 percent the foreign direct investment stocks that India amassed between 1996 and 2004, India has since diversified more widely. See United Nations Conference on Trade and Development, "FDI Stocks in Africa from Selected Developing Asian Economies," 2002, http://www.unctad.org/templates/WebFlyer.asp?intItemID=4180&lang=1 (accessed 18 May 2010).

4. Both South Africa and Zimbabwe had developed a small industrial base by the 1940s. Prior to majority rule in 1994 and 1980, respectively, international sanctions impelled these countries toward even deeper industrial development. Their capacity for trade in manufactured exports, however, was substantially limited to their neighboring countries. Because their industries were grown under protectionism, they were uncompetitive at the global level. Later, sanctions against both apartheid South Africa and Rhodesia further constrained export potential.

5. For example, see Gretchen Bauer and Scott D. Taylor, *Politics in Southern Africa: Transition and Transformation,* 2nd ed. (Boulder, CO: Lynne Rienner, 2011).

6. As reported in Neil Ford, "Record FDI for Africa," *African Business,* 1 January 2008.

7. Stephen Gelb, "South-South Investment: The Case of Africa," in *Africa in the World Economy: The National, Regional and international Challenges* (The Hague: Fondad, 2005), 202–204.

8. Aykut Dilek and Andrea Goldstein, "Developing Country Multinationals: South-South Investment Comes of Age," in *Industrial Development for the 21st Century: Sustainable Development Perspectives* (New York: United Nations, 2007), 85–116.

9. It is worth noting, however, that despite these international norms putatively governing corporate behavior for OECD-based companies, some of the leading names in international business continue to engage in rampant bribery in the developing world; see David Hilzenrath, "Justice Department, SEC Cracking Down on U.S. Companies Engaging in Bribery Abroad," *Washington Post,* 24 March 2011.

10. John Henley, Stefan Kratzsch, Mithat Külür, and Tamer Tandogan, "Foreign Direct Investment from China, India and South Africa in Sub-Saharan Africa: A New or Old Phenomenon?," UNU-WIDER Research Paper 24, March 2008. http://www.wider

.unu.edu/publications/working-papers/research-papers/2008/en_GB/rp2008-24 (accessed 26 October 2011).

11. Gelb, "South-South Investment."

12. For example, measured by number of enterprises, small-and medium size enterprises with investments under $10 million outnumbered large-scale firms by five hundred to thirty in 2000 (United Nations Conference on Trade and Development, *Asian Foreign Direct Investment in Africa: Towards a New Era of Cooperation among Developing Countries* [New York: United Nations, 2007], http://www.unctad.org/en/docs/iteiia20071_en.pdf [accessed 18 May 2010]). See also Deborah Brautigam, *The Dragon's Gift: The Real Story of China in Africa* (New York: Oxford University Press, 2009).

13. Gelb, "South-South Investment."

14. Ibid.

15. Brenthurst Foundation, Chinese Academy of Social Sciences, Council on Foreign Relations, and the Leon Sullivan Foundation, *Africa-China-US Trilateral Dialogue*, 30.

16. See John A. Gould and Matthew S. Winters, "An Obsolescing Bargain in Chad: Shifts in Leverage between the Government and the World Bank," *Business and Politics* 9.2 (2007), doi: 10.2202/1469-3569.1199, and Alistair Fraser and John Lungu, "For Whom the Windfalls: Winners and Losers in the Privatisation of Zambia's Copper Mines," 2006, www.liberationafrique.org/IMG/pdf/Minewatchzambia.pdf (accessed 26 October 2011).

17. In late 2011, this began to change, with the publication of books such as Emma Mawdsley and Gerald McCann's *India and Africa: Changing Geographies of Power* (Cape Town: Pambazuka Press, 2011), for example.

18. Henley, Kratzsch, Külür, and Tandogan, "Foreign Direct Investment from China, India and South Africa in Sub-Saharan Africa," 6–8.

19. Brautigam, *The Dragon's Gift*, 224–229.

20. Gelb, "South-South Investment: The Case of Africa."

21. Henley, Kratzsch, Külür, and Tandogan, "Foreign Direct Investment from China, India and South Africa in Sub-Saharan Africa," 6.

22. Brautigam, *The Dragon's Gift*. She refers to successful examples of this in Nigeria and Kenya.

23. Note, however, that among university graduates employed by Indian firms, 40 percent are Indian, as reported in Henley, Kratzsch, Külür, and Tandogan, "Foreign Direct Investment from China, India and South Africa in Sub-Saharan Africa," 10.

24. Chris McGreal, "Thanks China, Now Go Home: Buy Up of Zambia Revives Old Colonial Fears," *Guardian* (Manchester, UK), 5 February 2007.

25. Yaroslav Trofimov, "New Management: In Africa China's Expansion Begins to Stir Resentment," *Wall Street Journal*, 2 February 2007.

26. Then minister of home affairs Ronnie Shikapwasha countered that the number of work permits given to Chinese was just 2,340 ("Govt refutes Sata's Claims over Chinese nationals in Zambia," *Lusaka Times* [Zambia], 27 October 2007, www.lusakatimes.com/?p=1469 [accessed 26 October 2011]). However, this misleading figure clearly understates the number of Chinese in Zambia, which others have estimated at around 30,000. See Darren Taylor, "Chinese Aid Flows into Africa," *Voice of America*, 8 May 2007.

27. Brautigam, *The Dragon's Gift*, 310.

28. See Adam Gaye, *Chine-Afrique: Le dragon et l'autruche* (Paris: L'Harmattan, 2006).

29. H. S. Morris, "Indians in East Africa: A Study of a Plural Society," *British Journal of Sociology* 7.3 (1956): 194–211.

30. Less than a tenth of its former peak, Uganda's Asian population now measures only about seven thousand residents (plus an additional five thousand Indian nationals). In 1992, President Yoweri Museveni actually issued a call to Asians to return to Uganda and restored their property ownership. Museveni has also appointed Uganda Asians to high office, including Nimisha Madhvani, the scion of one of Uganda's most prominent business families, as the country's high commissioner to India.

31. As of 2004, India's stocks were $1.97 billion, whereas China's (through 2004) were $1.6 billion (United Nations Conference on Trade and Development, "FDI Stocks in Africa from Selected Developing Asian Economies."

32. Henley, Kratzsch, Külür, and Tandogan, "Foreign Direct Investment from China, India and South Africa in Sub-Saharan Africa: A New or Old Phenomenon?"

33. Gijsbert Oonk, "Debunking the Indian Diasporas: Empirical Explorations and Theoretical Assumptions," Asians in Africa Position Paper (2006), 13–14. http://www.asiansinafrica.com/lijst_publications.php (accessed 19 May 2010) (referring to the Indian High Level Commission Report on the Indian Diaspora.). One measure of diminished connection to the Indian homeland is borne out by remittance figures, which have been negligible. Even accepting that unofficial channels can account for as much as 50 percent of official levels, official remittances from Africa in the 1997–2003 period, for example, ranged between just 0.6 percent and 4.5 percent of total remittances to India, which amounted to nearly $75 billion during that period, according to the Bank of India.

34. Morris, "Indians in East Africa," 194–211.

35. Oonk, "Debunking the Indian Diasporas," 13–14.

36. TATA Group was among the first Indian large-scale firms to invest in Africa with the establishment of TATA Zambia in 1977.

37. In general, this measured corporate social responsibility is as much a reflection of India's democratic domestic politics as of responses to shareholder concerns; the shares of leading multinational corporations are actually tightly held so shareholder pressure is relatively limited. Corporate social responsibility is hardly a universal norm, however, as the Indian *state* invests in Sudan's oil sector along with China.

38. Mark Sorbara, "India and Africa—It's Old Friends, New Game and Rules," *Daily Nation* (Nairobi, Kenya), 9 February 2007, http://allafrica.com/stories/200702081111.html (accessed 24 October 2011).

39. Sushant Singh, "India and West Africa: A Burgeoning Relationship," Chatham House Africa/Asia Programme Briefing Paper, April 2007, http://www.chathamhouse.org/publications/papers/view/108471 (accessed 24 October 2011).

40. Ibid.

41. Vibhuti Hate, "India in Africa: Moving beyond Oil," *CSIS South Asia Monitor,* 10 June 2008, http://csis.org/files/media/csis/pubs/sam119.pdf (accessed 19 May 2010).

42. Now ArcelorMittal and headquartered in Luxembourg, Mittal was founded by Indian magnate Lakshmi Mittal and his family, though it had long been truly *trans-national*, and was headquartered in the Netherlands even before the merger with Arcelor.

43. Singh, "India and West Africa."

44. For example, India was one of the leading investors in Ghana between 1994 and 1996, accounting for 10 percent of newly registered projects—equaled only by China (United Nations Conference on Trade and Development, "FDI Stocks in Africa from Selected Developing Asian Economies"). In addition, India registered 185 "projects" in Ghana between 2002 and 2006 versus 177 for Britain and 161 for China, though many Indian investments were small-and medium-size enterprises and concentrated in the commercial sector (Sorbara, "India and Africa").

45. Mahajan, *Africa Rising: How 900 Million African Consumers Offer More Than You Think* (Upper Saddle River, NJ: Prentice Hall, 2009), 179.

46. Note that the Senegalese Transporters Union (and others) initially protested the deal and even went on strike, suggesting that Tata buses were less safe than French buses (who started this rumor, the French?). See Siddarth Varadarajan, "India Inc Makes Inroads in the Heart of Africa," *Times of India* (New Delhi), 1 March 2004.

47. Mahajan, *Africa Rising*, 179. See also, Singh, "India and West Africa."

48. Sorbara, "India and Africa."

49. Sudha Ramachandran, "India Pushes People Power in Africa," *Asia Times* (Hong Kong), 13 July 2007, http://www.atimes.com/atimes/South_Asia/IG13Df03.html (accessed 19 May 2010).

50. Heather Timmons and Vikas Bajaj, "Indian Iron-Ore Exporter is Target of Fraud Inquiry," *New York Times*, 30 October 2009.

51. Transparency International, "Foreign Bribery by Emerging Export Powers 'Disconcertingly High,'" http://www.transparency.org/policy_research/surveys_indices/bpi/bpi_2006 (accessed 26 November 2011). In the subsequent survey in 2008, Russia, China, and Mexico ranked lower than India (Transparency International, *Bribes Payer's Index, 2008* [Berlin: Transparency International, 2008], 5).

52. Henley, Kratzsch, Külür, and Tandogan, "Foreign Direct Investment from China, India and South Africa in Sub-Saharan Africa: A New or Old Phenomenon?"

53. Raphael Kaplinsky, "What Does the Rise of China Do for Industrialisation in Africa?," unpublished paper, October 2007.

54. Qtd. in McGreal, "Thanks China, Now Go Home."

5. FROM PATRIMONIALISM TO PROFIT?

1. This chapter deals mainly with black African business, which in the view of most observers is closely identified with corruption, patronage, and "briefcase" business-people.

2. Perhaps the extreme warlordism that characterized Sierra Leone and Liberia during the depths of their respective civil wars or the regional strife that has long plagued Eastern Congo are examples, although certainly some forms of "business" persisted even in these wholly inhospitable environments.

3. John Lloyd Chipembere Lwanda, *Promises, Power, Politics and Poverty: Democratic Transition in Malawi (1961–1999)* (Glasgow, Scotland: Dudu Nsomba Publications, 1997).

4. Henry Chilobwe, "Malawi: Muluzi's Empire Collapsing," *Nation* (Blantyre, Malawi), 7 May 2006.

5. Ibid.

6. John Grobler, "Namibia: Mafia Linked to Namibian Gems," *Namibian* (Windhoek), 23 March 2007, http://allafrica.com/stories/200703230749.html (accessed 3 May 2007).

7. Although Mobutu himself mainly *extracted* rents, a select few of his cronies used Africanization ("Zaireanization") "to build enduring business empires" (Steve Askin and Carole Collins, "External Collusion with Kleptocracy: Can Zaïre Recapture Its Stolen Wealth?," *Review of African Political Economy* 20.57 [1993]: 76). Moi himself appeared more careful to use intermediaries.

8. Richard A. Joseph, *Democracy and Prebendal Politics in Nigeria: The Rise and Fall of the Second Republic* (Cambridge: Cambridge University Press, 1988); Smith, *A Culture of Corruption*.

9. Stephen Bevan, "Obasanjo, Hailed as a Saviour by Blair, Leads Nigeria to despair," *Telegraph* (London, UK), 21 May 2006, http://www.telegraph.co.uk/news/worldnews/africaandindianocean/nigeria/1519014/Obasanjo-hailed-as-a-saviour-by-Blair-leads-Nigeria-to-despair.html (accessed 19 May 2010).

10. Freedom House, *Countries at the Crossroads 2006—Nigeria,* 3 August 2006, http://www.unhcr.org/refworld/docid/4738691264.html (accessed 21 May 2010).

11. See, for example, Naijapolitics or Elendureports.com.

12. "Politicians Buy," *Profit* (Zambia) 15.3 (1996): 40.

13. See Madelaine Drohan, *Making a Killing: How and Why Corporations Use Armed Force to Do Business* (Guilford, CT: Lyons Press, 2004), 300–303.

14. Kutesa has served Museveni in a number of roles, including as attorney general. He is an in-law of the president's.

15. Parliament of Uganda, parliamentary testimony, 21 March 1999.

16. Efforte Aviation and Global Airlinks ultimately became the controlling shareholders, and by 2003, Global Airlinks held 75.5 percent of shares, whereas Efforte held 17 percent. Sabena and its successors held 5 percent and CAA employees 2.5 percent.

17. Parliament of Uganda, parliamentary testimony, 21 March 1999; Drohan, *Making a Killing,* 301–302.

18. Parliament of Uganda, parliamentary testimony, 21 March 1999.

19. Of course, the Asian population found greener pastures in manufacturing, finance, tourism, and construction, higher value sectors they continue to dominate today (Himbara, "Domestic Capitalists and the State in Kenya," in *African Capitalists in African Development,* ed. Bruce Berman and Colin Leys [Boulder, CO: Lynne Rienner, 1994], 86).

20. Scott D. Taylor, "Indigenization, Black Economic Empowerment, and Affirmative Action in Zimbabwe and South Africa," in *Black Business and Economic Power*, ed. Alusine Jalloh and Toyin Falola (Rochester, NY: University of Rochester Press, 2002), 347–80.

21. Henning Melber, "Poverty, Politics, Power and Privilege: Namibia's Black Economic Elite Formation," in *Transitions in Namibia: Which Changes for Whom?*, ed. Henning Melber (Uppsala, Sweden: Nordic Africa Institute), 110–29.

22. Interview notes summary, in "Asset Ownership Study," unpublished paper, September 2000, Harare, Zimbabwe, 35. This research was conducted and circulated by a member of the international aid community in Zimbabwe who wished to remain anonymous.

23. Vadim Volkov, *Violent Entrepreneurs: The Use of Force in the Making of Russian Capitalism* (Ithaca, NY: Cornell University Press, 2002), esp. 40 and 85.

24. Ibid., 41.

25. Ibid., 33. In the Russian case, by the mid-1990s criminal groups had gained control over some forty thousand businesses, including stock companies, banks, and co-operatives (Svetlana Glinkina, "Russia's Underground Economy During Transition," in *Underground Economies in Transition: Unrecorded Activity, Tax Evasion, Corruption and Organised Crime*, ed. Edgar Fiege and Katarina Ott [Aldershot, UK: Ashgate, 1999], 101).

26. Volkov, *Violent Entrepreneurs*, 121–22.

27. Lydia S. Rosner, "Cracking Pandor's Box: The Soviet Breakup and the Onset of Buccaneer Capitalism," *Trends in Organized Crime* 6.2 (2000): 141.

28. It is possible that they bit off more than they could chew and exceeded their expertise. Alternatively, it may be that their firms and any contracts they secured were simply not viable absent the government connection, as in the Muluzi and Mwila cases suggest. Or the economic environment in the 1990s perhaps proved too inhospitable to sustain their firms. These explanations are hardly mutually exclusive.

29. Partenariat pour le Développement Municipal, "Les acteurs de la décentralisa-tion en Afrique de l'Ouest et du Centre," Burkina Faso, October 2001.

30. World Bank, "Thailand—Contracts Awarded, " January 2003, http://www .worldbank.or.th/external/default/main?pagePK=64027236&piPK=64027233&theSitePK =333296&menuPK=333334&contractid=1227769 (accessed 21 May 2010); Danielle Knight and Edward T. Pound, "Anatomy of a "Bribe," *U.S. News and World Report*, 27 March 2006, http://www.usnews.com/usnews/biztech/articles/060327/27bribe.htm (ac-cessed 22 May 2010). The bank cited evidence that in 1994, Idani received about $58,000 from the Mauritian accounting firm De Chazal Du Mee to "obtain" a $580,000 World Bank contract for training entrepreneurs in Guinea-Bissau. The accounting firm was awarded the grant, but once training had begun, bank staff began to complain immedi-ately about the poor quality of the contractor. During the controversy, Idani received an-other $15,000 from De Chazal Du Mee in traveler's checks and then paid $12,000 of that to Pean. Investigators determined this was a bribe to ensure that the contract was not ter-minated owing to the poor performance of the accounting firm. Idani claimed that the payments were unrelated: the payment from De Chazal Du Mee was for his consultancy services and his payment to Pean was reimbursement for a prior personal loan.

31. Danielle Knight and Edward T. Pound, "Cleaning Up the World Bank," *U.S. News and World Report*, 26 March 2006, http://www.usnews.com/usnews/biztech/articles/ 060403/3worldbank_print.htm (accessed 22 May 2010). Additionally, one report re-ferred to Idani as "boss" of Faso-Baara, the World Bank-Burkinabé partnership charged with implementing public works projects in 1993. See Jean-Pierre Béjot, "Chronique de la métamorphose du Burkina Faso de Blaise Compaoré (12)," *LeFaso.net*, 23 September 2005, http://www.lefaso.net/spip.php?article9675 (accessed 16 April 2007), although this is contested.

32. Nouvel Espace Technologies, "Qui sommes nous?," 10 February 2005, http:// web.archive.org/web/20040926065256/www.net2you.bf/quisommenous.htm (accessed 16 April 2007).

33. Nouvel Espace Technologies, "References," 10 February 2005, http://web.archive .org/web/20041119080457/www.net2you.bf/REFFO.HTM (accessed 16 April 2007).

34. African Development Bank, *2005 Annual Procurement Report*, June 2006, http://www.afdb.org/fileadmin/uploads/afdb/Documents/Project-related-Procurement/ 03440219_EN_2005%20PROCUREMENT%20ANNUAL%20REPORT.PDF (accessed 22 May 2010); Dell Inc., "Emerging Markets: EMEA," http://www1.euro.dell.com/ content/topics/topic.aspx/emea/contact/edb/burkina_faso?c=ed&l=en&s=bsd (accessed 22 May 2010).

35. Scimpex, "Fiche de présentation: NET," http://www.scimpex-bf.com/membres/ fiche-membre.php?Id_Mbre=1 (accessed 22 May 2010); Philippe Bama, "Burkina Faso: Formation et emploi des jeunes, les insuffisances relevées par le CES," *Le Pays* (Ouagadougou, Burkino Faso), 5 April 2007, http://fr.allafrica.com/stories/200704050182.html (accessed 24 October 2011); Koumia Alassane Karama, "Journée internationale de lionisme: Communion avec les plus démunis à Ouagadougou," *Faso Presse* (Ouagadougou, Burkino Faso), 11 October 2006, http://www.lefaso.net/spip.php?article16863 (accessed 22 May 2010).

36. "Première Édition des Faso-NTIC-Awards 2005: Les meilleurs professionnels des TIC récompensés," *Sidwaya Quotidien* (Ouagadougou, Burkina Faso), 28 December 2005, http://fr.allafrica.com/stories/200512290001.html (accessed 27 October 2011).

37. In addition to the recent recognition by the International Labour Organisation, in 2004 Tytens received a gold medal for the national defense of France for ENHAS's service to French troops during their Operation Artemis intervention in the Democratic Republic of Congo.

38. The company charged fees for imports that were ultimately destined to support the Ugandan war effort in the Democratic Republic of Congo. The Uganda government therefore switched to using its armed forces to move cargo bound there (Republic of Uganda, "Judicial Commission of Inquiry into Allegations into Illegal Exploitation of Natural Resources and Other Forms of Wealth in the Democratic Republic of Congo 2001," final report, November 2002).

39. In January 2004, for example, Chiyangwa was investigated for his role in trying to prevent the arrest of two directors of ENG Capital and a legal inquiry into their activities. ENG was a banking startup that also had some family connections to ZANU-PF. The firm had invested heavily in the financial sector, and it collapsed during the currency crisis. The two directors were accused of trying to offset losses through investing in foreign currency, a practice that was outlawed the previous year, and other fraudulent activity ("Chiyangwa Named in ENG scandal," *NewZimbabwe.com*, 1 August 2004, http:// www.newzimbabwe.com/pages/banks5.1282.html [accessed 21 May 2010]). Chiyangwa, who was rumored to be a 40 percent stakeholder in ENG, was accused of threatening a policeman during a court inquiry and of having the investigator followed by "hit men" ("Chiyangwa Arrested in ENG Scandal," *NewZimbabwe.com*, 1 October 2004, http:// www.newzimbabwe.com/pages/banks8.1293.html [accessed 21 May 2010]). In a another incident, Chiyangwa was again arrested in December 2005, accused of being the leader of a ring of prominent Zimbabweans giving information to acknowledged South African spy Aubrey Wilkin. Held incommunicado for two weeks, Chiyangwa claimed that he was tortured by police and suffered a minor stroke in custody. See Andrew Meldrum, "Zanu-PF High Flyer Caught in Mugabe Purge," *Guardian* (Manchester, UK), 6 January

2005, http://www.guardian.co.uk/zimbabwe/article/0,2763,1384056,00.html (accessed 21 May 2010). Chiyangwa was released by the court; however, the attorney general opted to keep the case open but inactive, perhaps as an insurance policy for keeping Chiyangwa in line (Dumisani Muleya, "Spy's Release Ends Diplomatic Tug of War," *Business Day* (Johannesburg, South Africa), 14 December 2005, http://www.intelligence.gov.za/MediaStatements/Articles/SpyRelease.htm, [accessed 21 May 2010]).

40. Nelson Banya, "Chiyangwa Sells Firm to AG's Family," *Financial Gazette* (Harare, Zimbabwe), 8 February 2006.

41. ENHAS chief Sam Kutesa was also owner of East African Airlines, which Kenya Airways considered a rival carrier.

42. Importantly, not all of Sam Kutesa's enterprises have been successful. East African Airlines was unsustainable, having only one international route, Entebbe to Johannesburg. Further, Kutesa and his fellow shareholders in Global Airlinks were banned by the international travel body IATA for their ownership of the Uganda Travel Bureau, which was accused of operating with forged documents and of writing bad checks.

43. ENHAS has drawn considerable praise from the International Labour Organisation for workers' rights, and so forth (International Labour Organization, "Uganda: ENHAS Airport Ground Handlers," 6 June 2008, http://www.ilo.org/global/About_the_ILO/Media_and_public_information/Broadcast_materials/Video_News_Release/lang—en/WCMS_093948/index.htm [accessed 21 May 2010]).

44. Patrick Bond, lecture, 10 October 2008, Georgetown University. See also "Blue Lines," *Africa Confidential* 51.7 (2010): 1.

45. Susan Rose-Ackerman, *Corruption and Government: Causes, Consequences, and Reform* (Cambridge: Cambridge University Press, 1999), 121–22.

46. See Nicolas van de Walle, *African Economies and the Politics of Permanent Crisis, 1979–1999* (Cambridge: Cambridge University Press, 2001) and Colin Leys "African Capitalists and Development: Theoretical Questions," in *African Capitalists in African Development,* edited by Bruce Berman and Colin Leys (Boulder, CO: Lynne Rienner, 1994), 24.

6. GOING CONTINENTAL, GOING GLOBAL

1. There are countless other examples of such hyperbole. Equally outrageous was Roben Farzad's cover story on the 29 November 2007 issue of *BusinessWeek* magazine: "Can Greed Save Africa? Fearless Investing Is Succeeding Where Aid Often Hasn't."

2. Leslie Sklair and Peter Robbins, "Global Capitalism and Major Corporations from the Third World," *Third World Quarterly* 23.1 (2002): 90.

3. Sklair and Robbins use the *Fortune* magazine rankings as their standard for what constitutes a "major corporation." Although *Fortune* is based on revenues, "there are several ways of measuring and comparing corporations, for example by revenues (sales), by employees, by market shares, by numbers of production and/or sales points, or by market capitalisation" ("Global Capitalism and Major Corporations from the Third World," 85). A revenue measure may be better but also problematic, since it is to an extent based on official exchange rates. See also Richard T. Mpoyi, Troy A. Festervand, and Sean K. Sokoya, "Creating a Global Competitive Advantage for Sub-Saharan African Companies," *Journal of African Business* 7.1/2 (2006): 119–37.

4. This same sentiment obtains in West Africa among Levantine residents. See Chris Bierwith, "The Lebanese Communities of Cote d'Ivoire," *African Affairs* 98.290 (1999): 79–99, esp. 94.

5. See the Dow Jones Africa Titans 50 Index, http://www.google.com/finance?client =ob&q=INDEXDJX:DJAFK (accessed 27 October 2010), and the Down Jones African Titans Index fact sheet, jindexes.com/mdsidx/downloads/fact_info/Dow_Jones_Africa _Titans_50_Index_Fact_Sheet.pdf (accessed 3 December 2011)

6. See "Africa's Top 200 Companies," *African Business*, April 2007, http://www .highbeam.com/doc/1G1-162237528.html (accessed 1 April 2009).

7. Ibid.

8. And some, like Illovo, have gained sufficient visibility to be seen as attractive takeover targets: Associated Foods, Plc. bought a controlling stake in South Africa's Illovo Sugar in 2006.

9. Some may be more obvious: Azeb Mesfin's Mega Corporation, for example; others are less explicitly linked to political patrons/benefactors, including presidents.

10. Jerry Uwah, "Dangote Signs US 228 Million Contracts for Cement," *Leadership*, 16 October 2009, http://allafrica.com/stories/200910160857.html (accessed 22 May 2010).

11. Kunle Aderinokun, "Transcorp to Sell 51 Percent Stake in Nitel," *This Day* (Lagos, Nigeria), 26 February 2009, http://allafrica.com/stories/200902260162.html (accessed 21 May 2010).

12. "Africa Calling," *Economist*, 24 May 2007, http://www.economist.com/people/ displaystory.cfm?story_id=9218181 (accessed 21 May 2010).

13. Emphasis added. See company profile at http://www.africarecruit.com/transcorp/ index.php (accessed 27 October 2011).

14. After selling Celtel, for example, Mo Ibrahim provided capital of $150 million to establish the African Enterprise Fund in 2007, which invests in promising emerging-market companies in areas such as mobile communications, energy, and mining (see www.africafundltd.com); the fund aims for an average investment amount of $20 million.

15. See, for example, Ibrahima Thioub, Momar-Coumba Diop, and Catherine Boone, "Economic Liberalization in Senegal: Shifting Politics of Indigenous Business Interests," *African Studies Review* 41.2 (1998): 63–89, and Chris Bierwith, "The Lebanese Communities of Cote d'Ivoire."

16. Himbara, "Domestic Capitalists and the State in Kenya," in *African Capitalists in African Development,* ed. Bruce Berman and Colin Leys (Boulder, CO: Lynne Rienner, 1994), 84.

17. Bierwith, "The Lebanese Communities of Cote d'Ivoire," 94.

18. Sreenivas Janyala, "Nightmare in Kampala, Sleeplessness in Saurashtra," *Indian Express* (New Delhi), 14 April 2007, http://www.indianexpress.com/news/nightmareinkampala -sleeplessinsaurashtr/28415 (accessed 22 May 2010).

19. Ibid.

20. Ibid.

21. J. K. S. Makokha, "Kenya; Differences between Africans and Asians," *East African Standard* (Nairobi, Kenya), 5 May 2007, http://allafrica.com/stories/200705070502 .html (accessed 21 May 2010).

22. Anthony Kanyika, "Uganda; What Has Mehta Done for Country?," *New Vision*

(Kampala, Uganda), 10 April 2007, http://allafrica.com/stories/200704110053.html (accessed 21 May 2010).

23. David S. Fick, *Entrepreneurship in Africa: A Study of Successes* (Westport, CT: Quorum Books, 2002), 349.

24. Nimisha Madhvani, granddaughter of the Madhvani patriarch and group founder Mulijibhai Madhvani, served as Uganda's high commissioner to India; in Zambia, Suresh Desai serves as national treasurer of the ruling Movement for Multiparty Democracy, and Dipak Patel has held several ministerial positions and a parliamentary seat.

25. Jeremy Seekings and Nicoli Nattrass, *Class, Race, and Inequality in South Africa* (New Haven, CT: Yale University Press, 2005), 411. The manufacturing sector was the largest formal sector employer with 1.5 million workers (representing 19.3 percent of the workforce), followed by agriculture, mining, and the financial sector, which accounted for 11, 7.4 and 6.4 percent of formal employment, respectively. As of 2000, manufacturing represented 20.2 percent of GDP, and the agriculture, mining and financial sectors comprised 4.5 percent, 6.5 percent, 17.6 percent, respectively. See South African Institute of Race Relations, *South Africa Survey 2000/01* (Johannesburg, South Africa: South African Institute of Race Relations, 2001), 45, http://www.sairr.org.za/research-and-publications/the-south-africa-survey (accessed 21 May 2010).

26. Hein Marais, *South Africa: Limits to Change: The Political Economy of Transition* (London: Zed Books, 2001), 30.

27. Duncan Innes, *Anglo American and the Rise of Modern South Africa* (New York: Monthly Review Press, 1984), 221.

28. In 1987, Anglo controlled 60.1 percent of the Johannesburg Stock Exchange's market capitalization, followed by Sanlam (10.7 percent), SA Mutual (8.0 percent), Rembrandt Group (4.3 percent), Anglovaal (2.4 percent), and Liberty (2.0 percent). See Jos Gerson, "Should the State Attempt to Reshape South Africa's Corporate and Financial Structures?," in *State and Market in Post-Apartheid South Africa*, ed. Merle Lipton and Charles Simkins (Boulder, CO: Westview, 1993), 165.

29. Neo Chabane, Andrea Goldstein, and Simon Roberts, "The Changing Face and Strategies of Big Business in South Africa: More Than a Decade of Political Democracy," *Industrial and Corporate Change* 15.3 (2006): 553–54.

30. Ibid., 573.

31. Black-*controlled* companies (often with considerably less than 50 percent ownership) numbered just twenty-one in 2003, down from thirty-eight in 1999. See Lucille Gavera, ed., *Empowerment 2004: Black Ownership, Risk or Opportunity?* (Johannesburg, South Africa: BusinessMap Foundation, 2004), 55, http://www.transformationaudit.org.za/research-database/civil-society/advocacy-organisations/2000-2006/busmapbee2 (accessed 21 May 2010).

32. Seekings and Nattrass, *Class, Race and Inequality in South Africa*, 343–45. See also Okechukwu Iheduru, "Black Economic Power and Nation Building in Post-Apartheid South Africa," *Journal of Modern African Studies* 42.1 (2004): 1–30.

33. African Development Bank, "The Middle of the Pyramid: Dynamics of the Middle Class in Africa," Market Brief, 20 April 2011, 13.

34. See Dilek Aykut and Andrea Goldstein, "Developing Country Multinationals:

South-South Investment Comes of Age," in *Industrial Development for the 21st Century: Sustainable Development Perspectives* (New York: United Nations, 2007), 98–101, and Stephen Gelb, "South-South Investment: The Case of Africa," in *Africa in the World Economy: The National, Regional and International Challenges* (The Hague: Fondad, 2005), 204.

35. Daniel Malan, "Corporate Citizens, Colonialists, Tourists or Activists? Ethical Challenges Facing South African Corporations in Africa," *Journal of Corporate Citizenship* 18 (Summer 2005): 49–60. Note that the table he provides (see p. 52) seems a bit misleading, as some of the companies are subsidiaries or affiliates and thus arguably being "double counted."

36. Ibid., 514.

37. United Nations Conference on Trade and Development, *FDI in Least-Developed Countries at a Glance, 2005–2006* (New York: United Nations, 2007), http://www.unctad.org/en/docs/iteiia20057_en.pdf (accessed 21 May 2010).

38. Dianna Games, "The Experience of South African Firms Doing Business in Africa," *Regoverning Markets,* 8 January 2007, http://www.regoverningmarkets.org/en/resources/s_africa/the_experience_of_south_african_firms_doing_business_in_africa (accessed 21 May 2010).

39. Daniel Malan, "Corporate Citizens, Colonialists, Tourists or Activists? Ethical Challenges Facing South African Corporations in Africa," *Journal of Corporate Citizenship* 18 (Summer 2005), 50.

40. And South Africa's blacks are hardly immune from demonstrating such behaviors themselves, as demonstrated by the wave of xenophobia unleashed in 2008 against other Africans residing and working in South Africa.

41. Malan, "Corporate Citizens, Colonialists, Tourists or Activists?," 54.

42. Graham Mackay, interview by Jack Ewing, *Businessweek,* 28 June 2004.

43. For example, the Bench Marks Foundation argued that these practices in Zambia meant that "sustainable economic development was not taking place, leaving host communities angry and poor." The body also accused Shoprite of failing to provide a living wage to its own staff and of repatriating all profits back to South Africa (Nicola Mawson, "NGO Criticises Shoprite," *Business Day* [Johannesburg, South Africa], 15 April 2009, http://allafrica.com/stories/200904150092.html [accessed 27 October 2011)]). Despite the publication date, however, the report does not appear to take account of the measurable progress made by Shoprite in Zambia and elsewhere.

44. Thomas Reardon, "The Rapid Rise of Supermarkets in Developing Regions: Implications for Agricultural Development," paper, Conference on Supermarkets and Agricultural Development in China: Opportunities and Challenges, 24–25 May 2004, Shanghai.

45. Regardless, it is difficult to imagine Shoprite or its policies *increasing* poverty, even if Bench Marks Foundation criticisms proved true. After all, before the arrival of the South African grocery chains, few farmers were selling produce to Mwaiseni or the Zambia Consumers' Buying Corporation.

46. Timothy de Waal Malefyt and Brian Moeran, *Advertising Cultures* (New York: Berg, 2003).

47. See also Catherine Kinney, "Snug US Fit for Africa," *Africa Investor*, September–October 2008, 129, http://www.nyse.com/pdfs/africa_investor_issue24_129.PDF (accessed 21 May 2010).

48. Kinney, "Snug US Fit for Africa," 129.

49. Chabane, Goldstein, and Roberts, "The Changing Face and Strategies of Big Business in South Africa," 560.

50. Aykut and Goldstein, "Developing Country Multinationals," 88.

51. Mittal Steel was founded in India and run by an Indian and widely considered to be "Indian" despite being headquartered in Europe and having worldwide operations. Did it remain "Indian" after its combination with Luxembourg-based Arcelor in 2006? (It is worth noting, however, that Chrysler continued to be referred to as an American carmaker even after its purchase by Germany's Daimler-Benz.)

52. See Anglo American website: http://www.angloamerican.co.uk/about/ataglance.

CONCLUSION

1. These are Botswana, Burkina Faso, Cape Verde, Ethiopia, Ghana, Lesotho, Mali, Mauritius, Mozambique, Namibia Rwanda, Sao Tome and Principe, Seychelles, South Africa, Tanzania, Uganda, and Zambia.

BIBLIOGRAPHY

Ackerman, Kenneth. *Boss Tweed: The Rise and Fall of the Corrupt Pol Who Conceived the Soul of Modern New York.* New York: Carroll and Graf, 2005.

Aderinokun, Kunle. "Transcorp to Sell 51 Percent Stake in Nitel." *This Day* (Lagos, Nigeria), 26 February 2009. http://allafrica.com/stories/200902260162.html.

"Africa Calling." *Economist,* 24 May 2007. http://www.economist.com/people/displaystory .cfm?story_id=9218181.

African Development Bank. "The Middle of the Pyramid: Dynamics of the Middle Class in Africa." Market brief, 20 April 2011.

———. *Selected Statistics on African Countries.* Vol. 27. Tunis: African Development Bank, 2008.

———. *2005 Annual Procurement Report,* June 2006. http://www.afdb.org/fileadmin/uploads/ afdb/Documents/Project-related-Procurement/03440219_EN_2005%20PROCUREMENT %20ANNUAL%20REPORT.PDF.

"Africa's Top 200 Companies." *African Business,* April 2007. http://www.highbeam.com/ doc/1G1-162237528.html.

Afrobarometer Network. "Citizens of the World? Africans, Media and Telecommunications." Briefing Paper 69, May 2009.

Anderson, Allan. "The Pentecostal Gospel, Religion, and Culture in African Perspective." Paper, history of religion seminar, University of Oxford, 29 May 2000. http://artsweb .bham.ac.uk/aanderson/Publications/pentecostal_gospel.htm.

Anti-Corruption Commission (ACC) News. January–March 2003.

Arthur, Peter. "The State, Private Sector Development, and Ghana's 'Golden Age of Business.'" *African Studies Review* 49.1 (2006): 31–50.

Askin, Steve, and Carole Collins. "External Collusion with Kleptocracy: Can Zaïre Recapture Its Stolen Wealth?" *Review of African Political Economy* 20.57 (1993): 72–85.

Austen, Ralph. *African Economic History.* Berkeley: University of California Press, 1987.

Austin, Gareth. "African Business in Nineteenth-Century West Africa." In *Black Business and Economic Power,* edited by Alusine Jalloh and Toyin Falola, 114–44. Rochester, NY: University of Rochester Press, 2002.

Ayittey, George B. N. *Africa Betrayed.* New York: St. Martin's, 1993.

Aykut, Dilek, and Andrea Goldstein. "Developing Country Multinationals: South-South Investment Comes of Age." In *Industrial Development for the 21st Century: Sustainable Development Perspectives,* 85–116. New York: United Nations, 2007.

Baah, Gaddiel. "Minister Says The Future of the Private Sector in Ghana is 'Beautiful.'" www .AllAfrica.com, 3 February 2006.

Bama, Philippe. "Burkina Faso: Formation et emploi des jeunes, les insuffisances relevées

par le CES." *Le Pays* (Ouagadougou, Burkina Faso), 5 April 2007. http://fr.allafrica
.com/stories/200704050182.html.

Banya, Nelson. "Chiyangwa Sells Firm to AG's Family." *Financial Gazette* (Harare, Zimbabwe), 8 February 2006.

Barajas, Adolfo, Ralph Chami, Connel Fullenkamp, and Anjali Garg. "The Global Financial Crisis and Workers' Remittances to Africa: What's the Damage?" IMF Working Paper 10/24, January 2010.

Basildon Peta. "Lesotho Textile Workers Left in Rags." *Star* (Johannesburg, South Africa), 28 April 2005.

Bauer, Gretchen, and Scott D. Taylor. *Politics in Southern Africa: Transition and Transformation.* 2nd ed. Boulder, CO: Lynne Rienner, 2011.

Bayart, Jean-François. *The State in Africa: The Politics of the Belly.* New York: Longman, 1993.

Bayart, Jean-François, Stephen Ellis, and Béatrice Hibou. *The Criminalization of the State in Africa.* Bloomington: Indiana University Press, 1999

Baylies, Carolyn, and Morris Szeftel. "The Fall and Rise of Multiparty Politics in Zambia." *Review of African Political Economy* 54 (1992): 75–91.

Becker, David. "Business Associations in Latin America: The Venezuelan Case." *Comparative Political Studies* 23.1 (1990): 114–38.

"Begin, Believe, Become: Kenya's National Business Plan Competition." 12 November 2007. http://www.believe-begin-become.com/Kenya/morenews.asp?NewsID=97.

Béjot, Jean-Pierre. "Chronique de la métamorphose du Burkina Faso de Blaise Compaoré (12)." *LeFaso.net,* 23 September 2005. http://www.lefaso.net/spip.php?article9675.

Bevan, Stephen. "Obasanjo, Hailed as a Saviour by Blair, Leads Nigeria to Despair." *Telegraph* (London, UK), 21 May 2006. http://www.telegraph.co.uk/news/worldnews/africaandindianocean/nigeria/1519014/Obasanjo-hailed-as-a-saviour-by-Blair-leads-Nigeria-to-despair.html.

Bierwith, Chris. "The Lebanese Communities of Cote d'Ivoire." *African Affairs* 98. 290 (1999): 79–99.

Birrell, Ian. "It's Time the World Listened to New Stories out of Africa," *Guardian* (Manchester, UK), 20 February 2011.

"Blue Lines." *Africa Confidential* 51.7 (2010): 1.

Blundo, Giorgio, and Jean-Pierre Olivier de Sardan. *Everyday Corruption and the State.* London: Zed, 2006.

Boeh-Ocansey, Osei. "Private Sector Development in Ghana: The Challenges and the Lessons." PowerPoint presentation, roundtable meeting on promoting private sector development, 17 July 2005, Accra, Ghana. http://web.idrc.ca/en/ev-85356-201-1-DO_TOPIC.html.

Bond, Patrick. Lecture, Georgetown University, 10 October 2008.

———. *Uneven Zimbabwe: A Study of Finance, Development, and Underdevelopment.* Trenton, NJ: Africa World Press, 1998.

Bratton, Michael. "Micro-Democracy? The Merger of Farmer Unions in Zimbabwe." *African Studies Review* 37.1 (1994): 9–37.

Bratton, Michael, and Peter Lolojih. "Rationality, Cosmopolitanism, and Adjustment Fatigue: Public Attitudes to Economic Reform in Zambia." Afrobarometer Working Paper 105, April 2009.

Bratton, Michael, Robert Mattes, and Emmanuel Gyimah-Boadi. *Public Opinion, Democracy, and Reform.* New York: Cambridge University Press, 2005.

Bratton, Michael, and Nicolas van de Walle. *Democratic Experiments in Africa: Regime Transitions in Comparative Perspective.* Cambridge: Cambridge University Press, 1997.

Brautigam, Deborah. *The Dragon's Gift: The Real Story of China in Africa.* New York: Oxford University Press, 2009.

Brenthurst Foundation, Chinese Academy of Social Sciences, Council on Foreign Relations, and the Leon Sullivan Foundation. *Africa-China-U.S. Trilateral Dialogue: Summary Report.* Washington, DC: Council on Foreign Relations, 2007.

Brett, E. A. *Colonialism and Underdevelopment in East Africa.* New York: NOK Publishers, 1973.

Brubaker, Rogers. *The Limits of Rationality: An Essay on the Social and Moral Thought of Max Weber.* London: Allen and Unwin, 1984.

Bundy, Colin. *The Rise and Fall of the South African Peasantry.* Berkeley: University of California Press, 1979.

Callaghy, Thomas. "The State and the Development of Capitalism in Africa: Theoretical, Historical, and Comparative Reflections." In *The Precarious Balance,* edited by Donald Rothschild, 67–99. Boulder, CO: Westview, 1988.

Carmody, Pádraig. *Globalization in Africa: Recolonization or Renaissance?* Boulder, CO: Lynne Rienner, 2010.

———. *Tearing the Social Fabric: Neoliberalism, Deindustrialization, and the Crisis of Governance in Zimbabwe.* Westport, CT: Greenwood, 2001.

Casson, Mark. *Entrepreneurship and Business Culture.* Aldershot, UK: Edward Elgar, 1995.

Chabal, Patrick, and Jean-Pascal Daloz. *Africa Works: Disorder as Political Instrument.* Bloomington: Indiana University Press, 1999.

Chabane, Neo, Andrea Goldstein, and Simon Roberts. "The Changing Face and Strategies of Big Business in South Africa: More Than a Decade of Political Democracy." *Industrial and Corporate Change* 15.3 (2006): 549–77.

Chege, Michael. "Introducing Race as a Variable into the Political Economy of Kenya Debate: An Incendiary Idea." *African Affairs* 97.387 (1998): 209–30.

Chilobwe, Henry. "Malawi: Muluzi's Empire Collapsing." *Nation* (Blantyre, Malawi), 7 May 2006.

"Chiyangwa Arrested in ENG Scandal." *NewZimbabwe.com,* 1 October 2004. http://www.newzimbabwe.com/pages/banks8.1293.html.

"Chiyangwa Named in ENG Scandal." *NewZimbabwe.com,* 1 August 2004. http://www.newzimbabwe.com/pages/banks5.1282.html.

Chua, Amy. *World on Fire: How Exporting Free Market Democracy Breeds Ethnic Hatred and Global Instability.* New York: Random House, 2003.

Clark, Gracia. "Gender Fictions and Gender Tensions Involving 'Traditional' Asante Market Women." *African Studies Quarterly* 11.2/3 (2010): 43–66.

Cohen, Abner. *Custom and Politics in Urban Africa: A Study of Hausa Migrants in Yoruba Towns.* Berkeley: University of California Press, 1967.

Conaghan, Catherine. "Capitalists, Technocrats and Politicians: Economic Policy Making and Democracy in the Central Andes." In *Issues in Democratic Consolidation: The New South American Democracies in Comparative Perspective,* edited by Scott Mainwaring,

Guillermo O'Donnell, and Samuel J. Valenzuela, 199–42. Notre Dame, IN: University of Notre Dame Press.

Cooper, Frederick. "What is the Concept of Globalization Good For? An African Historian's Perspective." *African Affairs* 100.399 (2001): 189–213.

Davis, Melissa. "Is Africa Misbranded?" *Brand Channel*, 13 August 2007. http://www.brandchannel.com/features_effect.asp?pf_id=381.

DeGrassi, Aaron. "'Neopatrimonialism' and Agricultural Development in Africa: Contributions and Limitations of a Contested Concept." *African Studies Review* 51. 3 (2008): 107–33.

Dell Inc. "Emerging Markets: EMEA." http://www1.euro.dell.com/content/topics/topic.aspx/emea/contact/edb/burkina_faso?c=ed&l=en&s=bsd.

de Waal Malefyt, Timothy, and Brian Moeran. *Advertising Cultures*. New York: Berg, 2003.

Dixon-Fyle, Mac. "Agricultural Improvement and Political Protest on the Tonga Plateau, Northern Rhodesia." *Journal of African History* 18.4 (1977): 579–96.

Djankov, Simeon, Caralee McLeish, and Rita Maria Ramlho. "Regulation and Growth." *Economics Letters* 92.3 (2006): 395–401.

Driman, Luyton. *Going the Extra Mile: A Guide to Trading in Africa*. East London, South Africa: Bradmanton Trading and Publishing, 2005.

Drohan, Madelaine. *Making a Killing: How and Why Corporations Use Armed Force to Do Business*. Guilford, CT: Lyons Press, 2004.

Easterly, William. "How the Millennium Development Goals are Unfair to Africa." Brookings Institution Working Paper 14, November 2007. http://www.brookings.edu/~/media/Files/rc/papers/2007/11_poverty_easterly/11_poverty_easterly.pdf.

Emsley, Ian. *The Malaysian Experience of Affirmative Action: Lessons for South Africa*. Johannesburg, South Africa: Tafelberg, 1995.

Erdmann, Erdmann, and Ulf Engel. "Neopatrimonialism Reconsidered: Critical Review and Elaboration of an Elusive Concept." *Commonwealth and Comparative Politics* 45.1 (2007): 95–119.

Evans, Martha, and Ian Glenn. "'TIA—This is Africa': Afropessimism in Twenty-First Century Narrative Film." *Black Camera* 2, n.s., 1 (2010): 14–35.

Evans, Peter. *Embedded Autonomy*. Princeton, NJ: Princeton University Press, 1995.

———. "Indian Informatics in the 1980s: The Changing Character of State Involvement." *World Development* 20.1 (1992): 1–18.

Ewing, Jack. "Upwardly Mobile in Africa: How Basic Cell Phones Are Sparking Economic Hope and Growth in Emerging and Even Non-Emerging Nations." *Businessweek*, 24 September 2007.

Farzad, Roben. "Can Greed Save Africa? Fearless Investing Is Succeeding Where Aid Often Hasn't." *BusinessWeek*, 29 November 2007.

Ferguson, James. *Global Shadows: Africa in the Neoliberal World Order*. Durham, NC: Duke University Press, 2006.

Fick, David S. *Africa: A Continent of Economic Opportunity*. Johannesburg, South Africa: STE Publishers, 2006.

———. *Entrepreneurship in Africa: A Study of Successes*. Westport, CT: Quorum Books, 2002.

Ford, Neil. "Record FDI for Africa." *African Business*, 1 January 2008.

Fore, Henrietta. Opening remarks. Partnerships for Promoting the African Entrepreneur panel discussion, 19 October 2007, Washington, DC.

Fraser, Alistair, and John Lungu. "For Whom the Windfalls: Winners and Losers in the Privatisation of Zambia's Copper Mines," 2006. www.liberationafrique.org/IMG/pdf/Minewatchzambia.pdf.

Freedom House. *Countries at the Crossroads 2006—Nigeria,* 3 August 2006. http://www.unhcr.org/refworld/docid/4738691264.html.

Friedman, Thomas L. *The Lexus and the Olive Tree: Understanding Globalization.* New York: Farrar, Straus, and Giroux, 2000.

Fukuyama, Francis. *The End of History and the Last Man.* New York: Avon, 1992.

Fomunyoh, Christopher. "Democratization in Fits and Starts." *Journal of Democracy* 12.3 (2001): 37–50.

Fyle, C. Magbaily. "Indigenous Values and the Organization of Informal Sector Business in West Africa." In *Black Business and Economic Power,* edited by Alusine Jalloh and Toyin Falola, 29–40. Rochester, NY: University of Rochester Press, 2002.

Galvan, Dennis. "Political Turnover and Social Change in Senegal." *Journal of Democracy* 12.3 (2001): 51–62.

Games, Dianna. "The Experience of South African Firms Doing Business in Africa." *Regoverning Markets,* 8 January 2007. http://www.regoverningmarkets.org/en/resources/s_africa/the_experience_of_south_african_firms_doing_business_in_africa.

Gavera, Lucille, ed. *Empowerment 2004: Black Ownership, Risk or Opportunity?* Johannesburg, South Africa: BusinessMap Foundation, 2004.

Gaye, Adam. *Chine-Afrique: Le dragon et l'autruche.* Paris: L'Harmattan, 2006.

Gelb, Stephen. "South-South Investment: The Case of Africa." In *Africa in the World Economy: The National, Regional and International Challenges,* 202–204. The Hague: Fondad, 2005.

Gerson, Jos. "Should the State Attempt to Reshape South Africa's Corporate and Financial Structures?" In *State and Market in Post-Apartheid South Africa,* edited by Merle Lipton and Charles Simkins, 161–201. Boulder, CO: Westview, 1993.

"Ghana Moves Ahead." *Business in Africa Online,* 3 March 2005.

Gibbon, Peter. "Present-day Capitalism, the New International Trade Regime and Africa." *Review of African Political Economy* 29.91 (2002): 95–112.

Gifford, Paul. *Ghana's New Christianity: Pentecostalism in a Globalizing African Economy.* Bloomington: Indiana University Press, 2004.

Glinkina, Svetlana. "Russia's Underground Economy During Transition." In *Underground Economies in Transition: Unrecorded Activity, Tax Evasion, Corruption and Organised Crime,* edited by Edgar Fiege and Katarina Ott, 101–16. Aldershot, UK: Ashgate, 1999.

Gould, John A., and Matthew S. Winters. "An Obsolescing Bargain in Chad: Shifts in Leverage between the Government and the World Bank." *Business and Politics* 9.2 (2007), doi: 10.2202/1469-3569.1199.

Government of Ghana. *National Medium-Term Private Sector Development Strategy, 2004–2008.* December 2003.

"Government Refutes Sata's Claims over Chinese Nationals in Zambia." *Lusaka Times* (Zambia), 27 October 2007. www.lusakatimes.com/?p=1469.

Graham Mackay. Interview by Jack Ewing, *Businessweek*, 28 June 2004. http://www .businessweek.com/magazine/content/04_26/b3889412.htm.

Green, Reginald Herbold. "The IMF and World Bank in Africa: How Much Learning." In *Hemmed In: Responses to Africa's Economic Decline*, edited by Thomas Callaghy and John Ravenhill, 54–89. New York: Columbia University Press, 1993.

Grobler, John. "Namibia: Mafia Linked to Namibian Gems." *Namibian* (Windhoek), 23 March 2007. http://allafrica.com/stories/200703230749.html.

Gupta, Akil. "Blurred Boundaries: The Discourse of Corruption, the Culture of Politics and the Imagined State." *American Ethnologist* 22.2 (1995): 375–402.

Hansen, Karen Tranberg. *Salaula: The World of Secondhand Clothing and Zambia*. Chicago: University of Chicago Press, 2000.

Hate, Vibhuti. "India in Africa: Moving beyond Oil." *CSIS South Asia Monitor*, 10 June 2008. http://csis.org/files/media/csis/pubs/sam119.pdf.

Heilbrunn, John R. "Commerce, Politics, and Business Associations in Benin and Togo." *Comparative Politics* 29.4 (1997): 473–92.

Heilman, Bruce, and John Lucas, "A Social Movement for African Capitalism? A Comparison of Business Associations in Two African Cities." *African Studies Review* 40.2 (1997): 141–71.

Henley, John, Stefan Kratzsch, Mithat Külür, and Tamer Tandogan. "Foreign Direct Investment from China, India and South Africa in Sub-Saharan Africa: A New or Old Phenomenon?" UNU-WIDER Research Paper 24, March 2008. http://www.wider.unu.edu/ publications/working-papers/research-papers/2008/en_GB/rp2008-24.

Herbst, Jeffrey. *State Politics in Zimbabwe*. Berkeley: University of California Press, 1990.

Himbara, David. "Domestic Capitalists and the State in Kenya." In *African Capitalists in African Development*, edited by Bruce Berman and Colin Leys, 69–94. Boulder, CO: Lynne Rienner, 1994.

Hodges, Tony. *Angola: Anatomy of an Oil Economy*. 2nd ed. Bloomington: Indiana University Press, 2003.

Hoff, Karla, and Arijit Sen. "The Kin System as a Poverty Trap?" World Bank Policy Research Paper 3575, April 2005.

Hopkins, A. G. "Big Business in African Studies." *Journal of African History* 28.1 (1987): 119–40.

———. "Imperial Business in Africa: Part I, Sources." *Journal of African History* 17.1 (1976): 29–48.

Iheduru, Okechukwu. "Black Economic Power and Nation Building in Post-Apartheid South Africa." *Journal of Modern African Studies* 42.1 (2004): 1–30.

Iliffe, John. *The Emergence of African Capitalism*. Minneapolis: University of Minnesota Press, 1983.

Inikori, Joseph E. "The Development of Entrepreneurship in Africa: Southeastern Nigeria during the Era of the Trans-Atlantic Slave Trade." In *Black Business and Economic Power*, edited by Alusine Jalloh and Toyin Falola, 41–79. Rochester, NY: University of Rochester Press, 2002.

Innes, Duncan. *Anglo American and the Rise of Modern South Africa*. New York: Monthly Review Press, 1984.

International Labour Organization. "Uganda: ENHAS Airport Ground Handlers," 6 June

2008. http://www.ilo.org/global/About_the_ILO/Media_and_public_information/ Broadcast_materials/Video_News_Release/lang—en/WCMS_093948/index.htm.

Interview notes summary. In "Asset Ownership Study." Unpublished paper, September 2000, Harare, Zimbabwe.

Jalloh, Alusine. *African Entrepreneurship: Muslim Fula Merchants in Sierra Leone.* Athens: Ohio University Center for International Studies, 1999.

Janyala, Sreenivas. "Nightmare in Kampala, Sleeplessness in Saurashtra." *Indian Express* (New Delhi), 14 April 2007. http://www.indianexpress.com/news/ nightmareinkampala-sleeplessinsaurashtr/28415.

Johnston, Michael. *Syndromes of Corruption: Wealth, Power, and Democracy.* Cambridge: Cambridge University Press, 2006.

Joseph, Richard A. *Democracy and Prebendal Politics in Nigeria: The Rise and Fall of the Second Republic.* Cambridge: Cambridge University Press, 1988.

———, ed. *State, Conflict, and Democracy in Africa.* Boulder, CO: Lynne Rienner, 1998.

Kang, David C. *Crony Capitalism: Corruption and Development in South Korea and the Philippines.* Cambridge: University Press, 2002.

Kanyika, Anthony. "Uganda; What Has Mehta Done for Country?" *New Vision* (Kampala, Uganda), 10 April 2007. http://allafrica.com/stories/200704110053.

Kaplinsky, Raphael. "What Does the Rise of China Do for Industrialisation in Africa?" Unpublished paper, October 2007.

Karama, Koumia Alassane. "Journée internationale de lionisme: Communion avec les plus démunis à Ouagadougou." *Faso Presse* (Ouagadougou, Burkino Faso), 11 October 2006. http://www.lefaso.net/spip.php?article16863.

Kaufman, Daniel. Speech. Governance Matters: Debunking the Afropessimism Myth Conference, 28 November 2007, Washington, DC. http://www.cgdev.org/doc/events/11.28.07/ Governance_Matters_Transcript_2007.pdf.

Keim, Curtis. *Mistaking Africa: Curiosities and Inventions of the American Mind.* 2nd ed. Boulder, CO: Westview, 2010.

Kinney, Catherine. "Snug US Fit for Africa," *Africa Investor,* September–October 2008. http://www.nyse.com/pdfs/africa_investor_issue24_129.PDF.

Knight, Danielle, and Edward T. Pound. "Anatomy of a 'Bribe.'" *U.S. News and World Report,* 27 March 2006. http://www.usnews.com/usnews/biztech/articles/060327/27bribe.htm.

———. "Cleaning Up the World Bank." *U.S. News and World Report,* 26 March 2006. http:// www.usnews.com/usnews/biztech/articles/060403/3worldbank_print.htm.

Korten, David C. *When Corporations Ruled the World.* Rev. ed. Bloomfield, CT: Kumarian Press, 2001.

Kraus, Jon. "Capital, Power and Business Associations in the African Political Economy: A Tale of Two Countries, Ghana and Nigeria." *Journal of Modern African Studies* 40.3 (2002): 395–436.

Kurokawa, Kiyoto. Fletcher Tembo, and Dirk Willem te Velde. "Donor Support to Private Sector Development in Sub-Saharan Africa: Understanding the Japanese OVOP Programme." ODI/JICA Working Paper 290, April 2008. http://www.odi.org.uk/resources/ download/1116.pdf.

Lancaster, Carol. "The Lagos Three." In *Africa in World Politics,* 2nd ed., edited by John Harbeson and Donald Rothchild, 189–206. Boulder, CO: Westview, 2009.

Leys, Colin. "African Capitalists and Development: Theoretical Questions." In *African Capitalists in African Development*, edited by Bruce Berman and Colin Leys, 11–38. Boulder, CO: Lynne Rienner, 1994.

Lindberg, Staffan. *Democracy and Elections in Africa*. Baltimore, MD: Johns Hopkins University Press, 2006.

Little, Eric, and Carolyn Logan, comps. "The Quality of Democracy and Governance in Africa: New Results from Afrobarometer Round 4." Afrobarometer Working Paper 108, May 2009.

Lubeck, Paul. "The African Bourgeoisie: Debates, Methods, and Units of Analysis." In *The African Bourgeoisie: Capitalist Development in Nigeria, Kenya, and the Ivory Coast*, edited by Paul Lubeck, 3–26. Boulder, CO: Lynne Rienner, 1987.

Lwanda, John Lloyd Chipembere. *Promises, Power, Politics and Poverty: Democratic Transition in Malawi (1961–1999)*. Glasgow, Scotland: Dudu Nsomba Publications, 1997.

MacGaffey, Janet. *Entrepreneurs and Parasites: The Struggle for Indigenous Capitalism in Zaïre*. Cambridge: Cambridge University Press, 1988.

MacGaffey, Janet, and Rémy Bazenguissa-Ganga. *Congo-Paris: Transnational Traders on the Margins of the Law*. Bloomington: Indiana University Press, 2000.

MacIntyre, Andrew, ed., *Business and Government in Industrialising Asia*. Ithaca, NY: Cornell University Press, 1994.

Mahajan, Vijay. *Africa Rising: How 900 Million African Consumers Offer More Than You Think*. Upper Saddle River, NJ: Prentice Hall, 2009.

Makokha, J. K. S. "Kenya; Differences between Africans and Asians." *East African Standard* (Nairobi, Kenya), 5 May 2007. http://allafrica.com/stories/200705070502.html.

Malan, Daniel. "Corporate Citizens, Colonialists, Tourists or Activists? Ethical Challenges Facing South African Corporations in Africa." *Journal of Corporate Citizenship* 18 (Summer 2005): 49–60.

Marais, Hein. *South Africa: Limits to Change: The Political Economy of Transition*. London: Zed Books, 2001.

Mawson, Nicola. "NGO Criticises Shoprite." *Business Day* (Johannesburg, South Africa), 15 April 2009. http://allafrica.com/stories/200904150092.html.

Maseko, Sipho Sibusiso. "From Pavement Entrepreneurs to Stock Exchange Capitalists: the Case of the South African Black Business Class." DPhil thesis, University of the Western Cape, Bellville, 2000.

Mawdsley, Emma, and Gerald McCann, eds. *India and Africa: Changing Geographies of Power* Cape Town, South Africa: Pambazuka Press, 2011.

McGreal, Chris. "Thanks China, Now Go Home: Buy Up of Zambia Revives Old Colonial Fears." *Guardian* (Manchester, UK), 5 February 5 2007.

McIntosh, Marjorie. *Yoruba Women, Work, and Social Change*. Bloomington: Indiana University Press, 2009.

McVey, Ruth. *Southeast Asian Capitalists*. Ithaca, NY: Cornell Southeast Asia Program Publications, 1992.

Melber, Henning. "Poverty, Politics, Power and Privilege: Namibia's Black Economic Elite Formation." In *Transitions in Namibia: Which Changes for Whom?*, edited by Henning Melber, 110–29. Uppsala, Sweden: Nordic Africa Institute, 2007.

Meldrum, Andrew. "Zanu-PF High Flyer Caught in Mugabe Purge." *Guardian* (Manchester, UK), 6 January 2005. http://www.guardian.co.uk/zimbabwe/article/0,2763,1384056,00.html.

Mkandawire, Thandika, and Charles Soludo. *Our Continent, Our Future.* Trenton, NJ: Africa World Press, 1998.

Moran, Theodore H. *Harnessing Foreign Direct Investment for Development.* Washington, DC: Center for Global Development, 2006.

Morris, H. S. "Indians in East Africa: A Study of a Plural Society." *British Journal of Sociology* 7.3 (1956): 194–211.

Morten Beyer and Agnew. "Daallo Airlines: Transformation of an African Airline." Power-Point presentation, 17 March 2007.

Moss, Todd. *African Development: Making Sense of the Issues and Actors.* Boulder, CO: Lynne Rienner, 2007.

Moyo, Dambisa. *Dead Aid: Why Aid Is Not Working and How There Is a Better Way for Africa.* New York: Farrar, Straus and Giroux, 2009.

Mpoyi, Richard T., Troy A. Festervand, and Sean K. Sokoya. "Creating a Global Competitive Advantage for Sub-Saharan African Companies." *Journal of African Business* 7.1/2 (2006): 119–37.

Muleya, Dumisani. "Spy's Release Ends Diplomatic Tug of War." *Business Day* (Johannesburg, South Africa), 14 December 2005. http://www.intelligence.gov.za/MediaStatements/Articles/SpyRelease.htm.

Mushi, Theo. "How the Private Sector Fares in Tanzania." *Guardian* (Manchester, UK), 7 March 2007.

Nellis, John. "Privatization in Africa: What Has Happened? What Is to Be Done?" Center for Global Development Working Paper 25, February 2003.

———. "Public Enterprises in Sub-Saharan Africa." In *State-Owned Enterprises in Africa,* edited by Barbara Grosh and Rwekaza Mukandala, 3–24. Boulder, CO: Lynne Rienner, 1994.

Noorbakhsh, Farhad, and Alberto Paloni. "Structural Adjustment Programs and Industry in Sub-Saharan Africa: Restructuring or De-Industrialization?" *Journal of Developing Areas* 33.4 (1999): 549–80.

Nouvel Espace Technologies. "Qui sommes nous?" 10 February 2005. http://web.archive.org/web/20040926065256/www.net2you.bf/quisommenous.htm.

———. "References." 10 February 2005. http://web.archive.org/web/20041119080457/www.net2you.bf/REFFO.HTM.

Olukoshi, Adebayo O. ed. *The Politics of Structural Adjustment in Nigeria.* London: James Currey, 1993.

O'Meara, Dan. *Forty Lost Years: The Apartheid State and the Politics of the National Party, 1948–94.* Randberg, South Africa: Ravan Press, 1995.

Öniş, Ziya, and Fikret Şenses. "Rethinking the Emerging Post-Washington Consensus." *Development and Change* 36.2 (2005): 263–90.

Oonk, Gijsbert. "Debunking the Indian Diasporas: Empirical Explorations and Theoretical Assumptions." Asians in Africa Position Paper, 2006. http://www.asiansinafrica.com/lijst_publications.php.

Oshikoya, Temitope W. "Macroeconomic Determinants of Domestic Private Investment in Africa: An Empirical Analysis. *Economic Development and Cultural Change* 42.3 (1994): 573–96.

Ostergaard, Tom. "The Role of the 'National' Bourgeoisie in National Development: The Case of the Textile and Clothing Industries in Zimbabwe." In *African Capitalists in African Development,* edited by Bruce Berman and Colin Leys, 115–38. Boulder, CO: Lynne Rienner, 1994.

Partenariat pour le Développement Municipal. "Les acteurs de la décentralisation en Afrique de l'Ouest et du Centre." Burkina Faso, October 2001.

Pew Research Center. *Spirit and Power: A 10-Country Survey of Pentecostalists.* Pew Research Center/Pew Forum on Religion and Public Life, October 2006.

Phiri, Isaac, and Joe Maxwell. "Gospel Riches: Africa's Rapid Embrace of Prosperity Pentecostalism Provokes Concern—and Hope." *Christianity Today,* July 2007. http://www.christianitytoday.com/ct/2007/july/12.22.html?start=3.

Pineau, Carol. "A Changing Continent: The Africa You Never See." *Washington Post,* 17 April 2005.

Pitcher, Anne. *Transforming Mozambique: The Politics of Privatization, 1975–2000.* Cambridge: University of Cambridge Press, 2002.

Pitcher, Anne, Mary H. Moran, and Michael Johnson. "Rethinking Patrimonialism and Neopatrimonialism in Africa." *African Studies Review* 52.1 (2009): 125–56.

Platteau, Jean-Philippe, and Yujiro Hayami. "Resource Endowments and Agricultural Development: Africa versus Asia." In *The Institutional Foundations of East Asian Economic Development,* edited by Yujiro Hayami and M. Aoki, 357–410. Basingtoke, UK: Macmillan, 1998.

"Politicians Buy." *Profit* (Zambia) 15.3 (1996): 40.

"Première Édition des Faso-NTIC-Awards 2005: Les meilleurs professionnels des TIC récompensés." *Sidwaya Quotidien* (Ouagadougou, Burkina Faso), 28 December 2005. http://fr.allafrica.com/stories/200512290001.html.

Radelet, Steven C. *Emerging Africa: How 17 Countries Are Leading the Way.* Washington, DC: Center for Global Development, 2010.

Rakner, Lise, Nicolas van de Walle, and Dominic Mulaisho. "Aid and Reform in Zambia." In *Aid and Reform in Africa: Lessons From Ten Case Studies,* edited by Shantayanan Devarajan, David R. Dollar, and Torgny Holmgren, 533–625. Washington, DC: World Bank.

Ramachandran, Sudha. "India Pushes People Power in Africa." *Asia Times* (Hong Kong), 13 July 2007. http://www.atimes.com/atimes/South_Asia/IG13Df03.html.

Ramachandran, Vijaya. "Indigenous Investment and Participation in Africa's Economy." Lecture, Society for International Development, 20 November 2006, Washington, DC.

Ramachandran, Vijaya, Alan Gelb, and Manju Kedia Shah. *Africa's Private Sector: What's Wrong with the Business Environment and What to Do about It?* (Washington DC: Center for Global Development, 2009. http://www.cgdev.org/content/publications/detail/1421340.

Reardon, Thomas. "The Rapid Rise of Supermarkets in Developing Regions: Implications for Agricultural Development." Paper, Conference on Supermarkets and Agricultural Development in China: Opportunities and Challenges, 24–25 May 2004, Shanghai.

Republic of Uganda. "Judicial Commission of Inquiry into Allegations into Illegal Exploitation of Natural Resources and Other Forms of Wealth in the Democratic Republic of Congo 2001." Final report, November 2002.

Rose-Ackerman, Susan. *Corruption and Government: Causes, Consequences, and Reform.* Cambridge: Cambridge University Press, 1999.

Rosner, Lydia S. "Cracking Pandor's Box: The Soviet Breakup and the Onset of Buccaneer Capitalism." *Trends in Organized Crime* 6.2 (2000): 141–47.

Sampord, Charles, Arthur Shacklock, Carmel Connors, and Fredrik Galtung, eds. *Measuring Corruption.* Aldershot, UK: Ashgate, 2006.

Sardanis, Andrew. *A Venture in Africa: The Challenges of African Business.* New York: I. B. Tauris, 2007.

Schneider, Ben, and Sylvia Maxfield, eds. *Business and the State in Developing Countries.* Ithaca, NY: Cornell University Press, 1997.

Scimpex. "Fiche de présentation: NET." http://www.scimpex-bf.com/membres/fiche-membre .php?Id_Mbre=1.

Seekings, Jeremy, and Nicoli Nattrass. *Class, Race, and Inequality in South Africa.* New Haven, CT: Yale University Press, 2005.

Sergeant, Barry. "Zimbabwe's Pale Barons." *Moneyweb,* 30 June 2008. http://www.moneyweb .co.za/mw/view/mw/en/page84?oid=212866&sn=Detail.

Shadlen, Kenneth C. *Democratization without Representation: The Politics of Small Industry n Mexico.* University Park: Penn State University Press, 2004.

Silva, Eduardo. "From Dictatorship to Democracy: The Business-State Nexus in Chile's Economic Transformation, 1975–1994." *Comparative Politics* 28.3 (1996): 299–320.

Singh, Sushant. "India and West Africa: A Burgeoning Relationship." Chatham House Africa/Asia Programme Briefing Paper, April 2007. http://www.chathamhouse.org/ publications/papers/view/108471.

Skalnes, Tor. *The Politics of Economic Reform in Zimbabwe: Continuity and Change in Development.* Basingstoke, UK: Macmillan, 1995.

Sklair, Leslie, and Peter Robbins. "Global Capitalism and Major Corporations from the Third World." *Third World Quarterly* 23.1 (2002): 81–100.

Smith, Daniel J. *A Culture of Corruption: Everyday Corruption and Popular Discontent in Nigeria.* Princeton, NJ: Princeton University Press, 2007.

Sorbara, Mark. "India and Africa—It's Old Friends, New Game and Rules," *Daily Nation* (Nairobi, Kenya), 9 February 2007. http://allafrica.com/stories/200702081111.html.

South African Institute of Race Relations. *South Africa Survey 2000/01.* Johannesburg, South Africa: South African Institute of Race Relations, 2001. http://www.sairr.org .za/research-and-publications/the-south-africa-survey.

Spring, Anita, and Barbara E. McDade, eds. *African Entrepreneurship: Theory and Reality.* Gainesville: University Press of Florida, 1998.

Stark, David, and László Bruszt. "One Way or Multiple Paths: For a Comparative Sociology of East European Capitalism." *American Journal of Sociology* 106.4 (2001): 1129–37.

"Start-Ups and Slow-Downs: What Impact Will Recession Have on Entrepreneurship" *Economist.com,* 18 November 2008. http://www.economist.com/displaystory.cfm?story _id=12625763.

Stein, Howard, ed. *Asian Industrialization and Africa.* New York: St. Martin's, 1996.

Stiglitz, Joseph. *Globalization and Its Discontents.* New York: Norton, 2002.

Strange, Susan. *The Retreat of the State: The Diffusion of Power in the World Economy.* Cambridge: Cambridge University Press, 1996.

Swainson, Nicola. "Indigenous Capitalism in Postcolonial Kenya." In *The African Bourgeoisie,* edited by Paul Lubeck. Boulder, CO: Lynne Rienner, 1987.

Tangri, Roger. *The Politics of Patronage in Africa: Parastatals, Privatization and Private Enterprise.* Trenton, NJ: Africa Word Press, 1999.

Taylor, Darren. "Chinese Aid Flows into Africa." *Voice of America,* 8 May 2007.

Taylor, Scott D. *Business and the State in Southern Africa: The Politics of Economic Reform.* Boulder, CO: Lynne Rienner, 2007.

———. "Indigenization, Black Economic Empowerment, and Affirmative Action in Zimbabwe and South Africa." In *Black Business and Economic Power,* edited by Alusine Jalloh and Toyin Falola, 347–80. Rochester, NY: University of Rochester Press, 2002.

———. "Labor Markets in Africa: Multiple Challenges, Limited Opportunities." *Current History* 108.718 (2009): 214–20.

———. "Race, Class, and Neopatrimonial Politics." In *State, Conflict, and Democracy in Africa,* edited by Richard A. Joseph, 239–66. Boulder, CO: Lynne Rienner, 1998.

Thioub, Ibrahima, Momar-Coumba Diop, and Catherine Boone. "Economic Liberalization in Senegal: Shifting Politics of Indigenous Business Interests." *African Studies Review* 41.2 (1998): 63–89.

Timmons, Heather, and Vikas Bajaj. "Indian Iron-Ore Exporter is Target of Fraud Inquiry." *New York Times,* 30 October 2009.

Transparency International. *Bribes Payer's Index, 2008.* Berlin: Transparency International, 2008.

———. "Foreign Bribery by Emerging Export Powers 'Disconcertingly High.'" 4 October 2006. http://www.transparency.org/policy_research/surveys_indices/bpi/bpi_2006.

Trofimov, Yaroslav. "New Management: In Africa China's Expansion Begins to Stir Resentment." *Wall Street Journal,* 2 February 2007.

Tsai, Kellee. *Capitalism without Democracy: The Private Sector in Contemporary China.* Ithaca, NY: Cornell University Press, 2007.

United Nations Conference on Trade and Development. *Asian Foreign Direct Investment in Africa: Towards a New Era of Cooperation among Developing Countries.* New York: United Nations, 2007. http://www.unctad.org/en/docs/iteiia20071_en.pdf.

———. *FDI in Least-Developed Countries at a Glance, 2005–2006.* New York: United Nations, 2007. http://www.unctad.org/en/docs/iteiia20057_en.pdf.

———. "FDI Stocks in Africa from Selected Developing Asian Economies." 2002. http://www.unctad.org/templates/WebFlyer.asp?intItemID=4180&lang=1.

United Nations Development Program. *Unleashing Entrepreneurship: Making Business Work for the Poor.* Commission on Private Sector and Development, report to the secretary general, 1 March 2004.

Uwah, Jerry. "Dangote Signs US 228 Million Contracts for Cement." *Leadership,* 16 October 2009. http://allafrica.com/stories/200910160857.html.

van de Walle, Nicolas. "Adjustment Alternatives and Alternatives to Adjustment." *African Studies Review* 37.3 (1994): 103–17.

——. *African Economies and the Politics of Permanent Crisis, 1979–1999.* Cambridge: Cambridge University Press, 2001.

Varadarajan, Siddarth. "India Inc Makes Inroads in the Heart of Africa." *Times of India* (New Delhi), 1 March 2004.

Villalón Leonardo A., and Peter VonDoepp. *The Fate of Africa's Democratic Experiments.* Bloomington: Indiana University Press, 2005.

Volkov, Vadim. *Violent Entrepreneurs: The Use of Force in the Making of Russian Capitalism.* Ithaca, NY: Cornell University Press, 2002.

West, Michael O. *The Rise of an African Middle Class: Colonial Zimbabwe, 1898–1965.* Bloomington: Indiana University Press, 2002.

White, Gregory, and Scott D. Taylor. "Well-Oiled Regimes: The Political Economy of Transition in Algeria and Nigeria." *Review of African Political Economy* 28.89 (2001): 323–44.

"Why Voting Is Good for You." *Economist,* 27 August 1994, 15.

Woo-Cumings, Meredith, ed. *The Developmental State.* Ithaca, NY: Cornell University Press, 1999.

World Bank. *Doing Business 2009: Comparing Regulation in 181 Economies,* September 2008. Doing Business Project. http://www.doingbusiness.org/~/media/fpdkm/doing%20business/documents/annual-reports/english/db09-fullreport.pdf.

——. "Economy Rankings," 2009. Doing Business Project. http://www.doingbusiness.org/EconomyRankings.

——. "Thailand—Contracts Awarded," January 2003. http://www.worldbank.or.th/external/default/main?pagePK=64027236&piPK=64027233&theSitePK=333296&menuPK=333334&contractid=1227769.

Zappile, Tina M. "Nonreciprocal Trade Agreements and Trade: Does the African Growth and Opportunity Act (AGOA) Increase Trade?" *International Studies Perspectives* 12.1 (2011): 46–67.

Zeleza, Paul T. "Beyond Afropessimism: Historical Accounting of African Universities" *Pambazuka News* (Cape Town, South Africa), 30 August, 2006. http://pambazuka.org/en/category/features/35832.

FURTHER READING

I have cited many sources in this book, probably more than I anticipated when the project began. Many other sources had a significant impact on my thinking about business and capitalism in Africa. I have listed below a number of books, both recent contributions and others now regarded as classics. Some lead to optimistic conclusions, some skew more toward pessimism, but each is rooted in a strong analytical framework. Although this is not an exhaustive list, all should be considered important if not required reading for those seeking to further understand the nexus of business, capitalism, and development in contemporary Africa.

Broadman, Harry G. *Africa's Silk Road: China and India's New Economic Frontier*. Washington, DC: World Bank, 2007.

Carmody, Pádraig. *The New Scramble for Africa*. Cambridge, UK: Polity Press, 2011.

Cheru, Fantu, and Cyril Obi. *The Rise of China and India in Africa: Challenges, Opportunities, and Critical Interventions*. London: Zed Books, 2010.

Collier, Paul. *The Bottom Billion: Why the Poorest Countries are Failing and What Can Be Done About It*. New York: Oxford University Press.

Dowden, Richard. *Africa: Altered States, Ordinary Miracles*. New York: PublicAffairs Books, 2010.

Falola, Toyin. *The Power of African Cultures*. Rochester, NY: University of Rochester Press, 2008.

Forrest, Tom. *The Advance of African Capital: The Growth of Nigerian Private Enterprise*. Charlottesville: University Press of Virginia, 1994.

Guyer, Jane. *Marginal Gains: Monetary Transactions in Atlantic Africa*. Chicago: University of Chicago Press, 2004.

Handley, Antoinette. *Business and the State in Africa: Economic Policymaking in the Neo-Liberal Era*. Cambridge: Cambridge University Press, 2008.

Iliffe, John. *The Emergence of African Capitalism*. New York: Palgrave, 1983.

Joseph, Richard. *Democracy and Prebendal Politics in Nigeria: The Rise and Fall of the Second Republic*. Cambridge: Cambridge University Press, 1987.

Kennedy, Paul. *African Capitalism: The Struggle for Ascendancy*. Cambridge: Cambridge University Press, 1988.

Kitching, Gavin. *Class and Economic Change in Kenya: The Making of an African Petite-Bourgeoisie*. New Haven, CT: Yale University Press, 1980.

Mbeki, Moeletsi. *Architects of Poverty: Why African Capitalism Needs Changing*. Johannesburg, South Africa: Pan Macmillan, 2009.

Miguel, Edward. *Africa's Turn*. Cambridge, MA: MIT Press, 2009.

Rodney, Walter. *How Europe Underdeveloped Africa*. Washington, DC: Howard University Press, 1981.

Rodrik, Dani. *The Globalization Paradox: Democracy and the Future of the World Economy*. New York: Norton, 2011.

Sklar, Richard, *Corporate Power in an African State: The Political Impact of Multinational Mining Companies in Zambia*. Berkeley: University of California Press, 1975.

In addition, two recent reports on Africa also make for highly illuminating reading:

Aker, Jenny, and Isaac Mbiti. "Mobile Phones and Economic Development in Africa." Center for Global Development Working Paper 211, June 2010. http://www.cgdev.org/content/publications/detail/1424175

McKinsey Global Institute. "Lions on the Move: The Progress and Potential of African Economies." 2010. http://www.mckinsey.com/mgi/publications/progress_and_potential_of_african_economies/pdfs/MGI_african_economies_ExecSumm.pdf

INDEX

Page numbers in italics represent illustrations.

Abacha, Sani, 18, 54, 110
Abusita, Mohamed Abdillahi, 88–89
affirmative action, 139–40
Affirmative Action Group, 142
Africa: A Continent of Economic Opportunity (Fick), 77
Africa: Francophone countries, 120, 122, 125; investment-friendly economies, 10–11; share of world trade, 66, 70
Africa Global Competitiveness Initiative, 74
Africa: Open for Business (Pineau), 10, 71, 89, 94, 181–82, 183, 188
Africa Works: Disorder as Political Instrument (Chabal and Daloz), 39, 40
African business, 194n5; economically dominant minorities as, 33; existing firms, 19–20; level of political commitment to, 11; multiple cultures of, 6; as phrase, 3, 20, 156, 181, 183–84; positioned for long-term success, 20–21, 130–31. *See also* black African business; diversity of African big business; minority-owned business
African Business, 10, 158–59, 160
African Business Roundtable, 10
African Development Bank, 70
African Economic History (Austen), 30
African Economies and the Politics of Permanent Crisis: 1979–1999 (van de Walle), 62, 186
African Entrepreneurship (Spring and McDade), 184
African Entrepreneurship: A Study of Successes (Fick), 77

African Growth and Opportunities Act (AGOA), 68–69, 70–71, 105
African Investor index, 159
African National Congress (ANC), 37, 57, 169
African Petroleum Plc., 160, 163
Africanization, 31, 32, 40, 102, 106, 119, 140, 196n3. *See also* indigenization; nationalism
"Africa's Top 200" index, 158–59, 160
Afrobarometer, 17, 58, 62, 79, 84
Afro-Marxist states, 30, 46, 196n2
Afro-optimism, xiv, 4–5, 9–11, 93
Afropessimism, xiv, 4, 5–9, 93, 183, 194n9; "backwardness," views of, 4, 6, 39, 41; determinism, 5–6, 8, 12–13, 156; undermined by historical perspective, 23
agricultural subsidies, 70, 71, 203n22
aid and debt regimes, 13
airlines, 86, 87, 88–89, 137–38
Algeria, 27, 32
Amin, Idi, 32, 119
Anglo American Plc., 19, 163, 169, 180–81
AngloGold, 163
AngloGold Ashanti, 163
Angola, 27, 30, 32, 55, 196n2; foreign direct investment in, 102, 123–24
antimarket backlash, 36–37
Asante people, 28
Ashanti Goldfields, 163
Asia, 31; investment partners in Africa, 101, 157; Western beliefs about, 6–7. *See also* China; India
Asian financial crisis, 1997, 64
Asians: Kenya and, 167; Uganda and,

32, 166, 211n30. *See also* Madhvani
  Group; Mehta Group (Uganda)
Association of African Business Schools
  (AABS), 77
Austen, Ralph, 25, 30
Austin, Gareth, 26
authoritarian regimes, 53–55, 139
automotive sector, 125

banking, 167, 174
Bartels, Kwamena, 81–82
Bayart, Jean-Francois, 39
BEE companies, 170
Benchmarks Foundation, 178, 219n43
Benin, 57
Bharti Airtel Ltd., 20, 125, 164
black African business: cultural constraints
  on, 5; historical restrictions on, 23, 27–
  29, 160; marginalization of, 15, 23, 28,
  31–32; minority-owned business as
  precursor, 70–71; state as, 37; under-
  development of, 23, 26, 111. *See also*
  African business; giants, corporate
black economic empowerment, 33, 139,
  141, 170–72, 176, 181; broad-based,
  170–72
blacklisting, 146–47
Blair, Tony, 70
Blundo, Giorgio, 39
Bond, Patrick, 153
Bongo, Omar, 38
Botswana, 10, 30, 109, 207n2, 208n2
branding problem, Africa's, 12, 94, 178
Bratton, Michael, 57
Brautigam, Deborah, 71, 107, 112, 118
Brazil, 101–102
Bredenkamp, John, 34
Bribe Payers' Index, 127
bribes, 127
BRICs, 101
briefcase businessmen, 13, 133
Broadman, Harry, 107
Bull, Theo, 60
bureaucratic bourgeoisie, 19, 38, 41, 132
Burkina Faso, 38, 146–47

business: benefits of democracy, 58–60;
  as a class, 57–58; role in democratic
  transitions, 56–58. *See also* legitimate
  business
Business and State in Southern Africa, 51
business associations, 51, 80, 81
BusinessAction for Africa, 74
business/entrepreneurial cultures, 4–5, 14,
  76–77, 184–87; adaptability and persistence, 85; globalization and, 65–66;
  South Africa, 175–78. *See also* entrepreneurialism

Callaghy, Thomas, 5, 39, 187
capitalism: African, xiv, xv; adjectival, 29,
  41; African as culturally deficient, 6,
  12, 29, 39; class of capitalists, 35–36;
  Western views of, 6–7
Carothers, Thomas, 29
cellular technologies, 79, 87–88, 125, 163–64
Celtel International, 19–20, 163–64
Chabal, Patrick, xiv, 39, 40
Chanakira, Nigel, 142
Chandaria Group, 167
China, 6, 36, 54; black African business
  and, 161; demand for industrial
  metals, 103; diversified investments,
  111–12, 114; economic growth, 71,
  72; export-import bank, 114; foreign direct investment, 15, 17, 18,
  66, 101, 103, 110–18, 127; infrastructure and, 112; labor, investment in,
  112, 114–17; labor tensions in Africa,
  115–16, 118, 128–29; manufacturing
  dominance, 109; nature of investment
  in Africa, 113–14; neocolonialism
  concerns, 110–11; politics of Africa
  strategy, 112–13, 127; positive potential, 110–11; resource seeking, 111;
  resource-seeking investment, 108–
  109; rise of, 107; special economic
  zones, 107; textile sector, 71. *See also*
  Asia; foreign direct investment (FDI);
  immigrant and foreign firms; multinational corporations (MNCs)

China National Petroleum Corporation, 123
Chinese diaspora, 112, 117–18, 128
Chiyangwa, Philip, 141–43, 148, 149–50, 215n39
Chua, Amy, 36, 58, 165
Citizens Empowerment Act of 2006 (Zambia), 140
Cohen, Abner, 25, 26
Cold War, xv, 66
colonialism, 14–15, 106; attempts to provide infrastructure, 28; damage to black business interests, 22–23; exploitation, 26–30; MNCs, 23–24; partition of Africa after 1884, 26
Commission on Private Sector and Development (United Nations), 74
commodities, primary, 17; China and, 111; dependence on, 99–100; as liability, 102. *See also* extractive sectors
commodity prices, 66, 69, 71, 72, 90–91, 100
communication technology, 78–79, 163–64
Communist Party, Chinese, 114
competition, 149, 150–52
Competitive and Private Sector Development Project (Mozambique), 81
compradors, 38, 76, 100, 133
computer businesses, 86–87
Confederation of Indian Industries, 122–23
Confucian culture, 6–7
Congo Basin, 99
consumerism, 105
contagion effects, 92, 94, 202n9
Cooper, Frederick, 65
Corporate Council on Africa, 10, 74
corporate social responsibility, 109–110, 166, 176, 210n37
corruption, 3, 38, 195n21; cost of doing business, 19; democratization and, 59–60; deterministic view, 5–6; economically dominant minorities and, 33, 34–35; as economically suboptimal, 36, 144; neopatrimonial view, 5; Nigeria, 135–36; not insurmountable, 19, 21, 94; Russia, 144–45, 150; syndromes, 8; as time of independence,

31; transparency and, 59; Uganda, 137–39, 217n38
Corruption Perceptions Index, 84, 156
Cote d'Ivoire, 15, 28, 30, 55, 199n4; import substitution industrialization, 103; Ivoirité, 140
Council for Mutual Economic Assistance, 49
credit, 25, 33; changes in volume of, 85, *190*
crony capitalism, 63, 130; adjustment of behavior, 19; bargains, 148–50; big men, 5, 15, 18, 34, 130, 145; conventional path to, 132, 133–36; as doing business, 35; economic spillover effects, 150–52; economically dominant minorities and, 33, 34–35, 131; evidence of redemption and legitimation, 145–48; indigenization programs and, 132, 139–43, 197n33; institutional change and, 19; legitimate business and, 5, 7–8, 131–32; legitimization, 132–33; levels of, 131; mechanism of transformation, 143–44; not limited to Africa, 7–8, 12, 24, 34, 40, 131, 154; origins of, 24, 133–43; privatization and, 132, 136–39; process of transformation, 143–50; as rational alternative to marginalization, 15, 34–35; SAPs and, 52; state, dependence on, 37–38; state, transformation of, 152–54; value of, 153–54
Crony Capitalism (Kang), 185
cultural deficiency arguments, 6, 12, 29, 39
cultural globalization, 66–67, 73, 76, 93
culture, African: analytical clarity about, 6–7; not monolithic, 6, 8, 130–31
currency controls, 46, 61

Daallo Airlines, 86, 87, 88–89
Dairo Air Services (DAS), 151
Daloz, Jean-Pascal, xiv, 39, 40
Dangote, Aliko, 161, 172
Dangote Group, 160–61, 163
de-Africanization, 164, 178–81
debt forgiveness, 9, 16, 61, 67, 90, 113; PRSPs and, 69–70

deindustrialization, 61, 103, 104, 109
democracy: not required for business success, 53–54; as political norm, 17
Democracy and Elections in Africa (Lindberg), 58
Democratic Republic of Congo, 61, 85, 88, 114, 139, 151–52
democratization, 13–14, 15, 53–60; ambiguous role, 62–63; benefits for business, xv, 16, 58–60; business role in, 56–58; corruption and, 59–60; creation of opportunity, 55; drawbacks for businesses, 58–59; failures, 45; private sector development and, 83–84. *See also* economic liberalization
determinism, 8, 12–13, 39, 156; neopatrimonial, 5–6
developmentalism, 55, 68, 197n29
diasporas: Chinese, 112, 117–18, 128; Indian, 117, 119–20, 126, 140, 168; Nigerian, 136
Didi, Agad, 138
diversity of African big business, 6, 14, 17, 24–25. *See also* foreign direct investment (FDI); giants, corporate
Djankov, Simoen, 92
Doha Round, 222n22
Doing Business surveys (World Bank), xi, 3, 10–11, 53, 59; factual indicators, 74–75; Ghana, 82; gross domestic product comparison, 90–92, *91;* Tanzania, 80
"Dollars and Danger: Africa, the Final Investment Frontier" (CNBC), 155, 182, 207n83
domestic markets, 3, 79, 104, 172
donor agencies, 9, 12, 16, 20, 46, 49, 73
Dow Jones Africa Titans 50 Index, 158, 159
The Dragon's Gift: The Real Story of China in Africa (Brautigam), 71, 112
Dubai Ports World, 89
Dutch East India Company, 157

East African Standard, 166
Eastern Bloc, 49

Econet Wireless, 86, 87–88, 93–94, 142, 160
economic globalization: adapting to new environment, 84–90; business environment, 90–93; evolution of, 67–73; examples, 86–90; key elements of new model, 69–73; measures of change, 85–86, *189, 190, 191. See also* globalization; private sector development (PSD)
economic liberalization, xv, 13–16, 36, 49–53, 104; government spending reduced, 52–53; privatization, 132; shifting roles, 50–53; trends in, 46–49. *See also* democratization
economic policy, 13–14, 67, 85
economic statism, 31
education, business, 77
efficiency-seeking strategies, 105
Egypt, 158
embedded autonomy, 31, 198n29
Emerging Africa (Radelet), xiii, 10, 35, 186
The End of History (Fukuyama), 66
energy sector, 87
Entebbe Airport, 137–38
Entebbe Handlings Services, Inc. (ENHAS), 138–39, 147–48, 151–52
Enterprise Africa, 74
Enterprise Surveys (World Bank), 62
entrepreneurialism: historical legacy, 23; at private level, 11; translation into firms, 14; in weak states, 85. *See also* business/entrepreneurial cultures
Ethiopia, 30, 56, 124, 125
Euronext, 179
Evans, Peter, 31, 51
exports, 13–14, 70–71, 82–86, 104–105, 118, *189;* China, 108, 109, 111, 114; crony capitalism, 133, 135, 148–49, 151, 153; India, 124–25
expropriation, 32, 153, 195n3
external shocks, 13, 100
Extractive Industries Transparency Initiative, 108
extractive sectors, 3, 17, 56, 71, 72; foreign investment in, 99–100. *See also* commodities, primary

Ferguson, James, 66, 76, 79–80
Fick, David, 10, 77, 89, 188
financial services companies, 27
Forbes Global Billionaires, 161
foreign direct investment (FDI), 17–18,
    66, 85–86, 99, *191;* Africa's share, 101;
    China, 15, 17, 18, 66, 101, 103, 110–
    18, 127; colonial era, 106; diversifica-
    tion, 104–105, 111–12, 114, 126–27;
    extractive sectors, 99–101; from global
    North, 100–101; India, 101, 107, 110,
    118–26, 212n44; labor and, 114–17;
    market-seeking, 105, 108, 120, 122,
    124–26; nationalist rhetoric, 103–
    105; nontraditional sectors, 100, 101,
    103–105, 105–106; resource-seeking,
    101, 108–109, 123–24, 172–73; so-
    cial responsibility, 109–110; by South
    Africa, 173; Southern advantage,
    108–110; South-South, 101, 107–108;
    value addition, 100. *See also* diversity
    of African big business; immigrant
    and foreign firms
formal sector, 82–83
Fortune Global 500, 3
Forum on Africa-China Cooperation, 113,
    114, 121–22
Francophone countries, 120, 122, 125
Freedom House index, 58, 59
Frelimo (Mozambique), 32
Friedman, Thomas, 65, 66
Fukuyama, Francis, 66

G and D Shoes, 143, 148, 149
G-8 summit, 2005, 70
Games, Dianna, 174
Gecamines, 114, 126
Gelb, Alan, xiii, 37, 62, 77, 86, 94, 155, 157
Gelb, Stephen, 108
Ghana, 10, 80; corporate giants, 163; eco-
    nomic liberalization, 48, 53, 61; In-
    dian investment in, 124–25; private
    sector development, 80, 81–84, 85;
    state machinery, 30
giants, corporate, 155–56; Asian-owned,

164–68; black-identified firms, 160–64;
    black-owned, 157; de-Africanization,
    164, 178–81; in domestic markets,
    159; failures, 161–63; FDI into Africa,
    173–78; measurement of, 156, 158–
    60; minority-owned, 156–57; Nigeria,
    158, 160–61; non-South African,
    158–68; South African, 157, 168–81.
    See also African business
Global Airlinks, 138
Global Entrepreneurship Week, 76
global recession, 2008, 61, 72, 84, 91, 100,
    103, 117
globalization, xv; business cultures and,
    65–66; cultural, 66–67, 73, 76, 93; as
    liberalization, 66; new mode of, 16–
    17, 72; post-Washington Consensus,
    16, 68–69; South Africa and, 68, 178–
    81; technology and, 78–79. *See also*
    economic globalization
Globalization and Its Discontents (Stiglitz), 66
globalizationists, 9–11, 13, 16, 17, 35, 185
Godsell, Bobby, 163
going concerns logic, 8, 132, 133, 134, 154
Gold Coast (Ghana), 28
gold mining, 83, 163
Golden Gate Group, 117–18
Goldenberg scandal, 135
Gowon, Yakubu, 136
Greater Nile Petroleum Oil Company, 123
gross domestic product (GDP), 90–92, *91,*
    103, 111
Guebuza, Armando, 83
Gula-Ndebele, Sobusa, 149

Harare International Airport, 134
highly indebted poor countries (HIPC),
    69, 70
Himbara, David, 28, 36, 165
historical perspective, 14–15; Afro-
    pessimism undermined by, 23; black
    capitalism, 37–40; immigrant and for-
    eign firms, 23–24; independence, era
    of, 30–32; India's trade with Africa,
    118–19; justification of skepticism,

22; legacy of, 25–26; legitimate trade, 22, 26; minorities, economically privileged, 32–37; precolonial business, 17, 22–23, 25; restrictions on black African business, 23, 27–29, 160; toward in inclusive African business, 35–37; trans-Saharan trade, 22, 25–26; underdevelopment of black African business, 23, 26, 111
hot-money flows, 68
Houphouet-Boigny, Felix, 38
Hu Jintao, 113
Huntington, Colis P., 146
hydropower projects, 102

Ibrahim Mohammed Yassin, 88–89, 125, 146, 163–64, 172, 217n14
Idani, Seydou, 146–47, 213n30
Ilovo Sugar Malawi, 159
immigrant and foreign firms, 23, 86; Africanization laws, 31, 32, 40, 102, 106, 119; colonial era, 26–27. See also China; foreign direct investment (FDI); minority-owned business
imperialism, 22, 26–30
import substitution industrialization (ISI), 103–104, 172, 196n2, 197n31
import-sensitive sectors, 51–52
independence, era of, 30–32
India, 66, 179, 209n3, 220n51; corporate giants in Africa, 164–68; dimensions of investment in Africa, 123–26; foreign direct investment, 101, 107, 110, 118–26, 212n44; historical perspective, 118–19; linkages with resident diaspora, 120, 126; market-seeking investment, 120, 122, 124–26; MNCs, 120–21; not monolithic, 121; politics of Africa strategy, 122, 127; resource-seeking investment, 123–24; state and foreign investment, 121–23. See also Asia; multinational corporations (MNCs)
India-Africa Partnership Conference, 122
Indian diaspora, 117, 119–20, 126, 140, 168

Indian High Level Commission, 120–21, 211n32
indigenization, 132, 139–43, 167, 197n33. See also Africanization; nationalism
informalization, 82
infrastructure, 3, 12, 30, 79–80, 89; China and, 112, 114; India and, 124; power generation, 94–95
Inikori, Joseph, 26
Initiative to End Hunger in Africa, 74
institutional change, 13–14, 184–85; approaching consensus, 47–49; business and democracy, 53–60; as chronological process, 45–46; comparison with OECD countries, 46–47; homegrown adjustment programs, 47; preconditions, 48–49; structural adjustment programs, 46, 47; supply of patronage, 19. See also democratization; economic liberalization; political liberalization
International Development Association, 70, 81. See also World Bank
International Energy Insurance Co. Plc., 87
International Finance Corporation, 73, 74. See also World Bank
international financial institutions (IFIs), 47
International Fund for Agricultural Development (United Nations), 76
International Labour Organisation, 152
International Monetary Fund (IMF), 49, 66, 69
internet access, 79–80
Investors Advisory Council (Ghana), 82
Islam, 25

Johannesburg Stock Exchange, 169, 179
Johnston, Michael, 8, 195n21
Jonah, Sam, 163
Journal of African Business, 10

Kampala Document, 47
Kang, David, 185
Kaplinsky, Raphael, 128
Kaufman, Daniel, 11

Kaunda, Kenneth, 30, 38, 83
Kenya, 11, 15, 30; business successes, 55; crony capitalism, 34, 38; GDP growth, 92; import substitution industrialization, 103; Madhvani Group, 36, 167; restrictions on black business, 27, 28; SAPs and, 52, 53; youth business plan competition, 76, 204n33
Kenya debate, 28
Khan, Mushtaq, 144
Khoza, Reul, 146
Kibaki, Mwai, 83
Kingdom Holdings, 142
kinship, 78, 138, 142, 143, 149
kleptocratic regimes, 83, 131, 132, 135
Korea, Republic of, 54
Kraus, Jon, 83
Kufuor, John, 81–82, 83
Kutesa, Sam, 138–39, 147, 149, 151

labor: China and tensions in Zambia, 115–16, 118; China's investment in, 112, 114–17; costs, 94; high standards, 152; India's investment in, 126
Lagos Plan of Action, 47
Latin America, 54, 55
legitimate business: cronyism and, 5, 7–8, 131–32; cultural constraints on, 6, 12; in failed states, 88–89; historical perspective, 22, 26
Lesotho, 70, 71
The Lexus and the Olive Tree (Friedman), 65, 66
Leys, Colin, 30, 39, 153
Liberia, 11
Lindberg, Staffan, 58
"Lions on the Move" (McKinsey), 10, 35
Lubeck, Paul, 30
Lwanda, John, 134

Mabira Forest Reserve, 166
MacGaffey, Janet, 184
Mackay, Graham, 175
macroeconomic conditions, 15, 16, 37, 61, 62, 90

Madhvani Group, 36, 167
mafiosi, 144
Mahajan, Vijay, 10, 125, 188
Makamba, James, 150
Malawi, 134
Mali, 25
Mandela, Nelson, 83
manufacturing sector, 27, 82–83, 104; high-volume, 109; Indian investment, 119, 124–25
market-dominant minorities (MDMs), 165
market-seeking investment, 105, 108, 120; India, 120, 122, 124–26; South Africa, 172–73
Marx, Karl, 29, 40
Masiyiwa, Strive, 87–88, 93–94, 142, 146
Massmart, 106–107, 172, 174, 176, 178
Matani, Rajan, 34
Mauritania, 25, 92, 209n3
Mauritius, 10, 117, 121, 308n3
Mawere, Mutumwa, 142, 150
Mbeki, Thabo, 83, 171, 175
Mbulo, George, 78
McDade, Barbara, 184
McVey, Ruth, xii, 6–7
Mehta, Mahendra, 166
Mehta Group (Uganda), 81, 166
Melber, Henning, 141
Mexico, 58–59
middle class, 51, 57, 139, 172
Midiron Investments, 148, 149
millennium development goals, 9, 90
Mills, John Atta, 82, 84
Mining Charter of 2002 (South Africa), 171
mining sector, 27, 83, 87, 99, 180
Ministry of Private Sector Development (Ghana), 81–82
minority-owned business, 5, 15, 24, 32–33, 196n28; as African business, 15, 24, 32–37, 40, 70; credit, access to, 33; cronyism and corruption, 33, 34–35; homeland networks, 33; positive effects, 36–37; SAPs and, 52; settler capital, 15, 32–37. See also immigrant and foreign firms

Mississippi Masala (film), 119
Mittal Steel, 124, 220n51
Mobutu Sese Seko, 32, 38, 40, 83, 135
Mohammed Enterprises Tanzania Ltd., 86
Moi, Daniel arap, 38, 135
Morocco, 158
Movement for Democratic Change (Zimbabwe), 57
Movement for Multiparty Democracy (Zambia), 58
Mozambique, 15, 32, 49, 53; foreign direct investment in, 102; private sector development, 81; restrictions on black business, 27
MSI Cellular Investments, 163
MTN, 173–74
Mugabe, Robert, 34, 40, 134, 142
Multi Fibre Arrangement, 71, 109
multilateral debt relief initiative (MDRI), 69
multinational corporations (MNCs), 17, 159, 163; colonial era, 23–24; Indian, 120–21; legacy of, 107–108; as minority shareholders, 102. *See also* China; foreign direct investment (FDI); India
Muluzi, Bakili, 134, 135, 145
Museveni, Yoweri, 138–39, 149, 167, 211n30
Mutharika, Bingu wa, 134
Mwaiseni Stores, 177
Mwiinga, Bennie, 137
Mwila, Ben, 137, 145

Namibia, 10, 134–35, 141
Nasasira, John, 151
National Board for Small-Scale Industries (Ghana), 82
National Democratic Congress (Ghana), 84
National Economic Consultative Forum (Zimbabwe), 142
nationalism, 140; rhetoric, 103–105. *See also* Africanization; indigenization
neoliberalism, 104; decline of, 64–65; modification of, 9, 67–69; strictures of, 16, 64–65. *See also* structural adjustment programs

neopatrimonialism, xiv, 4–5, 18, 34–35, 130, 195n14; implications for business culture, 5–9
New Africa Investments Ltd., 143
New Partnership for Africa's Development (NEPAD), 10, 74, 203n25
New Patriotic Party (Ghana), 81–82
New York Stock Exchange, 179
NFC Africa Mining Plc., 116
Nigeria, 15, 26, 30, 53; business successes, 55; cell phone use, 79; Chinese in, 117–18; company case studies, 86–87; corporate giants, 158, 160–61; corruption, 135–36; economic liberalization, 47; import substitution industrialization, 103; power generation, 94
Nigerian Telecommunications Ltd. (NITEL), 161, 162
Nigerianization Decree of 1971, 140
Nkrumah, Kwame, 30
nontraditional sectors, 100, 101, 103–106
Nouvelle Espace Technologies (NET), 147
Nujoma, Sam, 134
Nujoma, Zacky, 134–35
Nyerere, Julius, 30, 38, 83

Obasanjo, Olusegun, 83, 86–87, 118, 136; Transcorp and, 161, 162
Obasanjo Farms Ltd, 136
Obiang, Teodoro, 38
oil and gas production, 105, 106, 123–24
Oil and Natural Gas Corporation (ONGC), 123–24
oil crisis, 1973, 102; of 1979, 49
Okereke-Onyuike, Ndi, 162
Omatek-Nigeria computers, 86–87
Oonk, Gijsbert, 120
Organization of African Unity, 47
Osafo-Maafo, Yaw, 82

partial reform syndrome, 76, 80
Patriotic Front (Zambia), 116
patronage: bureaucratic sector and, 31; immigrant and foreign firms, 27. *See also* crony capitalism

patronage resources, 8; decline, 19, 143
patron-clientelism, 5–6, 18, 34–35; inter-
    racial, 34, 35. *See also* neopatrimo-
    nialism
Pattni, Kamlesh, 34
Pean, Leslie Jean-Robert, 146–47
Pineau, Carol, 10, 71, 89, 94, 181–82,
    183, 188
Pinnacle Property Holdings, 148, 149
Plateau Tonga community (Zambia), 28
Platteau, Jean-Philippe, 78
political liberalization, 13–14, 15–16, 30,
    53–60. *See also* democratization
political protection, 34, 35
Poly Group, 124–25
postcolonial regimes, 14–15, 24
postcolonial state, bureaucratic bloat and,
    30–31
post-Washington Consensus, 16, 68–69,
    93; poverty-reduction imperative, 71–
    73. *See also* Washington Consensus
poverty: crony capitalism contributes to,
    38; SAPs associated with, 16, 60–61
poverty reduction, 9, 16, 50, 61, 67, 68;
    post-Washington Consensus, 71–73
poverty reduction strategy papers (PRSPs),
    69–70
power generation, 94–95
private sector development (PSD), 10, 11,
    13, 62, 67, 73–84, 186; cultural global-
    ization and, 67; democratization and,
    83–84; as externally influenced, 73; at
    national level, 16–17; state roles, 80–
    84; unfavorable outlook, 20
Private Sector Foundation (Ghana), 81
privatization, 132, 136–39, 164, 201n17
property rights protections, 59
protectionism, 71, 104; Russia, 144–45
Putin, Vladimir, 150

Radelet, Steven, xiii, 10, 35, 91, 186
railways, 112, 121, 126
Ramachandran, Vijaya, xiii, 37, 62, 77, 94,
    155, 157
Rautenbach, Billy, 34

Rawlings, Jerry, 61, 81, 82, 83
religion, 25, 77–78
rent seeking, 4, 7, 8, 37–38, 63, 88, 161,
    208n2
resource-seeking investment, 101, 108–
    109, 123–24; South Africa, 172–73
Rhodesia, 27
robber barons, 146
Robbins, Peter, 155
Roberts, Simon, 170
Rodney, Walter, 111
Rose-Ackerman, Susan, 144, 153
Royal Dutch Shell, 54, 123
Russia, corruption, 144–45, 150
Rwanda, 10, 59

SAB-Miller, 19, 174, 180
Saleh, Salim (Caleb Akandwanaho), 138,
    139, 147, 149, 150
Sankara, Thomas, 38
Sanlam, 36
Sasol, 174
Sata, Michael, 116
Scott, Guy, 128
Senegal, 25, 32, 117, 118; Indian invest-
    ment, 125–26, 212n46
settler capital, 15, 27, 32–37, 168; anti-
    market backlash, 36–37; niche, 32–34
Shah, Manju Kedia, xiii, 37, 62, 77, 86, 94,
    155, 157
Shaik, Schabir, 34
Shining Century, 70, 71, 94
Shoprite Holdings, 174, 176–78
Sierra Leone, 15, 32
Singapore, 101
Sinoma International Engineering, 161
Sklair, Leslie, 155
slave trade, 22, 26
small- and medium-scale enterprises
    (SMEs), 67–68, 74, 81, 155, 210n12;
    in formal sector, 82–83; micro- and
    small- and medium-scale enter-
    prises (M/SMEs), x–xi, 12, 16, 36, 68;
    stereotypes of, 185–86
Somalia, 59, 61, 85, 88–89

Somaliland, 89
Sorbara, Mark, 126
south, global, 18
South Africa, 10, 15, 17, 92; apartheid, 27,
57, 172, 173, 197n29; black superrich,
171–72; business cultures, 175–78;
company study, 87; conglomeration,
169–70; continental impact, 173–74;
corporate giants, 157, 168–81; cronyism, 34; cultural dualism, 168; democratization, 57; economically dominant
minorities, 32; elites, 83; globalization
and, 68, 178–81; import substitution
industrialization, 103–104; Indian investment, 125; investment partnerships, 36–37, 102; as investor, 107, 108;
new black big business, 170–72; restrictions on black business, 27; Sanlam, 36; search for new markets, 172–
73; structural adjustment program,
200n14; unbundling, 169–70
South African Breweries. See SAB-Miller
Southern African Development Community, 173
South-South investment, 101, 107–108,
157; advantages, 108–110
special economic zones, 107, 118
spillover effects, 69, 133, 146, 150–52
Standard Bank (South Africa), 174
Stanford, Leland, 146
state, 30–32; as black African business, 37;
bureaucratic, 30–31; crony capitalism
and, 37–38, 152–54; damage to black
business interests, 23, 28, 37, 133,
142; economic liberalization, 50–53;
governed-market interventionism, 51;
outsized economic role, 15, 52–53;
regulatory restrictions, 53; shift in
worldview, 17; weak institutional environment, 38–39
state-led development models, 30
state-owned enterprises (SOEs), 38, 52, 61,
72; preservation of, 68; privatization
of, 136–39
Stevens, Siaka, 38

Stiglitz, Joseph, 66
Stitch Wise, 81, 87
structural adjustment programs (SAPs),
9, 11, 16, 46, 47, 60; business support for, 50–51; criticism of, 49–50,
53; poverty associated with, 16, 60–
61; South Africa, 200n14; weak states
and, 51–52. See also neoliberalism
Sudan, 60, 123
Sunflag Group, 167
Swaziland, 59
Syndromes of Corruption (Johnston), 8

Taiwan, 122
Talisman Energy, 123
Tangri, Roger, 164–65
Tanzania, 15, 53; company case study, 86;
crony capitalism, 38; economically
dominant minorities, 32; hostility
toward private business, 56; import
substitution industrialization, 104;
private sector development, 80; PSD
strategy, 80; SAPs and, 51; state machinery, 30; state sector, 31; Ujamaa
(Tanzania), 140
Tanzania National Business Council, 80
Tanzania Private Sector Foundation, 80
Tata Group, 121, 125
tax reform, 80
Techno-Economic Approach for Africa-
India Movement (TEAM-9), 122
technology, 66, 78–80
technology transfers, 108–109, 111, 122
telecommunications, 79, 94, 173–74, 179
Telkom, 179
textile sector, 70, 71, 95, 109
townships, 29
Transnational Corporation of Nigeria Plc.
(Transcorp), 161–63, 164
transparency, 54, 59
Transparency International, 84, 127
trans-Saharan trade, 22, 25–26
Tsai, Kellee, 54
Turanwe, Dick, 138
Tytens, George, 147–48, 152, 215n37

Uganda, 32, 36, 119; Asians and, 32, 211n30; corporate giants, 81, 166; corruption, 137–39, 217n38; Entebbe Handlings Services, Inc. (ENHAS), 138–39, 147–48, 151–52; transformation of cronyism, 147–49
Uganda Airlines Corporation (UAC), 137–38
Ujamaa (Tanzania), 140
UN Development Program, 94
UN Economic Commission of Africa, 47
United Nations, 68, 74
United States, cronyism, 146
U.S. Foreign Corrupt Practices Act of 1977, 108
USAID, 74

value addition, 100
values: accumulation and, 78; indigenous, 78, 93
van de Walle, Nicolas, 52–53, 57, 62, 68, 154, 186
Venezuela, 58
vicious circles, 31, 39–40, 102–103, 183, 194n9
violent entrepreneurship, 144–45
Volkov, Vadim, 144

Walmart, 106–107, 174
warlords, 8, 19, 145, 212n2
Washington Consensus, 48, 49, 51, 61, 62, 64. See also post-Washington Consensus
weak institutions, 5, 12, 31, 38–39, 94
weak states, 51–52, 85
Weber, Max, xii, 6, 7, 8
West Africa, 25, 26
Western beliefs, 66; about Asia, 6–7; exacting standards for Africa, 18, 131; valorization of, 4
women in business, African, 28
Wood, Jacob (Hu Jieguo), 117–18, 128

World Bank, 3, 10–11, 49, 69; bogus contracts scandal, 146–47; International Finance Corporation, 73, 74; International Finance Corporation, 73, 74; Private Sector Unit, 74
World Investment Report 2007 (United Nations), 105
World on Fire (Chua), 165
worldviews, shift in, 11, 17, 60, 62, 71, 84

xenophobia, 165–66, 219n40

Yoruba women traders, 28

Zain, 20, 125, 164–65
Zaire, 32, 40
Zambia, 10, 28, 53, 219n43; China, labor tensions with, 115–16, 118, 128; copper mining, 103; corruption, 137; crony capitalism, 34, 38; democratization and, 57, 58, 60; economic liberalization, 47, 48, 90; foreign investment in, 100, 103; hostility toward private business, 56; import substitution industrialization, 104; indigenization, 139–40; SAPs and, 51; South African investment in, 177–78; state machinery, 30
Zappile, Tina, 71
Zimbabwe, 15, 28, 134; company case studies, 87–88, 93–94; cronyism, 34; economic liberalization, 48, 201n27; economically dominant minorities, 32; import substitution industrialization, 103–104; indigenization, 141–42; Movement for Democratic Change, 57; SAPs and, 51, 52; state sector, 31
Zimbabwe African National Union-Patriotic Front (ZANU-PF), 57, 140, 142, 149
Zuma, Jacob, 34

SCOTT D. TAYLOR is Associate Professor in the School of Foreign Service at Georgetown University. He is author of *Business and the State in Southern Africa and Politics in Southern Africa: State and Society in Transition.*